EDITING MODERNITY:
WOMEN AND LITTLE-MAGAZINE CULTURES IN CANADA,
1916–1956

DEAN IRVINE

Editing Modernity

Women and Little-Magazine Cultures in Canada, 1916–1956

UNIVERSITY OF TORONTO PRESS
Toronto   Buffalo   London

© University of Toronto Press Incorporated 2008
Toronto Buffalo London
www.utppublishing.com
Printed in Canada

ISBN 978-0-8020-9271-7
(Studies in Book and Print Culture)

Printed on acid-free paper

Library and Archives Canada Cataloguing in Publication

Irvine, Dean, 1971–
    Editing modernity : women and little-magazine cultures in Canada,
    1916–1956 / Dean Irvine.

    (Studies in book and print culture)
    Includes bibliographic references and index.
    ISBN 978-0-8020-9271-7

    1. Canadian poetry (English) – Women authors – History and criticism.
    2. Women periodical editors – Canada – History – 20th century.   3. Little
    magazines – Canada – History.   4. Right and left (Political science) in
    literature.   5. Modernism (Literature) – Canada.   6. Canadian poetry
    (English) – 20th century – History and criticism.   I. Title.   II. Series.

    PN4914.L62I79 2008   C811'.5209358   C2007-903245-1

University of Toronto Press acknowledges the financial assistance to its
publishing program of the Canada Council for the Arts and the Ontario
Arts Council.

This book has been published with the help of a grant from the Canadian
Federation for the Humanities and Social Sciences, through the Aid to
Scholarly Publications Programme, using funds provided by the Social
Sciences and Humanities Research Council of Canada.

University of Toronto Press acknowledges the financial support for its
publishing activities of the Government of Canada through the
Book Publishing Industry Development Program (BPIDP).

for Ava,
forever emergent

The EDGE of the PRISM

The point is
I firmly believe
CIV/n is not a one man job
Hence CONTACT
Is important
So please answer
YES
As your FIRST STATEMENT
To 451 Clarke Avenue
Saturday January 8
Where the Scott's will provide
Lunch
And
Supper
Liquid and solid
Come at Noon
And be carried out
After Midnight
There is plenty of EVIDENCE
That our ALPHABET
Is helped by EXCHANGE
And COMBUSTION
So on the DELTA of Montreal
I plan a review
Of PREVIEW
So we may CATAPULT
All available FIDDLEHEADS
Into CONTEMPORARY VERSE
Into NEW PROVINCES
Even though
THE CANADIAN MERCURY
hits twenty below
Forcing us to take
A NORTHERN REVIEW
HERE AND NOW

F.R. Scott, party invitation (Jan. 1966, FRSP, box 65, file 4)

The 'little magazines.' Nothing in the world could sound more pitiful to the uninitiated than that term.

P.K. Page, letter to Sybil Hutchison (c. Sept. 1949, EBP, box 11, file 67)

Contents

Acknowledgments

I want to give thanks to those who have stood by me for the duration of this book's composition: to my parents, Ray and Helen Irvine, for their encouragement during all these years of learning; to my mentor and doctoral supervisor, Brian Trehearne, for his keen editorial eye, expert advice, and passion for Canadian modernism; and to my wife, Ava Kwinter, for everything.

Many of these pages found inspiration in conversation with my friends and colleagues while I was a graduate student at McGill University: Chris Holmes, John McIntyre, Colin Hill, Heather Bean, Sue Elmslie, Wes Folkerth, Brad Clissold, Jennifer Lokash, Tamara Bates, Kristin Lucas, Colene Bentley, Kevin Flynn, Marie-Thérèse Blanc, and Alex MacLeod. At McGill I received support and advice from a fine cohort of professors in the Department of English: Robert Lecker, Peter Ohlin, Nathalie Cooke, Miranda Hickman, Maggie Kilgour, and Dorothy Bray. To this McGill community I owe much for creating an academic environment never lacking in generosity. In my subsequent travels to and from the University of Ottawa and Dalhousie University, I have met with scholars at conferences who have offered invaluable advice, assistance, and feedback, especially David Bentley, Sandra Djwa, Zailig Pollock, Seymour Mayne, Marilyn Rose, Candida Rifkind, Heather Murray, and Gregory Betts. At Dalhousie my research assistant, Kelley Lewis, devoted hours and hours to help me recover fugitive poems from newspapers on microfilm.

I should like to acknowledge those authors, editors, and literary executors who have kindly granted me permission to quote from unpublished poems, correspondence, and other archival materials: Paul Arthur, Catherine Harmon, Irving Layton, P.K. Page, and Miriam Waddington; also Jennifer Whitby, Wailan Low, David Crawley, Jay

Stewart, Bruce McLaren, Marya McLellan, and William Toye on behalf of Patrick Anderson, Earle Birney, Alan Crawley, Dorothy Livesay, Floris McLaren, Anne Marriott, F.R. Scott, and A.J.M. Smith.

I have been hosted by many while I conducted archival research. I simply could not have completed my research for this book without the gracious hospitality of Betty and Lynn Holmes and Sal Nensi and Dileep Rangan in Toronto; Tim Conley in Kingston; Russ Bugera, Shona Hughes, and Russ Rickey in Winnipeg; Blaine Kyllo in Vancouver; and rob mclennan in Ottawa. Bruce and Diane McLaren of Victoria were most welcoming hosts, inviting me into their home and allowing me to consult the private collection of Floris McLaren's papers; their daughter, Cynthia McLaren, deserves many thanks for her hours of archival work on these papers and for helping me to piece together the chronology of her grandmother's correspondence with Alan Crawley. To Alf and Gayle Kwinter I give thanks for their fondness for what they endearingly call 'poultry' and for their kindness and generosity to their poetry-loving son-in-law.

A number of archivists and librarians have been especially helpful with my research: George F. Henderson of Queen's University Archives; Patricia Anderson and Gaby Divay of the Department of Archives and Special Collections, University of Manitoba; Carl Spadoni of the William Ready Division of Archives and Research Collections, McMaster University; George Brandak of the Department of Special Collections, University of British Columbia; Edna Hajnal of the Thomas Fisher Rare Book Library, University of Toronto; the staff of Library and Archives Canada, especially Anne Goddard, Catherine Hobbs, and Linda Hoad. David McKnight of the Department of Rare Books and Special Collections, McLennan Library, McGill University, deserves special thanks for lending me copies of little magazines from his personal collection and for his bibliography of little magazines in Canada. I am also grateful to the Interlibrary Loans staff of the McLennan Library, who obtained rare copies of little magazines, among dozens of other items, for this study.

My research was funded by doctoral and postdoctoral fellowships from the Social Sciences and Humanities Research Council of Canada; a Margaret Gillett Graduate Research Scholarship from the McGill Centre for Teaching and Research on Women; a research grant from the Social Sciences and Humanities Grants Sub-committee, Faculty of Graduate Studies and Research, McGill University; and a research travel grant from the Department of English, McGill University. I express my deepest gratitude to these funding bodies for their financial support.

My thanks to editors Robert Lecker and Kevin Flynn of *Essays on Canadian Writing* and Imre Szeman, guest editor of the 'Materializing Canada' issue, for publishing a shorter version of the first half of chapter 1: 'Among *Masses*: Dorothy Livesay and English Canadian Leftist Magazine Culture of the Early 1930s,' *Essays on Canadian Writing* 68 (1999): 183–212. The *CV2* editorial collective deserves acknowledgment for publishing a longer version of the second section of the conclusion, which appeared in the Dorothy Livesay special issue: 'Dorothy Livesay's Perspectives, Retrospectives, and Prospectives: "A Putting Down of Roots" in *CVII*,' *Contemporary Verse 2* 21.3 (1999): 65–78. And thanks to Sandra Djwa and Zailig Pollock for publishing a section of chapter 3 – 'The Two Giovannis: P.K. Page's Two Modernisms' – in the P.K. Page special issue of the *Journal of Canadian Studies*.

Finally, thank you to my editors at the University of Toronto Press, Siobhan McMenemy and Frances Mundy, and my copy editor, Elizabeth Hulse, for their patience and advice at various stages of editing and production.

Abbreviations

The abbreviations for archival collections listed here have been used throughout the text in parenthetical references. Full citations of archival collections appear in the list of works cited. Other abbreviations and acronyms adopted in the text follow.

Archival Collections

ACP	Alan Crawley Papers
AJMSP-TU	A.J.M. Smith Papers, Trent University
AJMSP-UT	A.J.M. Smith Papers, University of Toronto
AMKP	A.M. Klein Papers
AMP	Anne Marriott Papers
AWP	Anne Wilkinson Papers
CLCF	Canadian Literature Club Fonds
DLC-UM	Dorothy Livesay Collection, University of Manitoba
DLP-QU	Dorothy Livesay Papers, Queen's University
EBP	Earle Birney Papers
FMDP	Flora MacDonald Denison Papers
FMP	Floris McLaren Papers
FRSP	F.R. Scott Papers
ILP	Irving Layton Papers
LDF	Louis Dudek Fonds
LPP	Lorne Pierce Papers
MA	Macmillan Archives
MEPP	M. Eugenie Perry Papers
MFP	Margaret Fairley Papers
MWP	Miriam Waddington Papers
PAP	Patrick Anderson Papers

PKPP   P.K. Page Papers
PMMP   PM Magazine Papers
RC   Royal Commission on National Development in the
            Arts, Letters and Sciences briefs and submissions
RGP   Ralph Gustafson Papers

Other Abbreviations and Acronyms

CAA   Canadian Authors Association
CAC   Canadian Arts Council
CBC   Canadian Broadcasting Corporation
CCF   Co-operative Commonwealth Federation
CPC   Communist Party of Canada
CPUSA   Communist Party of the United States of America
CWC   Canadian Writers Committee
FCW   Federation of Canadian Writers
LPP   Labour Progressive Party
LSR   League for Social Reconstruction
NFB   National Film Board of Canada
NFC   New Frontier Club
PAC   Progressive Arts Club
VPS   Vancouver Poetry Society
WCC   Writers' Craft Club
WLL   Women's Labor League
YCL   Young Communist League

EDITING MODERNITY:
WOMEN AND LITTLE-MAGAZINE CULTURE IN CANADA,
1916–1956

Introduction

Every host knows that the trick to any successful party is its guest list. When F.R. Scott drew up the guest list for his party in January 1966, he invited a familiar group of past and current Montreal literary couples – Louis Dudek and Aileen Collins, Irving and Aviva Layton, Ralph and Betty Gustafson, A.J.M. and Jeannie Smith, and John and Elma Glassco – as well as some newcomers: Leonard Cohen, Eldon Grier, D.G. Jones, Al Purdy, Wynne Francis, and Michael Gnarowski. Predictably, the guest list names the men first and appends the names of wives in parentheses. Scott sent out invitations in the form of a poem ('The EDGE of the PRISM') incorporating the names of Canadian little magazines, many of them edited by the guests – and by their host (FRSP, box 65, file 4). Like many of these magazines, the invitation was typed, mimeographed, and distributed in a limited number of copies, only a handful of which survive in archival collections. Of the eighteen magazines Scott catalogues in his invitation, the majority (sixteen) were edited by men, the minority (two) by women. Only one of these women attended the party – one of the 'wives,' Aileen Collins. However arbitrary and anecdotal, these statistics are typical of the way in which the little magazine in Canada has entered into our cultural memory, but not in the least representative of Canadian women's extensive engagements in little-magazine cultures since the early twentieth century.

In the 1910s Canada witnessed the emergence of a little-remarked period of activity among women editors of literary, arts, and cultural magazines. Between 1916 and 1956 an unprecedented number of Canadian women established and edited these kinds of periodicals. Many of these editors were themselves poets who published in their own magazines and in those of their contemporaries. Dorothy Livesay,

Anne Marriott, Floris McLaren, Doris Ferne, P.K. Page – all of these women helped either to found or to edit magazines in which they also published their own poetry. Other women also established, edited, and contributed occasional poems, fiction, articles, and reviews to their own magazines: Flora MacDonald Denison, Mary Kinley Ingraham, Laura and Hilda Ridley, Mary Davidson, Margaret Fairley, Eleanor Godfrey, Myra Lazechko-Haas, and Aileen Collins. Still other women never published their own poems but edited magazines: Florence Custance, Catherine Harmon, and Yvonne Agazarian. Numerous other women joined editorial boards, magazine-affiliated writers' groups, and organizations involved in the production of literary, arts, and cultural magazines in Canada. The kind of periodical these women edited is commonly called the little magazine: a type of non-commercial literary, arts, or cultural-interest periodical whose history is co-extensive with the rise of literary modernism in the late nineteenth and early twentieth centuries. In Canada the little magazine first appeared in the mid-1910s, coincidentally with the ascendancy of modernism in European and American literary cultures. Despite their major contributions to the making of such magazines since the early twentieth century, however, women have so far remained peripheral to historical narratives of the little magazine in Canada.

Though most commentators agree upon the historical co-emergence of little magazines with the advance of literary modernism in the late nineteenth and early twentieth centuries, their generic classification remains open to debate. According to Renato Poggioli's *The Theory of the Avant-Garde* (1962; trans. 1968), 'their most symptomatic characteristics are limited printings and sparse, though highly selective, circulation' and 'the non-commercial nature of their publishing; that is their natural condition (and the no less natural reason for the failure of each of them or, at least, for their short lives)' (22). Poggioli's identification of the little magazine's defining traits is faithful to the now-standard characterization of the genre delineated more expansively in Frederick J. Hoffman, Charles Allen, and Carolyn F. Ulrich's *The Little Magazine: A History and a Bibliography* (1946; see Hoffman et al. 2–6). Not only in these seminal texts but also in much of the scholarship based upon their findings, the little magazine appears to be not so much non-commercial as *anti*-commercial: its chief function is to serve as a combative instrument of the avant-garde, 'an independent and isolated military unit, completely and sharply detached from the public' (Poggioli 23; see also Hoffman et al. 3–4). Conversely, as Mark S. Morrisson argues in *The Public Face of Modernism: Little Magazines, Audiences, and Reception, 1905–1920* (2001), modernist periodicals of the early twentieth century were not always antipathetic to the general public or to commercial culture but rather adapted techniques of mass marketing, advertising, and self-promotion to the non-commercial interests of little-magazine culture. Morrisson's counter-argument provides a useful point of departure for the reconsideration of little-magazine historiography in Canada, where the categorical emphasis on the aggressive, avant-garde, anti-commercial, and typically masculinist character of the little magazine has led to the exclusion of other magazines from the historical record, especially those whose founders, editors, and contributors were predominantly women.

From the mid-1910s to the mid-1950s, little magazines in Canada presented non-commercial alternatives to the dominant national mass-circulation magazines of the period, including the *Canadian Home Journal*, *Saturday Night*, *Chatelaine*, *Maclean's*, and the *Canadian Magazine*. That Canadian women seized the opportunity to edit modernist and leftist little magazines is in part attributable to their exclusion from editorial positions in the mass-circulation magazine's normative, middle-class, male-produced, dominant culture. Although women were frequent contributors to Canadian mass-circulation magazines in the 1920s (both those of general interest and those specifically intended for women readers), '[t]he editors of these magazines were not only themselves middle class but middle aged and male' (Vipond, 'Image' 117). While some of these magazines, notably *Chatelaine* and the *Canadian Home Journal*, did in fact employ women as editors by the late 1920s and early 1930s (see Korinek 43–7), they were largely uninterested in the publication and promotion of women's modernist and leftist poetry. Though some women poets occasionally published free verse in the pages of these and other Canadian commercial magazines of the early to mid-twentieth century, the typically masculinist and anti-bourgeois rhetoric aimed at these periodicals by little-magazine groups actively discouraged poets from publication in mass-circulation magazines. For the majority of Canadian modernists and leftists involved with little magazines, mass-circulation magazines and the poetry they published became objects of derision, variously disparaged as examples of bourgeois, consumerist, and feminized mass culture. That many of the late-nineteenth-century inventions for printing mass-market periodicals (cheap paper, the rotary press, the Linotype machine) effectively enabled the production of inexpensive little magazines is one of the ironies that modernists and leftists more often than not chose to ignore and one of the contradictions that subtends their tendentious attitudes toward commercial magazine culture (see Morrisson 3–4; Dudek, 'Role' 206).

Well before the founding of the first little magazines in Canada, the earliest modernist and leftist little magazines had appeared in England and the United States in the late nineteenth and early twentieth centuries. Among the most influential of the early twentieth century were those founded, funded, and/or (co-)edited by women: Emma Goldman (*Mother Earth*), Harriet Shaw Weaver (the *New Freewoman* and the *Egoist*), Harriet Monroe and Alice Corbin Henderson (*Poetry*), Margaret Anderson and Jane Heap (the *Little Review*), Maria Jolas (*transition*), Marianne Moore (the *Dial*), Ethel Moorhead and Kay Boyle (*This Quarter*), Katherine Mansfield (*Rhythm*, the *Blue Review*, and the *Signature*), H.D. and Bryher (*Close-up*), and Mary McCarthy (the *Partisan Review*). Scholarship on these and other women editors of modernist and leftist little magazines has evolved into a field of significant proportions.[1] While there have been no sustained attempts to introduce Canadian women's literary and editorial work into this area of modernist and leftist studies, the recognition of Canadian women poets and editors among their British and American counterparts is contiguous with current critical and literary-historical projects that seek to decentre the dominant, masculinist, and exclusionary narratives of modernist and leftist literary cultures. Early- to mid-twentieth-century Canadian women editors and poets should not be regarded as detached local or national figures, for the international contexts of modernist and leftist little-magazine cultures permeate the literary and editorial work of women in Canada. After all, the poets included in this study published in American and British little magazines, and many editors (both male and female) in Canada designed their magazines on the models of their predecessors and contemporaries in the United States and England. Nor should these Canadian women be considered merely belated followers of the international scene, since the character of their little-magazine cultures is not just imitative but innovative, not merely replicative but generative of alternative local and national communities of writers, editors, and readers.

In documenting the historical marginality of women editors and contributors to little magazines in Britain and the United States, critics and literary historians have returned to the emergent formations, as Raymond Williams says, of radical and avant-garde movements whose 'marginal or rejected artists become classics of organized teaching' (*Politics* 34). While certain women modernist writers and magazine editors, such as Monroe, Anderson, Moore, Mansfield, and H.D., have moved from the margins to the canonical centres of national and international modernisms, others remain peripheral to modernist literary-historical narratives and outside the domain of dominant European and American national literatures. The corollary of European and American modernisms' transition from emergent to dominant cultural positions has been the historical exclusion of 'marginal modernisms' (Kronfeld 4); this exclusionary practice in turn motivates Williams's proposal to 'search out and counterpoise an alternative tradition taken from the neglected works left in the wide margin of the century' (*Politics* 35). That alternative tradition could account for the conjuncture of co-emergent cultural formations contemporary to the interwar period of European and American modernisms, including leftist and other modernist literary cultures whose historical marginality poses counter-narratives to those of canonical modernisms. As alternative traditions, Canada's modernist and leftist little-magazine cultures emerge on the peripheries of European and American cultural modernities. Hence Canadian women magazine editors and poets represent a doubly marginalized group in relation to international literary cultures. The historical and literary-historical marginality of these women and their little magazines, at once marginal to Canadian modernist and leftist literary cultures and to their international counterparts, covers the full dispersion of 'alternative' (modernist, internationalist, non-commercial) and 'oppositional' (anti-modernist, avant-garde, leftist, feminist, nationalist, anti-commercial) dispositions that Williams identifies in emergent cultures (*Marxism* 123–5). Their alterity oscillates between these alternative and oppositional positions, between these complementary and, at times, contradictory cultural orientations. In conjunction with the recovery of an *alternative* tradition that Williams posits, therefore, the concomitant materialization of an *oppositional* tradition among Canadian women poets and little-magazine editors necessitates the expansion of revisionist literary-historical frameworks to address the relationships among these co-emergent cultural formations.

Numerous histories of Canada's little magazines have accumulated since the late 1950s. Previous research has already produced a sizeable archive of theses, dissertations, bibliographies, indexes, essays, and books, many of which refer to women's literary and editorial work.

Even though the range of scholarship on little magazines of this period is far more extensive than that on previous generations of Canadian periodicals, women magazine editors and poets who were members of little-magazine groups between 1916 and 1956 have continued to be minor figures in the historical record. Consequently, feminist scholars such as Carole Gerson and Donna Pennee have characterized literary histories of this period as masculinist, even claiming that Canadian modernism itself has been gendered in the historical record as a masculinist aesthetic (Gerson, 'Literary' 65; Pennee). Pauline Butling has likewise argued that literary historians have defined Canadian modernist little magazines using 'masculinist' terms ('Hall' 62), an argument echoed in Barbara Godard's critique of a male-dominated literary-magazine culture in Canada prior to the formation of feminist literary magazines in the 1970s ('Women' 260). The object of this feminist critique is a definition of the little magazine that privileges a masculinist literary-historical discourse. From the perspective of queer studies, Robert K. Martin, David Leahy, Justin D. Edwards, and Peter Dickinson have analysed the masculinist discourses circulating among Montreal little magazines of the 1940s and among literary histories of the period. What these studies all hold in common is a persistent questioning of normative gender categories; only Edwards, however, has interrogated the 'masculinist position' of the little magazine in histories of literary modernism in Canada and elsewhere (67). Even among these critics, the assumption of Canadian modernism's dominant masculinist character has impeded the consideration of alternative histories of women's involvement with the Montreal little magazines.

It is not enough to reject the masculinist histories and cultural practices of the period without assessing the origins and impact of their gendered discourse. By situating Canadian women modernists in the gendered contexts in which they modified the périod's dominant, normative, masculinist modernism, we bear witness to an emergent women's modernism. Certain masculinist tendencies are clearly evident, both in editorials, reviews, and articles by Canadian modernists and in literary-historical narratives about little magazines and modernism in Canada, and these deserve further inquiry. The result of that critical inquiry should not be a solidification of the literary-historical myth of Canadian modernism and its magazine culture as masculinist phenomenon, however. Rather, Canadian modernism's dominant masculinist discourses, whether evidenced by the editing of little magazines or by the practice of modernist poetics, should be viewed in dialogic relation to the articulation of an emergent women's modernism. What I present in this study, then, is a reconfiguration of critical and literary-historical perspectives on the relationships among poetics, gender, and little-magazine production that inform women's participation in modernist literary cultures in Canada. This reconfigured history attends to the doubly gendered contexts of Canadian women's modernist poetry and poetics: namely, the sociality of gender in modernist magazine culture and the gender of their modernisms.

Another history of women's literary *modernism* in Canada, however, cannot fully account for the numbers of women active on the cultural *left*. Histories of cultural magazines of the left in Canada may in fact serve as models for critics and literary historians in search of alternatives to an apparently masculinist narrative of modernist little magazines. Inspired by the careers of literary women such as Dorothy Livesay and Margaret Fairley, historians of Canada's cultural left have produced wide-ranging scholarship on women and periodicals from the 1920s to the 1950s. Following Joan Sangster's foundational study *Dreams of Equality: Women on the Canadian Left, 1920–1950* (1989), Douglas Scott Parker, David Kimmel, Gregory S. Kealey, Caren Irr, and James Doyle have contributed studies of women editors and writers involved with *Masses* (1932–4) and *New Frontier* (1936–7) in the 1930s and *New Frontiers* (1952–6) in the 1950s. These histories supplement the predominant studies of Canada's modernist little magazines, a field of scholarship that has tended to disregard or disparage the literary content of leftist magazines. Conversely, histories of the cultural left have been reluctant to acknowledge contemporary modernists – except, of course, those authors sympathetic to or active on the political left.

Louis Dudek, Michael Gnarowski, Wynne Francis, Ken Norris, and James Doyle have surveyed and catalogued Canada's modernist little magazines, but none of these general surveys incorporates leftist periodicals. Gregory Peter Schultz, J. Lee Thompson, Richard F. Hornsey, and Peter Stevens have also composed histories of Canadian periodicals after the First World War; their work includes thematic analyses and/or close readings of the poetry published in magazines and journals, addressing both leftist and modernist periodicals, among others. Their studies are comparative in approach, covering a wide range of periodicals. One could also add a sizeable list of indexes, articles, theses, and books devoted to one or two periodicals. Many of these are relevant to the study of the most recognized little magazines included in this study: *Contemporary Verse* (1941–52), *Canadian Poetry Magazine*

(1936–63), *Preview* (1942–5), and *First Statement* (1942–5). Literary historians, biographers, and bibliographers who have specifically addressed women's editorial and literary contributions to these and other magazines are predictably far fewer.

By bringing together leftist and modernist literary histories, this study negotiates between competing cultural discourses, allowing their coextensive narratives to engage in dialogue and reanimating leftist and modernist critiques of one another's literary practices. This dialogic approach to modernist and leftist magazine cultures seeks to address women's contradictory responses to the historical conditions of modernity in early- to mid-twentieth-century Canada, a dialogism that recognizes the anti-modernism and social-political radicalism of the cultural left as mediating discourses in the fashioning of women's modernisms. If, as Jackson Lears argues, late-nineteenth- and early-twentieth-century anti-modernism consists of the reactionary masculinist critique of modernity embodied by 'overcivilized,' feminized, bourgeois, mass culture (xiii; see also Willmott 162–7), it follows that leftist women poets and magazine editors naturally subscribed to this form of gendered culture critique. At the same time, modernist women poets and magazine editors also expressed their ambivalence toward the discursively gendered character of historical and cultural modernity; this species of anti-modernism exposes one among many sites of contradiction within women's modernisms and dispositions toward modernity. Where modernist and proletarian avant-gardes typically defined themselves using a masculinist discourse and rhetoric in opposition to a genteel, feminized bourgeoisie and mass culture, radical leftists went further in simultaneously attacking and distancing themselves from an effete, feminized, and decadent modernist literary culture. Women modernists, conversely, frequently sought to align their aesthetic practices with the progressive (feminist, anti-fascist) politics of the cultural left. Women's negotiations with these contradictions in the gendered discourses of modernity, modernism, and anti-modernism and their social, political, and cultural formations have been examined at considerable length since the mid-1980s by a broad and growing range of literary critics and cultural theorists.[2] Rather than accepting binaristic oppositions of masculinist and feminzed cultural formations, contemporary critics and theorists have moved toward 'retheorizing the modern by breaking down traditional distinctions between a radical avant-gardism (often codified as masculine) and a mass culture that has often been depicted as sentimental, feminine, and regressive' (Felski, *Gender* 29).

Given the evident differences among women's critiques of the gendered discourses of modernity, the types of literary modernism and anti-modernism exhibited in early- to mid-twentieth-century magazine cultures require some preliminary differentiation. The 'literary strategy of antimodernism' (McKay 227) found in early-twentieth-century folk-poetry culture, for instance, is not anti-modernist because its predominantly male late-romanticist poets rebelled against the modernists, but because they resisted the effects of modernization through their poetry. Groups such as the Song Fishermen of Halifax – who contributed to the *Song Fishermen's Song Sheets* (1928–30), a poetry magazine edited by Andrew Merkel – resolved to conserve traditional modes of poetic expression and to preserve folk poetry's rural, masculinist cultural values against the corrosive social and economic forces of modernity (Davies, *Studies* 164–6; see also Gerson, 'Literary,' and Kizuk, 'Molly'). Anti-modernist practice among women poets and editors in the context of leftist cultural organizations and periodicals of the 1930s and 1950s, however, is specifically directed against not only the aesthetics of literary modernism but also the tendentially feminized, bourgeois forms of modern mass culture. The aesthetic practices adopted by anti-modernists – socialist and social realism, as well as socialist and revolutionary romanticism – were devised as oppositional strategies, yet not without internal contradictions, for they are informed not only by the belligerent masculinist discourses of the proletarian avant-garde and the militant labour movement but also by the discourses of women's suffrage, socialist feminism, pacifism, maternalism, utopianism, premodern nostalgia, and sentimentalism. Certain anti-modernist tendencies among women modernists are therefore riven by ambivalence in that these women at times enjoin the leftist critique of the feminization of bourgeois culture and the progressive politics of socialist feminism but reject the conservative, masculinist reaction to literary modernism and nostalgia for traditional poetic modes. In addition, the profusion of multiple, coextensive, and dialectically counterposed modernisms (imagist and expressionist, primitivist and futurist, aestheticist and socialist, mythical and social, maculinist and feminist, objectivist and subjectivist, personalist and impersonalist) is indicative of the tensions and contradictions in women's aesthetic engagements with the social, poltical, and cultural conditions of modernity. For Marianne DeKoven, the unavoidable state of 'unresolved contradiction' among women's literary responses to early twentieth-century modernity is constitutive of literary modernism that enacts a 'radical remaking of culture' in concert with the social-political radicalism of left-wing – and, in the literary sense, anti-modernist – movements (*Rich* 4, 20). The irresolution of DeKoven's formulation is apposite to Canadian women's involvement in modernist and leftist magazine cultures, for it positions these women in a medial space between the dominant masculinist discourses of modernist aesthetics and anti-modernist leftism, a space that provokes a 'radical remaking' of Canadian little-magazine histories.

Literary-historical practices have not been scrutinized often enough in scholarship on leftist and modernist periodicals in Canada. As a corrective to little-magazine histories by Dudek, Gnarowski, Francis, and Norris, Brian Trehearne has initiated revisionary study of 1940s literary culture by calling into question 'the apparent need to categorize and hierarchize the various magazines important to Canadian modernism according to unacknowledged, certainly unarticulated, prescriptions for "real" little magazines' ('Critical' 24). Trehearne's interrogation of these histories represents an 'attempt to supersede the little-magazine alignments so familiar in the period,' though it is not 'a rejection of Canadian literary history, only one of its prominent and least compelling narratives' (*Montreal* 12). If one takes his repudiation of little-magazine-based narratives to signal the need for the revision of Canadian literary history as it has been written in the past, then his polemic may in fact point to a new phase in the making of little-magazine histories, rather than an abandonment of the project altogether. Trehearne's critique of the Dudek-Gnarowski-Francis-Norris lineage of little-magazine scholarship also indicates his predecessors' complicity in 'the exclusion of vital magazines and journals from extensive study' ('Critical' 24); that recognition underpins my own research on Canadian women editors and their little magazines, even those deemed to be 'antithetical to the "little magazine"' in previous histories (Dudek, 'Role' 207).

Canadian little-magazine historiography as it stems from Dudek – including Trehearne's critique – has so far privileged a Montreal-based literary culture emergent in the early 1940s. Most commentators will provisionally admit the *McGill Fortnightly Review* (1925–7) and the *Canadian Mercury* (1928–9) into their little-magazine histories, though not without the qualification that these 1920s periodicals were not 'real' little magazines but rather precursors to those of the 1940s (Dudek, 'Role' 206; Gnarowski, 'Role' 214–19; Norris, *Little* 12, 19). According to Dudek's restrictive definition of the little magazine, 'Canada in the 1930s had no "little magazine" or "little press" movement: no magazines of poetry and experiment representing the rebellion of the creative minority against the profit-motive literature of mass-readership and cultural appeasement' ('Role' 207). His exclusionary practice thus omits periodicals of the 1930s such as *Masses*, *New Frontier*, and the *Canadian Forum* (1920–2000), whose leftward orientations nonetheless subscribe to his notion of the little magazine as 'the embattled literary reaction of intellectual minority groups to ... commercial middle-class magazines' (206). Dudek's emphasis on the 'literary' disqualifies these magazines supported by the Canadian left, all of which published writing about social, political, economic, and non-literary arts matters as well as poetry, short fiction, and literary reviews. Given that these magazines were the chief repositories of modernist and/or leftist writing, especially poetry, in Canada during the 1930s, one might question the value of Dudek's 'literary' category of little magazine. The impact of his categorical strictures is visible in Norris's *The Little Magazine in Canada 1925–80: Its Role in the Development of Modernism and Post-Modernism in Canadian Poetry* (1984). Norris's history bridges the gap between the 1920s and the 1940s with references to *Canadian Poetry Magazine*, *New Provinces: Poems of Several Authors* (1936), *New Frontier*, and a catalogue of poetry collections. Only the entirely male cast of poets included in the anthology *New Provinces*, however, seems to merit analysis: *Canadian Poetry Magazine* he dismisses in a disparaging parenthetical comment; *New Frontier* he quotes only to provide historical context (20–1). According to Norris's narrative, a decade of silence intervenes in the history of the Canadian little magazine.

The wholesale omission of the 1930s from little-magazine-based histories has contributed to the marginalization of women's literary and editorial activities. Canadian literary and cultural magazines of the 1930s featured women editors such as Hilda and Laura Ridley of the *Crucible* (1932–43), Mary Davidson of the *Twentieth Century* (1932–3), and Eleanor Godfrey of the *Canadian Forum*, none of whom appears in historical surveys of Canadian little magazines (though Godfrey has received sporadic recognition in histories and memoirs specifically related to the *Canadian Forum*). On *New Frontier*'s staff, women constituted a majority: its founder (Jean Watts), two of its four editors (Dorothy Livesay and Margaret Gould), and its business manager (Jocelyn Moore). Likely as a result of the high proportion of women involved in its production, it served as an important forum for women's writing. As Douglas Parker claims, 'During its short life, from April 1936 to 1937, no other magazine in Canada published as many articles, poems, short stories and plays written by women, not even *Chatelaine'* (46). Hilda and Laura Ridley were equally diligent in printing women writers in the *Crucible*. During its decade-long run, from 1932 to 1943, a significant majority of its contributors were women, especially its poets: roughly 75 per cent of poems published in the magazine were written by contributors identified as women. *Canadian Poetry Magazine* posted a similar majority of women poets. As the official organ of the Canadian Authors Association (CAA), *Canadian Poetry Magazine* predictably represented the parent organization's proportion of women members: just under 60 per cent of poems published in the magazine during the 1930s were written by contributors identified as women (some issues reached as high as 80 per cent), a gender ratio the magazine sustained into the 1940s and 1950s. (Only during Earle Birney's editorship from 1946 to 1948 did the percentage of women – and CAA – contributors decrease.) While the succession of *Canadian Poetry Magazine*'s male editors – E.J. Pratt, Charles G.D. Roberts, Watson Kirkconnell, Earle Birney, Arthur Bourinot – was only interrupted by Amabel King's two-issue stint as an acting editor in 1944, its exclusion from literary-historical narratives of Canadian little magazines warrants further scrutiny and consideration of ways in which the little magazine's masculinist historiography has not been limited to omissions based on biological gender.

Under Dudek's 'literary' category of little magazine, the *Canadian Forum*, *Masses*, and *New Frontier* would be omitted on the grounds that none is primarily literary. Yet his definition of the little magazine also guards against other kinds of literary magazines. Dudek even singles out *Canadian Poetry Magazine* as a periodical 'antithetical to the "little magazine"' ('Role' 207). Factoring in its high percentage of women contributors, one could infer that his characterization of *Canadian Poetry Magazine* is itself predicated upon a masculinist definition of the little magazine. Even more revealing of his masculinist categorization is his derisive commentary on the 'poetry of appeasement, of gullible sentimentality' published in *Canadian Poetry Magazine* ('Role' 207): for modernists such as Dudek, as Suzanne Clark has shown, the sentimental is a discourse gendered feminine (2). Hence his masculinist definition of *Canadian Poetry Magazine* as the antithesis of the little magazine renders it modernism's sentimental, feminized, and excluded other. Neither Dudek nor his successors have considered the *Crucible*, even as an object of contempt: its predominantly female poets' sentimental tendencies would have just as readily received uncharitable jeers as their counterparts in *Canadian Poetry Magazine*. Both the marginalization of *Canadian Poetry Magazine* and the invisibility of the *Crucible* in the historical record are indicators of the extent to which a masculinist discourse has so far shaped the historiography of Canadian little magazines.

Having bracketed out the 1930s, little-magazine historians have focused on Canada's modernist literary culture of the 1940s. Primary attention to little magazines of the latter decade has been directed toward three Montreal publications: *Preview*, *First Statement*, and *Northern Review* (1945–56). Critics and literary historians have regularly assigned these little magazines a central role in Canadian literary culture of the 1940s, the consequence of which has been the neglect of their contemporaries. Butling locates the origins of this historiographic tendency in Dudek's history of the little magazine ('Role'), calling into question his brief mention of the first little magazine established in Canada in the 1940s, *Contemporary Verse* ('Hall' 62). Founded by a committee of four women (Livesay, Marriott, Ferne, and McLaren) and edited by a man (Alan Crawley) who published more modernist poetry by women than any other Canadian magazine editor of the period, *Contemporary Verse* makes plain Dudek's exclusionary, masculinist narrative of the modernist little magazine. Dudek states that *Contemporary Verse* was superseded by a 'more aggressive "second stage"' of little magazines, *Preview* and *First Statement*; he determines the 'defect' of *Contemporary Verse* was that it 'was not a fighting magazine with a policy' ('Role' 208). According to Butling's critique of Dudek, *Contemporary Verse* eludes his 'masculinist' definition of the little magazine 'as an aggressive, assertive, fighting, militant instrument of the avant-garde' ('Hall' 62). If, as Butling contends, Dudek's definition is masculinist, its gender bias is not specifically directed against the group of women poets who founded *Contemporary Verse*, nor against the high proportion of women poets who published in it, but against any literary periodical that fails to meet his conspicuously gendered criteria for little magazines. Conversely, his preference for an avant-garde, 'fighting magazine' (208) does lead him to emphasize the typically masculine traits of those that fit under this rubric; hence he praises the Montreal-based *CIV/n* (1953–5), edited by Aileen Collins, for its 'vigour and aggressiveness' ('Role' 210). Just as he employs a feminizing discourse to designate those publications 'antithetical to the "little magazine,"' so he enlists a masculinist discourse to certify those he includes in a category of the 'real "little magazine"' ('Role' 207, 209). Such gendered categorizations and oppositions are by no means limited to Dudek; he is, however, the progenitor of a masculinist little-magazine historiography in Canada, later reproduced in Gnarowski's description of *Northern Review*'s 'more virile grouping of poets in Montreal' ('Role' 221) and Francis's assessment of *First Statement*'s 'masculine, virile "poetry of experience"' ('Montreal' 27). This Dudek line of little-magazine history can be traced back to his involvement with the *First Statement* group in the early 1940s. The group's masculinist editorial practices are exhibited in chapter 3, where we witness *First Statement*'s female contributors (including Page, Waddington, and Kay Smith) subjected to gender-specific attacks.

Because definitions of the Canadian little magazine in the early to mid-twentieth century have valorized a masculinist literary-historical discourse and because feminist critiques of that historiography have narrowly characterized literary modernism and the literary left in Canada as predominantly masculinist, the need for counter-narratives to offset these prevailing narratives is crucial to understanding Canadian little-magazine culture of the period. Some basic readjustments of terminology and historiography should help to counteract the promulgation of these masculinist literary-historical myths. A redefinition of the little magazine in Canada should properly incorporate those non-commercial literary, arts, and cultural-interest magazines whose editors facilitated and participated in the construction of a magazine culture for their contributors and readers – but not, primarily, for profit. Others might query this categorical emphasis on the economy of the little magazine rather than its ideological position, its aesthetic values, or its proportion of literary content, but the implementation of this broader generic category will enable less-guarded readings of modernist and leftist magazine cultures in Canada than adherence to circumscribed definitions has encouraged in the past. This revision of little-magazine historiography in Canada is not altogether alien to standard definitions of the little magazine in the Anglo-American context (cf. Hoffman et al. 2–6), though it subordinates the little magazine's aesthetic and/or ideological character to material concerns related to the means and conditions of its production.

Placing an accent on the little magazine's economic base also serves to locate women in relation to the material histories of cultural production in early- to mid-twentieth-century Canada. This approach calls attention to the business of little magazines, which has so far been misrepresented and undervalued in Canadian literary histories. When Francis addresses the subject of little-magazine production in Canada, she claims that little-magazine editors are unbothered by business matters, unconcerned by money, indifferent to production values, and 'most often antipathetic to the public' ('Literary Underground' 65–6). Insofar as little magazines of modernist and leftist orientation habitually define themselves against the commercial values and markets of mass-produced magazines, they may project an image of unbusinesslike practices and inattentive public relations. Yet the women poets and magazine editors included in this study were actively and variously involved in the business of little magazines: they conducted promotional tours, solicited and collected subscriptions, courted advertisers, typed stencils, cut and pasted dummies, answered correspondence, and so on. Most little magazines routinely employed women (and, less frequently, men) in clerical roles, sometimes acknowledged on the masthead, often not. Though crucial to the little magazine's non-commercial economy, these menial jobs have regularly been deemed inferior to editorial work and summarily disregarded by little-magazine historians. The predominantly clerical labour involved in little-magazine production is, in this historical context, gendered female; this characterization, too, demonstrates that literary history has so far marginalized not only women editors and members of magazine groups but also their feminized forms of labour. Though I recognize women's non-editorial, as well as editorial, contributions to modernist and leftist little magazines, I have not sought in this study to catalogue all the women involved as editors, associate editors, regional editors, business managers, and subscription agents. In cases where women's editorial and non-editorial duties overlap – as in the case of Page, for example – I have documented the impact of their labour on the making of little magazines.

According to Francis's description of the little magazine's unbusinesslike policies, its antipathy to the 'public' is counterbalanced by its '"given" audience, more often seeking than sought out by the magazine' ('Literary Underground' 66). While little magazines initially assume a 'given' readership, they also enlist marketing techniques of self-promotion and advertising as a means of expanding their audiences. Modernist and leftist critiques of mass culture and mass-market magazines do not block little magazines from public engagement: Canadian modernists and leftists alike participate in a non-commercial magazine culture whose actual audience is limited, but whose ideal audience is often imagined in terms of the 'masses' or the 'public' or the 'people.' To argue that their actual audience was always a 'given' is to misrepresent little-magazine cultures of the period. One may take for granted that *Canadian Poetry Magazine* counted on subscriptions and contributions from members of the CAA, that the *Woman Worker* (1926–9), *Masses, New Frontier, New Frontiers,* and the *Canadian Forum* depended on the same from cultural and political organizations of the left; but to say that these magazines merely took these 'given' audiences for granted and solicited no others is to contradict statements made by editors in the magazines themselves. Francis contends that the little magazines she names – *Contemporary Verse, First Statement, Preview,* and *CIV/n* among them – are disseminated among a 'given' audience only and that their 'readers are self-initiated members of a cult who recognize each other by certain attitudes and enthusiasms' ('Literary Underground' 66). Yet the editors of Canadian little magazines initiated schemes – whether shifting from typescript/mimeograph to print (the *Woman Worker,* the *Crucible, First Statement, CIV/n*), or publishing a broadsheet and educating readers with an explanatory issue (*Preview*), or going on speaking tours and broadcasting poetry on radio (*New Frontier, Contemporary Verse*), or holding readings and fund-raisers (*Canadian Poetry Magazine, here and now*) – in order to gain public exposure, to attract more readers, and to increase circulation levels. Such activities clearly indicate that these little-magazine editors were neither underground dealers of 'cult' magazines nor content with 'given' or 'self-initiated' audiences.

The question of modernism's and the cultural left's audiences is central to Morrisson's revision of Anglo-American little-magazine historiography, in which he delineates specific intersections between commercial culture and little magazines and offers a thorough reconsideration of the material means of little-magazine production and design, techniques of advertising and self-promotion, and methods of targeting readers and markets. Among the key issues he raises is 'whether the tools of publicity offered by the mass market represented a crisis of publicity or a new opportunity' (7) for the promotion of aesthetic, cultural, social, and political modernities through little magazines. Calling attention to the early twentieth-century modernists' and leftists' ambivalence toward the proliferation of commercial magazines and mass-market advertising, he recognizes 'a sense of crisis in some – and an expectation of opportunity in others' (16). For some, the mass market and mass culture represented threats to modernism and the cultural left as well as to their little magazines; for others, they held new possibilities. But even if the mass market offered tools to increase publicity for modernism and the cultural left, an atmosphere of crisis prevailed among little-magazine editors and contributors. The crisis felt by these modernists and leftists was exacerbated by the fact that the little magazines they founded were often short-lived ventures with limited circulations. As Morrisson puts it, 'Despite attempts to reach broad audiences, because of problems of reception and finances, and the logic of the mass market, ultimately these modernist [and leftist] magazines found only small readerships and led brief lives' (16). Little magazines reached a circumscribed community of readers, sub-scribers, and contributors, but even those ambitious magazines that sought an audience of 'masses' were forced to accept that this was only an imagined audience. Whatever uplift the implementation of mass marketing, advertising, and distribution techniques may have brought to modernist and leftist little magazines, their persistent financial and organizational crises remained constant.

According to Jayne E. Marek's feminist critique of Anglo-American little-magazine histories, the literary-historical construction of early twentieth-century modernism as a period of religious, psychological, philosophical, social, economic, and/or political crisis 'reflects the values of a masculinist viewpoint that reinforces hierarchy' in that 'the familiar modernist dissonances expressing "crisis" necessarily under-girded a drive toward an encompassing consonance' (6). If, to extrap-olate from Marek, literary-historical narratives of modernist disso-nance and crisis are masculinist constructions of deviation from and return to normative, consonant cultural formations, the obverse is also true: the emergence of women's modernisms and women-edited little magazines represents critical ruptures and sites of critique within the histories of dominant, masculinist cultures. In place of masculinist nar-ratives of modernism as the cultural history of crises and conflict, Marek posits the histories of women's editorial collaborations and little-magazine communities. 'Collaboration and community serve as recurrent themes in examining the work of these women,' she observes, adding that 'history has neglected the cooperative work found in women's editorial operations, a teamwork less common in men's' (21, 19). Placing emphasis on modernist women's editorial col-laborations, she points to certain formations of little-magazine culture as the product of women's (and, to a lesser extent, men's) communal enterprises. While community, collaboration, and cooperation may be distinct features of selected women's editorial relations, there is ample evidence to demonstrate that these editorial practices and communal formations apply to both male *and* female modernists, though the ten-dency among male editors to dominate rather than collaborate within mixed-gender little-magazine communities or to establish and edit magazines independently is certainly pronounced. Even so, for modernist and leftist little-magazine groups, the histories of crisis are indelible: the dissolution of community – whether signalled by insolvency, by the decline in contributions and readership, by transformations in editorial policy and organization, by the addition and/or resignation of editors, or by the termination of the magazine – is always a prominent episode in little-magazine histories.

Because little-magazine cultures are emergent phenomena – not only in Williams's sense of alternative and oppositional cultures but also in the secondary sense of that which is 'urgent, pressing,' or 'required for emergencies' (*OED*) – they frequently appear in response to communal experiences of social and political crisis. To claim that every little magazine issues from a state of social or political emergency is, admittedly, to paint a rather dramatic backdrop to their more typically commonplace, though often romanticized and retrospectively revolutionized, origins. Still, expressions of pressing need for alternative and oppositional publication forums were integral to the self-definition of modernist and leftist little magazines at their moment of emergence. For instance, as Floris McLaren attests, recalling the Canadian periodicals in circulation just before *Contemporary Verse* appeared in the early 1940s, 'The chances of publication in Canada for an unknown writer, or for a writer experimenting with new verse forms, or concerned with social or political themes, were almost nonexistent' ('*Contemporary*' 55). The development of the little magazine as a forum for new, formally innovative, and socially or politically conscious authors frequently results from these conditions of cultural *necessity* – if not, given their editors' and contributors' urgent sense of need, *emergency*. Equally, when little-magazine cultures enter into periods of decline or change, these critical junctures often prefigure the advent of new magazines. This cycle of continual emergence – at once a process of cultural renewal and a sign of structural instability – is attributable to various material and social conditions of the early- to mid-twentieth-century little magazine: its precarious economic base, its limited circulation, its restricted pool of contributors, and fractures in its collaborative production and its communal reception.

For arts, social, and political groups, little magazines constitute material sites of socio-cultural mediation among editors, authors, and audiences. Little-magazine editors and authors are often self-conscious about their circumscribed audiences: the 'littleness' of the little magazine's social and cultural circles encourages its editors and writers to participate in internal dialogue and debate, by way of editorials, poems, stories, letters, or reviews. This self-consciousness also materializes from an unsettling awareness of the little magazine's isolation from its ideal or imagined audience, often articulated by editors and authors in terms of crises of communication. So the leftist poet will write of her failure to communicate her political or social consciousness to the masses or the people through a populist poetic and proletarian poetry; the modernist poet will write of her inability to express her social solidarity or personal empathy with others through an impersonal poetic and depersonalized poetry. For leftist and modernist poets alike, the articulation of these experiences was often related to the means of communication itself: the poet's crises find correlatives in the socio-cultural mediations of the little magazine, particularly in its reaching out for audiences beyond its own communities of contributors, editors, and organizations.

Among mid-century Canadian poets, perhaps the best-known auto-critical expression of the poets' and their little-magazine culture's state of solipsistic crisis is A.M. Klein's 'Portrait of the Poet as Landscape,' in which both he and his contemporaries are subjected to trenchant satire: at once self-aggrandizing leftists, who, 'patagonian in their own esteem, / and longing for the multiplying word, / join party and wear pins, now have a message, / an ear, and the convention hall's regard' (2: 637), and 'convolute and cerebral' (2: 637) modernists, 'Who live for themselves, / or for each other, but for nobody else' (2: 637). Given that the sociality of gender in Klein's satire of modernist and leftist literary culture is actually homosocial and exclusively male, the unintended irony of his typically masculinist portrait is that the truly 'incognito, lost, lacunal' poet is not his anonymous 'Mr. Smith in a hotel register' (2: 635) but his female contemporaries, whose signatures have been left unrecorded. Although less celebrated than Klein and his canonical 'Portrait,' women poets central to Canada's early- to mid-twentieth-century little magazines adopted similar self-reflexive and autocritical positions, writing poetry about their own and their magazine culture's crises of communication and about their self-consciousness as women among both male- and female-dominated and mixed-gender communities of writers and editors. While less personally and psychologically devastating than Klein's lapse into silence after the mid-1950s, these women's interrogation of their poetry's relationship to its actual and imagined audiences also led to a series of impasses – for Livesay in the early 1930s and in the 1950s, for Marriott and Waddington in the 1940s, and for Page in the

1950s. By the mid-1950s, all four women had withdrawn from little-magazine cultures; their collective withdrawal coincided with the collapse of the magazines that had appeared in the early 1940s.

These intersecting histories of emergent modernist and leftist women poets and of little magazines constitute one of the formative narratives of literary culture in Canada from the 1910s to the 1950s. I have sought here to demonstrate how transitions and crises in each poet's creative career often coincide with, and can sometimes be caused by, moments of transition or crisis – or, in other words, emergent conditions – in Canadian modernist and leftist little-magazine cultures. In correlating these histories of individual poets and little magazines, I have brought together four of the most prominent Canadian women poets of this period (Livesay, Marriott, Page, and Waddington) and the principal little magazines in which they published their poetry (*Masses*, *New Frontier*, *Contemporary Verse*, *Canadian Poetry Magazine*, *First Statement*, and *Preview*). These poets' individual circumstances come together in the collective contexts of the period's little magazines: chapter 1 deals with Livesay's editorial activities and poetry in the context of two magazines of the cultural left, *Masses* and *New Frontier*, between 1932 and 1937; chapter 2 concerns Livesay, Marriott, their involvement in poetry groups in Victoria and Vancouver, and their publications in *Contemporary Verse* and *Canadian Poetry Magazine* between 1935 and 1956; chapter 3 addresses the poetry of Page and Waddington published in *Preview* and *First Statement* from 1942 to 1945, their poetry appearing in *Contemporary Verse* from 1941 to 1952–3, and their editorial activities in and/or relationships to these Montreal and Victoria-Vancouver magazine groups between 1941 and 1956. At once a history of poets, editors, and their respective groups, of local, national, and international literary cultures, and of their confluence in cities from Victoria in the west to Montreal in the east, these chapters examine little-magazine cultures in deliberately circumscribed and overlapping temporal periods and particularized locations in order to foreground the critical importance of the frequently disregarded quotidian events and ordinary routines involved in the physical and editorial production of modernist and leftist magazines.

Even as I reassemble this articulated network of affiliated poets, editors, and literary groups, I relate these women's editorial work and/or poetry to a remarkable series of crises and transitions in Canada's leftist and modernist little-magazine cultures. This historical pattern of crisis and transition pertains at once to the poetry of Livesay,

Marriott, Page, and Waddington and to the little-magazine groups in which they and other women were active as editors, founders, and/or contributing members. If these histories attend to fine details of literary production, they do so in order to comprehend some of the intricacies and complexities of relations among poets, editors, and the concomitant formation and breakdown of Canadian modernist and leftist little-magazine cultures. This approach has enabled me to integrate readings of each poet's early trials and turning points into a history of Canada's modernist and leftist little magazines.

If literary critics and historians have not yet recognized the extent to which these women addressed poetic and cultural crises, it is in part because so many of the poems in which they voice these concerns were published in periodical form but not included in their early poetry collections of the 1930s, 1940s, and 1950s. Retrospective collections by Page, Livesay, and Waddington have now recovered some of these periodical poems from their early years. Most of Marriott's early poetry, however, has been out of print since the 1940s; her uncollected poems are still scattered among the pages of magazines and newspapers. Numerous other poems have been left unpublished in any form: much of Page's, Marriott's, and Waddington's early poetry remains hidden, relegated to archives. Literary history cannot accomplish the complementary work of scholarly editors; I cannot expect here to retrieve the poems themselves from their periodical and archival sources, nor will I instigate a process of collecting such stray poems by putting together appendices (see Ringrose, '*Preview*'; Boylan; Schultz; Stevens, 'Development'). Even when these poems have subsequently been collected in retrospective volumes by Livesay, Marriott, Page, and Waddington, they have not appeared in scholarly editions. Without even a minimal editorial apparatus, these retrospective collections have not represented the historical origins of poems originally published in little magazines. Fortunately, annotated bibliographies of Livesay, Page, and Waddington have traced the print histories of these poems. For Marriott, though, there is no such bibliography available; so I have reconstructed the publishing histories of her poems. My method here, then, has been to integrate these print histories and critical readings of the poems, taking account of their contexts in Canadian little-magazine cultures of the 1930s, 1940s, and 1950s.

This method stems from Cary Nelson's strategies of literary-historical recovery in the context of modern American poetry, attending to those poems omitted from the historical record and even those left out of a poet's collections: 'Uncollected poems may point to historical realities that seem irrelevant or counter-productive only at the particular moment that the poet is assembling a collected volume ... Uncollected poems can also often define the outer edges of a poet's enterprise, directions a poet may have pursued for a time then rejected' (*Repression* 192). Another methodological innovation here is to consider those poems never published by Livesay, Marriott, Page, and Waddington but composed at the same time as their activities as little-magazine editors, founders, and/or contributors during the 1930s, 1940s, and 1950s. Taken together, these methods for the study of the four poets allow me to present readings of their poems either never collected or published at the time or only later collected in retrospective volumes; these poems I resituate in relation to Canadian little magazines and their communities, their editorial policies and practices, and their historical context in international modernist and leftist magazine cultures from the 1910s to the 1950s.

Few literary critics and historians read backwards to discover the published origins of poems and their contexts in periodicals. Even fewer consider the value of those texts published in periodicals but never collected by the author in book form. Fewer still read those texts left unpublished, sometimes destined for a retrospective or posthumous book, sometimes consigned to a file among an author's archival papers. These kinds of 'lost' periodicals and texts constitute the basis of an alternative history of Canadian literary culture, a history to which this study of Canadian modernist and leftist women poets and magazine editors of the twentieth century contributes. There is no doubt that this is an unconventional history, especially in view of its eccentric focus on women's fugitive poems, short-lived magazines, and little-known print cultures, but its preoccupation with the archives, marginalia, and ephemera of these magazine cultures seeks to decentre dominant literary-historical narratives and, in doing so, to present alternatives to those narratives generated by the poets' canons and consecrated by editors, anthologists, critics, historians, and academic institutions. By calling attention to which kinds of textual material are cast aside at a given historical moment, we may begin to reassess the processes of cultural selection that shape the canons, histories, and critical traditions that we have for the most part passively accepted without ever knowing what was left out in the first place and what interests and values motivated these originary acts of omission. This revisionist literary-historical approach not only reconstructs the

material contexts in which these women's fugitive poems were originally written and published but also reconstitutes the circumstances
that contributed to their exclusion from chapbooks, books, and little
magazines of that time. Attention to the minutiae of little-magazine,
book, and chapbook production is imperative in such recovery work.
This overarching concern for the textual, bibliographic, and editorial
processes of cultural production is fundamental to my method of refin-
ing and redefining the histories of Canadian women modernists and
leftists. Manuscripts, typescripts, correspondence, and other archival
documents as well as poems, letters, editorials, articles, reviews, and
advertisements published in the little magazines themselves contain
an abundance of information about these women – as poets, editors,
and/or members of little-magazine groups. From these materials, I
assemble a series of narratives about the formation and disintegration
of Canadian little-magazine cultures and about the editorial construction of women's leftist and modernist poetry in Canada.

Although correspondence with Livesay, Marriott, Page, and
Waddington reveals women employed as editors for Canadian publishing houses (Sybil Hutchison of McClelland and Stewart and Ellen
Elliott of Macmillan), these women and their male counterparts (John
Sutherland of First Statement Press, Jack McClelland of McClelland
and Stewart, Hugh Eayrs of Macmillan, and Lorne Pierce of Ryerson
Press) enter into consideration here only insofar as their editorial decisions have an impact on the publication of women's leftist and modernist poetry in Canada. Records of their editorial interventions are
crucial, though, to any attempt to assess the discrepancies between the
poetry that Livesay, Marriott, Page, and Waddington published only in
little magazines and the poems included in their books and chapbooks.

While women poets who were also editors of little magazines
and/or members of little-magazine groups are featured in the first
three chapters, women little-magazine editors who were not themselves poets (or not primarily poets) are introduced in chapters 4 and
5. These chapters examine how women editors of literary, arts, and
cultural magazines initiated and facilitated the formation of Canadian
leftist and modernist magazine cultures between 1916 and 1956. Contemporary with the emergence of modernist little magazines in the
United States in the second decade of the twentieth century and in
Canada in the 1920s, Flora MacDonald Denison established the *Sunset
of Bon Echo* (1916–20) and Florence Custance founded the *Woman*

Worker (1926–9), which mark the beginnings of a line of little magazines edited and co-edited by women in Canada. Denison and Custance were followed by editors Hilda and Laura Ridley of the *Crucible*
(1932–43), Mary Davidson of the *Twentieth Century* (1932–3), Eleanor
Godfrey of the *Canadian Forum* (1935–47), Catherine Harmon of *here
and now* (1947–9), Myra Lazechko-Haas of *Impression* (1950–1), Yvonne
Agazarian of *pm magazine* (1951–2), Aileen Collins of *CIV/n* (1953–5),
and Margaret Fairley of *New Frontiers* (1952–56). Marginalized by literary historians, these women editors form the cast of an alternative narrative contiguous with the predominant masculinist histories of little
magazines in Canada.

By examining a diverse range of women editors and little magazines, chapters 4 and 5 attest to the multiplicity and complexity of
cultural discourses that circulate among literary, arts, and cultural
magazines in Canada throughout the forty-year period under consideration. Modernism and leftism are variously inflected by regionalist,
nationalist, and internationalist interests in the context of Canada's
little magazines. Feminism, too, plays a significant part in these emergent modernist and leftist cultural formations. In fact, the chronologi-
cal limits of this study are marked by feminist magazines: the fourth
chapter opens with studies of the suffragist feminism and socialism of
the *Sunset of Bon Echo* after 1916 and the proletarian feminism of the
Woman Worker in the 1920s, which anticipate the conclusion's remarks
on the emergence of a feminist literary-magazine culture in Canada in
the 1970s and 1980s.

Proceeding chronologically from 1916 to 1956, the main trajectory of
this little-magazine history moves toward and passes through
Canada's major national cultural event at mid-century: the Royal
Commission on National Development in the Arts, Letters and Sciences (1949–51) – or, as it is commonly known, the Massey Commission. As the Massey *Report* of 1951 indicates, the principal story of
Canada's little magazines is their constant state of economic crisis. Its
economic instability is the one universal condition of the little magazine in Canada prior to the founding of the Canada Council in 1957.
About the Massey Commission, the Canada Council, and the little
magazine's continuance in the post–Canada Council era, I reserve
comment until chapter 5, though I should note here that the decision
to end the present study with the folding of Margaret Fairley's *New
Frontiers* in 1956 owes much to a radical shift in Canadian literary-
magazine culture after 1957. While I look ahead to the emergence of

Canadian feminist literary periodicals of the 1970s and 1980s in the conclusion, I proceed there only with the understanding that the material basis of these periodicals is fundamentally different from the little magazines edited by women prior to 1957.

Although the narrative arc of this study might suggest a progressive story about the little magazine's evolution from masculinist to feminist cultural formations, this interpretation would effectively reinforce some of the current literary-historical narratives about Canadian modernism and the cultural left that the following chapters call into question. As I demonstrate in the conclusion, the appearance of feminist literary periodicals in the 1970s coincides with a sharp decline in the number of women editing little magazines after 1957. Along with a marked increase in little-magazine production after that year, the proportion of women editors steadily dropped. Given the demographics of the post-1957 little magazine in Canada, the establishment of feminist literary magazines edited by women for the publication of women's writing is indicative of the ways in which the sociality of gender in magazine cultures contributes to the formation of alternative and oppositional cultural phenomena, whether (post)modernist, leftist, or feminist. By situating Canadian feminist literary magazines founded by editorial collectives in the 1970s and 1980s – *CV2*, *Fireweed*, *Room of One's Own*, and *Tessera* – in relation to their modernist and leftist predecessors, the conclusion reflects on the women editors and poets of earlier generations to consider the transhistorical contexts of women's efforts to redress gender inequity in magazine cultures at moments of cultural crisis and transition.

The return to Livesay in the conclusion, where she resurfaces as a founder and editor of the magazine *CV/II*, speaks to her overarching presence in Canadian little-magazine cultures from the 1930s to the 1970s. While the other women included in this study were affiliated with one or at most two magazines, Livesay was involved in various capacities with at least six. Her recurrence in this history provides a linking device that allows the whole to cohere as a narrative rather than a series of episodic case studies. She bridges the histories of modernist and leftist magazine cultures in a way that no other figure included in this study does; she is the one individual who persistently traverses modernist and leftist cultural formations and reappears at key moments of crisis and transformation of magazine cultures. Moreover, Livesay is partly responsible for the renewed critical and literary-historical attention paid to both modernist and leftist little magazines in the 1970s, primarily through her work on *CV/II* and the recovery and publication of her own fugitive works in retrospective collections. Her career thus provides a literary-historical narrative frame that opens near the beginnings of modernist-leftist little-magazine culture in the early twentieth century and extends to the emergence of feminist literary magazines that continue into the early twenty-first century.

Not only prefiguring the formation of Canada's feminist periodicals in the later twentieth century but also coinciding with the publication of early- to mid-twentieth-century European and American little magazines edited by women, the four key decades (1916–56) I have bracketed here constitute the period during which Canadian women modernists and leftists facilitated the 'radical remaking of culture' (DeKoven, *Rich* 4) and the growth of an emergent culture. This historical conjuncture of modernist and leftist little magazines, a confluence of alternative, oppositional, and sometimes contradictory cultural formations, marks a pivotal era in Canadian women's literary and cultural history. It situates the country's women modernists and leftists in a medial space – between the cultural activities of their American and European counterparts, between the dominant forms of feminized mass culture and the masculinist modernisms and anti-modernisms of their contemporaries, between early-twentieth-century bourgeois feminism and late-twentieth-century feminisms. *Emergent Women* thus documents the ways in which the production of little magazines in Canada mediated women's acts of cultural emergence, whether in conjunction with normative masculinist discourses and practices in modernist and leftist magazine cultures or in resistance to dominant forms of masculinist modernism and leftism; whether in opposition to commercialized mass culture or in league with socialist, proletarian alternative mass-cultural formations; or whether in critique of early twentieth-century feminisms and middle-class women's cultures or in sympathy with socialist women's social, political, and cultural movements. These spaces of contradiction foreground the recurrent crises in women's editing of modernist and leftist little magazines and their advocacy of women's poetry. As distinctive cultural phenomena conspicuously absent from the historical record in Canada, these magazines and their crises constitute one of the emergent narratives of Canadian women's cultural history. To recognize this absence is to acknowledge a crisis in the writing of Canadian cultural history itself, one that may facilitate a transition in the historiography of English Canada's modernist and leftist literary cultures.

1 Invitation to Silence: Toronto Montreal Vancouver, 1932–1937

The news reels flashed by as if unrolling from her own mind: war, breadlines, crisis, drought – and yet again those letters in thundering black type – CRISIS.

Dorothy Livesay, 'Case Supervisor' (*Right Hand* 103)

Histories of the Cultural Left

Ruth McKenzie's pronouncement in her 1939 article 'Proletarian Literature in Canada' continues to be representative of literary-historical attitudes toward proletarian culture of the 1930s: 'Since few members of the labouring classes are articulate in the literary sense, practically no literature of that origin exists in Canada or in any other country' (49; cf. Hynes 11). Even among members of the cultural left, an author as committed to proletarian literature as Dorothy Livesay questioned its material existence. Writing in 'Proletarianitis in Canada' around 1936, she anticipated McKenzie's later verdict: 'There is no proletarian literature in Canada; but there is no Canadian literature either. It is my theory (and as one of thousands of Canadians writing verse I am entitled to have my theory) that until we look to the people, and the industries, and the economics of our social set-up, we will have no original contribution to make. Until our writers are social realists (proletarian writers if you will) we will have no Canadian literature' (*Right Hand* 230). By 1936 Livesay had already taken part in a failed attempt to establish a Canadian proletarian literature through the leftist cultural magazine *Masses* (1932–4). Between the collapse of *Masses* in April 1934 and the formation of *New Frontier* in April 1936, she witnessed and contributed to the transformation of the Canadian left's magazine culture. Her theory about the absence of a proletarian literature in

Canada is symptomatic of that period of transition: the cultural left had shifted away from the class-based proletarianism characterizing the Third Period (1928–34) of the Communist International (Comintern) toward the anti-fascism of the Popular Front (1935–9). Livesay's analysis of proletarian literature in Canada was part of an ongoing project of self-definition conducted in Canadian magazines of cultural left, particularly in *Masses* and *New Frontier*.

Crucial to this project were deliberations over the meaning of the term 'proletarian literature.' Within leftist literary culture, it was often defined as class-conscious and revolutionary literature written from the point of view of the working class. Because the working class was in the minority among writers sympathetic to the cultural and political left, the definition of proletarian literature was not limited to literature of working class authorship. Livesay's interpretation points to the apparent lack of Canadian working-class authors: 'All of our writers today come from an educated, middle-class group. Their experience is almost wholly confined to one aspect of life, the consumer's.' Middle-class writers, she contends, have 'no understanding of the producing groups'—that is, the working and labouring classes (*Right Hand* 231). Livesay exempted herself, of course, setting herself as an example to the middle class: she was a convert to communist 'producing groups' and herself a producer of proletarian literature. Yet at mid-decade she presented herself not as a communist nor as a socialist realist, but as a 'social realist,' a term she identified with 'proletarian writers.' This correlation of the proletarian and the social realist bypassed the political association between socialist realism and communism in the 1930s; her redefinition of 'proletarian literature' around 1936 maintained its class significations, but muted its political affiliations with a communist literary culture. Livesay's exegetical strategies can be attributed to the conditions of mid-1930s cultural politics: the emergent Popular Front coalition of communists, social reformers, and progressive liberals necessitated the reinvention of cultural keywords. Where she erred in 'Proletarianitis in Canada,' however, was that her definition of the working and labouring classes as cultural producers precluded their function as cultural consumers. Typical of her contemporaries in the Canadian left's magazine culture, she devoted full attention to the authors but little attention to the audience of proletarian literature.

Just as the question of authorship was problematic in the development of proletarian literature in Canada, so was the question of audience. This latter problem became acute when, as McKenzie observed of Canadian proletarian writers en masse, Livesay, among other writers of revolutionary verse who wanted 'a Canadian audience,' had 'to rely almost solely on magazines for publication' (49). For poets writing proletarian poetry in Canada, audience was mainly generated through magazine publication and distribution. Fortunately for Livesay, her publication history coincided with the emergence of a Canadian magazine culture on the left in the 1930s.

Having authored two collections of poetry, *Green Pitcher* (1928) and *Signpost* (1932) – both published by Macmillan with the stipulation that the Livesays cover the printing costs (Stevens, *Dorothy Livesay* 29) – Livesay did not see another collection until Ryerson Press published *Day and Night* (1944).[1] Her correspondence with Lorne Pierce at Ryerson began on 8 June 1936, and her first letter alluded to her current arrangement with Macmillan: 'I am sending you herewith a new manuscript of mine which I want to have published in the autumn. I believe it is a significant advance over my previous poetry, and should have considerable effect in developing a new trend in Canadian poetry as a whole. Quite regardless of its worth, because of its particular *direction* I feel it is essential to have it published now, and have made arrangements to do so myself' (LPP, box 6, file 6, item 5; original emphasis). Pierce was not as eager as Livesay to see the new collection in print. Their correspondence concerning the collection continued until 2 July 1937, after which a hiatus of several years ensued.[2] On 13 March 1943 Livesay submitted to Pierce a new collection called 'Day and Night,' which was published the following year. The reserved tone of her cover letter whispers compared with that of her first contact with Pierce in 1936: 'I think, after ten years of silence (from the book point of view), I really should have something to offer' (LPP, box 9, file 10, item 39).[3]

From 1932 to 1944, therefore, Livesay depended entirely on periodical publication to reach her audience. Beginning in 1932, she learned the magazine trade in the company of authors and magazine editors of Canada's cultural left. Founded in Toronto in 1931, the Progressive Arts Clubs of Canada (PACs) had formed the leftist cultural group that Livesay joined and where in turn she found an audience through its magazine culture. In the autumn of 1932 she started to work with the first of three different PACs – first in Toronto, later in Montreal (1933–4), and then in Vancouver (1936–9).[4] Having participated in the Toronto PAC writers' group, she began in November 1932 to contribute reviews, 'agitprop' (agitation-propaganda) plays, and proletarian poems to *Masses*, the magazine published and edited by members of the PAC from April 1932 to April 1934.

Compared with other Canadian magazines of the cultural left in the 1930s, such as *New Frontier* and the *Canadian Forum*, *Masses* has not yet enjoyed significant literary-historical attention. What sparse coverage it has received more often than not attacks its adherence to the cultural directives of the Communist Party of Canada (CPC) and belittles its minor production of proletarian literature. Even Livesay herself mentions *Masses* only briefly in her recollections in *Right Hand Left Hand* and *Journey with My Selves*. But we need look no further than her own poetry collections for her evaluation of her proletarian poems of the early 1930s, much of which she published in *Masses* but all of which she left uncollected until she assembled her retrospective volumes *Collected Poems: The Two Seasons of Dorothy Livesay* (1972) and *Right Hand Left Hand* (1977). Just as *Masses* has been relegated by literary historians and by Livesay herself to a minor role in Canadian cultural history, so has her proletarian poetry of the early 1930s.

With an eye for critical principles of selection, George Woodcock once suggested, 'One way of approaching Livesay's poetry of the Thirties is to consider the pieces that were left out of *Collected Poems* and included in *Right Hand Left Hand*' ('Transmuting' 241). Another related approach is to import Nelson's literary-historical method of recovering and recontextualizing periodical poetry, but with the specific intent of targeting those poems Livesay left out of her collections altogether (Nelson, 192; see also Hornsey; Schultz; and Stevens, 'Development'). One further advance in method is to consider those poems never published by Livesay but written between 1932 and 1937 during her years with *Masses* and the PACs in Toronto and Montreal and with *New Frontier* and the New Frontier Club (NFC) in Vancouver. Taken together, these methods for the study of Livesay's proletarian verse will allow me to present readings of her collected, uncollected, and unpublished poems from the years 1932 to 1937 in relation to *Masses* and *New Frontier*, their editorial policies, and their historical contexts in an international magazine culture of the left.

Among *Masses*: Livesay and Leftist Magazine Culture

Prior to *Masses*, PAC writers published poems and articles in proletarian papers such as the CPC's weekly *Worker* and the Canadian Labor Defense League's organ the *Canadian Labor Defender*. But these were not cultural organizations and publications; this cultural gap on the Canadian left was filled by the PACs and *Masses*. What started in Toronto as 'a Saturday afternoon discussion circle which began meeting in 1928 at the home of Abraham Nisnevitz, the operator of a small upholstery plant and author of poetry in Yiddish and English' (Endres xxiii), expanded in the fall of 1931 into 'the Progressive Arts Club of Toronto, with about 35 members in an artists' group, a writers' group, and a dramatic group' (Ryan). After 1932, the Toronto PAC evolved into a national PAC network extending to Halifax, Montreal, East Windsor, London, Winnipeg, and Vancouver, interconnected by the Toronto-based cultural magazine *Masses*.

One such organization of leftist cultural groups was already active in the United States, the John Reed Clubs (JRCs), founded in 1929. The Canadian PACs were contemporaries of the JRCs, which also supported local magazines in the late 1920s and early 1930s. The earliest of these was the New York–based *New Masses* (1926–48). Canada's *Masses* took at least its name from one of its American predecessors – the *Masses* (1911–17) or *New Masses*; this claim can be substantiated by a comparison of graphic design (see Carr 133–4). In addition to *Masses'* linocut prints for cover art and cartoons, its typeface and layout also mirror *New Masses*. Unlike its American comrade, however, *Masses* itself never experienced active government repression in Canada, though its very existence was partly attributed to the censorship of *New Masses* by Canadian customs officials ('Cultural Reaction in Germany' [2]; 'Weekly "New Masses"'). Nor were the *Masses* editors trying to reach an audience beyond Canadian borders, since the JRC magazines already met the demands of the American market. Rather, they were attempting to introduce an international proletarian culture – writers, workers' press, visual artists, theatre groups – to left-wing Canadian workers, writers, and intellectuals in order to develop the nascent proletarian cultural movement in Canada.

What *New Masses* and *Masses* did hold in common was their desire to discover and promote working-class voices – that is, to allow the historically repressed access to means of literary expression and production. They also shared the consequence of giving voice to the historically silenced masses: the attempted silencing of those voices raised in opposition to the proletarian movement. Those voices were shouted down at the time by populist enthusiasm for revolutionary modes such as mass chants, workers' songs, and agitprop poetry and theatre. Reticent bourgeois intellectuals and artists were equally censured within the proletarian movement for what was perceived to be willed silence on issues of concern such as poverty, unemployment, labour rights, and civil liberties.

With polemical rhetoric and incisive commentary on the cultural milieu in which *Masses* was conceived, the first editorial broadsided Canadian intellectuals and artists in an attempt to goad them into following their American, Soviet, and French contemporaries who had already expressed support for the proletarian movement. The unsigned editorial was penned by Toronto playwright, theatre critic, and newspaperman Oscar Ryan (Gordon Ryan 27). Ryan placed rhetorical emphasis on the comparative silence of Canadian artists and intellectuals both to elaborate common cultural tropes in the Depression era – sterility, drought, wasteland – and, paradoxically, to enumerate such silences in order to give voice to the working class:

> This development has not as yet very forcibly manifested itself in Canada. Possibly it is because Canada has been so culturally sterile. But there are a number of Canadian writers, painters, – intellectuals of greater or lesser achievement. Are they *eternally to remain silent*? Will they perhaps actively engage in the social life of Canada, – but in the drawing rooms of our social pillars? Or will a few be found who will go among the workers, try to understand the sufferings of the workers, their struggles, their hopes? Will they continue *to remain silent*, or at best stifle their indignation when workers are massacred, as in Estevan, when workers are jailed under sedition laws, under Section 98, under every manner and form of anti-labor statute? Can they *remain silent* and 'impartial' when workers are starving in tens of thousand[s], when farmers are evicted, when foreign-born jobless are deported en masse? (Ryan, emphasis added)

By naming their silences, Ryan also attacked Canadian bourgeois artists and intellectuals for their passivity and irresponsibility toward the working class and the unemployed. While his editorial purported to recruit so-called fellow-travellers – that is, progressive bourgeois sympathetic to revolutionary proletarian organizations and objectives – his tendentious manifesto style counteracted the intent to convert anyone other than the already converted. In giving voice to the emergent proletarian culture, Ryan condemned what he believed to be a dying bourgeois culture 'eternally to remain silent.'

His editorial communicated policies reminiscent of the Soviet Proletarian Cultural·and Educational Organization – Proletcult for short –

which flourished immediately after the October Revolution in 1917 and viewed worker-writers as the only legitimate producers of proletarian literature.[5] Although already in decline by 1922, the Soviet Proletcult exerted residual influence upon both the Canadian PACs and the American JRCs and their respective periodicals, *Masses* and *New Masses*. As Barbara Foley says of 'the strong Proletkult influence on U.S. literary radicalism,' its legacy continued in North America long after its official demise in the Soviet Union (90, 146–7). Ryan's treatment of bourgeois intellectuals and artists represented this early stage in the development of twentieth-century proletarian culture, a stage most prominently documented in the cases of the editors of the *Masses* and *New Masses* in the United States (see Aaron; Foley; Gilbert; Murphy). That stage was commonly and broadly characterized by the term 'leftism,' one aspect of which was a tendency toward proletarian sectarianism, while another was a propensity toward anti-bourgeois propaganda (Murphy 1). During the parallel developmental stage in Canadian proletarian culture, the PAC and *Masses* dismissed bourgeois literati and emphatically encouraged industrial workers, farmers, and the unemployed to generate an autonomous cultural movement: '[The PAC] does not seek the applause of the select literati, nor does it ask for their tolerance. It is a movement of workers. It is a movement that will find its greatest encouragement in the approval, by the workers, of its work. It addresses itself to the workers, to the poor farmers, to the jobless man in the bread-line ... The workers will produce, and are today producing, their own writers, their artists, their revolutionary intellectuals. MASSES is the first publication of its kind to appear on Canadian soil, produced from the life of Canada's factories, farms, – and breadlines' (Ryan). The *Masses* manifesto could only ensure a non-sympathetic response from a predominantly conservative population to an emergent proletarian culture in early 1930s Canada. Even if Ryan's message had managed to reach an audience of 'select literati,' their response – like McKenzie's pronouncement on proletarian literature – was commonly one of incredulity toward working-class writers. An aggressive demand for autonomy of proletarian writers, artists, and intellectuals could only guarantee for *Masses* a reciprocal autonomy of proletarian readers. This autonomy translated into a self-imposed entrapment of the Canadian proletariat producing and consuming only among themselves. At this moment in the history of Canadian proletarian culture, then, we witness the artists and writers of *Masses* assigning themselves to a culture of their own.

Anxieties among the PACs over the cultural identity and autonomy of the proletariat were translated in specific ways to the field of literary production. Livesay, in particular, communicated these anxieties in her proletarian poetry of the 1930s. She was one of the fellow travellers who wanted to move beyond sympathy to activism, and she pledged herself to the proletarian cause by choosing not to remain silent. To prove her commitment to the working class, Livesay recognized, in her published letter of July 1932 to Jean Watts, that she would have to repudiate her bourgeois heritage in order to participate in an autonomous proletarian culture: 'As for communism, it's a working-class movement and I realize now that it's no use trying to spread it anywhere except within the proletariat. It is alien to the other classes, they do not *feel* that way and so they cannot think that way. I want to think and belong to, work for the proletariat' (*Right Hand* 45; original emphasis). Full commitment to the proletarian movement effectively required Livesay to repress her personal history and identity as a bourgeois poet. As such, she had been prolific, but her desire for solidarity with the working class as a proletarian writer drew her away from writing poetry and toward political, social, and cultural activism. The repression of her bourgeois identity and history contributed to her preoccupation with problems of language, communication, and audience in the proletarian poetry that she did manage to write in the years coincident with the publication of *Masses*. These personal issues, connected to her conversion to communism in 1932, were tied to communal issues concerning the authorship, autonomy, and audience of proletarian culture. In Dennis Cooley's words, 'Livesay's political conversion can be seen then as a crisis in language as much as a crisis in social formation' (237). These crises Livesay most often presented in her poetry through figures of silence.

Studies of figurative silences in Livesay's poetry have been common among her critics. Only Nadine McInnis and Beverley Mitchell have intentionally diminished, even negated, the presence of silence in Livesay's poetry from the 1930s (McInnis 38; Mitchell 519); other critics – namely, Margaret Ann Munton and Peter Stevens – have identified silence as the dominant and unifying poetic figure of Livesay's oeuvre (Munton 146; Stevens, 'Out' 580). Dennis Cooley and Caren Irr have also isolated figural silences in Livesay's 1930s poetry, Irr even extending her readings to include some previously uncollected and unpublished poems (220, 225). Both Cooley and Irr acknowledge and extrapolate from the thematic reading of Livesay's early poetry in terms of 'arrested or twisted voices' (Cooley 257) and 'muted or thwarted voices' (Irr 220), originally formulated by Stevens as 'the silence within that struggles to break out into poetry, a poetry that tries to use the silence but somehow fails to' ('Out' 585). Where Cooley and Irr differ from Stevens is in their gradual shift away from thematic and psychologistic criticism and toward cultural criticism that seeks to interpret Livesay's figural silences as signs of aesthetic and socio-political expression and repression in Canadian proletarian culture of the 1930s.

Because Livesay's figural silences signify both expressive and repressive, positive and negative forces in and around Canadian proletarian culture, they become signifiers of ambivalence. In her anti-fascist poem 'Broadcast from Berlin,' from the September 1933 issue of *Masses*, for instance, silence acquires both positive and negative valences of meaning. In opposition to the symbolic representations of German fascism, silence is associated in the poem with the physical embodiments and implements of labour and of communism. While workers' implements such as hammer and sickle are common communist symbols, they are presented in the poem not as symbols but as metonyms of labour, thus rendering the 'hammer's swing, the sickle's harvesting,' as physical rather than symbolic (*Archive* 42). The physical, material language of communism in the poem thus counters the symbolic, abstract language of fascism; this emphasis on the physical necessitates communication through the workers' universal gestures of manual labour. To interpret their gestures, the audience addressed in the poem is drawn rhetorically into a position of solidarity with the workers, into their work space 'behind closed doors' (42). In tandem with the speaker, whose second-person address to an audience opens the poem, the reader initially views the workers from the distance of the third person in the first and second stanzas. As the poem progresses to the third and fourth stanzas, both speaker and reader enter the workers' space. Access to it has been granted to the speaker, who in the fourth stanza actually speaks on behalf of the workers and directs the reader with imperatives to interpret the workers' labour and their point of view. Even though their 'work' and their 'searching glance' are physical manifestations of silence, both express a positive aspect of silence as the kind of universal knowledge understood by communist '[w]orkers of the world' (42). But because their work is hidden from the brown-shirted fascists who run the communists out of the streets to shelter 'behind their doors,' the 'silent searching glance' of the workers also indicates their scrutiny and distrust of outsiders to the proletarian movement (42). Therefore the silence of the workers also marks the negative and repressive social conditions experienced by organized labour under German fascism in the early 1930s; the communist workers must remain in secret and in silence as they plot strategies of resistance and revolution against the ruling fascists. At least rhetorically and imaginatively, the poem attempts to counteract the repressive force of fascism, for it is presented as a 'broadcast,' a global radio transmission in which speech is freed from physical restraint in a disembodied medium. Unlike what we know to be the limited circulation of *Masses*,[6] Livesay's imagined broadcast was directed to the masses as an audience of 'millions' (47).

'Broadcast from Berlin' puts forward the image of the masses as an autonomous proletarian body, an image that Ryan invoked in his opening editorial and that *Masses* editors reproduced in subsequent issues. That the poem was originally published in *Masses* but subsequently omitted from later poetry collections speaks to the consequences of Livesay's ideological choice to represent the cultural autonomy of a sectarian proletariat. Her articles for *Masses*, beginning with the November 1932 issue, had already exposed her appreciation only of artists 'whose work tends towards a comprehension of present-day conditions, of the life of the working class' ('Art Exhibition'). Similarly, her review of Edmund Wilson's book *Devil Take the Hindmost* challenged the author on the basis that he was only a fellow-traveller and 'that his position as an observer is untenable, that a writer must be a revolutionary.' Livesay's intolerance of such fellow-travellers is again raised in her article on the Art Students' League of Toronto: 'The aim of the artists of the proletariat is not seclusion and individualism. Not "co-operation" with bourgeois wealth, but solidarity with the workers' struggle' ('Guild'). Each review article Livesay signed only with her initials, a shield of pseudo-anonymity that she maintained until the final issue of *Masses*.[7] These review articles sharply reiterated the typically leftist sectarianism of PAC members and magazine contributors. Her desire to protect herself behind an impersonal signature among the ranks of *Masses* contributors, however, signalled a patent contradiction in her service to proletarian culture and her attack on bourgeois culture: she secluded herself among the proletariat rather than among the bourgeoisie.

Livesay published three other poems in *Masses*: 'Pink Ballad' (December 1932), 'A Girl Sees It!' (March–April 1933), and 'Canada to the Soviet Union' (March–April 1934). 'Broadcast from Berlin' was never collected by Livesay herself, though it was reprinted during her lifetime in *Dorothy Livesay and the CBC: Early Texts for Radio by Dorothy Livesay* (1994). Both 'Pink Ballad' and 'Canada to the Soviet Union' she excluded from *Collected Poems* but included in *Right Hand Left Hand*. For both poems, she could expect sympathetic reception only from leftist audiences. 'Pink Ballad' makes no concessions to non-communists and addresses no audience other than CPC members, those 'workers' to and by whom the final 'chorus' is spoken (*Right Hand* 177). Congruent with Livesay's criticism of fellow-travellers in her articles for *Masses*, 'Pink Ballad' is an uncompromising polemic against Co-operative Commonwealth Federation (CCF) leader J.S. Woodsworth and MP Agnes Macphail, politicians supported by the rival 'pink' socialist magazine, the *Canadian Forum* (*Right Hand* 176).[8] As Douglas Scott Parker has commented on 'Pink Ballad,' 'Livesay's dedication to her cause, the urgency to create a voice for the workers against their enemies, and her adherence to CPC strategy all shaped this poem into a polemical diatribe rather than a persuasive piece' (65). This polemic is couched in a feminizing discourse typical of the Comintern's Third Period; it initially deploys female-gender stereotypes and sexist expressions circulating in mass culture ('Hot stuff, baby! Hot stuff, baby!') to caricature the CCF and finally recycles the same phrasings ('Hot stuff, worker! Hot stuff, worker!!') for the closing 'chorus' (*Right Hand* 176) – perhaps that of a vaudevillian, all-female chorus line. In any case, the chorus effectively feminizes the worker, drawing obvious parallels between the 'baby' of the opening lines and the 'worker' of the close, hailing him as an emasculated product of the CCF's 'pink' socialism and as a participant in a feminized culture, whether that of social-democratic politics or that of mass entertainment. 'Pink Ballad' exerts repressive force on those CCF voices raised in opposition to the CPC and, in so doing, aligns those voices with a tendentially feminized political discourse and mass culture. In a style indicative of CPC tactics of the early 1930s, Livesay attacks the CCF for conducting political action '[b]y "reason," not by force' (*Right Hand* 176); she thereby applies the revolutionary rhetorical 'force' of CPC politics, armed with a masculinist-leftist strategy of denigrating the feminized other.

With an adjusted political strategy, 'Canada to the Soviet Union' makes plain its expressive intentions and identifies repressive forces with church, bourgeois, and capitalist figures. The poem is a mass chant documenting how underprivileged Canadians suffer under capitalism and aspire to the social conditions of their idealized Soviet comrades living under communism. Presented as a recitation by Canadian masses to an audience of Soviet masses, the poem seems almost forced to justify *itself* to its intended audience in its final lines: 'We shall be unashamed to face you, comrades! / For our children will have songs, at last / To spur their eager feet!' (*Right Hand* 72). Like political ballads and workers' songs, the mass chant was developed for proletarian voices; their audiences, of course, were also proletarian. Because of their intended pro-communist audiences, Livesay wisely reserved both 'Pink Ballad' and 'Canada to the Soviet Union' for a collection such as *Right Hand Left Hand*, in which readers are given some indication of the historical and socio-political contexts in which such proletarian poetry was originally published.

Of Livesay's poems printed in *Masses*, only 'A Girl Sees It!' was republished in *Collected Poems* – and then only because the poem was brought to her attention by a young socialist correspondent who wrote to Livesay when she was reviewing the galleys.[9] Substituted for the previously unpublished poem 'Testament,' 'A Girl Sees It!' was selected by Livesay to open 'The Thirties' section of the collection. Appropriate to its position in *Collected Poems*, 'A Girl Sees It!' represents her early 1930s views on proletarian culture as a revolutionary movement constituted by members of the working class and by middle-class converts to communism. Since it was published in the collection under the title 'In Green Solariums,' the gendered title of 'A Girl Sees It!' is effaced; here we can begin to see how the publication history of such a poem raises issues of gender representation in *Masses*. The revised title substitutes an image of the bourgeoisie, 'In Green Solariums,' for a proletarian declamation, 'A Girl Sees It!' Like Livesay's other *Masses* poems 'Broadcast from Berlin' and 'Canada to the Soviet Union,' 'A Girl Sees It!' opens with a second-person address to its audience, but now the implied audience is bourgeois and the speaker's tone is accusatory: 'You don't know the city, / You who sit in green solariums' (*Collected* 72). The poem is largely the first-person narrative of a young female servant, Annie, who becomes pregnant by the son of her bourgeois employers, who receives care during her pregnancy from the Salvation Army, and who after giving birth is inspired as a witness of social injustice to incite revolutionary action. Unlike other young women who are rehabilitated by the Salvation Army and 'clamber back to green solariums' (73), Annie rejects servility among the bourgeoisie and opts instead for liberation through solidarity with the workers' movement:

We will march up past green solariums
With no more fear, with no more words of scorn:
Our silence and the onrush of feet
Will shout for us: the International's born! (75)

Like the speaker of 'Broadcast from Berlin,' Annie valorizes 'silence' and physical action as the workers' means of communication. In fact, the poem is written in blank verse and is therefore indebted to the literary tradition of the bourgeois; hence Annie declares at the beginning of the poem to her bourgeois audience, 'I have learned to talk like you' (72). Her final declaration of silence and the sound of marching feet offers an alternative means of communication for the workers' movement, a form of proletarian action rather than bourgeois speech. As in 'Broadcast from Berlin,' verbal silence may take on a positive meaning in the context of proletarian culture.

However we may view Livesay's revisionist degendering and depersonalizing of the title, the social issues of concern in the poem are congruent with her critique of middle-class feminism printed in the same issue of *Masses* as 'A Girl Sees It!' The masculinist bias of proletarian culture as it manifests itself in *Masses* is unavoidable: a masculine proletariat is dominant in the cover designs and in the articles devoted to the question of what constitutes proletarian art and culture. For *Masses*, whatever proletarian art is, it is the socially conscious art of the working man; whatever bourgeois art is, it is decadent, effete, the 'pink' art of 'literary poseurs, scoundrels, eccentrics, and sex maniacs of the bourgeois intelligentsia' ('To All Subscribers'). Livesay, in her review of *Ann Vickers* by Sinclair Lewis in the March–April issue of 1933, thus accommodates the cultural program of *Masses* to her critique of middle-class feminism and individualism:

Feminism was essentially a middle-class movement. The economic 'rights' of the proletarian woman had been decided in the eighteenth century, when the textile mills seized her. The feminists of the twentieth century, on the other hand, were individualists seeking economic equality and political power for their own class. To say they have won either would be ridiculous. The middle-class female will always be obliged to give up her career if she is to be considered as a woman and mother. Only in Soviet Russia, only in a socialist state, can real equality between the sexes be established.

That Livesay writes of twentieth-century feminists in the past tense is perhaps telling enough; that gender parity can only be fulfilled by the establishment of a classless socialist state further signals her indoctrination into a leftist ideology that cannot value any form of middle-class feminist individualism. What her critique entails is a reaction against suffragette feminism, a rejection of the middle class, and a censure of individualism.[10] Livesay's reading of Friedrich Engels's *Origin of the Family, Private Property, and the State* had strongly influenced her thinking about the roles of women in proletarian culture (*Right Hand* 22). Just as her review of Lewis reflects ideas inspired by Engels, so her poem 'A Girl Sees It!' enables a female speaker to voice the idea, shared by her 1930s contemporaries, that 'a revolutionary working-class women's movement was the only true vehicle for women's emancipation' (Sangster 18).

The conviction with which 'A Girl Sees It!' announces a young woman's conversion to the workers' movement is conspicuously absent from the poem that it replaced in *Collected Poems*. Composed on 28 July 1934, approximately three months after the demise of *Masses*, 'Testament' records a far more tentative and troubled conversion to the cause of the working class than its substitute in *Collected Poems*. Certainly, the folding of *Masses* after its March–April 1934 issue must have shaken Livesay's faith in the successful establishment of a radically leftist proletarian culture in Canada or at least one devised by the CPC members of *Masses*. Without the optimism of 'A Girl Sees It!' then, 'Testament' reiterates the need for the proletarian movement to recruit rather than ridicule members of the bourgeoisie. Where 'A Girl Sees It!' embodies the agonistic leftist approach toward the bourgeoisie, 'Testament' expresses the trepidation of those bourgeois sympathetic to the proletarian movement, a major obstacle in the formation of a non-sectarian proletarian culture that stems from working-class scepticism toward middle-class converts to communism.

'Testament' is a parable-poem primarily about the conversion of two bourgeois lovers – the speakers of the poem – to communism. At first Livesay presents the lovers as socially alienated and sexually repressed office employees who remember their sexual intimacies in the marshland country and who desire release from their workplace in the city. To express their social alienation while working in offices, Livesay borrows a metaphor from the newspaper industry:

Business of living crushing us, until
We come out from between the rollers

Flat as newspapers, with a few headlines
For recognition, someone's photograph, and a 'lost' column. (*Archive* 43)

Effectively pressing the speakers into what they materially are on a page – print-media constructions – Livesay reflects upon ways in which the machinery of capitalism reproduces 'flat,' impersonal, dehumanized images of mass humanity in its mass print culture.[11] At least figuratively, the office workers are processed into a print commodity; their alienation is compartmentalized into a newspaper '"lost" column.' Formally, Livesay isolates the conceit in a four-line stanza of its own, signifying their social alienation in a way analogous to the segmented format of newspapers. Immediately preceding and following this stanza, the office workers' experience of social alienation in the city is juxtaposed with their physical release from the city to the country, though this release is presented as escapism, another form of social alienation. The balance of the poem is dedicated to a parable about their conversion to class consciousness. Through natural images suitable to the conventionality of a parable, the lovers' escapes to the country are continually rendered through sun imagery, meant to represent the bourgeoisie, in contrast to shadow imagery, intended to stand for the working class and unemployed. Analogously to the black-and-white image of the newspaper, the sun and shadow imagery depicts stark divisions between classes, divisions that the speakers are keen to eliminate, but only by projecting a screen of bourgeois self-loathing and self-questioning. Their subsequent gesture to join the working-class masses is neither easily given nor accepted, and is again punctuated by self-doubt and self-interrogation:

Moving over then, with the masses
Afraid to touch, and be friendly,
Afraid to be found out, and jeered at:
'You – you came from the sun!'
Fear dwindles, in the growing knowledge
The growing oneness of work to be done.
We look at the sun, and are not blinded
The sun our attainment, and its parasites
Blades of burnt grass to be trampled.
Was it so once for us? Were we once so,
Parasites burnt with a false possession? (*Archive* 44)

Here Livesay makes explicit the paralysis that besets sympathetic bourgeois intellectuals and artists who, like herself, remained silent about their social privilege and who feared ostracism from the proletarian movement for not passing as authentic working-class. Once more the sympathetic bourgeois recall their former social alienation, figured as 'parasites,' consumers of capitalist culture 'burnt with a false possession' of and by a mystified commodity like the 'sun.' Yet the speakers' rhetorical questioning of their past lives as 'parasites' of capitalist culture indicates the rigorous class consciousness that proletarian culture demands of its partisans; here their self-reflection is carried out rhetorically, and the final two stanzas of the poem reinforce such self-inspection.

In the penultimate stanza, the speakers' conversion to class consciousness is presented through their return to the marshland. Their return to a place where 'there is no longer isolation' (*Archive* 44) signifies a rebirth of sensibility, joining sensation and thought in a new knowledge and themselves in a new union. Employing structures of repetition to imitate the movement of this return, Livesay reflects their shift in consciousness not only imaginally by revisiting the opening images of the lovers' escape but also formally: the poem is structured so that the form of the second and third stanzas (four and six lines apiece) is inverted and repeated in the final two stanzas. Where the isolation of the four-line stanza in the first instance had communicated the alienated condition of the office workers, the formal repetition in the concluding four-line stanza serves to show their emergence from that earler social condition. Their new union within the proletarian movement is, unlike the lifeless and 'flat' image of the newspaper, now imagined as fecund and 'rounded.' Their new knowledge, however, much like the codes of the poem itself, is not openly communicated: 'Look,' they declare, 'we have secrets comradely yielded' (*Archive* 44). Those 'secrets' may serve to alienate the non-partisan readers of the poem, perhaps to place them in a position of social alienation and to tempt them into following the speakers. Non-partisans are left with a 'false possession' or nothing at all; they cannot share the secrets encoded in this proletarian parable, communicated figuratively: 'the wind for all city lovers and children / Is a banner upshaken' (*Archive* 44).

As a poem that elaborates crises of sectarianism and communication – among the working- and middle-class left and among communists and non-communists – 'Testament' is a complex form of proletarian literary expression. Its figurative language, imaginative ambiguities, and formal principles are by no means antipathetic to techniques of literary modernism; it could hardly be a poem written by or for one of the worker-writers to whom *Masses* editors wanted to appeal (see Thompson, 'Emphatically' 119–20). 'Testament' offers a critique of the form, if not the content, of proletarian poetry in particular and proletarian culture in general, countering leftist sectarianism, anti-modernism, and didacticism. Its aesthetic principles accord with what Candida Rifkind calls 'socialist modernism' ('Labours' 6), a politically inflected modernist poetics that provides an alternative to the creative strictures of leftist anti-modernism and the communicative impasse of Third Period cultural politics.

Masses editorialists and reviewers were, of course, often strongly biased toward cultural leftism. Ryan's 1932 manifesto statement – 'Art is propaganda, or more precisely, a vehicle of propaganda' – typified their leftism. Specific to proletarian poetry, M. Granite's July–August 1932 article 'On Canadian Poetry'[12] represented the *Masses* editorial line on propaganda and poetry:

> Poetry must become the inspiration of the masses; it must be a powerful weapon in the hands of the workers.
>
> The beginning of the movement towards this poetry may seem crude, incomplete, bombastic ...
>
> The poet of today must sing about the demonstrations of the workers in such a way that workers will want to repeat his poems and march the streets to the beat of their rhythm.
>
> Poems of miners, and strikes, and the sufferings and triumphs of the working class. Poems against police terror, against section 98, against the imprisonment of workers, against deportation.
>
> Propaganda? Yes! But is this not life? Is not life propaganda?

Arguments concerning the relationship between propaganda and proletarian art reached their apex in the debate between Ed Cecil-Smith and Stanley Ryerson published in the magazine's final issues of January and March–April 1934. Cecil-Smith's critique of leftism for its disregard of aesthetics and technique and for its propaganda-for-propaganda's-sake conception of proletarian art ('Propaganda' 11) was met by Ryerson in a leftist riposte in which he condemned his fellow CPC and PAC member for accepting 'at face value the meaning which the bourgeoisie gives to the word "propaganda," i.e., "the spreading of subversive, untrue ideas"' (6). Cecil-Smith's rejoinder in the final issue of *Masses* pointed to the danger that an anti-bourgeois, leftist stance posed to the continuation of Canadian proletarian culture: 'the narrow and sectarian line in this regard ... has a very retarding effect on such artists as are drawn into the class struggle. We have ample proof of this both in Montreal and Toronto, where artists and writers coming under this influence actually tend to cease to produce ... More than one competent writer and critic in the Progressive Arts Clubs has practically quit writing altogether, because he has come under this influence and believes that the little he knows of the class struggle is "utterly insufficient"' ('Let's' 7, 16).

Livesay certainly counts among the leftists who contributed to *Masses*; her sectarian, anti-bourgeois, and anti-modernist attitudes are prominent in her reviews and poems. Cecil-Smith's criticism of leftism was intended to encourage *Masses* editors, writers, and readers to embrace proletarian art, but under the rubric of socialist realism, which subsumed proletarian art as a subcategory and allowed for 'the development of art from the point where the bourgeoisie ha[d] left off' ('Propaganda' 11). Unlike sectarian leftist definitions of proletarian art – that is, revolutionary art by working-class authors and artists – his definition of socialist realism did not exclude non-proletarian or non-communist fellow-travellers.[13] According to Cecil-Smith, leftism threatened the very core of PAC writers and artists, leaving fellow-travellers to abandon progressive art to the revolutionary working class.

Some consequences of Livesay's leftism are visible in the sharp decline in her poetic production during her *Masses* years. Lee Briscoe Thompson's archival report on Livesay's poetry worksheets from the early 1930s details the drastic reduction: 'After having produced an average of nearly one hundred poems every year from 1926 through 1931, ... [Livesay] drafted a total of barely two dozen poems in the pre–New Jersey phase of 1932, 1933, and 1934 ... Only four of her poems made it into print in those three years, the depths of the Depression, and all in the Marxist periodical *Masses*' (*Dorothy Livesay* 34–5). Of those 'barely two dozen poems' that Thompson locates among Livesay's 1930s poetry worksheets, 'Pink Ballad' was the only political poem that she published in 1932, but she had published five poems – typical in style and content of her romanticist and imagist lyric poetry collected in *Green Pitcher* and *Signpost* – in the January 1932 issue of the *Canadian Forum*. Among her recollections of her 1931–2 year at the Sorbonne in Paris, Livesay mentions her cultural and political associations, which consisted of 'attending meetings and watching parades' (*Right Hand* 36), but which were far from the feverish political and social activism in which she became engaged on her return to Toronto.

With the exception of one social documentary of impoverished Paris denizens in her poem 'Old Trees at Pere La Chaise [sic]' (Right Hand 41), Livesay did not record her Paris experiences of social and political protest in verse. Compared with her single poetry publication on her return to Toronto in the summer of 1932, her year in Paris was relatively productive in terms of writing poetry. Having completed her thesis on modernist poetry and symbolist poetics at the Sorbonne, Livesay returned to Toronto in June 1932, but not to write either lyrical or political poetry. After she entered the School of Social Work at the University of Toronto in the autumn of 1932,[14] her poetry was largely displaced by her social, political, and cultural activism. This trend continued over the next three years as she finished her first-year social work studies in Toronto and moved to Montreal in 1933 to commence her second-year fieldwork at the Family Service Bureau. These years in Toronto and Montreal from 1932 to 1934 coincided with her cultural and political work for the PACs and Masses, the Young Communist League (YCL) and later the CPC, the Canadian League against War and Fascism, and the Workers' Unity League of Toronto. It follows that the most significant consequence of Livesay's leftism was the shift in her priorities away from the personal pursuits of writing poetry and toward the public roles of social, political, and cultural action. What little poetry she did produce during her extreme leftist years of the early 1930s was consumed with and by these public roles.

After Livesay moved from Toronto to Montreal in the autumn of 1933, she was promoted from the YCL, which she had joined the previous year, to full membership in the CPC. As she records in her memoirs, she 'was chosen [by the CPC] to contact organizations such as the YMCA, YMHA, church groups and welfare groups' (Journey 82). Contrary to appearances in the 'Montreal 1933–1934' section of Right Hand Left Hand, Livesay did not write many poems during her ten months in Montreal. Given the dates on her extant worksheets, it seems rather that her social, political, and cultural work in that city was less conducive to writing poetry than to collecting documentary material for later composition.[15] On the basis of extant archival evidence, Livesay appears to have written only seven, possibly eight, poems while living in Montreal: 'Broadcast from Berlin' and 'Canada to the Soviet Union,' which she contributed to Masses while working as secretary for the Montreal branch of the PAC; 'Montreal: 1933,' which she first drafted in October 1933;[16] an untitled and unpublished poem dated October 1933 (DLC-UM, box 80, file 4); 'An Immigrant,' which she based on the shooting of an unemployed immigrant worker, Nick Zynchuk, at an eviction by the RCMP on 8 March 1933 in Montreal;[17] 'Rain in April,' which she probably composed prior to May Day 1934;[18] and two other unpublished poems, 'Montreal – 1934' and 'Repeal.'[19] Of these eight poems, 'Montreal: 1933' and 'An Immigrant' appeared in *Collected Poems*, and 'Canada to the Soviet Union' and 'Rain in April' in *Right Hand Left Hand*; only 'An Immigrant' appeared in both collections.[20]

When 'An Immigrant' was first published in the CPC's weekly paper the *Worker* on 14 March 1936, Livesay identified a necessary public function of proletarian poetry. The poem was published as an elegy for Nick Zynchuk (subtitled 'Commemoration: Montreal, March 8, 1933') and specifically addressed a working-class audience. It therefore functioned as a form of working-class cultural memory – that is, the public documentation of proletarian history in poetry. Although she records events particular to an individual historical figure, Livesay renders Nick Zynchuk a typical proletarian martyr analogous to figures such as Sacco and Vanzetti, Tom Mooney, or the Scottsboro Boys in American proletarian literature. By staging the conflict between the 'silent' workers, ready to defend, and the police sergeant, 'at his words,' giving orders to attack, 'An Immigrant' speaks *for* the historically repressed and silenced masses (*Collected* 79). Having first been published in the *Worker*, the poem also speaks *to* the masses. Given that its publication in the *Worker* was an exception to Livesay's typical practices in the early to mid-1930s (since she contributed poems to *Masses* but not to Canadian leftist papers such as the *Worker* [1922–36], the *Daily Clarion* [1936–40], and the *Canadian Labor Defender* [1930–5] [Irr 227]), we should discern a shift in her recognition of the relationships among poetry, mass media, and mass audiences around mid-decade.

According to Cary Nelson, the publication of poetry in working-class newspapers – frequently on the features page, along with letters to the editor, notices of events, and recipes – marks the broader transformation of poetry's public and cultural function during the 1930s:

> Mass readership reinforced the shift in emphasis from the production to the consumption of poems, shifting ownership from author to audience. What mattered to the audience, moreover, was not an effort to capture what an author meant but to take responsibility for how poems could change their own lives. Publishing poems in newspapers suggested not so much that poems were utterly expendable and transitory – the same

.   poems, after all, might later be collected in books – but rather that their
claims to transhistorical values mattered only if they were taken up in
people's daily lives. For poets, therefore, a wide popular readership
demonstrated that poetry mattered; compromising its elite status was a
gain, not a loss. (*Revolutionary* 145)

While it seems doubtful that Livesay would have been inclined to
hand over *ownership* of her poems to her working-class audience, it is
evident that she was conscious of the need to address the contradiction
in poets from middle-class backgrounds writing proletarian poetry for
the working class, or what she identifies as members of the 'consumer'
class writing for the 'producing' class (*Right Hand* 231). By shifting
emphasis from working-class production to consumption, from producing to consuming poetry, from authorship to audience, the publication and reception of proletarian poetry in working-class newspapers assigns value to what Raymond Williams calls 'common' culture
– that is, in the double sense of mutual (culture as the products and
processes of social relations) and ordinary (culture as everyday phenomena and social practices) ('Culture' 11). For instance, poems published in the *Worker* between 1935 and 1936 frequently appeared on the
same page as cartoons, sports, recipes, and the column 'With Our
Women,' suggesting not only the insertion of poetry into a public
space directed specifically (though not exclusively) at women but also
the gendering of poetry and mass culture in leftist newspapers.
Livesay's 'An Immigrant' is among the poems that appeared on the
Worker's eclectic mass-culture pages, alongside the women's column,
which included advice and commentary on women's issues, labour
and working conditions, domestic management, child rearing, and so
on. These poems, like advice columns, could be read as part of the
quotidian events of daily living, integrated into a 'common' proletarian culture.

When 'An Immigrant' was later published in *Collected Poems*, it continued to function in terms of cultural memory, though no longer
limited to proletarian culture and working-class audiences. The same
perennial cultural function cannot be attributed to the bulk of Livesay's
proletarian poetry from the early 1930s. All her poems from the Montreal period adhere to the leftist tendencies of agitprop; they are didactic poems, directed to proletarian audiences, communicating worker-
related political and social events, and inciting revolutionary action by
the working class. Yet only three of these poems appeared in print in

the 1930s. As Irr has written about Livesay's proletarian poetry of the 1930s, the poems may have served a legitimate function, but only for a political minority: 'The discovery of this horror is still fresh enough in the didactic poems to be taken personally; perhaps this is why these poems were not especially powerful for readers outside Livesay's political subculture, for readers who had not experienced a similar revelation. The didactic poems do not communicate her crisis in language as well as they reflect it' (227). Here Irr reiterates the problem of audience as central to Livesay's early failure to find a broad readership among the masses, given that the actual audience of her poems published in *Masses* was in reality a marginal, not a mass, culture.

Livesay's unpublished poetry from this period reveals her difficulties in writing poetry for leftist publications and proletarian audiences. Around the time she moved to Montreal and took full membership in the CPC, Livesay marked the occasion with a poem of October 1933 that begins with a denunciation of bourgeois individualism and ends with an encomium for Lenin (DLC-UM, box 80, file 4). Like her 1934 poem 'Growing Up,' which opens the 'Montreal 1933–1934' section of *Right Hand Left Hand*, this untitled and unpublished poem follows a pattern of opening apologia for bourgeois individualism and concluding celebration of proletarian solidarity.[21] Despite the speaker's claim 'I must fight, not with myself at all,' the poem's strength lies in the internal struggle with the self to reject bourgeois individualism and to accept communism; its telltale leftist weakness lies in its 'unflinching certainty of right' and evangelical 'belief and faith' in Lenin. Oscillating between an individualist 'I' and a collective 'we' voice, the poem possesses the kind of polyvocality found in mass chants that 'workers of the world create and sing' in labour halls: by shifting between individual and collective voices, the poem stages the process of transition from individualism to communism. Its intended audience, however, would not have been at the labour hall, since it addresses the need to convert those individuals who would not have been there in the first place. It is primarily a didactic poem that instructs its audience to forego individual struggle with the self and to join the communist struggle against the ruling class. That the poem never appeared in *Masses* may be explained by the fact that it is untitled and probably unfinished; but that the poem was never finished may be more to the point: its value to Livesay could have been personal, not public.

Livesay's poetic expression of personal crisis is intimately tied to the problems of communication and organization among leftist political, cultural, and labour groups of the early 1930s. If we take into account her organizational roles within these groups and her casework within social agencies, it is natural that her poetry of the period should reflect immediate problems of action and planning in these contexts. Able neither to sustain an autonomous working-class culture nor to maintain an acceptable meeting ground between working-class and progressive middle-class artists and intellectuals, Canadian leftists became intensely self-conscious about their state of cultural and political crisis.

Also never published, 'Montreal – 1934' is a topical poem that points to failures among leftist organizations, emblematized by the collapse of *Masses* after April 1934. To say that 'Montreal – 1934' reflects such failures is also to suggest that it contributes to the problem. A didactic poem such as this may propose collaboration between intellectuals and artists to plot the destruction of capitalist cities and construction of socialist utopias, even though its imagined audience is composed of intellectuals and artists, not of workers. Artists and intellectuals are invited to join the speaker as Shelleyan legislators and organizers of 'beauty,' but they would not carry out the labour necessary to construct such a city (DLC-UM, box 80, file 4). Even as it calls for solidarity, the poem reinscribes definite lines of division – between thinkers and workers, intellectual and manual labour, 'we' and 'they.' How these two groups communicate in order to perform their labour is not made entirely clear in the poem: this ambiguity is its impasse, its crisis of communication and organization. Livesay's resolution to this problem in the final stanza is to trust in universal symbols of labour as a means of communication between the artists and intellectuals and the workers: 'The hammer beats, and the sickle has its song.' She attempts with this figuration to transform the tools of manual labour into the verbal tools of the poet's craft: by abstracting these implements from their material contexts, she redeploys them to represent the work of her verses; and conversely, by attributing 'beat' and 'song' to the workers' tools, she identifies analogues to the metrics and lyrics of her verse. The poet's craft and the worker's labour are thus rendered in a mutually communicable, universal language. Such communicability and universality is finally intended to transcend not only divisions of labour within the proletarian movement but also divisions of nationality and of language. Livesay does not ultimately legislate a resolution for Montreal in 1934, but for a socialist utopia of the future; her aesthetic of 'beauty' in a 'WORLD of cities' develops from the utopian tendencies of 'socialist romanticism.'[22] Even an aesthetic of socialist romanticism, which inflects much of her poetry of the 1930s and presents an alternative to rigid Third Period proletarianism, does not resolve the problems of its sectarianism. 'Montreal – 1934' may attempt to negotiate the division of labour within the proletarian movement, but it fails to address a wider public.

Because of its intended audience, that poem may have been unsuitable for publication in *Masses* or in any other proletarian periodical of the time. 'Canada to the Soviet Union' could have been selected for publication in the final issue of *Masses* for its qualities as a mass chant about the 'beauty' of workers in the Soviet Union in contrast to the 'ugliness' of the unemployed in Canada, spoken by and addressed to the workers, instead of 'Montreal – 1934,' which duplicates many of the same tropes but is spoken by and addressed to the artist and intellectual. Another consideration is that Livesay could have written 'Montreal – 1934' after the collapse of *Masses* and thus have faced difficulty finding an appropriate Canadian periodical to publish her poem and even more trouble finding an American one to accept such a localized piece. One final possibility, to which Irr alludes, is that a poem such as 'Montreal – 1934' does not communicate but reflects the failure of language and form in revolutionary verse. The poem mixes archaic and present-day diction, rhyming couplets and *vers libre*. It is not socialist realism but socialist romanticism. In terms of poetic language and verse form, it is an imperfect alloy of nineteenth- and twentieth-century verse, a confusion of the conventional and the contemporary.

Livesay was particularly sensitive to this transitional character of proletarian verse in the early 1930s. Reviewing *When Sirens Blow*, a collection of verse by Leonard Spier, in the March–April 1934 issue of *Masses*, she called attention to the crisis of language and form faced by the proletarian poet: 'In any new literature that is rising with the rise of a new class to power there is much of the old forms and the old words that will be used, even when the thought behind it is new and revolutionary. We cannot expect a new way of writing all at once. So we find the writers of these poems struggling to think the way the worker thinks and yet putting his thoughts into forms that were used during the nineteenth century' (15). For all its aesthetic imperfections, 'Montreal – 1934' is itself a perfect example of the contradictions in language and form that Livesay identified in the proletarian poetry of her American contemporary. Even as she criticized others for faults present in her own poetry, and even though she did not relent from her typically leftist line of argument (refusing to admit the value of influence from revolutionary nineteenth-century romantic poets), Livesay advanced her own poetics toward socialist romanticism. The shift of audience from workers to artists and intellectuals in 'Montreal – 1934' was particularly strategic, then, since she could incorporate literary traditions and innovations outside the immediate experience of the worker-writer. This is not to say, however, that she was ready to cast aside her leftism and accept contemporary modernist experiments in language and form. Taking issue in the same review article with the practice of modernist poetics in the anthology *We Gather Strength*, by Herman Spector, Joseph Kalar, Edwin Rolfe, and Sol Funaroff, Livesay subjected their poetry to her anti-modernist and anti-bourgeois criticism: 'What happens, on the other hand, when the worker-poet has steeped himself in "modernism"'? When the fantastic language, obscure thinking, and chaos of decadent bourgeois (such as T.S. Eliot) has made a deep impression on his mind? The little anthology "We Gather Strength" is the answer' (15). Just as she admonished Spier for displaying residual effects of nineteenth-century poetry, so she panned the anthology for presenting proletarian poets of the early 1930s in transition from modernist poetry of the 1910s and 1920s: 'They grope, they are overloaded with words and traditions which they have not succeeded in fusing with their thought' (16). Whether Livesay would have considered the anthology successful had the poets merged modernist poetics and revolutionary proletarian thought is uncertain, though the direction of her poetry after the demise of *Masses* indicates that she soon followed her American contemporaries with her own attempts – beginning with 'Testament' in 1934 – to resolve the proletarian poet's crisis in language and form by accommodating her poetics to a post-Eliot, socialist modernism.

What Livesay deemed the greatest value in the poetry of her American contemporaries was less its content than its format. Reviewing pamphlets of American poetry at a time when proletarian literature met 'an impassable barrier' at the Canadian border ('Cultural Reaction Continues'), she praised their American publishers and urged Canadian presses to follow suit: 'Such pamphlets are a challenge to Canadian revolutionary writers to get together and print the same type of thing, whatever the odds' (Rev. of *When Sirens* 16). With the collapse of *Masses* imminent, Livesay's call to the workers' press in Canada to take up the project of publishing proletarian verse was necessary but unsuccessful. The Canadian workers' press had produced some publications, including plays performed by the Workers' Experimental Theatre and workers' song sheets, published by the PAC, and political pamphlets published by the Canadian Labor Defense League. With the exception of the lyrics of workers' song sheets, the Canadian workers' press did not devote its energy or capital to the production of poetry pamphlets. Yet contrary to the literary-historical myth that persists in reference to the economic hardships faced by publishers in the 1930s, there was no material lack of poetry collections published during the Depression. J. Lee Thompson's survey of Canadian poetry in the 1930s is salutary in its corrective to this myth, at once reiterating McKenzie's claim for the necessity of periodical publishing at a time when 'book publishing was undeniably impeded by economic conditions' and advancing her own unexpected findings on the material conditions of poetry production: 'In view of the acute financial problems of the Depression, one would expect very few books to have been published in the thirties, and particularly poetry, a sphere regarded by many as purely ornamental. It was after reading four, five, six hundred volumes that I began to suspect that the urge to self-expression transcends dollar reality' ('Emphatically' 6, 7). Thompson leaves to the imagination the economic output required to produce such vast quantities of verse. To take Livesay's publishing history as representative of Canadian poets (proletarian or not) of the 1930s, we should expect that the 'urge to self-expression' was more often than not self-financed (see n1). Since the workers' press in Canada was not producing poetry, nor were worker-poets in a financial position to pay for their own collections, the economic burden of publishing proletarian poetry largely fell on cultural periodicals such as *Masses* and the *Canadian Forum*.

When *Masses* ceased publication after only twelve sporadic issues over two years, it did so at a perceived moment of triumph. Commemorating its two-year anniversary in the March–April 1934 editorial pages ('Your Task and Ours'), the editors claimed to be confident in their accomplishments: 'With this number we become the leading cultural magazine in Canada with respect to circulation, having now surpassed "The Canadian Forum" which has held that honour for many years.' Despite their claim of superiority in terms of circulation, they complained of the need for 'prompt payment of bills,' a 'subscription drive in the localities and the ordering of regular bundles' in order to improve the quality and guarantee the regular appearance of what was supposed to be a monthly magazine. Their recognition of financial instability was compounded by their continued anxieties over the distribution of the magazine to their target audiences: 'We still remain largely isolated from the masses of workers in shop, mine and farm who are daily becoming more conscious of the need for struggle. We have not yet reached the large numbers of the intelligentsia who are becoming dissatisfied.' Having identified the problem of audience, the editors suggested that its solution could be found in the demographics of contributors: 'Broadening out of the circle of contributors to include dozens more from among you who work in the industries, slave camps, mines and farms of Canada will assure that the contents of our magazine will be close to the daily struggles.' Given that they had heralded their success as a 'cultural magazine' and that they had obtained financial support through the PACs – not groups of workers or intelligentsia but groups of artists – the editors may have intended to elicit 'the support of the readers and of the cultural groups who see their first copy of MASSES with this issue' (March–April 1934). Because *Masses* ceased publication after this issue, we can only assume that the appeal to readers and cultural groups outside the PACs met with little success.

That the termination of *Masses* was not accompanied by the disbanding of the PACs points to the economic underpinnings of leftist cultural magazines in Canada. Unlike the American magazines affiliated with the JRCs, *Masses* was not dependent on the Communist Party for funding. When the party withdrew its financial support from the JRCs toward the end of 1934, the clubs folded along with the majority of the cultural magazines that they had published. The two exceptions were *New Masses* and *Partisan Review*. Founded in 1934 but forced to suspend publication two years later after the dissolution of the JRCs, *Partisan Review* was refounded without party support in 1937. Even though *Masses* had folded prior to these changes on the American scene, its failure to reach audiences beyond the PACs marked a crisis in Canadian proletarian culture similar to that in the United States after the disbanding of the JRCs. Because the American clubs had been largely composed of working-class amateurs, the decision to liquidate the JRCs and their magazines indicated the shift in policy away from support for young proletarian writers and prefaced the international move toward the more liberal policies of the Popular Front. In a parallel development to the refounding of *Partisan Review* during the rise of the Popular Front, the successor to *Masses* – *New Frontier: A Canadian Monthly Magazine of Literature and Social Criticism* – was established in April 1936. Along with editor-in-chief William (Lon) Lawson and editors Margaret Gould, Jocelyn Moore, Leo Kennedy, and J.F. White, Livesay served as a co-founder and a regional editor of *New Frontier*, which she later described as 'a "united front"' magazine set up in contradistinction to another, more radically communist magazine *Masses*. It was to rally the middle class intellectuals and artists to the cause of the international working class against war and fascism' (*Right Hand* 219). Similarly, in the American context, the new *Partisan Review* founded itself as a Popular Front magazine in opposition to *New Masses*, which *Partisan Review* editors artificially constructed as their leftist scapegoat (Murphy 195). Although *New Frontier* did not single out *Masses*, its editorials and articles sometimes reacted against the former sectarian cultural policies of the CPC. While *Masses* had not been officially affiliated with or funded by the CPC, it was strongly partisan and merits distinction as a communist cultural magazine. According to Livesay, *New Frontier* 'was not a strictly Communist Party organ'; its finances were secured through her long-time friend and the wife of the editor-in-chief, Jean Watts Lawson, whose inheritance from her capitalist grandfather paid for the magazine (*Right Hand* 219). While *Masses* was entirely dependent on the PACs for financial support and largely so for contributions, *New Frontier* received assistance and contributions not only from the PACs but also from intellectuals and artists of broad political persuasion and class orientation. With the widening of authorship and audience that accompanied *New Frontier*'s support for the Popular Front, the magazine's advance toward the incorporation of progressive (liberal and left-wing) members of the middle class indicated, not its retreat from the working class, but its reorganization of proletarian authors and audiences into new relations within Canadian magazine culture of the left.

New Frontier's Popular Front

Remembering 1935, Livesay often remarked in her memoirs and retrospectives a break with her leftism of the early 1930s. She also recalled 1935 as the occasion of a nervous breakdown which, during her period of convalescence in the autumn months, allowed her to write and, for the first time since the collapse of *Masses*, to publish her poetry. Consequently, her recollections of the early 1930s were often tainted by reactionary anti-leftism and functioned as disclaimers for her activism in support of Stalin (Irr 216).[23] Her memories of 1935 record innovations in her poetry that coincided with a shift on the left toward the politics of the Popular Front, an international movement among communists, socialists, and progressive liberals that supported workers and the unemployed and protested against war and fascism. In a headnote written for *The Documentaries: Selected Longer Poems* in 1968 and revised for *Right Hand Left Hand* in 1977, Livesay strategically bracketed her leftist years (1932–4) between two significant events: her rejection of Eliot and bourgeois poetry in 1932 and her introduction to post-Eliot modernist poetry in 1934–5. This account chronicles her introduction to poetry written by British fellow-travellers in the early 1930s. She claimed to have discovered these poets for herself while she was employed as a caseworker at Memorial House in Englewood, New Jersey, from late 1934 to late 1935:

> All these social work years I had abandoned writing any poetry which was personal. But in New Jersey, so near New York, in trips to Greenwich bookshops I delved about – perhaps seeking some relief from the orthodox Marxian literature I had been consuming for so long – [*New*] *Masses*, *The Daily Worker*, and countless pamphlets and political tracts along with some heavier economics and Engels, Lenin and Stalin. What was my astonishment and unbelief to find some slim volumes of English poetry – revolutionary poetry but full of lyricism and personal passion! C. Day Lewis first, then Spender, then Auden and MacNeice. There was nothing like it in America and Canada, but it was a movement that followed exactly where I had left off with my Paris thesis – it threw Eliot aside and proclaimed a brave new world. (*Right Hand* 153)

By foregrounding her repudiation of Eliot in 1932, Livesay obviously intended to draw attention to the coincident and sympathetic tendency in British poetry of the time and the subsequent publication of collections by second-generation, post-Eliot modernists: W.H. Auden's *The Orators* (1932), C. Day Lewis's *The Magnetic Mountain* (1933) and *A Time to Dance* (1935), Stephen Spender's *Poems* (1933) and *Vienna* (1934), Louis MacNeice's *Poems* (1935), and the anthologies *New Signatures* (1932) and *New Country* (1933), edited by Michael Roberts. In counting the so-called MacSpaunday (MacNeice, Spender, Auden, Day Lewis) group among her contemporaries in a post-Eliot movement, Livesay re-established some of the bonds she had broken with bourgeois literary culture in 1932 by embracing British fellow-travellers in 1935.[24]

In the fall of that year she composed the title poem for the collection she tentatively called 'The Outrider and Other Poems' (see n1). A tripartite poem in multiple sections and verse forms, 'The Outrider' was intended to be her 'revolutionary' advance in Canadian poetry to match that of her British contemporaries; she even adopted her title, epigraph, and serial verse structure from Day Lewis's *The Magnetic Mountain*. Yet 'The Outrider' itself did not come out in print until the September 1943 issue of *First Statement*.[25] The 'revolutionary' poem she did publish after twenty months of absence from magazine culture was 'Day and Night,'[26] which appeared in the inaugural issue of *Canadian Poetry Magazine* in January 1936. In returning to magazine publication, Livesay also overcame the problem of cultural isolation that had stifled *Masses*, the PACs, and leftist literary culture of early 1930s: she presented her proletarian poetry to a predominantly bourgeois, *Canadian Poetry Magazine*, CAA audience. This reconciliation with the CAA and its bourgeois literary-magazine culture was only temporary. At the 1936 CAA convention, held that summer in Vancouver, she reasserted her leftism to that same audience and 'insisted that young poets should take their spiritual sustenance from participation in the daily life going on around them in the factories, mines and farms of the Dominion, and especially that they should become socially and politically conscious' (Macnair 23).[27] Just three months after her appearance in *Canadian Poetry Magazine* in January 1936, Livesay and her fellow *New Frontier* editors recoiled from Canada's bourgeois, CAA literary culture and founded an alternative national magazine for socially and politically progressive authors.

As a forum for the Popular Front in Canada, *New Frontier* attempted to facilitate communication among members of working and middle classes, among leftists and fellow-travellers, and among an international bloc of sympathetic authors and readers leaning toward the political left. *New Frontier* avoided the sectarianism of *Masses*, at once maintaining a rigorous scepticism of the bourgeoisie and welcoming those literary fellow-travellers who had committed themselves to the Popular Front. *New Frontier*'s inaugural April 1936 editorial closes with an invocation of that international contingent of 'middle road writers' or fellow-travellers, 'those who have been sitting on the fence lining up in support of culture and civilization.' 'If NEW FRONTIER is able to assist their progress in any way,' the editors announced, 'we feel we will have more than justified our existence.' *New Frontier* did print an international range of progressive-minded authors, including many prominent leftists and fellow-travellers already published in American and British magazines of the cultural left – *New Masses, Partisan Review & Anvil, New Verse,* and *Left Review,* among others. With the May–June 1936 issue, Jack Conroy and Edwin Seaver were added to *New Frontier*'s list of associate editors, at a time when both were still editing *Partisan Review & Anvil* (Carr 135). Beginning in October 1936, *New Frontier* ran a campaign that offered new subscribers deals on books by American, British, and Canadian authors who had published in the magazine. Even the title of the magazine evokes tacit associations with the landmark anthologies of the Auden group, *New Signatures* and *New Country,* an internationalist affiliation that the *New Frontier* editors were keen to exploit. What we may infer from its composite of influences, contributors, associate editors, and marketing strategies is that *New Frontier* was organized as an international cultural magazine, yet specifically aimed at Canadian audiences.

Its internationalism was obviously well suited to Livesay's mid-1930s realignment with the modernist poetry and poetics of British fellow-travellers. Her debts to the poetry of the Auden generation (the MacSpaunday group) are unquestionable, and at times her poetry's indenture to some of their best-known poems is that of an apprentice's imitations; these are not just exercises in poetic imitation but localized rearticulations of an international cultural practice on the left.[28] Livesay's poetry of the mid to late 1930s issues from a progressive conception of culture on the left as a 'collective project' whose 'commonality and shared cultural mission' run counter to what Cary Nelson calls 'the sacramental devotion to exceptionalism that has shaped the dominant culture's literary memory' (*Revolutionary* 6, 8). If we attend to the counterpoint between the poetry of the Auden generation and of Livesay as the collective voice of a 'poetry chorus' (Nelson, *Revolutionary* 141), rather than the discrete voices of individual poets, we may begin to hear the polyvocality and intertextuality of her mid-1930s poems as that of communal, contrapuntal 'masses.'

The *New Frontier* poetry she published either in *Day and Night* or later in *Collected Poems* and *Right Hand Left Hand* clearly reflects her internationalist outlook and literary affiliations during the mid-1930s. With the declamatory title 'Yes!' Livesay's first poem in *New Frontier* appeared in the May 1936 issue; its title appropriately announced her mid-decade conversion to a 'revolutionary poetry' of 'lyricism and personal passion' (*Right Hand* 153). She followed 'Yes!' with 'Doom Elegy' in the July 1936 issue; this elegiac poem documents the impact of an imperialist ideology on the daily lives of her own interwar generation. This personalist poetry not only rejected Eliot's and others' mode of modernist impersonality but also superseded her own mode of leftist impersonality – that is, her abandonment of 'writing any poetry which was personal' during her nearly two-year period of publication silence after the collapse of Masses (*Right Hand* 153). Livesay's personalist mode of socially and politically conscious poetry is characteristic of the Auden generation's modernism; this late modernist mode soon became dominant among the fellow-travelling poets of the Popular Front.

When it was later recovered by Livesay for her *Collected Poems*, 'Yes!' was arranged in a longer poetic structure ('Queen City') typical of the Auden generation. This is also true of 'Doom Elegy,' which was collected in the sequence 'Seven Poems' in *Day and Night*. Like her other poetic sequences of the 1930s – 'Depression Suite,' 'The Outrider,' and 'Day and Night' – both 'Queen City' and 'Seven Poems' are formally fragmented, ranging from rhymed stanzas to blank verse to free verse. Day Lewis's *The Magnetic Mountain* provided Livesay's modernist model not only for 'The Outrider' but for all her longer sequences of the mid-1930s. Although she never printed her longer multi-sectioned poems in *New Frontier*, she did follow Day Lewis's practice in this regard: both poets regularly published individual poems in magazines prior to their integration into poetic sequences (see Hynes 117; Irvine, 'Editorial' 264n23).[29] It seems evident, then, that Livesay's exposure to the Auden generation's innovations in poetic form facilitated her transition from leftism to modernism, and that *New Frontier* provided an outlet for this transformation in her poetry and poetics.

Abandoning the depersonalized, collectivist voice of her early-1930s proletarian poetry, 'Yes!' is a modernist interior monologue, a mode that may have led Stevens to suggest that 'the title [is] perhaps an echo of Molly Bloom's affirmation of love' in the final chapter of Joyce's *Ulysses* ('Development' 258). The declamatory title could likewise be traced back to the signature Joycean epiphany. Stevens's proposition is certainly plausible insofar as an allusion to Joyce's modernism coincided with the mid-1930s shift in Livesay's poetics away from the anti-modernist tendencies of her Masses years. Beyond the titular allusion and the interior monologue form, though, evidence of Joyce's specific influence is less substantial. With 'Yes!' Livesay concatenates unusual juxtapositions of images, employing the common modernist stream-of-consciousness technique. The opening of 'Yes!' *in medias res* is also typical of the modernist foregrounding of the poem as fragment, as in Pound's *The Cantos*. Not only structured as an internally coherent fragment like the first of *The Cantos*, 'Yes!' also exploits fragmentation as the technical means of mixing voices, images, and verse forms in radical discontinuity, which in turn generates new connections through juxtaposition.

'Yes!' establishes its formal discontinuity in its fragmented opening line, where the initial conjunction implies its rhetorically logical but absent antecedent:

> But there must be beauty somewheres, somewheres,
> Kid yourself, keep telling yourself, Kid.
> The steel-helmeted bird, relentless to Honolulu
> Pilot spanning blue's outdistance,
> They lie low together, loving. They know,
> They speed in intimate connection
> Pilot in plane, man in woman. (*Collected* 84)

Shifting from the colloquialisms of the internal monologue to the elevated diction of the poetic conceit, this opening stanza epitomizes the vocal juxtapositions and class intersections throughout 'Queen City.' While changing vocal registers, the speaker imagines the figurative passage from street to sky and the transcendence of both class and economic barriers. With the ascent to the sky, juxtaposed images of airplane in sky, pilot in airplane, man in woman travel with 'speed in intimate connection' in classless freedom; but with the return to the street, images of obstructed movement present 'a hard street and a smashing hatred / Enemy shoulders brushing' in class conflict. Pursuing beauty not in stasis but in movement, the speaker constructs the second and final stanza by means of anaphora, creating rhetorical connections as the continuous sentence accumulates images of beauty, culminating in 'the warm scent of the breath bent on a woman.' These juxtapositional images build to this 'beauty with connection caught / My fruit content in a warm womb.' That the final line break creates discontinuity – by terminating the rhetorical figure of anaphora and by juxtaposing the abstraction of beauty to the concrete final image by way of apposition – only reasserts the poem's creation of new continuities. Furthermore, Livesay's introduction of the personal pronoun ('my') in the final line not only underscores her conversion to a modernist poetry of 'lyricism and personal passion' (*Right Hand* 153) but also enables an empathetic response from the reader through the personation of the speaker and of his/her desires. The personal pronoun is, in itself, 'with connection caught': its gender ambiguity suggests the 'intimate connection' of 'man in woman.' Their sexual congress is a metonymic form of intimacy, one that Livesay herself achieves through her poem's embodiment of a personalist poetic. Coincident with a moment of formal breakdown in the poem, the closing lines gesture toward Livesay's acceptance of the formally fragmented character of modernist poetics, her adaptation to personalist modes of expression under the influence of the Auden circle, and her poetry's accommodation of gendered identities and personal eroticism during a period of mid-decade transition away from the masculinist gender and cultural politics of the CPC-allied organizations with which she had been affiliated during the early 1930s.

Given her auspicious debut in the magazine, it is disconcerting to discover that of her *New Frontier* poems, only 'Doom Elegy' was collected in *Day and Night*, that only three additional *New Frontier* poems appeared in 'The Thirties' section of *Collected Poems* ('Yes!' rpt. in 'Queen City'; 'And Still We Dream' rpt. as 'Deep Cove: Vancouver'; and 'Spain'), and that the 'New Frontier 1936–1937' section of *Right Hand Left Hand* contains no poetry whatsoever. Even after the publication of *Collected Poems* and *Right Hand Left Hand*, Livesay left uncollected over half the poems (five of nine) she contributed to the magazine. That she suppressed more than half of the poems she published in *New Frontier* can surely be attributed to their failure to meet the criteria of social realism she demanded of 'proletarian literature' at the time (*Right Hand* 230). Were these poems reproduced in her poetry collections, we could have seen the disparity between her mid-1930s pronouncements on social realism and her poetry's proclivities toward a socially and politically conscious modernism and, by late 1936, a return to socialist romanticism. Just months into her *New Frontier* period, her nascent radicalized modernism was displaced by a revival of her leftism, a transition to socialist romanticism triggered by the declaration of war in Spain on 18 July 1936.

For Livesay and other Popular Front poets and activists, Republican Spain in the early months of the Spanish Civil War represented a socialist utopia, a romantic topos onto which she and her comrades projected their dreams of revolution. Her earliest poems about the Spanish war are predictably suffused with socialist romanticism. As Nicola Vulpe observes, 'Livesay supported the Republic as a matter of course and transferred it to her utopias' (45); he also notes that she was not alone among non-Spanish poets in her inclination to write 'at once about the Spanish War but only rarely about Spain,' and that even Auden's 'Spain,' probably the most famous English-language poem on the war, 'appropriates the Spanish War ... through a *displacement*, a transposition of the most pressing issues of the time' (32; original emphasis). Elaborating upon the historical conditions that contributed to the displacement of issues central to the Spanish war from Spain, Vulpe concludes: 'The international and acutely ideological nature of the Spanish War, as did political and ideological conditions at home, facilitated, even demanded such a displacement ... Spain was the theatre only, and to Spain and the very concrete and immediate struggle there for political and economic democracy the poets (and not only the poets) transposed from Canada, as from the rest of the world, their hopes and dreams which at home could only belong to a remote and abstract future' (32). The internationalism of the Popular Front's struggle against fascism certainly encouraged the effacement of national distinctions. In Canada the Popular Front was predicated upon the fact that the rise of fascism in Spain was but an indication that the same could happen in this country. *New Frontier* articles documenting the fascist press and political activities in Quebec were aimed at an acquiescent Canadian populace that steadfastly believed the fascists could never take political power in Canada (see Betcherman; Robin Martin). So when the *New Frontier* editorial of September 1936 reported on the Spanish Civil War, it concluded with the displacement of the ideological conflict from Spain to Canada: 'For Canadians the lesson in Spain is clear: the only hope for democracy, peace and progress in this country is a People's Front including all sections of the working and middle class' ('Civil War' 3).

This practice of transnational displacement is effected in Livesay's early romanticist poems about the Spanish war – 'And Still We Dream' and 'Man Asleep' – published together in the October 1936 issue of *New Frontier*. For both poems, the dream is the figurative vehicle through which people escape from war to utopias. In 'And Still We Dream' the speaker warns a fellow dreamer on the mountainside that 'we, who like to lie here hushed, immobile / ... Can have no rest from clash of arms' and that they must take collective action: 'rise up, Comrade, / It is death to rest' (*Collected* 94). The speaker in 'Man Asleep' addresses a figure 'hunched in grass': a homeless man, the 'dreaming one' whose figurative Spanish guerrilla 'brothers raise the dust / Over Madrid.' The homeless man is then urged to behold the utopian prospect of a Republican victory in Spain:

> See, the world's home they build in Spain –
> The fireside stone you never had, the arms
> You snatched at, but could not maintain.
>
> Now hunched in sleep, you dream the battle's done
> But still your bones shall spring to life like steel
> Clamp down on victory, behold the sun! (*Archive* 45)

Here the bond of comradeship between the homeless man and the guerrillas effects the displacement of social and economic problems of homelessness in North America to the political arena in Spain. As inspiration for the homeless man, who dreams his 'battle's done' and so passively accepts defeat, the war in Spain is presented as another struggle for a utopian 'world's home.' Because 'Man Asleep' was written at an early stage of the war when 'the triumph of Republican and especially revolutionary Spain seemed, and indeed was, a distinct possibility' (Vulpe 46), it communicates an optimism unique among Livesay's war and anti-war poems of the 1930s. Since her optimism had been so premature and, in the end, mistaken, it is not surprising that she chose to suppress 'Man Asleep' from her subsequent collections and to omit 'And Still We Dream' from the 'Spain 1936–1939' section of *Right Hand Left Hand*.

'In Preparation,' Livesay's next Spanish war poem in *New Frontier*, was published in the February 1937 issue. In contrast to the socialist romanticism of 'And Still We Dream' and 'Man Asleep,' 'In Preparation' presents a romanticized portrait of lovers undercut by its wartime context. Not until the poem's final lines is it revealed that the poem is set at time of war. At first we perceive the lovers concealed in the 'dark,' looking at the 'intermittent spark / Of sun shaft hitting out at snow.' We encounter this striking image of natural beauty not knowing its violent origin. That the lovers are holed up in blackout during an air raid is suspended until the final couplet: 'Look fearless at these searchlight suns, / Unblinking at the sound of guns.' Read as an imperative, the lovers' command ('Look') implores the reader to behold the wartime reality behind the poem's romanticized images of natural beauty. So the poem itself is constructed 'in preparation' of its audience for the reality of anti-aircraft floodlights and guns. That the poem could ever adequately prepare its audience for the reality of war is doubtful. Apparently, Livesay was herself uncertain about 'In Preparation,' because she never reprinted the poem.

Nor did she reprint the other two poems that accompany 'In Preparation' in the February 1937 issue of *New Frontier*: 'The Dispossessed' and 'In Praise of Evening.' While 'The Dispossessed' may have been written as early as 1934 or 1935, when the majority of Livesay's verse was directed toward issues related to her social work, its subject matter is still consistent with the social concerns of the Popular Front. Livesay had at one time collected 'The Dispossessed' among the poems in the unpublished typescript entitled 'The Down and Out Series' (c. 1934–5; DLC-UM, box 80, file 4), which contains poems she later published as part of 'Depression Suite.' 'The Dispossessed' shares certain formal features with some of the verse in 'Depression Suite,' lyrics reminiscent of Industrial Workers of the World ballads and workers' songs. The distinctive formal character of the poem, however, is not its derivation from the working-class ballad but from the Elizabethan pastoral lyric. It is in part a parody of Christopher Marlowe's 'The Passionate Shepherd to His Love'; it is also an imitation of Day Lewis's 'Two Songs,' published in *A Time to Dance* (1935), the second of which parodies Marlowe's lyric. 'The Dispossessed' signals a departure from Livesay's previous social and political poems in its evocation of courtly poetry of the sixteenth century; this departure represents not so much a problem of audience – for Marlowe's poem had long been the object of parody and would have been familiar to many readers of *New Frontier* – as one of voice. The speakers of the poem are the urban homeless, not intellectuals, artists, and writers. Another related problem with the poem is its objectification of the homeless for a predominantly poetry-literate, educated audience of *New Frontier* readers. As a homeless speaker declaims in the final stanza:

O come with me and be my love!
Here in the crowd, break free:
The world's eye shall our pleasures prove
And lust at misery. (7)

The speaker's attempt to convince a *New Frontier* audience to join the homeless crowd is of course ironic, undercut by the final lines, which objectify and ironize (and so establish the audience's distance from) the miserable conditions of the homeless. Coupled with the parody of

Marlowe's courtly lyric, the speaker's objectification of the homeless is therefore not empathetic but rather ironic. The speaker, who appears in the guise of the collective 'we' in the opening stanza, is revealed to be an individual 'me' in the final stanza. What we are left with is the speaker's impersonation of the homeless, an ironized lyric subject speaking as a member of the homeless crowd.

'In Praise of Evening' appears to have been the third section of a sequence, possibly together with 'In Preparation' and 'The Dispossessed.'[30] The typescript of this 'sequence' as such is no longer extant, but all three poems were printed together in *New Frontier*, and all thematize 'love' as a social force, whether ironized ('In Preparation,' 'The Dispossessed') or idealized ('In Praise of Evening'). Where 'In Preparation' and 'The Dispossessed' employ techniques to undercut poetic romanticization, 'In Praise of Evening' fully embraces the aesthetics and ideology of socialist romanticism. If these poems were indeed part of a sequence, they constitute a contradictory social vision.

While the speaker of 'The Dispossessed' ironizes the conditions of poverty, the speaker of 'In Praise of Evening' empathizes with the homeless, seeing beyond their privation to their endurance and to their future:

> The excitement of evening, bare relief
> In living, and thrusting the hand out
> In taut silhouette against sunset
> As a tree on the rim of horizon:
> The liveness of breathing, clenched against hunger
> Leaving defeat behind on the doorstep
> The heart resilient with April's motion
> Contracting, expanding to earth's own rhythm. (*Archive* 49)

Composed in one continuous sentence, this first half of the poem furnishes a sense of movement by stringing together a series of verbs in the present tense, giving form to the speaker's hope for progress. Assonance here creates continuities, presenting a formal pattern of social solidarity among the homeless. These unified gestures of the homeless are juxtaposed to 'famine's gesture' in the second half of the poem. The conspicuous disappearance of organic imagery so prevalent in the first half of the poem underscores the non-pastoral reality that the urban homeless experience day to day. Absence of assonance further emphasizes the harassed and unsettled condition of the homeless, which is brought into relief with the return to an assonantal pattern, together with tree imagery, in the final lines:

> The will to be rooted, but like a tree waving
> Sifting the air through boughs and branches
> Leaning to lover, urgent with blossom
> In wise embracing shielding the seed. (*Archive* 49)

Given order through image and sound, these final lines rearticulate 'earth's own rhythm,' springtime plenitude counterposed to barren 'famine's gesture.' In particular, the repetition of the tree image – the static silhouette of a tree at sunset, which becomes the dynamic gesture of a tree in the wind – communicates the ideas of progress and regeneration propelled by 'April's motion.' Like the silence of the workers in Livesay's Third Period proletarian poems, the homeless communicate here through gestures. These gestures are not coded in the courtly pastoral language of 'The Dispossessed' (those homeless who, ironically, probably never possessed such language) but in nature imagery, the language of a common people. The final lines embody the socialist-romantic vision of the poem: they shift into the romanticized language of lovers, whose 'seed' or children represent a utopian generation of the future.

That Livesay never placed 'In Praise of Evening' in any of her collections may be attributed to her tendency to suppress her socialist romanticism of the 1930s. 'In Praise of Evening' was published (and perhaps written) in early 1937, when Livesay's poetic interests were shifting away from social poetry about the unemployed and the homeless and revolutionary romanticist poetry about the Spanish war toward anti-war and elegiac poetry about the victims of war. This shift in poetic sensibility may explain why she left uncollected all three poems published in the February 1937 issue of *New Frontier*. Indeed, the next two poems she published in the April and June issues – 'A Mother, 1918' and 'Spain' – were both anti-war pieces.

'A Mother, 1918' returns to a wartime context through an elegiac mode of anti-pastoral and anti-war poetry. This is not uncommon among poets of the Popular Front, who often drew upon images of the First World War to serve as anti-war propaganda (Dowson 19). As a poem about a mother who recalls the wartime loss of her son, 'A Mother, 1918' was likely also influenced by the policies of the Canadian League against War and Fascism, a Popular Front group of which

Livesay was member and organizer. 'Women who joined the League,' writes Joan Sangster, 'believed one could be anti-war and anti-fascist at the same time, for few were absolute pacifists' (143–4). With the onset of the Spanish Civil War in July 1936, the league moved away from pacifism to support a war for peace and democracy in Spain, eventually changing its name in 1937 to the League for Peace and Democracy (Sangster 143). Yet the only way one could read 'A Mother, 1918' as both anti-war and anti-fascist is to establish that the poem was originally published in a Popular Front magazine such as *New Frontier*. Because 'A Mother, 1918' was never collected by Livesay, we might conclude that its governing allusion to the First World War diverged too sharply from the immediate historical events documented in her other anti-war poetry of the 1930s. Another reason that she might have left it uncollected is the speaker's romanticization of her dead son, imagined through the conceit of a 'deflowered' flower (*Archive* 50). Livesay relies throughout the poem upon the primary sentimental value of the flower imagery to communicate secondary political significations. The mother's romanticization of her son's death may be a faint political gesture, but her elegiac act of commemoration is personal, not communal.

Livesay's poetic sentimentality soon came under attack in an article submitted by Vernon van Sickle to *New Frontier*, entitled 'Dorothy Livesay and A.A. [Audrey Alexandra] Brown.' Van Sickle was a member of the Vancouver New Frontier Club (NFC), founded in June 1936 and chaired by Livesay (DLC-UM, box 15, file 3). In his letter of 5 April 1937 to the Vancouver NFC, *New Frontier* editor William Lawson summarized van Sickle's article (never published and no longer extant), saying, 'Dorothy's work is criticized for its sentimentality. But there is no attempt to substantiate this criticism (with which I am in complete agreement)' (DLC-UM, box 60, file 37). Given the appearance of 'A Mother, 1918' in the April 1937 issue, the timing of van Sickle's article and Lawson's letter suggests that Livesay's most recent poem may have provoked this critique of her 'sentimentality.' From this reference we may infer from the balance of Lawson's summary that he means van Sickle's critique of Livesay's romanticism both before and after her conversion to communism. The assault on her poetry's sentimentality, moreover, is a signal masculinist reaction to an overtly feminized poetry (as in 'A Mother, 1918'); this form of anti-sentimentalism, symptomatic of both modernist and anti-modernist contempt for feminized forms of culture, not only demonstrates the period's disavowal of the feminine but also exemplifies the ways in which women poets on the left were subject to gender-specific attacks.

Between December 1936 to April 1937, correspondence between the Vancouver NFC and Lawson had been dominated by arguments over *New Frontier* publication policies. Lawson's justification for not publishing the Vancouver group's offerings was based on what local NFC secretary Duncan Macnair, in his January 1937 letter to Lawson, claimed the Toronto editor had called the "sectarianism" of the Vancouver NFC (*Right Hand* 237). 'We were considered to be too individualistic and anarchistic,' Livesay later reflected (*Right Hand* 234), a view that was met by Lawson's decision to promote aggressively his own leftist political beliefs – anti-Trotskyite and anti-CCF[31] – and which resulted in his rejection of some contributions by members of the Vancouver NFC. Even so, Lawson's assessment of Livesay's sentimentalist and individualist tendencies does not seem to have impeded her publication in *New Frontier*, though it is still worth remarking that she published only one more poem in the magazine after April 1937.

'Spain,' the last poem Livesay published in *New Frontier*, appeared in the June 1937 issue. Possibly written in reaction to van Sickle and Lawson, it abnegates her poetic sentimentality and individualism. Given this context, we may read the poem as a masculinist, anti-sentimentalist critique of feminized, bourgeois culture. 'Spain' accosts its projected audience of bourgeois aesthetes, assailing their appreciation of an apolitical art for art's sake: 'You who hold beauty at your fingertips / Hold it because the splintering gunshot rips / Between your comrades' eyes' (*Collected* 98). Rather than allowing aesthetics to subordinate Popular Front politics (as in 'A Mother, 1918'), 'Spain' engages leftist tactics to censure aestheticism. Later in the poem Livesay specifies her intended bourgeois audience – 'You who live quietly in sunlit space / Reading The Herald after morning grace' (*Collected* 98) – but this reference merely serves to exculpate middle-class readers of *New Frontier* and other fellow-travellers. Less than a year after she published 'And Still We Dream' and 'Man Asleep,' the revolutionary romanticism of Livesay's early Spanish war poetry had dissipated, replaced by an extreme anti-bourgeois leftism.

Her poetic critique of aestheticism is consistent with *New Frontier* editorial policy. Its inaugural April 1936 editorial, for instance, targeted the aestheticist's retreat to 'the ivory tower, in which some artists in general and so many poets in particular have taken temporary refuge.' *New Frontier*'s editorial board strongly opposed what was perceived to be bourgeois, aestheticist, *l'art pour l'art* leanings of Canadian writers, artists, and intellectuals. Livesay's own critiques of aestheticism can be found in two prose documents from her *New Frontier* period published in *Right Hand Left Hand*: 'Proletarianitis in Canada,' probably the text for one of her public talks about *New Frontier* in 1936 (see *Right Hand* 220–4), and 'Decadence in Modern Bourgeois Poetry,' the transcript of her CBC radio broadcast that same year. As the title of her broadcast suggests, Livesay was preoccupied at the time with a leftist critique of aestheticism and decadent – that is, in her terms, non-progressive – modernist poetry. According to her thesis, 'modern poetry reflects the decadence of bourgeois society' (*Right Hand* 61). 'All modern poetry has this same tendency,' she adds, 'which arises from the theory of art for art's sake: namely, to appeal to a very small group of people who happen to have had the same prolonged education and the same refinement of the senses' (*Right Hand* 63). In typically leftist fashion, her broadcast ends with the pronouncement that such aestheticist and decadent 'bourgeois art is dead, [and] that a new art, the art of the proletariat is being born' (*Right Hand* 67).

Never published by Livesay herself, 'Invitation to Silence' (c. 1936–7) is a suppressed poem from her *New Frontier* period that represents the continuation of her leftist (anti-bourgeois and anti-modernist) tendencies after the collapse of *Masses*. It performs the leftist critique of decadent modernism that she implemented in 'Decadence in Modern Bourgeois Poetry' and demonstrates her own poetry's failure to meet the criteria of social realism (or, in her terms, proletarian literature) that she detailed in 'Proletarianitis in Canada.' The poem opens with its proletarian speaker's oration to an audience of 'befuddled poets and prophets ... / convinced of decadence' (*Archive* 47). Though she uses the term 'decadence,' Livesay does not limit its denotation to *fin de siècle* culture. For her, the term signifies the condition of modern bourgeois culture in decline; her decadent 'poets and prophets' are therefore representatives of what she and other leftists believed to be a literary culture and capitalist economy in a state of decay. Language itself, her speaker laments, has deteriorated in this historical context: 'Words! I am ashamed to use words, you have so abused them / They were lovely once: now they have been corrupted / Crushed under the weight of too many meanings.' According to Livesay, the language of decadent modernist poetry consists of an erudite diction (*Right Hand* 63–4). As her speaker says of that language toward the beginning of the second stanza: 'Forget the tinklings and the jangle: there is volume behind them.' The 'volume' behind a decadent poetic language is the sound and mass of the proletariat – agricultural labourers, miners, and factory workers. For the balance of the second stanza and the whole of the lengthy third, Livesay records the sounds of labour and protest from the proletariat in the fields, the mines, and the factories. It is in these stanzas that she chronicles events which concern the militant working class and make the poem, if only in part, a document of social realism – or, in Livesay's lexicon, proletarian literature.

That social realism gives way to socialist romanticism in the latter half of the poem. As in her leftist poetry of the early 1930s, Livesay's proletariat in 'Invitation to Silence' communicates by non-verbal means. Opening the fourth stanza, the speaker calls out to the bourgeoisie to 'shake off your radio-trained ears / And hear the thunder of non-broadcast sounds' (*Archive* 48). Like the 'volume' behind the bourgeoisie's decadent language, the 'thunder' above the radio is that of the proletariat; their 'non-broadcast sounds' are the products of their labour and their means of communication. In the final two stanzas, the proletariat gain control over the means of communicative production – that is, the means of production *as* the means of communication (Williams, 'Means' 57). Replacing the bourgeois 'poets and prophets,' the proletariat become the 'singers of this world' (*Archive* 48). These stanzas describe the silence of a decadent bourgeoisie whose culture and economy have come to a standstill and, at the same time, the silence of a proletariat whose seizure of the means of production brings about a general strike. In contrast to the first stanza, in which the bourgeois 'poets and prophets' are said to have accumulated words with too many meanings, in the final stanza words are said to be emptied of all meaning: 'Until one word comes hurling, striking at the root of you ... / Until from ploughed lands, the mines or the factories / "Revolution"'s sounded out in marching feet' (*Archive* 48). Communicated in a non-verbal form, recalling the final lines of 'In Green Solariums,' 'Revolution' is signified by the action and sound of 'marching feet.' This non-verbal means of proletarian communication manifests the utopian aspect of Livesay's socialist romanticism, yet it also represents a crisis for her leftist poetry. That this poem is, after all, an 'Invitation to Silence' bears repeating.

Radical proletarian poetry such as 'Invitation to Silence' threatens the liberal-democratic tenets upon which *New Frontier* and the Popular Front were founded: it is an agitprop poem that speaks unashamedly and exclusively for the revolutionary proletariat. Even though the poem is addressed to a bourgeois audience, its proletarian speaker does so to convert the 'dying bourgeoisie' to the revolutionary cause of the proletariat (*Right Hand* 67). There is little chance that 'Invitation to Silence' would have been published in *New Frontier*, a Popular Front magazine aimed at drawing support from the class that Livesay's poem attacks and intends to eliminate.

Published in the June 1937 issue of *New Frontier*, Livesay's article 'Poet's Progress' better serves the social and political interests of the Popular Front. This article could even be read as an apologia for her *New Frontier* poetry, a mediation between 'revolutionary' modernism and socialist romanticism in the historical setting of the Popular Front. Livesay purports here to determine the 'functions' of the progressive poet: 'He must have individual personality[;] he must associate himself with "pure ideas"; [and] he must be the conveyor of emotional values' (23). She defines each of the three functions, taken in order. Instead of modernist and leftist practices of poetic impersonality, the first function accentuates the poet's personality: 'No modern poet can be accused of trying to lose his individualism in the "collectivist spirit"' (23). Individualism, once anathema to Livesay's leftism, is reaccommodated in the 'collectivist' context of the Popular Front. In her concept of individualism, the personality of the poet is sublimated by the poem itself: 'A poet's individual mark appears not in his thought content, but in his style, form, and technique. This is as true of T.S. Eliot as it is true of Auden and Spender' (23).[32] The poet's second function is concerned with 'the problem of what we mean by experience and the expression of "pure ideas,"' or traditional poetic themes ('love, death and nature'). Here the poet's role is to associate what Livesay calls "pure ideas" and "poetic experience" with the philosophical, political and social concepts of his time' (23). The poet's third function is to render the 'ideational content' of poetry not as abstractions but as expressions of 'emotional value' in the portrayal of social, economic, or political issues and, at the same time, in the arousal of 'aesthetic sense' (23). Having defined the three elements of progressive poetry – 'formal expression, philosophical content, and emotional value' (23) – Livesay then observes their correlation with the two functions of that poetry's audience: 'The three are related together in such a fashion as to create in the hearer a sensation of identity with others, and to release in him an individual creative comprehension' (23–4).

These concepts of social solidarity and aesthetic response make plain the socio-political character and cultural function of her progressive poetry: it is at once collectivist and individualist. Accordingly, the three functions of the poet and two functions of the audience constitute the theoretical underpinnings of not only modern poetry's progress but also socio-political progress. Livesay's concluding remarks on this progressive movement resound with revolutionary romanticism:

> If these premises are accepted we can go on more fearlessly to an understanding of what modern poets are attempting. Recognizing that we are living in a time of transition, their concern is to identify themselves with those forces in society which are working towards human development and expression, as opposed to other groups, identified with capitalism, which are seeking to hold the clock back ... To those who still cling to the more static conception of society such poetry is 'propaganda.' Fifty years hence it will not seem so, and the critics will again have time to concern themselves with the highly varied individual differences between poets who are now lumped together as being ruined by the 'collectivist complex.' (24)

Because Livesay's apologia was the last item she contributed to *New Frontier*, her words obtain an uncanny sense of closure. In conceptualizing the functions of progressive poetry and its audience, she ventured to offer her contemporaries and historians the critical tools with which they could separate her 'individualism' from the mass of versifiers on the cultural left. Like the progressive modernist poets of the Auden generation whom she emulated, Livesay has emerged more than fifty years after the collapse of the Popular Front as one of the distinctive voices among Canadian poets of the literary left. Yet also in common with the Auden generation, she retreated from the cultural left at the end of the 1930s. By the end of the decade these revolutionary modernist poets of the Popular Front found their socialist utopias in decline.

Left in Crisis

As Dorothy Livesay tells the story in her memoir and dramatic monologue addressed to Jean Watts Lawson (Gina in *Journey with My Selves*), the founder and financial backer of *New Frontier*, the collapse of the magazine after the September 1937 issue was the first in a chain of calamitous events for political and cultural groups of the left in the late 1930s:

Nineteen thirty-eight must have been the watershed of our youth. What we had worked for and dreamed it could lead into was a decade without war, without dictatorship, when man's urge for power and destruction might be curbed for good. Instead the scene was dominated by Mussolini, Franco, Hitler and Stalin. You will remember, Gina, the tension of that year when all across Canada the forces of left and right were lining up, not for unity, but for power. Magazines like *New Frontier* folded, the United Front collapsed and in my seaport town, Vancouver, the Progressive Arts Club and the West End Community Centre ... were in disarray. (*Journey* 83, 85)

As much as international and national politics in 1938 could have devastated a Popular Front publication such as *New Frontier*, the magazine was already in trouble by late 1937, but not on the political front. The problems it encountered were less international and national than local, less political than financial and organizational. The organizational crises that Livesay recalled – among the Popular Front, the Vancouver PAC,[33] and the West End Community Centre – certainly contributed to the demise of *New Frontier*. But she neglected to mention the magazine's financial crisis, which was outlined, together with a plan for fiscal and editorial restructuring, on the final page of the September 1937 issue:

New Frontier is an independent venture, with the backing of no organization or party. Contributions from friends have supplemented its income from sales and subscriptions ... To continue we must have circulation, and so we have decided to launch a public drive for the establishment of a circulation fund ... We are re-organizing our editorial board and securing the services of a full-time business manager. We hope that the improvement in the magazine and in its business organization will raise circulation to a point where we will be self-sustaining. ('Message')

Given that no further issues of the magazine were published after September 1937, we can assume that the appeal for public funding proved unsuccessful. While the statement that *New Frontier*, like *Masses*, received no funding from political parties is true, the claim that the magazine lacked organizational support certainly diminishes the importance of the national network of NFCs, which the editorial describes as 'discussion groups in every Canadian province' ('Message').[34] The portrait in the September editorial of the 'new' *New*

Frontier as an 'independent venture' clearly conflicts with the statement that appeared at the foot of the every masthead until the July–August 1937 issue: 'NEW FRONTIER welcomes the work of Canadian artists and writers ... As NEW FRONTIER is a co-operative venture, it does not pay for contributors.' The removal of this policy statement from the September 1937 issue indicates the direction of the magazine's reorganization away from a 'co-operative venture,' whereby the NFCs contributed material and solicited subscriptions, toward an 'independent venture,' in which the NFCs were limited to the role of 'discussion groups.' Given the featured writers in the September 1937 issue – Sylvia Townsend Warner, Valentine Ackland, and C. Day Lewis – we can also witness how *New Frontier* played down 'the work of Canadian artists and writers' and exploited the value of internationally recognized authors in order to boost circulation. While these reorganization policies may appear to have been fiscally sound, they risked alienating the magazine's guaranteed reader and contributor base in the NFCs. In reality, *New Frontier* was already an 'independent venture' when it was founded and financed by Jean Watts Lawson's inheritance money; its reorganization strategy failed to estimate the potential loss of 'co-operative' support from the NFCs. With the campaign to solicit funds from public sources, to increase circulation, and to become an 'independent' and 'self-sustaining' magazine, *New Frontier* wrote its own invitation to silence.

Without support from organizations such as the PACs or the NFCs and without patronage, magazines of the cultural left such as *Masses* and *New Frontier* could hardly have lasted longer than a single issue. Both magazines terminated with an appeal for increased circulation, and both succumbed as a result of financial shortfalls. To blame the financial crises experienced by the two magazines on the economic difficulties of the Depression is the immediate temptation, if we seek an easy answer to the question of why neither magazine could maintain fiscal security. We could produce a comparable contemporary, the *Canadian Forum*, as a magazine that experienced financial instability but still survived under private ownership in the early 1930s and with backing from the League for Social Reconstruction (LSR) in the middle to late 1930s.[35] As an association of intellectuals with leanings toward British Fabianism, the LSR was well positioned to wage educational campaigns against the injustices of monopoly capitalism and present the alternative system of cooperative ownership and centralized state planning. With a middle-class membership of intellectuals, the league was far more financially secure than the predominantly communist and working-class PACs. Cultural rather than class affiliation of intellectuals, artists, and writers in the NFCs produced a composite left-wing membership of progressive liberals, socialists, and communists who supported the Popular Front. Neither the PACs nor the NFCs were political organizations like the LSR; both were essentially cultural organizations that supported magazines, without the financial resources of a political organization. Whatever the social and political agendas of these magazines on the cultural left, their organizational affiliations determined their solvency or their failure.

Instead of creating continuities and new means and modes of communication, instead of forging unities and new communities and organizations, the Popular Front and Canadian magazine culture of the left were faced at the close of the 1930s with a new state of fragmentation and new conditions of silence. Following the Hitler-Stalin non-aggression pact in August 1939, the CPC, the YCL, Popular Front organizations such as the League for Peace and Democracy, and all leftist publications were banned by authorities, and many leaders of CPC cells were jailed under the Defence of Canada Regulations. Even under section 98, which gave authorities the ability to halt performances by the PACs' theatre groups in the early 1930s, left-wing publications were not made illegal in Canada. August 1939 signalled a more rigorous era in the persecution of Canadian leftist culture, with the government repression of the CPC's national paper, the *Daily Clarion*, published illegally and distributed by an underground network until a new legal paper, the *Canadian Tribune*, was established in January 1940 by one of the regular reviewers for *New Frontier*, Margaret Fairley, among others. While the Canadian cultural left was entering this forceful and prolonged period of political repression, Livesay retreated to live as one of those fellow-travellers whom she had so mercilessly battered in *Masses* and *New Frontier*. As she remembered of herself and her husband in late 1939, 'We were isolated from hearing any Party "line," as I imagine were most people who had been active on the left. Our solution was to withdraw, to settle down to family life on the North Shore' (*Right Hand* 278). It was there, on the North Shore of Vancouver, that Livesay met Alan Crawley in 1938, and there that the organization of a different species of magazine and magazine culture – literary and devoted to poetry – was inchoate but poised on the threshold of the 1940s.

2 Marginal Modernisms:
Victoria Vancouver Ottawa, 1935–1953

Mrs. L. was shocked when she found in turn that I did not belong to the CAA, a Poetry group, The Arts and Letters Club, The Writers Club of Vancouver, or any other august body all of whose members were included in the general invitation and were at the party suitably tagged with printed or typed cards bearing their names and associations ... Why in God[']s name are these priestesses of rhyme so serious?

Alan Crawley, letter to Floris McLaren (n.d. [summer 1941], FMP)

Canadian Poetry Magazine, the CAA, and *Contemporary Verse*

Both *Canadian Poetry Magazine* and *Contemporary Verse* were products of the CAA and its predominantly female membership: the former at the national level, the latter at the local level. When the CAA launched *Canadian Poetry Magazine* under the editorship of E.J. Pratt in January 1936, it was the first periodical of its kind in Canada. Even so, literary historians have routinely omitted it from studies of Canadian little magazines, largely because of prevailing antipathies toward the CAA and its publications among critics and historians in the field of Canadian literary modernism (see Norris, *Little* 20; Dudek, 'Role' 207; McCullagh xxiii). Literary biographers David G. Pitt and Elspeth Cameron have contributed histories of *Canadian Poetry Magazine* editors Pratt and Earle Birney respectively, and historian Lyn Harrington has written of the magazine in *Syllables of Recorded Time: The Story of the Canadian Authors Association 1921–1981*; there are also Birney's memoirs about the CAA and its poetry magazine, collected in *Spreading Time: Remarks on Canadian Writing and Writers*. These histories and memoirs have offered us views of the CAA and its poetry magazine; they have not, for the most part, ameliorated current critical opinion of either the association or the magazine. They have served to elaborate episodes in the careers of Pratt and Birney but neglected the literary-historical significance of the poetry cultures that circulated around the CAA's poetry chapbooks, yearbooks, and magazine during the 1930s and 1940s. While Harrington documents meetings and conventions of the national executive, articles in the *Canadian Author* and the *Canadian Bookman*, and editorial changes on the board of *Canadian Poetry Magazine*, she does not record the histories of local CAA branches. Ever since F.R. Scott memorialized the association as a group of Miss Crotchets in his 1927 poem 'The Canadian Authors Meet,' his portrait has remained indicative of the pejorative ways in which it has been remembered and, moreover, feminized by critics and literary historians of Canadian modernism (see Vipond, 'Canadian'). That portrait of a predominantly female membership is, despite its misogyny, representative of the local branches and poetry groups of the CAA in the 1930s and 1940s. Neither the women of these local poetry groups nor their poetry yearbooks have received attention from historians of the CAA and *Canadian Poetry Magazine*; these omissions have also occluded the origins of *Contemporary Verse* in the association of the 1930s and early 1940s.

Even memoirs and histories of *Contemporary Verse* have failed to mention its evolution out of local poetry groups of those years. Joan McCullagh's history of *Contemporary Verse* admits no connection between the magazine and the 'annual yearbooks of non-modern poetry from various branches of the Canadian Authors' [*sic*] Association [that] continued to be published through the Depression' (xxi–xxii; see also McLaren, 'Contemporary'; Livesay, 'Foreword' and *Journey* 159–66). This categorization of the local CAA yearbooks as 'non-modern' poetry is indicative of the literary-historical refusal to recognize the publications of the association's poetry groups. While most of these yearbooks more often than not included poets of minor talent, there were notable exceptions. Singled out by Pratt as one of the most accomplished among the CAA branches ('News'), the Victoria and Islands poetry group began publication of its yearbook, the *Victoria Poetry Chapbook*, in 1935, followed by another in 1936 and three more in biannual instalments (1937–8, 1939–40, 1941–2). Having attended meetings of the Victoria poetry group since 1934, Alan Crawley was chosen to select the contents of the *Victoria Poetry Chapbook* in 1935 and 1936; he worked on the chapbook with a committee consisting of Floris McLaren, Doris Ferne, and branch president M. Eugenie Perry. For both McLaren and Ferne, their experiences with Crawley and the *Victoria Poetry Chapbook* were rehearsals for the development of editorial and production policies for *Contemporary Verse*. Both poets were apparently interested in expanding their readerships to a public beyond that of CAA publications.[1] One way to reach and create a broader public for poetry was to found a new poetry magazine. Coincident with the suspension of the *Victoria Poetry Chapbook* after 1941–2, McLaren, Ferne, and Anne Marriott – three of the core members of the Victoria poetry group – assisted in preparations for the first non-CAA-affiliated poetry magazine in Canada. Under Crawley's editorship, McLaren, Ferne, and Marriott were joined by Dorothy Livesay and helped to launch *Contemporary Verse* in September 1941.

If *Canadian Poetry Magazine* and *Contemporary Verse* were products of the CAA in the 1930s, they were also connected to an international modernist little-magazine culture that had emerged in the 1910s. That magazine culture originated with the work of women editors in the United States. *Contemporary Verse* was, like *Canadian Poetry Magazine*, not an avant-garde magazine in the tradition of Margaret Anderson and Jane Heap's the *Little Review* (1914–29), but rather a poetry magazine in the tradition of Harriet Monroe and Alice Corbin Henderson's *Poetry: A Magazine of Verse* (1912–). Both *Canadian Poetry Magazine* and *Contemporary Verse* were in fact fashioned in the image of that first modernist poetry magazine in the United States, *Poetry*, founded by Monroe in Chicago in 1912.

In his editorial for the inaugural issue of *Canadian Poetry Magazine* in January 1936, Pratt makes plain his desire to replicate the successes of American little magazines: 'The United States ... keeps alive, if not flourishing, more than forty magazines which publish nothing but verse and critical comments, and a few of these are responsible for the discovery of several major American poets of the twentieth century. The time is well advanced for Canada to initiate its own movements in the same direction' ('Foreword' 6). While *Poetry* has been memorialized by literary historians as the origin of the modernist little-magazine movement, *Canadian Poetry Magazine* has been denigrated by literary historians as a purveyor of CAA conservatism, boosterism, and mediocrity in verse. There is ample evidence to show that these pejorative traits characterize great quantities of verse published in *Canadian Poetry Magazine*, yet there is substantial verse by poets such as

Livesay, Marriott, Waddington, Page, Kennedy, Smith, Birney, Dudek, and Scott that proves the magazine was by no means bereft of emergent modernist poets.[2] In fact, Pratt published many of the poets in the 1930s who later developed their talents in the more fashionable Canadian little magazines of the 1940s.

As a non-commercial venture, *Canadian Poetry Magazine* was also in line with the financial organization of little magazines such as *Poetry*.[3] By June 1938 Pratt was appealing to the magazine's CAA readership for financial aid, instancing the economic struggles of *Poetry* and the efforts of its founding editor, Monroe, whose autobiography, *A Poet's Life: Seventy Years in a Changing World* (1938), was reviewed in the same issue (Pratt, 'Third'). If Pratt's comparison between *Canadian Poetry Magazine* and *Poetry* were not explicit enough, we need only consider the description of the Canadian magazine in Hoffman, Allen, and Ulrich's *The Little Magazine: A History and a Bibliography* (1946): 'The magazine admits the purpose of its beginning – to furnish Canadian poetry with a voice similar to Harriet Monroe's *Poetry* and other American poetry magazines' (399).

Contemporary Verse announced itself to some of its future contributors in June 1941 as a new (as yet unnamed) magazine 'inspired by the Chicago Poetry Issue' and conceived in reaction to 'the Canadian Poetry Magazine's very low standard' (Livesay to A.M. Klein, 9 June 1941, AMKP, M–3619, 146).[4] The appearance of the April 1941 issue of *Poetry*, the Canadian number edited by E.K. Brown,[5] precisely coincided with the original meeting of the four women founders of *Contemporary Verse* in Victoria on the Easter weekend of 1941 (McLaren, 'Contemporary' 55–6). As contributors to the April 1941 issue of *Poetry*, Livesay, McLaren, and Marriott were acutely aware of the prestige of the magazine, especially among Canadian poets seeking recognition from its established American audience.[6] Livesay and Marriott were featured and McLaren briefly mentioned in the survey article by Brown, 'The Development of Poetry in Canada, 1880–1940' (46–7); Marriott was additionally represented by W.E. Collin's review of her 1939 chapbook, *The Wind Our Enemy*. The April 1941 issue marked not only the first appearances by Livesay, McLaren, and Marriott in *Poetry* but also the last. Yet this distinction did not sever the informal correspondence between *Poetry* and *Contemporary Verse*. As an advocate of exporting Canadian poetry to the United States, Crawley made it his editorial priority to have poets send what he felt to be their best pieces to *Poetry* if, after his own reading, he felt they merited the sizeable audience the American magazine could offer. If rejected by the editors of *Poetry*, poets were encouraged by Crawley to resubmit their manuscripts to *Contemporary Verse*. Given its origins in the founding committee's response to the Canadian number of *Poetry* and its editor's practice of redirecting Canadian poets and their manuscripts toward *Poetry*, *Contemporary Verse* was unofficially opening lines of communication between poets and magazine editors in Canada and the United States. While it sometimes served as a repository for poems rejected by the pre-eminent North American poetry magazine of its time, *Contemporary Verse* in the 1940s was confronted with a modern poetry culture in much the same inchoate condition as that faced by *Poetry* in the 1910s.

Among histories and memoirs of *Contemporary Verse*, only minimal attention has been given to its relationship to *Poetry*. Only Mary Lee Bragg Morton conjectures that *Poetry* was a likely model for *Contemporary Verse* (based on her examination of the two magazines' size and format [44]), though her argument applies equally well to the Philadelphia-based poetry magazine *Contemporary Verse* (1916–29). Livesay has claimed that resuscitating the name *Contemporary Verse* was her suggestion, 'which [she] made remembering an earlier journal printed in the U.S. that [she] had seen on her mother's desk' (*Journey* 164).[7] In his 3 June 1941 letter to the founding committee, Crawley accepted the editorship of a magazine he refered to as 'Canadian Poetry Quarterly,' so named in a letter (since lost) from Marriott to Crawley (ACP, box 1, file 43). While Livesay's suggestion avoided confusion between their poetry quarterly and the CAA's poetry magazine, the rejected name gestures toward the American template for *Contemporary Verse*.

McLaren, in her 14 January 1952 letter to the editor of *Poetry*, Karl Shapiro, explained the nature of the decade-long association between their magazines: 'Both Alan Crawley and I are long[-]time readers and admirers of POETRY (and subscribers whenever we can raise the annual five dollars) and to both of us POETRY has been a more or less unofficial pattern of what we wanted CONTEMPORARY VERSE to be ... CV has existed for ten years to give the serious poets in Canada a place for their work and assurance of critical reading by the few people who feel that "modern" poetry is important' (FMP). McLaren and Crawley, whose extant correspondence dates from 1936, often mentioned issues of *Poetry* in their letters; they even shared a subscription during the 1940s. Writing to McLaren in 1939, Crawley alerted her to the July 1938 issue of *Poetry*, in which Archibald MacLeish printed the transcript of his speech on the state of modern poets and poetry 'In Challenge Not Defence.' 'It will help you I am certain,' Crawley wrote to McLaren, 'and set into actual conviction what I have tried to say so often and what I know you feel with me' (FMP). Crawley redirects MacLeish's challenge toward Canadian poetry and poets: 'what is Canadian poetry doing really? Will the poets never get away from the old expressions and longings and verbiage? Do so few of them really feel so little of [w]hat is going on about them in the world today and do they entirely overlook or ignore what a poet should feel is his mission, to put it highly, or his JOB at any rate?' (Crawley to McLaren [1939], FMP). Taking the pioneering editorial work of Monroe and *Poetry* as their American models, Crawley and McLaren produced *Contemporary Verse* as a magazine for modern poetry in Canada. Crawley even recommended that McLaren borrow a copy of 'Harriet Monroe's book of her life' – *A Poet's Life* (ACP, box 1, file 39, item 1). Having appropriated at least a page or two from Monroe's autobiography, McLaren was also a minor poet who, like Monroe, became a poetry-magazine editor. For both, a poet's life was exchanged for – if not sacrificed to – an editor's life; their poems have become footnotes to their editorial work in the service of modern poetry.

For Crawley and Monroe alike, the editorial vocation began with a common interest in modern British poetry of the 1910s. Both were introduced to modern poetry when the Georgians were in vogue (Livesay, Foreword ix–x; Monroe 255–6).[8] Of *Contemporary Verse* historians, Morton alone contends that although Crawley's interest in the Georgian poets had declined by the time he began editing *Contemporary Verse*, his editorial principles and critical sensibility continued to be influenced by modern British poets into the 1940s (2). She correlates certain of the Georgians' traits – simplicity, lyricism, pastoralism, eclecticism, nationalism (4–5) – and their popularity to Crawley's editorial practices and tastes: 'Their search for a wide audience and their emphasis on an unpretentious style appealed to Crawley and constitute his most enduring heritage from Georgian poetics' (4). Although the relation of Georgian poetics to Crawley's editorial principles is only sometimes pertinent, Morton does not mean to suggest that he was influenced to the point that *Contemporary Verse* replicates Edward Marsh's *Georgian Poetry* anthologies (1912–22). If Crawley were remembered solely as the compiler of the *Victoria Poetry Chapbook* (1935–6), there might be better justification for the comparison. Monroe, like Crawley, was an advocate of modern verse among late

Romantics, late Victorians, and Georgians – she among their midwestern American counterparts of the 1910s and 1920s, he among their western Canadian imitators of the 1930s. Like the Georgians with their popular anthologies, however, Monroe and Crawley sought wide audiences for modern poetry; through the medium of their poetry magazines, they endeavoured to create modern poetry's public.[9]

The modern poetry that Crawley introduced to the poetry group of the Victoria CAA was not Georgian but rather that of second-generation British modernists – the Auden generation – and their Anglo-American, Canadian, and Spanish contemporaries.[10] Such poetry was not yet in common currency among the CAA poets in Victoria. Nor were such moderns yet a major influence on the poetry scene when Crawley moved to Vancouver in January 1935. In the fall of that year he attended his first and only meeting of the poetry group of the Vancouver CAA, convened by Marion Isabel Angus, but left dismayed (Crawley to Perry [1935], MEPP, box 3, file 12). In the meantime, he continued to give readings of and talks on modern poetry to the CAA group in Victoria, and he later made contact in Vancouver with Livesay (Crawley, 'Dorothy' 117), with whom he could share his enthusiasms for modern poetry.

Crawley and Livesay had initially arranged – via their mutual acquaintance with McLaren – to get together at a meeting of the Vancouver Poetry Society (VPS) in October 1938. Both Livesay and her husband, Duncan Macnair, were members of the society, chaired by Ernest Fewster.[11] Among the society's accomplishments was the founding of *Full Tide*, a thrice-yearly magazine containing poems by members of the VPS, in December 1936. Livesay's contributions to the society and its poetry magazine consisted of delivering talks on poetry and publishing poems in the May 1938 and February 1939 issues. Crawley, however, had little patience with the society; his first attempt to rendezvous with Livesay at a VPS meeting in the fall of 1938 produced only feelings of exasperation with the poetry he heard, compounded by his disappointment at her absence from the meeting (Crawley to McLaren [1938], FMP). Crawley later submitted to Livesay's entreaties to attend another VPS meeting in 1939 and even give a reading with his 'own comment on the modern poetry and the writers' (Crawley to McLaren [1939], FMP).[12]

Crawley's letter of 3 June 1941 to the founding committee of *Contemporary Verse* emphasized his interest in modern poetry and poets: 'In spite of the distress of the times and the prospect of continued

disquiet and unsettled days to come, I feel that the idea of the publication of a magazine of Canadian poetry is a worthwhile and reasonable
venture that could if properly managed and edited do much to help
modern Canadian writers for I know of no publication that is now
giving this possible help to writers' (ACP, box 1, file 44). Implicit in his
assessment of the publishing field is his criticism of the CAA's poetry
yearbooks and its *Canadian Poetry Magazine*, as well as the VPS's *Full
Tide*. His emphasis on modern Canadian poets excluded many
members of the Victoria and Vancouver poetry groups and, moreover,
militated against Pratt's editorial compromise between modern and
traditional verse in *Canadian Poetry Magazine* (see Pratt, 'Comment' 6).
When Crawley wrote in his September 1941 editorial about spending
'two hundred hours reading poetry published in the preceding twenty
years in Great Britain, Canada and the United States' and 'half as many
hours in libraries and book shops and in searching through current
magazines to find and get together these poems,' he declared himself
a reader of the moderns ('Foreword').

   It may seem unfair to ask in hindsight why none of Livesay, Marriott, Ferne, or McLaren even contemplated taking on the editorship
herself, or even collectively. Instead they selected Crawley and
assumed roles on the founding-publishing committee. 'The founding
committee,' McLaren recalls, 'felt strongly that the choosing of poems
for the magazine was a one-man job; there should be no board of
editors or editorial advisors' ('*Contemporary*' 57). Crawley's insistence
on editorial autonomy probably stemmed from his prior dissatisfaction with committee interference during the process of selection for the
Victoria Poetry Chapbook in 1936.[13] He expressed his displeasure with
such mechanisms of selection and compromise – namely, the necessity
of including at least one poem by every poet in the group – by declining the Victoria poetry group's request that he choose the poems for its
1937 chapbook (Crawley to Perry [1937], MEPP, box 2, file 9). When
approached by Birney in 1946 with a proposal to amalgamate *Canadian
Poetry Magazine* and *Contemporary Verse*, Crawley again backed away
from the compromised editorial role in which an organization such as
the CAA would have placed him. He baulked at the offer of an associate editorship on the board of the proposed magazine because of his
belief in the necessity for editorial autonomy.[14] Crawley's notion of
editorial independence should, however, be understood only in terms
of his power to make final decisions on the selection of poems for *Contemporary Verse*. His sense of autonomy is somewhat misrepresentative

of the production of the magazine, especially his dependence on the publishing committee in Victoria. Within the *Contemporary Verse* group there was a definite division of labour between editorial work undertaken by Crawley in North Vancouver and production work conducted predominantly by McLaren, but also by Marriott and Ferne, in Victoria. McLaren took charge of the clerical work, circulation, and, in the fall of 1950, assistant editorship; McLaren, Livesay, Marriott, and Ferne all contributed reviews and poems and participated in discussions on matters of policy and management, including the decision not to amalgamate with *Canadian Poetry Magazine*. Crawley, who was visually impaired, had to have his wife, Jean Crawley, read manuscripts aloud to him so that he could transcribe them on his Braille typewriter. Without her, McLaren, Livesay, Marriott, and Ferne, *Contemporary Verse* might never have appeared at all.

So why would the four women found and publish but not edit *Contemporary Verse*? Perhaps Livesay, Marriott, McLaren, and Ferne were aware it was utopian that in 1941 a Canadian poetry magazine edited by four women living on the West Coast could gain respectability, and they anticipated that the male-dominated Montreal and Toronto literary establishments would scoff at the presumption of four 'poetesses.' Livesay's leftward politics and agitational persona made her a high-profile member of the founding committee, but not an impartial editor. Because Marriott, McLaren, and Ferne were poets still intimately associated with the Victoria poetry group, there was an immediate need to dissociate *Contemporary Verse* from the CAA if they wanted to attract the leading modern Canadian poets to publish in their magazine. Their ties to the predominating conservative CAA poets might discourage contributions from those modern Canadian poets who were already disinclined to publish in *Canadian Poetry Magazine*. Crawley alone among the founders belonged to no organizations, represented the interests of no cliques, and preached no political programs.

When P.K. Page reviewed *Contemporary Verse* in the eighth issue of *Preview*, the reasons for the four women on the founding committee to defer editorial responsibility for the magazine became evident. In her opinion, '[t]he first – Contemporary Verse – did not say a particular[ly] loud "boo" to the pink tea pretties but it was loud enough for one of their wags to dub it Contemptible Verse in a moment of irritation. That was probably its first real victory' ('Canadian'). Page's gender-inflected phrase 'pink tea pretties' was presumably aimed at the CAA. As well, the parodic name 'Contemptible Verse' is indicative of CAA attitudes toward contemporary experiments in free verse.[15] Page was likely aware of the CAA origins of *Contemporary Verse*, and her masculinist discourse is symptomatic of modernist little-magazine culture of the 1940s, where groups made up predominantly of women such as the CAA or the founding committee of *Contemporary Verse* were subject to gender-specific criticism. While the selection of Crawley as editor distanced the *Contemporary Verse* group from the CAA, the magazine was not immune to the masculinist discourse brandished by its contemporaries.

As Page's review attests, *Contemporary Verse* prompted criticism from the poets of the newly formed *Preview* group in Montreal. Immediately following the publication of *Preview*, the fourth issue of *Contemporary Verse* presented Crawley's statement of his editorial policies:

A glance at the note on contributors at the back of this number shows that CONTEMPORARY VERSE is not the chapbook of a limited or local group of writers. The contents of each number will at once dispel any charge that it exists to press political propaganda, particular social adjustment or literary trend. The aims are to entice and stimulate the writing and reading of poetry and to provide means for its publication free from politics, prejudices and placations, and to keep open its pages to poetry that is sincere in thought and expression and contemporary in theme and treatment and technique. ('Editor's Note' [1942] 3)

Here Crawley countered point by point the original manifesto 'Statement' of the *Preview* group: *Contemporary Verse* was neither parochial, militant, political, partisan, and agitational nor avant-garde. His only definitive statement of editorial policy required that poetry submitted to the magazine be 'contemporary' – or, to use an equivalent term, 'modern' ('Editor's Note' [1942] 3). Having for the first time printed in this issue the names of the members of the founding committee ('To Our Subscribers'), he also made certain to differentiate *Contemporary Verse* from a 'chapbook of a limited or local group of writers' such as the CAA poetry yearbooks or *Preview*, a self-proclaimed 'Literary letter' (Anderson, 'Note' [1942]).

When CAA president William Arthur Deacon wrote to offer Birney the editorship of *Canadian Poetry Magazine* on 8 July 1946, he too mentioned its problem of 'arising out of local chap-books put out by CAA Branches in Edmonton, Ottawa, Montreal, and elsewhere, but excluding Toronto.' Deacon felt dismayed that 'these local efforts, often connected with contests, represented distinct disloyalty to our own publication,' noting the recent Ottawa branch chapbook *Profile* as credible but detrimental to contributions and subscriptions to the national magazine (Deacon 231). Not so myopic as to ignore factors external to the CAA, he acknowledged the competition of magazines such as *Contemporary Verse, First Statement,* and *Preview,* founded in the early 1940s: 'We are also conscious of the fact that the starting up of several rivals by groups of younger poets at different points indicates very clearly that there is some lack in the service that the magazine is not performing' (230). Of the members on the CAA national executive, he cited Marriott as a representative voice of the 'younger poets' in favour of Birney's editorship: 'Miss Anne Marriott said that your influence with the younger poets would be of inestimable value. She saw now the one chance of uniting the poetic interest in Canada' (229–30). Deacon proposed to effect such unity by amalgamating *Canadian Poetry Magazine* with its rivals: 'We have not the capital to finance the purchase of other magazines, but you intimated that the suggestion might be the reverse, namely, that Mr. Alan Crawley is now financing *Contemporary Verse* at a loss and now might be willing to contribute to the costs of *The Canadian Poetry Magazine*' (230–1). We can only speculate whether such a merger might have produced a conflict like that so often documented (and exaggerated) in histories of the Montreal little magazines *Preview* and *First Statement.*

Despite their common ancestry in the CAA poetry yearbooks and derivation from *Poetry, Canadian Poetry Magazine* and *Contemporary Verse* remained separated by their different commitments to the making of modernist little-magazine cultures, particularly to the issue of gender. Crawley's personal correspondence, including editorial advice and recommendations for revision, inspired an entire generation of Canadian poets, especially women poets, to publish their poetry either in *Contemporary Verse* or in other little magazines. As Butling notes in her article on women and British Columbia little magazines, '*Contemporary Verse* is ... significant for the number of women writers that it published. Thirty to fifty percent of the poems in every issue were by women ... (Not until the eighties do we see such a high percentage again)' ('Hall' 61–2).[16] While she is emphatic that *Contemporary Verse* was not a 'women's magazine' (62), Butling speculates on the possible reasons for its attractiveness to women: 'Was it the greater prominence of women in wartime combined with the obvious presence of women contributors at the start of the magazine, or editor

Crawley's open and supportive manner, or the non-aggressive nature of the magazine?' (62). Writing in 1938 to McLaren, Crawley hinted at the gender orientation of his editorial work on *Contemporary Verse* when he announced 'what a feminist I am unconsciously' (FMP).

The extent to which he practised an 'unconscious' feminism and fostered an emergent women's modernism in an otherwise masculinist little-magazine culture can be measured by the significant volume of women's modernist poetry he published in *Contemporary Verse*. In fact, around the mid-point of the magazine's run, Crawley takes stock of the number of men and women poets represented not only in *Contemporary Verse* but also in the recent anthologies *Unit of Five* (1944) and *Other Canadians* (1947); he notes that in each case the men far outnumber the women and finds himself surprised to discover that 'in twenty-two numbers of Contemporary Verse covering a period of more than six years forty men have contributed considerably more poems than the women writers whose number is thirty' ('Notes' 20). If Crawley's initial 'unconscious' feminism facilitated the emergence of a respectable proportion of women poets, his statistical reflection on the magazine's contents bespeaks a gender consciousness that makes plain his advocacy of an increased representation of women at a time when Canada's modernist literary culture sustained its domninant masculinist character.

Conversely, Birney's apparent lack of gender consciousness as editor of *Canadian Poetry Magazine* speaks to the ways in which his emphasis on modernism alienated many women poets affilated with the CAA. During Birney's editorship (1946–8), the publication of modernist Canadian poets became a priority in *Canadian Poetry Magazine*; this had a reciprocal effect, however, of estranging many of its CAA contributors and subscribers, whose conservatism conflicted with its editor's modernism. It also had the concomitant effect of markedly reducing the number of women contributors and thereby reasserting an exclusionary, masculinist modernism. For just under two years, Birney transformed *Canadian Poetry Magazine* into a modernist little magazine aligned with *Contemporary Verse*, but without matching Crawley's consistent record of publishing women modernist poets.

For Birney, the primary editorial concern was not gender but regional representation. Consequently, he attempted to integrate a diversity of poets and regional concerns into the editorial organization of *Canadian Poetry Magazine*. While he edited the magazine from the University of British Columbia campus in Vancouver (with typing and filing assistance from his wife, Esther [Cameron, *Earle* 292]), it was still published and distributed by the management committee in Toronto. In August 1946 he wrote to poets 'selected with a view to regional representation' to form 'an editorial board of men and women who are themselves writing poetry of distinction' (Editorial 6). Letters went out to prospective associate editors: McLaren in Victoria, Marriott and Page in Ottawa, Charles Bruce and Philip Child in Toronto, Patrick Waddington and Leo Cox in Montreal. Page declined on 24 August, claiming conflict of interest: 'I believe that a person cannot work for two magazines – there was the possibility that N[orthern] R[eview] would fold. If it had I would have been delighted to be on your editorial board. As it hasn't, I must refuse' (EBP, box 15, file 21). McLaren followed on 29 August, citing similar circumstances: 'Although my work on C[ontemporary] V[erse] has been entirely non-editorial, my name has been on the magazine from the beginning, and it does take all the time and energy I have to give. I feel that I simply cannot associate myself with another poetry magazine and do justice to either' (EBP, box 14, file 2). Bruce, Child, Waddington, and Cox accepted Birney's offer. Marriott also accepted, though her response to Birney on 21 August betrayed her profound ambivalence and divided loyalties to both *Canadian Poetry Magazine* and *Contemporary Verse* (EBP, box 14, file 25).

Marriott's concurrent involvement with both *Contemporary Verse* and *Canadian Poetry Magazine* is emblematic of their intertwined histories. Her poetry of this period, published in both magazines, is informed by her negotiations between the competing interests of the *Contemporary Verse* group and those of *Canadian Poetry Magazine* and the CAA. Consequently, the tension between the innovative forms and idioms of her modernist poetry (prominent in her *Contemporary Verse* publications) and the derivative manner of her romantic and imagistic lyrics (prevalent in her *Canadian Poetry Magazine*, newspaper, and commercial-magazine publications) is central to her first two decades as a poet, stretching from 1934 to 1953. That tension is compounded by the fact that editors, critics, and reviewers associated with modernist little magazines adopted a gender-specific, feminizing discourse to dismiss the poetry of CAA members. John Sutherland's review of her 1945 collection, *Sandstone and Other Poems*, for instance, assailed Marriott's predominant style: he caricatured her so-called magazine verse – that is, derivative romantic and imagistic poetry typically published in commercial periodicals – and in doing so, exposed a masculinist condescension typical of his attitudes toward women's poetry when he claimed that she 'adopts a difficult modern style to express the philosophy of lady writers of the C.A.A' ('Anne' 100, 101). Despite this kind of criticism, Marriott maintained a tentative balance between her two poetic styles.

Rather than consolidate her poetic interests, she wrote for multiple print and radio outlets: for non-commercial and commercial magazines, for small-press chapbooks and books, for newspapers and radio. By 1941 the Ryerson Press could boast of her publications in 'over fifty magazines in Canada, England, and the United States' (Marriott, *Calling* [front cover]). With publications exceeding even that of the young Livesay, Marriott produced three chapbooks – *The Wind Our Enemy* (1939), *Calling Adventurers!* (1941), and *Salt Marsh* (1942) – and one book-length collection, *Sandstone and Other Poems* (1945), by the age of thirty-two. For her second collection, *Calling Adventurers!*, the CAA awarded her the Governor General's Award for Poetry; that collection contained her verse choruses from the CBC radio documentary drama *Payload* (1940). During the early 1940s Marriott collaborated with Margaret Kennedy on several CBC radio documentary dramas in prose and verse, including *Payload*, *Who's Johnny Canuck* (1941), and *We See Thee Rise* (1943). In the early 1940s she also broadcasted her poetry over local Vancouver radio stations and in 1943 conducted a cross-Canada school radio broadcast series called *My Canada*. Though she knowingly forfeited the complexities of her poetic modernism for these radio productions, she accomplished her goal of reaching a mass audience for her poetry. Throughout the 1940s Marriott attempted to reconcile her modernist poetic practices with her desire for a more popular, less difficult strain of modern lyric poetry; that project ultimately ended in crisis. After *Sandstone* was published in 1945, she did not publish another collection of poetry for thirty-six years. This period of withdrawal and silence was anticipated in her poems of the early to mid-1940s and chronicled in her uncollected poems of the late 1940s and early 1950s – especially in her modernist poetry, much of it still uncollected, published in *Contemporary Verse*.

Within this Victoria-Vancouver poetry-magazine culture, Marriott was joined by Livesay, Crawley, and Birney as advocates of modern poetry's broad dissemination through print and radio media. For Livesay, these prevailing concerns recall her own frustrated efforts to communicate her proletarian poetry of the 1930s to mass audiences through the magazine culture of the Canadian left. By the late 1930s, though, her publication strategies had changed in significant ways.

Following the collapse of *New Frontier*, she shifted her politics from communist to 'soft socialist' (Thompson, *Dorothy* 61), thus allowing her to expand her audience beyond the cultural left in Canada. In contrast to her *Masses* and *New Frontier* periods of 1932–4 and 1936–7, when she restricted her publications to periodicals of the cultural left, the late 1930s, 1940s, and 1950s witnessed her poetry's dissemination among an expanding number of commercial and non-commercial periodicals, a tactic – comparable to Marriott's – that enabled her to reach as wide an audience as possible. Earlier than Marriott, Livesay similarly sought to extend that audience through radio. Anticipated by 'Broadcast from Berlin' in 1932, her interest in writing for radio began in earnest as early as 1936 and continued through the 1940s and 1950s (Tiessen and Tiessen xi). Concurrent with her poetry's distribution through diversified print and radio media, her experimentation with new modes of poetic expression provided alternatives to her leftist modes of the early to mid-1930s. These alternatives developed out of her interest in populist forms of expression employed in other media – not only in radio but also in visual art and theatre – through which she might, if she was capable, reach out to greater audiences. Each of her poetry collections of the 1940s and early 1950s – *Day and Night* (1944), *Poems for People* (1947), *Call My People Home* (1950) – is characterized by her interest in poetry as a medium of mass communication. But even with her increased readership, publicity, reputation, and critical acclaim throughout the 1940s – Governor General's Awards for *Day and Night* and *Poems for People* and the Lorne Pierce Gold Medal of the Royal Society of Canada (1947) – this productive and distinguished period was curtailed by the early 1950s. For Livesay, like Marriott, experienced a decline in productivity at this time, most noticeably following the demise of *Contemporary Verse* in 1952–3.

Both women articulated crises of language and communication in their poetry of the late 1930s through the early 1950s. Even as they augmented the range of their poetry's reception, Marriott and Livesay compromised the linguistic density and formal complexity of their modernism in the interest of what Pratt, in his January 1936 *Canadian Poetry Magazine* editorial, called 'greater marketability' and 'public consumption' ('Foreword' 5). In the sections that follow, the readings of Marriott's and Livesay's poetry will focus on the apparent contradiction between the proliferation of modern poetry's media in Canada during the 1930s, 1940s, and early 1950s – including *Canadian Poetry*

Magazine and *Contemporary Verse*, Ryerson Press chapbooks and books, and CBC radio – and these poets' distinctive crises of communication.

Modernism Our Enemy? Marriott and 'Magazine Verse'

When John Sutherland reviewed *Sandstone* in the first issue of *Northern Review*, he characterized much of Marriott's collection as '"magazine verse" ... not essentially different from work appearing in *Good Housekeeping*, *American Magazine* and similar publications' ('Anne' 100). His derisive reference to 'magazine verse' was directed at the publishing practices of commercial periodicals – national monthlies, daily newspapers, Sunday supplements – in which some of her poems had been published prior to *Sandstone*. Such print organs encouraged a kind of crass commercialism with respect to poetry, often printing it 'as a kind of decorative cement to fill the gaps left by articles which fail to reach the bottom of a column,' as Birney once described the poems published in *Saturday Night* ('Has' 7). Related to his first criticism, Sutherland's second volley assails Marriott's predominant style in the collection: 'she gives the impression of trying to whip up an inspiration by compounding each word with every other word and by packing in modifiers until lines are bursting at the seams.' This 'difficult modern style,' he claims, is merely a mask for her adherence to what he calls the 'philosophy' of 'lady writers' affiliated with the CAA ('Anne' 101). If by 'philosophy' he means the typical CAA poet's inspiration by nature, producing imitative and belated Romantic, Victorian, Georgian, or imagist verse, his remark on Marriott's 'magazine verse' is apposite to the popularity of such poetry in commercial periodicals of the time – and, moreover, in *Canadian Poetry Magazine*. But in questioning her 'difficult modern style,' namely, her frequent hyphenations and modifications, he also challenges her for adopting the modernist idiom of poetry in other little magazines. If Sutherland is correct in his seemingly contradictory assessment of Marriott's 'magazine verse' written in a modernist style, then we can see how she landed herself in a double bind: she attempted at once to maintain artistic integrity (and reputation) by writing modernist poetry for little magazines and to gain financial rewards (pro rata and prizes) and other honours by writing 'magazine verse' for popular magazines, newspapers, and CAA publications.

This contradiction of aesthetic interests produced a crisis in language in Marriott's poetry of the 1930s and 1940s. Her modernist style of this period is characterized by its condensation of language: a poetry directed at those smaller and more specialized audiences of little magazines. At the same time, she often applied this style to her poetry published in periodicals of mass consumption, thus decorating such 'magazine verse' with the surface effects of modernist aesthetics. She produced far more of the latter type of verse, probably to the detriment of her reputation among editors and poets of little-magazine groups, but certainly to her benefit among CAA groups, whose local yearbooks and national poetry magazine alike honoured her with awards. Writing 'magazine verse' carried her through a boom period extending from 1934 to 1945, during which she published more than two hundred poems in periodicals and after which she entered a period of decline. She published only eighteen more poems between the appearance of *Sandstone* in 1945 and the closure of *Contemporary Verse* in 1952–3 and only nine more throughout the remainder of the 1950s.

Economic pressures also governed Marriott's prolonged decline in poetic production after 1945. This is not to say that economic forces were the determining factor in her retreat from writing poetry. Her departure to Ottawa, where she started work at the NFB in March 1945, detached her from the poetry communities in Victoria. Although she continued to write and publish poems in newspapers and magazines after 1945, she ceased publishing books and chapbooks of her poetry; her creative energies at the NFB were channelled into writing film scripts. After leaving the NFB in 1949, she concentrated on commercial media: writing radio dramas and documentaries for the CBC, editing the women's page of her local paper, and broadcasting poetry on Victoria radio. Having married Gerald McLellan in 1947, she moved with him to Victoria two years later and to northern British Columbia in 1951; this latter move isolated her altogether from literary communities. The separation did not, however, occasion a further drop-off in her poetry output comparable to that after her departure to Ottawa in 1945. The Victoria and Vancouver poetry groups of the CAA and of *Contemporary Verse* were the motivating forces behind her poetic production for roughly two decades – from the mid-1930s through the early 1950s. Her history and her poetry call attention to the vital cord that connects the poet to her community and that, if severed, may lead to alienation, invisibility, even silence.

The Victoria poetry group profoundly affected the progress of Marriott's early poetry. As early as 1934, she had joined the Victoria poetry

group, and by the end of the decade, she emerged at the forefront of
Canadian modernist poets. Marriott credits several figures connected
to the Victoria poetry group with the cultivation of her poetic technique at this time. Of the first, then CBC radio regional director Ira Dilworth, she recalls:

> [He] gave me one of the first real revelations of my life. One of the CAA
> ladies (most were ladies!) had a meeting at her house at which Ira gave a
> reading of T.S. Eliot's 'The Wasteland' [sic]. The Keats and Shelley et al[.]
> I had read at [private] school [in Victoria] fell away into the past and I sat
> there truly enthralled. I thought 'The Fire Sermon' was the most wonder-
> ful piece of writing I had ever heard. I really walked out of there a differ-
> ent person. I know it sounds melodramatic but it was like that. (Marriott
> to Geoff Hancock, 22 November 1984, AMP box 4, file 1; see also Marriott,
> *Anne*)

As Marriott's most recent critics have noted, Eliot's influence on her
long poem *The Wind Our Enemy* is thematically and stylistically
marked. Drawing on information given in Ruth Scott Philip's 1982
interview with Marriott (11), Anne Geddes Bailey even attempted to
track down Dilworth's critical reading of *The Waste Land* (55), but
could not find the source because his reading of Eliot to the Victoria
poetry group was no more than a recitation. D.M.R. Bentley has likewise proposed not only Eliot's but also Joyce's influence on *The Wind
Our Enemy*, noting Marriott's interpolation of modernism's 'various
techniques – montage, unfinished sentences, snippets of popular
culture, the comments of unidentified voices – that were assembled by
Joyce and Eliot to describe the spiritual deserts of early twentieth-
century Europe' (71).
 But based on Marriott's testimony, we should reconsider the question of Eliot's influence, which has proved salutary in both Bentley's
and Bailey's readings of modernist poetics in *The Wind Our Enemy*.
Marriott's exposure to Eliot's free verse – as she claimed during a 1974
panel discussion at Simon Fraser University – gave her 'a whole new
freedom to write the way [she] wanted to' (AMP, box 5, file 4). That
freedom to write in *vers libre* was not limited to *The Wind Our Enemy*
but developed throughout her successive collections of the 1940s.
While Dilworth's reading of Eliot offered Marriott the *vers libre* and
long-poem model for her composition of *The Wind Our Enemy* in the
fall of 1937, her poetry from the early 1940s was checked and meas-

ured against her first modernist long poem. Rather than reaffirming
Marriott's liberation from traditional modes of rhyming verse in the
1930s, the positive critical reception of *The Wind Our Enemy* demanded
that she continue to produce poetry in this socially conscious, modernist mode. Instead of giving her 'freedom to write the way she
wanted to,' modernist poetics increasingly weighed upon her as a
burden.

   Even the publication history of *The Wind Our Enemy* is connected to
the Victoria poetry group of the CAA. At one of its meetings in the fall
of 1938, Ferne, in her capacity as convener, gave a reading of the poem
to the group (Perry to Edgar, 6 January 1939, MEPP, box 5, file 23).
Livesay remembers being present at the meeting, along with her
father, J.F.B. Livesay, the general manager of the Canadian Press
(Livesay, 'Poetry' 87). After the reading, Ferne presented him with a
typescript copy of *The Wind Our Enemy*, which he in turn conveyed to
Toronto and brought to the attention of Pierce at the Ryerson Press.
Marriott's correspondence with J.F.B. Livesay between 26 November
1939 and 16 February 1939 documents his successful negotiations with
Pierce for the publication of *The Wind Our Enemy* (AMP, box 3, file 1).
Rather belatedly, Dorothy Livesay made the negotiations public
knowledge in 'An Open Letter to Sir Charles G.D. Roberts,' published
in the April–May 1939 issue of the *Canadian Bookman*.[17] She berated not
only Canadian publishers who allegedly refused to publish Marriott's
poem but also the CAA poetry group that received its first reading and
that, after all, facilitated its publication:

   I have been looking in vain, not for 'proletarian poets' – we are far from
   that – but for some genuine expression of experience, related to the way
   people live and struggle in Canada. I have found it only in isolated spots,
   cropping up in a shy way on the prairie and then being silent again. I
   have found it, most certainly, in Anne Marriott of Victoria, who has
   written a poem about the prairie which no one has seen fit to publish, but
   which is a voice from the people crying out. But woe unto her if she does
   not break free from critics and mutual admiration societies!

Livesay's raillery against the lack of objective criticism among CAA
poetry groups is probably accurate, and her advice to Marriott to lib-
erate herself from the shallow praise of such groups is wise. From
Livesay's dissatisfaction with the state of Canadian poetry groups
(whether the CAA or the VPS or any other poetry society, association,

club, or guild), we can detect the first stirrings of a different kind of group – led not by poets but by critics such as Crawley.

While connected to the Victoria CAA in the 1930s, Crawley markedly changed the direction of Marriott's poetry. He offered her objective criticism, even in the context of so-called mutual admiration societies such as the Victoria poetry group. Marriott later credited him with encouraging her to attempt a longer poem like *The Wind Our Enemy*. Commenting on his early editorial advice, she noted during a talk delivered in Saskatoon in 1971 that he 'did point out, right away, that what I wrote mostly, a catalogue of scenic effects, however nicely phrased did not really constitute a genuine poem' (AMP, box 4, file 1). By 1935 she had started the transition from rhymed quatrains and sonnets to verse forms favoured by the early modernists, particularly the haiku and its western correlative, the imagist lyric. These uncollected haiku and imagist poems from 1935 are not themselves distinctive, except insofar as they prefigure what Bentley has identified in *The Wind Our Enemy* as 'its use of techniques derived from Imagism' (69). As a stage in her development toward the accumulation of imagistic fragments in the long poem, Marriott's imagist lyrics represent her transition from the conventionalized subjects and verse forms of the CAA poets – for even the imagist lyric and haiku had been acceptable CAA fare since Louise Morey Bowman and Frank Oliver Call introduced them to Canadian poetry in the early 1920s – toward the integration of modernist techniques and social subjects. Crawley urged Marriott to work toward writing poetry in longer forms, so that she could organize her tendency toward the 'catalogue of scenic effects' into a larger structure such as the long poem, where she could attempt to catalogue the heterogeneity of social phenomena in a sequence of imagistic verses.

The only extant typescript of *The Wind Our Enemy* – a single sheet consisting of the first and final sections – is really the kind of catalogue that Crawley wanted Marriott to supersede. Originally entitled 'Dust Storm' and then 'Drought Area,' the early version is merely an imagistic portrait (AMP, box 15, file 4). Turning to Marriott's recollections of Crawley, we might speculate how he would have responded to this early version:

Alan used to criticize my poetry, and urged me to write something longer. *The Wind Our Enemy* was the result. But after that, nothing I could write measured up to 'The Wind –' and gradually I stopped showing him my work, in fact stopped writing poetry altogether, feeling nothing else I did would be good enough. I virtually stopped writing poetry for over twenty years. Though of course I was involved with other kinds of writing, and with people, as I hadn't been before, and that all used up my creative energy. (Marriott to Hancock, 22 November 1984, AMP, box 4, file 1)

Marriott's memory of her relationship with Crawley represents a clear difference from other women's memoirs of the editor of *Contemporary Verse*: McLaren, Livesay, and Ethel Wilson each contribute to the enduring portrait of his 'open and supportive manner' (Butling, '"Hall"' 62). Apparently, however, Crawley shared with Sutherland a certain distaste for Marriott's inclination toward what Marilyn Rose calls the 'short lyric – informed by modernist interests in economy, aestheticism, and imagism – that may have always been her true but unacknowledged métier' (244). Marriott's early attraction to the imagist lyric never abated, even under Crawley's influence, and his criticism of her so-called magazine verse speaks in part to the ways in which the practice of imagist poetics by modernist women poets contributed to the gendering of imagism as a mode of women's modernism. This gendering of imagism stems from its advent in Ezra Pound's now-legendary nomination of 'H.D., Imagiste' in 1912 and, more tellingly, from his infamous renomination of the movement during its 1914–17 period as 'Amygism' (after Amy Lowell). Pound's typically condescending, masculinist disavowal of the feminine anticipates the disparagement of belated imagist-influenced women poets in the Canadian context, especially women affiliated with the CAA.

Unlike her experiences with the core group of the Victoria CAA, Marriott's encounters with Crawley were not occasions for flattery. He never adopted the gender-inflected language of Sutherland,[18] nor could one say that Crawley's preference for Marriott's longer poetic works necessarily privileged a masculinist poetics. Nevertheless, he proved a demanding editor of her poetry, his expectations raised by her early long poems *The Wind Our Enemy* and *Calling Adventurers!* – poems that for obvious reasons bear little resemblance to her short imagistic lyrics. Both long poems were published prior to the appearance of *Contemporary Verse*. Marriott published a total of fifteen shorter lyric poems but only one long poem in the magazine. Her poetry from *Contemporary Verse* tells the story of her efforts and failures to produce another modernist long poem like *The Wind Our Enemy*. These crises most often manifest themselves in her poetry of the 1940s, particularly in her poetry published in *Contemporary Verse*, as failures of language and communication.

Printed in the first, September 1941, issue of *Contemporary Verse*, Marriott's uncollected 'Prayer of the Disillusioned' is among the earliest of her renewed efforts to write in the modernist manner of *The Wind Our Enemy*.[19] If *The Waste Land* presents a language of spiritual and cultural exhaustion in postwar Europe, 'Prayer' revisits Marriott's earlier transposition of Eliot's tropes of alienation and sterility to *The Wind Our Enemy*. Where her long poem translates Eliot's vision to the ecological, social, and economic conditions of the Canadian prairies during the Depression, her poem-prayer rearticulates his mood of disillusionment through her speakers' exhausted language. Her traveller-speakers in the poem-prayer undertake their quest through a spiritual desert in search of renewed sources of communication. 'Give us too a cause!' they exhort at the beginning of their journey, and then go on to describe their spiritual alienation and sterile speech:

> We who have talked through days, nights, barren seasons,
> Said everything, emptied our hearts and minds out
> In sourceless dry streams of words
> And still said nothing,
> Never found the one word
> Our speech ran after,
> The potent word, the complete answer
> To a billion circling questions.

The failure of communication that the speakers convey leads to their crisis of faith in language. As speakers of a prayer, they address an absent audience, a divine host whose 'potent word' would grant their 'cause.' If not the cause, then the ambiguous meaning of the speakers' quest is delivered in the final lines, as they emerge from their 'aimless desert':

> ... we come to the bound of the desert,
> The perpetual river set in unchangeable course,
> And deep in the current, the long strong water, lose
> The last dry grain from the ear, from the solaced eye,
> Most blessedly lose our selves.

Like the drowned Phoenecian sailor of *The Waste Land*, the drowned speakers of Marriott's poem are ambiguous figures: their death by water may signify no more than the last words and act of the 'disillusioned,' or it may symbolize their self-sacrifice as a prelude to rebirth in the 'perpetual river.' To pursue the latter reading, Marriott's poem, like Eliot's, concludes with a benediction – a paradoxical blessing, since her speakers' loss of self is 'blessed' only insofar as it is *self*-blessed. Without the 'potent word, the complete answer,' their loss of self is a leap of faith into an 'unchangeable course.' It ironically reiterates their loss of faith in language.

Of the seven poems that Marriott published in *Contemporary Verse* prior to the appearance of *Sandstone* in June 1945, only 'Prayer' was omitted from the collection. That it appears in *Contemporary Verse* is significant in so far as her return in 'Prayer' to the thematic concerns of *The Wind Our Enemy* was probably applauded by Crawley. Perhaps the defining characteristic and chief fault of 'Prayer' is its double derivation from two modernist long poems – not only from Eliot's but also from her own. Although 'Prayer' recaptures a symbolic world of spiritual drought that one encounters in *The Waste Land* and *The Wind Our Enemy*, the fragmented, multivocal, multilinear narrative of cultural and spiritual crisis in these long poems is not replicated in the structure of her prayer-poem. While the ironic and ambiguous close of 'Prayer' is indeed a signature modernist effect, its recycling of the thematics of *The Wind Our Enemy* is telling above all of Crawley's insistence that she write something that measured up to her first modernist long poem.

Although Marriott's *Calling Adventurers!* predates *Contemporary Verse*, its organization as a long poem seems to gesture toward Crawley's early influence on her modernist poetics.[20] *Calling Adventurers!* contains her verse choruses from *Payload*, the documentary drama in verse and prose co-written by Marriott and Margaret Kennedy, with music by Barbara Pentland. Originally broadcast on CBC radio on 8 November 1940, *Payload* was scripted for multiple voices and employed techniques of audio montage (see AMP, box 16, file 2). Instead of multivocality and montage, *Calling Adventurers!* produces a narrative that is lyrically univocal and occasionally interspersed with other voices carried over from the radio version.[21] Separated from their original radio format, the choruses compose a discontinuous narrative of sectional pieces, arranged in the fragmented manner of a modernist long poem. While the radio play was popular enough among CBC audiences to merit its second broadcast in 1943 (see Marriott to Frank Flemington, 17 January 1943, LPP, box 10, file 1, item 74), *Calling Adventurers!* did not demand a second printing, even after winning the Governor General's Award. Compared to *The Wind Our Enemy*, which had already sold out its run of 250 copies by the time *Calling Adventurers!* went to press, her second chapbook was not nearly so popular (see n22). Both author and publisher had evidently mistaken the limited readership of poetry chapbooks for the popular audience of radio.

Once Marriott had offered Ryerson Press the choruses from *Payload* on 7 December 1940 (LPP, box 8, file 1, item 96), Pierce suspended plans for the publication of her third collection, *Salt Marsh*. Originally submitted to Ryerson on 14 September 1940, *Salt Marsh* was the object of numerous revisions, additions, and deletions prior to its publication over two years later in October 1942 (Marriott to Pierce, 14 September 1940 and 13 October 1942, LPP, box 8, file 1, item 94, and box 30, file 3, item 58). Marriott's apparent uncertainties about the collection were reflected in its critical reception and, compared to the success of *The Wind Our Enemy*, its meagre sales.[22] Livesay's review of *Salt Marsh* in the June 1943 issue of *Contemporary Verse* renewed her earlier warning to Marriott about the dangers of writing poetry for 'mutual admiration societies' ('Open' 35) and even accused her of 'letting work be published which is adolescent verse' ('Recent' 13). *Salt Marsh* certainly reproduces a representative selection of what Sutherland later called her 'magazine verse' – that is, derivative imagist and romanticist nature lyrics. The collection also contains some of her more challenging modernist work from the late 1930s and early 1940s ('Night Travellers,' 'Station,' 'Traffic Light,' 'Prairie Graveyard'), though this material is far outnumbered by her prevailing poetic tendency to produce imagistic catalogues, romanticist reveries, and impressionistic portraits.

Given Livesay's sharp assessment of *Salt Marsh*, Marriott understandably baulked at the inclusion of juvenilia in her first book-length collection, *Sandstone*. Having submitted a selection of her poems to Ryerson on 24 May 1944, she later questioned her judgement. She received the proofs of the collection after moving to Ottawa at the end of March 1945 to start work for the NFB. At that time she alerted Pierce to changes she wished to make: 'I have completely deleted several poems. I have gone over the whole MS most carefully in my spare moments this past week, and, viewing it as a whole a year after sending it to you, I feel rather strongly that there are a few poems

included which I do not now want to have in a representative collection. I do not feel they would do the book or my "literary reputation"
any good' (LPP, box 12, file 7, item 60). The 'literary reputation' she
wanted to promote was not that of the prodigy of the Victoria poetry
group, but rather that of a poet who had released the apron strings
tying her to the so-called lady writers of the CAA (Sutherland, 'Anne'
101).

As early as April 1944, when she first selected the poems for *Sandstone*, Marriott had started to manifest anxieties about her poetic abilities. She found herself at that time on the cusp of poetic silence, her
creative energies for poetry sapped by writing plays for CBC radio (see
Marriott to Pierce, 17 April 1944, LPP, box 11, file 1, item 108). Just
prior to her move to Ottawa, she confessed to Pierce in a letter of 7
March 1945: 'As a poet, I'm beginning to think I've seen my best days
– though I hope that's not the case' (LPP, box 12, file 7, item 59).
Appended to this letter, she sent him a copy of her poem 'Portrait,'
recently published in the January 1945 issue of *Contemporary Verse*. It
appeared as the final poem in *Sandstone*; its placement at the end of the
collection, as much as its content, foreshadows the thirty-six-year
period that followed the publication of her book.

'Portrait' is not a Marriott self-portrait. Rather, it begins as an impersonal, even dehumanized, portrait of a librarian: 'Bloodless as paper
she, and lifeless / as dead words on dull binding are her eyes, looking
not in or out' (*Sandstone* 42). Debilitated by routine, the librarian has
fallen into a condition of silence, become as inarticulate as the inani-
mate books and implements of her occupation:

> ... mute
> as volumes never off the shelves her tongue –
> the rubbered pencil used to point
> the novel overdue, the scanty fine.

Like the speakers' pleas for the 'potent word' in 'Prayer of the Disillusioned,' the speaker of 'Portrait' calls out for something to reanimate
the librarian:

> O life – love – something – burst the resisting doors –
> ignore the silence sign – vault the tall desk
> and on her locked blank pages
> write a living tale.

If the impersonal portraiture early in the poem establishes the speaker's aesthetic distance, the closing apostrophe and imperatives here indicate her empathy for the librarian. With the image of writing evoked in the final lines, the poet-speaker declares her empathy, releasing both librarian and poet from their mutual conditions of silence. The poet-speaker's realization of her empathy for the librarian achieves the force of an epiphany: her 'living tale' at the close revitalizes the dead words of her initially impersonal portrait. But because this final poem in *Sandstone* was followed by a thirty-six-year gap, her poet-speaker's epiphany would lead nowhere.

'Portrait' was the final poem of Marriott's prolific early period – that is, prior to her move to Ottawa in March 1945. Her Ottawa period was not at all productive in terms of writing poetry, nor was she particularly effective as an associate editor of *Canadian Poetry Magazine*. Her editorial duties were limited to soliciting manuscripts from potential contributors and drumming up subscriptions; she was especially recruited to serve as a liaison with prairie poets.[23] Birney also wanted her to contribute her poetry to the magazine, giving it first priority. Her acceptance letter obviously angered him, since she stated that 'this is a tentative acceptance of the job – I don't know what I'll do if faced with a superb poem to be channeled towards Vancouver and have to decide whether to direct it to you or to Alan Crawley!' (EBP, box 14, file 25). Birney fired back a letter on 10 September 1946, first thanking her for accepting the position and sending a poem, then berating her for wanting to preserve ties to *Contemporary Verse*:

> I don[']t want you on the Board if your first loyalty is still to *Contemporary Verse*. I am having to get tough about this because too many people are saying to me – isn[']t it wonderful you are trying to make a go of C[anadian] P[oetry] M[agazine] – I am all for you – though of course my first loyalty is to C[ontemporary] V[erse] (or Northern Rev[iew], or what have you). So with Floris McLaren, Doris Ferne, Dee Livesay, Pat Page, etc. etc. Well, you must all make a choice. I can[']t carry the whole load myself. If you *want* a national magazine of poetry then you have to support it first, before you support local efforts. After all, it was I who tried to avoid this situation by an amalgamation with CV. And the CAA were willing. It was CV that turned it down. I'm not 'feuding' with Alan over that but I have no recourse now than [*sic*] to be tough and competitive; and I want you on my side. (EBP, box 14, file 25; original emphasis)

But Marriott managed to swing both ways, contributing poems to *Canadian Poetry Magazine* and *Contemporary Verse* during the tenure of her associate editorship.

After nearly a three-year hiatus from *Canadian Poetry Magazine*, she contributed 'Appeasers' to the September 1946 issue, the first edited by Birney. In sending her poem along with her acceptance of the associate editorship on 21 August 1946, she also submitted a caveat: 'As for unpublished verse of mine – would that I had some. I just can't write poetry any more – it's gone, and I haven't the remotest idea if it's ever coming back ... However – searching through the MSS I have here, I discovered the enclosed, which was written at least five years ago, polished it a bit, and am sending it. I don't know if it is any good at all – but it literally is the only thing I have' (EBP, box 14, file 25). Characteristic of her contributions to *Canadian Poetry Magazine* in the 1930s and early 1940s, 'Appeasers' is a romantic nature lyric, though far above the standard of verse accepted by Birney's predecessor, Watson Kirkconnell. Its central trope is a journey, an escape into a place of 'solace, ease for stress, soft peace': first, into the 'tropic wood,' where the speaker discovers there is 'No solace in the lush'; then, 'Into bare steep country,' where 'Peace is in sturdy leaves making no stain, / Ease in strong scent of stripped, storm-raked earth, / ... Comfort is the high sunlight on the peak.' Of her nature lyrics, 'Appeasers' is by no means distinguished and counts as one among dozens of her early uncollected poems, typical of her so-called magazine verse (Sutherland, 'Anne' 101).

After several months' break in correspondence, Birney became impatient with Marriott and asked in a letter dated 23 July 1947 whether she wished to continue as associate editor (EBP, box 14, file 25). Writing a long letter to him on 15 August 1947 – after a visit to Victoria and after missing the CAA annual convention in Vancouver – she explained that she still wanted to continue her associate editorship.[24] With respect to her failure to contribute poetry to the magazine, she confessed that over 'the last two and a half years, I have written possibly five small pieces of inferior verse' (EBP, box 14, file 25). Given Birney's strict position on Marriott's obligations to the magazine, however, we might suspect that the appearance of her poem 'Communication to a Friend' in the spring 1947 issue of *Contemporary Verse* may have led him once again to question her loyalties to *Canadian Poetry Magazine*.

Although her ties to *Contemporary Verse* were no longer editorial or managerial, her friendship with the Victoria-Vancouver group superseded her membership in the CAA and her editorial relationship to *Canadian Poetry Magazine*. Her failure to communicate with Birney during the first year of her associate editorship was symptomatic of her growing distance from the CAA; she remained a member and served on its national executive throughout the 1940s, but rarely contacted other CAA poets in Ottawa, never joining the Ottawa poetry group of the CAA or contributing to its poetry yearbooks. After 'Appeasers' appeared in *Canadian Poetry Magazine* in September 1946, she did not publish again until the spring of 1947, when the first of four poems written during her Ottawa period came out in *Contemporary Verse*. Perhaps to deflect readings of the poem as a coterie piece, Marriott revised and changed the title of 'For Friends Far Away' to 'Communication to a Friend' for publication in *Contemporary Verse* (AMP, box 15, file 5). In contrast to the way that the original title personalizes the poem in the manner of a dedication to the *Contemporary Verse* group, the changed title universalizes the poem. Its appearance in *Contemporary Verse* may have been occasioned by Crawley's visit to Ottawa as part of his ten-week reading tour hosted by the Canadian Clubs in the fall of 1946, which was advertised in the summer and fall issues of *Contemporary Verse* that year.[25] Marriott's encounter with Crawley, renewing her connection to a community of friends in Victoria and Vancouver, seems to have prompted her to write and, moreover, publish her strongest poem since her departure from Victoria in March 1945 and her last publication in *Contemporary Verse* in January that year.

'Communication to a Friend' foregrounds the travails of communication between two lovers separated by physical distance.[26] The means of communication in the poem is not verbal but physical. Its emphasis on exploration, maps, and settlement reads as a frontier narrative, where communication is conveyed through the lovers' journeys. It is a narrative of communication and miscommunication, tracking and backtracking, tracing and retracing:

Five thousand miles a broad wound between us
yet tonight we are closer
than within the hand's reach of first meeting.
For then, like two travelers in a vast wilderness,
sighting pin-size on the horizon another journeying,

we began the long exploratory march toward each other
over tortuous terrain and frequently mistaking map-readings.

The journey is, in the end, successful: the two travellers come 'face to face' and build a figurative 'hostel, storm proof, added to yearly, / with walls to stretch at need five thousand miles.' Reassured by the travellers' reunion, the reader may be 'mistaking map-readings,' for the 'hostel' is a temporary lodging, a site of physical impermanence – an unlocatable place, inhabited by mental travellers. This place exists only in the space of the poem, only in its act of communication: it is a lyrical correspondence between lovers and, for Marriott, between herself, the readership of *Contemporary Verse*, and her friends, its publishers.

In Ottawa at the NFB, Marriott found a new community of poets among co-workers P.K. Page and another fellow modernist poet, Kay Smith. 'This was almost as great as "The Fire Sermon,"' Marriott recalled. 'I found I *could* talk to them, about contemporary work and thoughts and feelings and topics' (Marriott to Hancock, 22 November 1984, AMP, box 4, file 1; original emphasis). However, her initial poetic response to Ottawa and the NFB returns to the prevailing narrative of alienation and communication breakdown that characterizes her modernist poetry of the early 1940s. Like Page's office poems of 1942–3 (see chapter 3: 138–45), Marriott's 'Ottawa Payday, 1945' portrays the conditions and effects of alienation in a bureaucratic office environment. In their Kafkaesque world, Marriott's civil servants are given only titles, no names, no faces; they exist only as entries in records, ledgers, and bank books. Even access to their paycheques is granted by bureaucratic means:

> Obedient to bank's unyielding sign
> with 'departmental pass' in hand,
> resigned, cattle-patient line
> Dominion civil servants stand.

'Ottawa Payday' does not document personal experience through a persona, but rather impersonally renders the bureaucratic order of civil servants. Combined with the impersonal mode of address, the incorporation of acronyms ('CS,' 'DBS') and job titles ('Grade One typist,' 'Grade Two file clerk,' 'Temporary Five') reminiscent of office memoranda reproduces depersonalized bureaucratic conditions. Civil servants obey and become signs. This is a poem of multiple solitudes, of individuals alienated from any sense of community. In place of community, civil servants live in bureaucracy; instead of communication, they line up in impenetrable silence. That Marriott published 'Ottawa Payday' in the spring 1948 issue of *Contemporary Verse* serves as a reminder of the poet's need for community to ensure the survival of the self in the face of such alienating and dehumanizing bureaucracies.

The same issue of *Contemporary Verse* also contained her poems 'Waiting Room: Spring' and 'Old Maid.' Marriott had already sent the latter to Birney on 2 February 1948, calling it 'a small bit of verse which suddenly arrived a couple of days ago – maybe the effect of marriage, I don't know, anyway it's the first for nearly a year' (EBP, box 14, file 25). He returned the poem on 11 February 1948 with a short letter explaining that the June 1948 issue was the last under his editorship and that any submissions were to be handled by the new editor (EBP, box 14, file 25). Marriott stayed on as associate editor during Arthur Bourinot's editorship, only leaving her position when she and her husband moved to Vancouver in the summer of 1949. She did not submit 'Old Maid' to Birney's successor at *Canadian Poetry Magazine*, but rather redirected it to Crawley for immediate publication in *Contemporary Verse*.

If her modernist poems of 1945–8 document crises of communication, dehumanization, and alienation, 'Old Maid' presents a breakthrough in its central figure's search for and discovery of a new means of communication. The poem begins with the image of a spinster figure, similar to the librarian of 'Portrait,' caught in her daily routines, wearied and trapped in her isolated world. This figure, like the speakers of 'Prayer of the Disillusioned' and 'Communication to a Friend,' embarks on a journey, though hers is conducted along '[c]orridors of loneliness,' not across deserts or continents. She is trapped in a domestic space where 'windows [have] turned to mirrors reflecting her own face,' her claustrophobic hallway marvellously transformed by the discovery of an 'incredible outlet' into an 'unsuspected spring.' This moment of revelation presents a new world where everything is as yet unnamed, a fabulous land where she is struck dumb, 'not knowing the language here / nor able to read even one pointing sign, / a speechless stranger in a land of love.' Instead of the exhausted landscape and language of her earlier poems from the 1940s, 'Old Maid' envisions rebirth and the promise of redemption. Like the poet-speaker at the close of 'Portrait,' the old maid is poised to cross the threshold of silence and answer the urge to 'life – love – something – burst the resisting doors.' Yet Marriott waited two years before learning how to write in the language of this new world, before interpreting the revelation of an unfamiliar landscape.

Nearly a decade after publishing *Calling Adventurers!* – a decade of failure to recapture the form of *The Wind Our Enemy* – Marriott at last wrote another modernist long poem in July 1950. McLaren and Crawley, who had urged Marriott to write another long poem, published 'Holiday Journal' in the fall-winter 1950 issue of *Contemporary Verse*. Her new long poem is a natural sequel to 'Old Maid,' because Marriott is no longer a 'speechless stranger' dumbfounded by a 'land of love,' but rather a documentarist reading the landscape of Quebec, New Brunswick, and Nova Scotia and communicating her perceptions in a journal dedicated to 'G.J.M.' (16) – her husband, Gerald McLellan. 'Holiday Journal,' moreover, provides a modernist counter-narrative to the drought, sterility, and alienation in *The Wind Our Enemy* and to the crises of communication articulated in the modernist poems that she composed throughout the 1940s and published in *Contemporary Verse.* 'Holiday Journal' resembles the kind of documentary writing in which she had been engaged during the war years and for which she was employed at the NFB. Its variance from such writing is most immediately apparent in the lyrical distortion of the documentary footage, recording both objective and subjective images. Its syntax and rhythms travel at the speed of trains and emotions: 'O lovely patterning lovely lovely the train sang / our hearts sang our eyes affirming' (16). Technologies of radio communication and train travel, as well as topography and vegetation, become elaborate 'patterning' to the speaker's eye:

> Soon then radio towers gawked from the Sackville marshes
> (crying unheard to us a loud Canada to the world)
> intricate cat's cradle cables spurning
> simpler twisting of red mud marsh channels.
> Then the flowers in the heart burst to bloom and rivaled those roadside,
> – for him homecoming, for me delight of discovery.
> Wheels at boundary chanted Nova Scotia Nova Scotia
> engine snorted Halifax Halifax
> our sea-born blood springing to outstrip. (16)

Marriott's juxtaposition of radio-tower cables and red mud channels connects communication technology and topography, the radio broadcast of CBC international and the local Sackville marsh. By similar means, she locates in the percept of roadside and trackside flowers an objective correlative to communicate the subjective experience of travelling through the marshlands. The repeated names of Nova Scotia and of its capital transform into onomatopoeic phrases imitating the auditory experience of train travel; this audible pattern is echoed by the rhythm of the travellers' blood. Every image in the speaker's experience – visual and auditory – represents some kind of communicative function; every image is anthropomorphic, mapping human language, emotions, and bodies upon Canadian geographies.

'Holiday Journal' is structured by the chronology of journal entries – 'July 2 ... July 3–11 ... July 12 ... July 16 ... July 25 ... July 31' – but its narratives are by no means linear chronicles. Memories, histories, itineraries all collide in multiple temporalities and perspectives. The temporal linearity of the journal structure is, moreover, shaped by the natural narrative circularity of a round trip. The Sackville marsh of July 2, viewed at speed and distance from the train, is then recycled into the narrative of the Amherst marsh of July 25, perceived up close. Typically modernist, the cyclical movements of time and history are foregrounded in this pattern of repetition. When the travellers rest at the edge of a dyke, their perception of the marsh mud recaptures not only the recent history of three weeks ago but also European imperial histories of exploration and settlement, and even Christian mythologies of creation:

            Sat there heels dangling
over mud red as the old blood of the first comers.
Under wind spined with salt implacable tide
turned, thrust a strong grey fist
up Digby Gut
and as the current bent our beginnings glimmered.
The spirit of God moved on the face of the waters
the ship of Champlain moved on the face of the waters,
waters that thrust up the inlet into the bloody land,
receded came again (requiring no reproduction).
We pulled our roots, found them set fast and tight
In the loose shifting sea of his of our discovering. (20)

Marriott's 'mythical method,' to borrow a phrase from Eliot ('Ulysses' 178), telescopes multiple histories and mythologies into a personal narrative of discovery. The linearity of the travel narrative resumes in the final entry of July 31, as the travellers leave Nova Scotia and return by bus to Quebec:

Poles trees houses unrolled faster than eye-blink.
Slowly ashismed [sic] from the world
with the old sensation 'the bus hung in space.'
With numb body bright brain grew nimble,
causes and patterns incredibly clear. (20)

Detached from the landscape, the travellers' perceptions become abstracted, just as before when they observed from the train the 'patterning' of the Sackville marshlands. Their clarity of perception is then ruptured by contact with the social world, so that 'causes and patterns' lose coherence. Other travellers interrupt their reverie and force the fragmentation of their travel narrative: the pieces of its pattern – likened to 'puzzle pieces' (20) – disintegrate into a series of discontinuous impressions. As befits a round trip, their narrative is reintegrated into an aesthetic whole, encircled by impressions of flowers – 'rose blue amber blurred together trackside' flowers that 'greeted' them upon departure (16) and flowers in the 'dingy terminal' upon homecoming (21). 'Festooned with memory,' the travellers continue homeward in a taxi, 'through a forest of flowers' (21).

Marriott's decision not to include 'Holiday Journal' in either her chapbook *Countries* (1971) or *The Circular Coast: Poems Selected and New* (1981) prompts consideration of the consequences of its exclusion. She may have believed the poem to be only meaningful to a closed audience of *Contemporary Verse* readers, many of whom would have been aware of her recent marriage (announced in the winter 1947–8 issue). Other concerns include her and her readers' historically contingent attitudes toward nation and empire, nationalism and imperialism. 'Holiday Journal,' which opens *in medias res* the day after Dominion Day, is a narrative driven by the travellers' romantic-nationalist desire to identify with the people and land of Canada, and it culminates in their meditation upon and identification with the imperial history of exploration and settlement in the new world. It is representative of what Jody Berland calls 'nationalist modernism' (28), that strain of Canadian modernist cultural production dominant in the 1950s and typical of the film scripts and radio plays that Marriott had written for the NFB and the CBC. Such narratives, directed to Canadian audiences engaged in the cultural and economic project of nation-building in the early 1950s, might appear ideologically naive to present-day readers. Even so, the omission of 'Holiday Journal' from Marriott's canon has obscured a crucial advance in her modernist poetics, a corrective to her poetic crises of communication throughout the 1940s.

While she did not publish a new collection until *Countries* in 1971, she outlined preliminary plans for another as early as 1949. Under the heading 'New Poems for a Chapbook Feb. 1949,' she listed twelve of a projected fifteen poems inside the back cover of a binder containing typescripts from the years 1939–53 (AMP, box 15, file 6).[27] All four poems published in *Contemporary Verse* after *Sandstone* in 1945 were listed, but not 'Appeasers' from *Canadian Poetry Magazine*. (This latter absence reconfirms the importance of *Contemporary Verse* as a forum for her modernist poetry through the late 1940s, even as she maintained ties to the CAA and wrote occasional reviews for *Canadian Poetry Magazine*.) Apart from the four poems from *Contemporary Verse* – 'Communication to a Friend' (listed as 'For Friends Far Away'), 'Waiting Room: Spring,' 'Ottawa Payday, 1945,' and 'Old Maid' – the list chiefly consists of nature lyrics, typical of her romanticist and imagist 'magazine verse' (Sutherland, 'Anne' 101). Rather than risk the harsh criticism that she had received from Livesay for *Salt Marsh* or from Sutherland for *Sandstone*, however, Marriott dropped the plan for a new chapbook. Had she added 'Holiday Journal' to this projected collection, one could speculate on her long poem's potential to anchor the other modernist poems slated for inclusion. If such a chapbook had been issued in the Ryerson Press series, it surely could have helped to recentre her within modernist poetry culture in Canada.

Combined with her withdrawal from little-magazine culture and decline in productivity after 1950, her decision not to publish another poetry collection for thirty-six years after *Sandstone* led to her subsequent marginalization in the literary-historical record. Without a collection containing 'Prayer of the Disillusioned,' 'Communication to a Friend,' 'Ottawa Payday, 1945,' 'Old Maid,' and 'Holiday Journal,' it is not surprising that we have so far failed to comprehend her trials with modernist poetry and poetics after writing *The Wind Our Enemy*. These uncollected poems consitute the basis of an alternative narrative of Marriott's involvement in modernist poetry-magazine culture of the 1940s and early 1950s. To recognize the evidence of that narrative, which has been hidden in her uncollected poems published in *Contemporary Verse*, is to chart the continued progress of her modernism in the decade after *The Wind Our Enemy*.

A People's Modernism: Livesay's *Contemporary Verse*

When Livesay championed *The Wind Our Enemy* as 'a voice from the people crying out' ('Open' 35), she might have identified Marriott as a poet at the forefront of Canadian proletarian literature. Aware of Marriott's heritage among CAA poets in the Victoria poetry group, Livesay hesitated at such a claim; she instead denied the existence of any proletarian poetry culture in Canada and called attention to the genteel poetry culture that had, ironically, produced a kind of people's poetry. After two failed attempts to establish a proletarian magazine culture in Canada in the 1930s, Livesay discovered 'a voice from the people' emerging not from a radical political culture but from a conservative poetry culture. Whatever criticisms she levelled at the CAA poetry groups, she could not deny the fact that they had aided the development of at least one poet of national significance. At the same time, even as she maligned those groups, she was herself a member of the equally conservative Vancouver Poetry Society. However forgettable the majority of their poets, such organizations as the CAA and the VPS proved valuable for their ability to fund and manage poetry magazines, essential to the dissemination of poetry. Livesay recognized the importance of such magazines to the development of a national poetry culture, even though the poetry itself could so often be negligible. Yet she grasped the need for exceptional poets such as Marriott to reach a national poetry-reading public – beyond that of CAA yearbooks or *Canadian Poetry Magazine* or Ryerson chapbooks.[28] Having witnessed in Marriott the promise of a people's poetry – a poetry accessible to the general public, a popular poetry written in the idiomatic style and diction of common speech – Livesay perceived the necessity for new means of publication, so that poems such as *The Wind Our Enemy* could profit from increased exposure to a Canadian poetry-reading public, regardless of the poet's affiliation with groups, associations, parties, societies, coteries, or clubs.

Contemporary Verse probably failed to satisfy Livesay's immediate expectations. Over the course of its first year of publication, she recommended to the founding committee the possibility of mergers with other magazines. Just as he was preparing the make-up of the third issue in the spring of 1942, Crawley wrote to McLaren to veto Livesay's suggestion of an amalgamation with *Canadian Poetry Magazine* (FMP). After her visit to Toronto in the summer of 1942, Livesay reported to Crawley the feasibility of a merger with *Canadian Review of Music and Art*, the Toronto-based journal founded by Marcus Adeney in the fall of 1941 (Crawley to McLaren [1942], FMP). These proposals for mergers with other national periodicals give some indication of Livesay's unrealized hopes for *Contemporary Verse*; both were printed and bound magazines, not mimeographed and saddle-stapled like *Contemporary Verse*, and they had the financial backing to cover production costs. Livesay's dealings also bespeak her initial dissatisfaction with the editorial organization of *Contemporary Verse*. As Crawley wrote to McLaren in the spring of 1942, 'I have been a bit worried as you appear to be as to how to prevent any feeling among the committee that you and I are taking over all the selection and complete charge of C[ontemporary] V[erse] and what to do about it ... I will do anything you suggest to do away with this feeling and for[e]stall it and if you think there should be an editorial com[m]ittee it is fine with me' (FMP).

If Livesay could not have her way with the editorial organization of the magazine, then she would leave her mark on *Contemporary Verse* by way of reviews and poems. For every year of its twelve-year run, she published at least one poem or review in the magazine. During this period she appeared in *Contemporary Verse* more often than in any other periodical. Of the twenty-four poems that came out in the magazine, only four were never collected by Livesay herself; and of those four, only one was a fully realized, discrete poem – that is, not part of a longer sequence. In other words, many of her prominent poems from the 1940s and early 1950s were first printed in *Contemporary Verse*. Even when she could not find another periodical to accept a poem, she was almost certain to find receptive readers among the *Contemporary Verse* group.[29] As we will witness, however, in the case of the one poem she published in *Contemporary Verse* but never collected herself, this unofficial policy of receptivity was vulnerable to editorial lapses.

Other Livesay poems discussed in this section never appeared in *Contemporary Verse* – not because Crawley formally rejected them but because they were aimed at audiences beyond the little magazine's readership; its print runs hovered around four hundred at its peak. In certain poems from her *Contemporary Verse* period, she looks beyond the medium of modernist poetry magazines to mass-communication media; these poems exhibit the pressures exerted by such media on modernist poetry and poetry-magazine culture during the 1940s and early 1950s. Either previously uncollected or unpublished and/or marginalized in the literary-historical record, these poems present case studies of Livesay's post-proletarian poetry for mass audiences.

Never collected by Livesay herself, 'Motif for a Mural' is a portrait of a poet in transition, a poet in search of post-proletarian modes of expression and means of mass communication. Even so, it is influenced by proletarian art. Dating from the 1940s, the poem invokes contemporary modes employed by modern visual artists for monumental public installations. Alluding in its title to the murals of Canadian artists in the 1930s and 1940s, 'Motif' evokes the work of Vancouver PAC muralists Jack Shadbolt, Charles Comfort, Fraser Wilson, and Margaret Carter (see Livesay, *Journey* 158). It even imitates the three-panel structure of a triptych – the traditional format of altarpieces but also common to murals – and depicts a triadic historical perspective on the poet's relationship to the public.

Its first panel, so to speak, is an idealized portrait of the urban working class, reminiscent of Livesay's proletarian verse of the early to mid-1930s. It depicts a street scene of unemployed men, comrades who 'Hurry from silence / Wear on their brow / The brand of a brother' (*Archive* 71). The 'silence' is that of 'streets / Shifted to low gear / Thrown in reverse' (71). The historical context and origin of this 'silence' is not specified, but the mechanical image likely refers to the shutdown of factories and slowdown or 'reversal' of economic progress during the 1930s. The furrowed brow of the unemployed men is a sign of brotherhood they bear in silence; they are united by 'deeds unsung / Alone / With the unnamed name / Burning the tongue' (71). Because they lack the means of communication and organization, the unemployed men 'walk in the street' alienated, anonymous, and silent. So this 'silence,' unlike that of the workers in Livesay's proletarian verse of the early to mid-1930s, is not an alternative system of communication among the unemployed. The 'deeds unsung' and the 'unnamed name' are not the revolutionary manifestations of 'silence' Livesay once attributed to the radicalized and organized actions of the proletariat. Silence is no longer loaded with revolutionary signification; rather, it is merely a sign of the potential for revolution. Given the significance of silence as a motif in Livesay's 1930s verse, its permutation in 'Motif' may reflect her ambivalence, as a poet of the 1940s, toward the naïveté of leftist agitprop rhetoric and cliché. While in this section the repetition of a phrase – 'So many young men' – invokes techniques common to proletarian mass chants, its tone is not agitational. Where in agitprop verse the poet typically impersonates a voice of the masses, in this opening section of 'Motif' the poet's proximity to the unemployed is not made explicit; its

purported objectivity is that of the documentary – or, in Michael
Denning's apt phrase, 'social modernism' (122).

The second section adopts a leftist mode of documentary –
reportage – in which a partisan speaker emerges as the voice of the
proletariat.[30] Objectivity and temporal immediacy in the first section
give way to subjectivity and temporal distance in the second. Events
recounted by the first-person speaker are now situated in the past; this
shift from first to second section, from present to past tense, is rein-
forced by the rhetorical repetition of the formulaic phrase 'In the time
of ...' This phrase introduces each subsection of a tripartite history: 'the
time of speech,' 'the time of action,' and 'the time of quiet' (71, 72). In
succession, each subsection portrays a proletarian history of leftist
propaganda, revolution, and then repression in the 1930s. The first
subsection introduces a proletarian figure – a speech-maker and leader
– now dismayed by the impotency of agitational propaganda and the
vacuousness of leftist rhetoric. Giving voice to disillusioned members
of the left in the early 1940s, Livesay's speaker embodies a range of
critical responses to leftism and its decline. Language itself is politically and rhetorically suspect: leftist propaganda is now 'liquid,' slip-
pery, deceptive. Speeches are staged before a proletarian audience
unable to move, stand, or speak for itself; it is an 'inert audience,' fashioned of the same elemental substance as language. So when the 'the
curtain fell / And the people melted,' their collapse dramatizes the
rhetorical construction of an imagined 'spineless' audience – supported by a figurative 'column of words' (71) – and the staging of that
audience necessary to the speech-maker's didactic mode. By exposing
the constructedness of such an audience, Livesay lays bare the foun-
dations of her own leftism and poetic practice in the 1930s.

Moving from speech to social and political action, the second subsection reflects upon the catastrophic effects of proletarian revolt. As
leftists, the revolutionaries attack institutional structures symbolic of
church ('Cathedrals') and capital ('Skycrapers'). Their violence
becomes their means of expression, obviating the role of speech-maker
and leader. The speaker is obviously ill-fitted to lead the crowd, as
demonstrated by the ostentatious mounting of a steed ('I pranced on a
black horse' [72]). This romantic gesture betrays the poetic speech-
maker as a truly 'unacknowledged' leader of the revolution. No longer
in control of the crowd, the speaker is figured as a rider upon the back
of the revolution. Bereft of all but a symbolic means of expression, the
speech-maker is ironically silenced. The 'crowd roared,' the 'guns

exhorted,' even the 'black horse snorted,' but the speaker has been 'routed' (72). Knocked off the horse and buried under the rubble of fallen skyscrapers and cathedrals, the speaker is, at least figuratively, overthrown by the 'mounting movement' itself. 'In the time of action,' there is no time for romantic revolutionary speech.

Symbolically entombed 'under a stone' (72) after the revolution, the speaker regains the capacity for self-expression in the third subsection. In a self-contained romantic landscape, the speaker's tears replenish the post-revolutionary wasteland so that 'the grass grew again / Green in a gold oasis / And the well was watered' (72). Just as the rider is a romantic symbol in 'the time of action,' so the post-revolutionary res-urrection bespeaks the speaker's romanticism in 'the time of quiet.' If this post-revolutionary world is utopia, it is an imaginary 'no place' where no one but the speaker bears witness ('No one listened / Nothing shouted'). Although the speaker does not fall into a condition of silence, there is no audience for this speech. It is not the speaker's emotive expression of tears but an archetypal power, figured here as a 'tongue / Of the ancient sun' or mythical language, that brings health to the wounded and 'infested' world (72). Alluding to the solar and vegetation myths upon which Eliot had drawn in *The Waste Land*, Livesay at last embraces his 'mythical method' (Eliot, 'Ulysses' 178). But her mythical vision is not of a wasteland, but of a *post*-wasteland; her recourse to mythical language is taken as a means of transcendence from the social and political wasteland in 'the time of action.' Myth is posited here as a means of communication, an ancient but always his-torically situated system of signs (Barthes 118). This second section of Livesay's 'Motif' illustrates how mythical language is always pro-duced 'in time,' how myth is a type of speech predicated upon (real or imagined) events in history. For here the transcendent function of myth is not ahistorical, not an escape from history, but rather the refig-uration of contemporary history in another sign system, a mythical language, an ancient 'tongue.'

That transcendence is depicted in a painterly fashion on the third 'panel' of the mural. Livesay not only transmutes history into myth but also refines mythic language. She reduces myth to the materiality of colour and abstract pattern, stripped of rhetorical apparatus. Unlike the proletarian speech-maker, the speaker of this third section never employs rhetoric to persuade an audience to take action. Even though the verbs in the first two stanzas of this section are predominantly imperative, there is little resemblance to the rhetorical imperatives of

Livesay's proletarian verse of the 1930s; these imperatives are self-reflexive. Like the first two 'panels,' the self-reflexive third is a species of documentary – that is, 'the making of' a portrait of the self. Of course, this third 'panel' is not objective documentary or social realism; nor is it socialist, revolutionary romanticism. With its tendency to iconic abstraction, its radical subjectivity, its eruptive palette (purple, blue, gold, dove grey, scarlet, yellow, green), its violent dynamism, and its spiritual utopianism, this self-portrait exhibits characteristics of modernist – specifically, expressionist – visual art.[31] Its closing motif is a signal expressionist image of conflagration and regeneration, an apocalyptic death and rebirth of the self:

> Bound in the bands of colour, burned
> A salamander, I:
> Or phoenix who
> In world['s] own ashes lie:
> Affirming the still firmament, the flame
> Leaping to meet the master sun
> Praising his fiery name! (73)

Expressionist or expressionistic, this portrait is nevertheless a spiritual expression of the self. It represents transcendence of the self from the material conditions of alienation; it signifies an ecstatic communion with the world. For the unemployed men depicted on the first 'panel,' this is the scene of self-revelation, the expression of 'the unnamed name / Burning the tongue.' For the speech-maker of the second 'panel,' this is mythical speech in the 'tongue / Of the ancient sun.'

Because the poem can be dated only approximately to the 1940s, we cannot know which of Livesay's collections from that decade might have included 'Motif.' Nor can we determine if she ever attempted to publish the poem in a periodical, since no extant correspondence mentions its submission or rejection. The fact that she decided not to publish 'Motif' during the 1940s may be attributed to its political and cultural context. Since the political magazine culture in which she had been writing in the 1930s was no longer active by the early 1940s, Livesay could not expect to find a sympathetic audience for a non-partisan poem such as 'Motif' in the underground leftist press in Canada during the war years. Nor could she really count on finding a forum in Canada interested in the dissident verse of disenchanted members of the left. Had she persuaded Crawley to publish 'Motif' in *Contempo-*

rary Verse, she might have reached some readers sympathetic to the disenfranchised left, but she could not have expected to capture her poem's intended mass audience.

None of Livesay's proletarian poems collected in *Day and Night* articulates the disillusionment prevalent among artists, intellectuals, and activists of the left after the Soviet-Nazi non-aggression pact in August 1939 or after the banning of leftist organizations and publications and jailing of leaders of CPC cells under the Defence of Canada Regulations implemented during the Second World War. By 1944 she had capitulated to the Canadian war effort, so that the proletarian poems published in *Day and Night* were either dated as historical artefacts of the cultural left from the 1930s ('Day and Night' [1935]; 'The Outrider' [1935]) or presented as labour poetry in support of the wartime workforce ('West Coast' [1943]). Just as L.A. Mackay observed 'the strained apocalyptic tone in the earlier part of the book' (16) in his review of *Day and Night* for the April 1944 issue of *Contemporary Verse*, so we could measure the resonance of 'Motif' against the revolutionary tone of Livesay's proletarian verse from the mid-1930s. Given its apocalyptic tone and revolutionary subject, 'Motif' resembles her mid-1930s proletarian verse in *Day and Night*; but its critique of mass action and its affirmation of the self contradict the collectivist ethos of her proletarian verse in the 1944 collection. This dissonance with the proletarian modes at work in *Day and Night* marks 'Motif' as a transitional poem: it not only turns toward the self as the centre of her poetry in a transitional period between *Day and Night* in 1944 and *Poems for People* in 1947,[32] but also anticipates the mythic bent of her modernist poetry in the 1950s.

By the mid-1940s Livesay had at once distanced herself from her proletarian verse of the 1930s and reoriented herself toward its intended mass audience. Hence the title of *Poems for People* echoes the social and political verse that she had written during the 1930s, yet none of its poems could be called proletarian. Nor is its intended audience proletarian. Rather, its poetry is populist, a democratic mode of modernism, a 'social modernism' (Denning 122) – or, in another phrase, a people's modernism. *Poems for People* is therefore post-proletarian.

Crawley, reviewing *Poems for People* in the summer 1947 issue of *Contemporary Verse*, presents a careful consideration of Livesay's intended mass audience: 'The title and contents of POEMS FOR PEOPLE suggests [sic] that its author has determined that her writing shall

bring the language and content of poetry into closer touch with the
average reader, and in this aim many of the poems have been simplified in form and expression' ('Two' 16). He contrasts such 'simplified'
poetry written for the 'average reader' with poetry written for poets,
quoting Robert Graves as an adherent of the latter tendency: 'I write
poems for poets ... for people in general I write prose' (qtd. in
Crawley, 'Two' 16). Although he does not entirely agree with Graves,
Crawley notes that Livesay's 'simplification is successful' in some
poems, 'but in others she comes dangerously near to writing down.
It is in the more complex poems that she strongly declares her care
for poetry as such, whereby language itself becomes a continuing
experience' (16).

Livesay's transitional period of the mid-1940s is related to her search
for post-proletarian modes and media suitable to a people's poetry.
During this period, she composed poetry about artistic mass-communication media such as visual art, radio, and stage. Of course, writing
a poem about radio, about the stage, about a mural, or about a painting does not in itself constitute mass communication. *Poems for People*
is exemplary of her poetry's restriction to limited-circulation print
media in the mid-1940s. While almost all these poems had previously
appeared in magazines between May 1943 and June 1947, only one
had appeared in a mass-circulation magazine. Her subsequent publication of *Poems for People* with Ryerson Press could not ensure its mass
circulation or its dissemination among the general public for which
her people's poetry was written. Not until she focused on writing *for*
mass-communication media – instead of writing *about* it – could she
hope to communicate her poetry to mass audiences.

Livesay endeavoured in the late 1940s and early 1950s to write both
'poems for people' and, to reiterate Graves's phrase, 'poems for poets.'
She planned to address mass audiences by broadcasting her poetry on
radio (see Tiessen and Tiessen xii–xiii) and to maintain contact with a
minority literary culture by publishing her poetry in a variety of literary, arts, and academic periodicals. Through *Contemporary Verse* in particular, she was able to bring together her poetry for radio and print
media; both the magazine and its editor were instrumental in
Livesay's integration of her poetry and mass-communication media in
the late 1940s. As Livesay told Crawley in conversation in 1948, 'Canadians still put an aura around a poet's head, yet they rarely read
poetry, let alone read it aloud. I believe that radio will change that
picture. We will become as used to the sound of poetry as we are to the

sound of classical music and, once uninhibited, people will not mind reading poetry aloud at home, or having a poet talk to them' (qtd. in Crawley, 'Dorothy' 122).

Crawley published Livesay's 'Call My People Home,' a documentary poem for radio about the expulsion of Japanese Canadians from the West Coast after Pearl Harbor, in the summer 1949 issue of *Contemporary Verse*. In his editorial afterword to this issue, he called attention to recent broadcasts of her poetry on CBC radio – a fifteen-minute version of 'Call My People Home' on CBC Vancouver, a thirty-minute version on CBC Montreal produced in collaboration with musicians from the Montreal Symphony Orchestra, and a thirty-minute reading of her poems over the CBC Toronto Trans-Canada network (see Tiessen and Tiessen xv) – and concluded that 'it is a grand thing that at last CBC gives an often [*sic*] chance to thousands of listeners to hear the reading of poetry' ('About' 24). Annoyed by the dramatic vocalization and musical accompaniment of the 'Call My People Home' broadcasts, he reserved his praise for the reading of Livesay's poems: 'The producers of the Toronto broadcasts realized poetry's one great need and gave it, quite simply, the means of communication ... The readers were content to be a mouthpiece for the poet in clear and intelligent speech' (23). Disengaged from the apparatus of radio production, Crawley's publication of 'Call My People Home' granted it another means of communication and so presented her work as an example of such 'poems worthy of publication which by reason of content or length are unlikely to get printing elsewhere' (24).

After *Saturday Night* and *Poetry* rejected 'Call My People Home' – to give another example of his tendency to encourage Livesay and others to submit to prominent magazines before *Contemporary Verse*[33] – Crawley set aside an entire number for her radio poem, making it the only issue ever devoted to one poet. Evidently Livesay had originally intended to reach a larger audience through periodical publication elsewhere. Her decision to release 'Call My People Home' in a Ryerson chapbook of the same title in October 1950 indicates that her radio documentary could in fact 'get printing elsewhere,' and that its publication in *Contemporary Verse* and later in chapbook form represented a strategy to reach as large an audience as possible through available print media. If Marriott's critical review of *Call My People Home* in the spring 1951 issue of *Contemporary Verse* is a reasonable gauge of the printed poem's reception at the time, one might question Crawley's judgment in handing over an entire issue of the magazine to Livesay.

As an experienced radio scriptwriter, Marriott delivered her criticism with authority: 'Writing for broadcast naturally demands a more simplified style than Miss Livesay's usually is, with meaning which may be instantly appreciated. But how even in the interests of radio directness, can a writer of such ability justify the dullness of some passages, or such outworn poetic stuff' ('New Crop' 19). Reading Marriott's critique of 'Call My People Home,' one is reminded of her own radio poetry in *Calling Adventurers!* published nearly a decade earlier as a Ryerson poetry chapbook, and her commentary on the problems of writing for radio (see n21). Like Livesay, Marriott sacrificed the complexities of her poetic modernism in order to reach a mass audience on national radio. And in a similar fashion to Marriott's attempts to reconcile her modernist style with more popular 'magazine verse,' 'Call My People Home' crystallizes Livesay's poetic project and crisis in the late 1940s and early 1950s: to write at once socially conscious 'poems for people' and modernist 'poems for poets.'

During the hiatus between the 'Call My People Home' issue in the summer of 1949 and the release of her Ryerson chapbook of that title in the fall of 1950, Livesay's poem 'Vancouver' came out in the spring 1950 issue of *Contemporary Verse*. It does not appear among the eight additional poems appended to the typescript of *Call My People Home*, submitted by Livesay to Ryerson on 21 September 1950 (DLP-QU, box 2, file 20). 'Vancouver' has the dubious distinction of being the only discrete poem – that is, not part of a longer sequence – printed in *Contemporary Verse* but never collected by Livesay herself. It is a poem that was, to borrow Crawley's words, 'unlikely to get printing elsewhere.' In this respect, Morton's assessment of Livesay's frequent appearances in *Contemporary Verse* is apposite to the publication of 'Vancouver,' if not 'Call My People Home': 'Crawley appears to have been influenced ... by his friendship with Livesay to publish the large amount of her work that appears in *Contemporary Verse*' (96).

Like 'Call My People Home,' 'Vancouver' is written in the mode that Livesay calls documentary – that is, poetry 'based on topical data but held together by descriptive, lyrical, and didactic elements' ('Documentary' 269). It is at once a personal documentary of the speaker's cross-Canada journeys to and from Vancouver and a social documentary of the city itself. It is, moreover, a feminist and leftist documentary of the city, an exposé of explicitly *male* forms of urban violence. The poem opens with the declaration 'The city is *male*' and proceeds to document a feminist critique of male violence. As a documentary, 'Vancouver' diverges from standard leftist, documentarist tenets of social realism; it simultaenously exhibits Livesay's tendency to incorporate mythical motifs in her modernist poems of the 1950s. The poem closes with a report on gang violence in Vancouver's Chinatown, with a dead body that is not real but symbolic of the city personified and, in this final stanza, apostrophized:

> O body lying shattered, limbs of man
> Tossed in a doorway for the maggot sun:
> City unburied, shall I approach you now
> Open and undeterred?
> What, if your arms say nothing and your mouth
> Cries out unheard
> Can you awaken yet, out of this sleep
> And proclaim the Word? (*Archive* 91)

Now the publication of the poem in a Vancouver-based periodical becomes significant: it addresses a localized audience, figuratively embodied as a city of the dead. Here the documentarist speaker shifts into a didactic voice, reminiscent of Livesay's leftist verse of the 1930s, addressing the city itself. The exposed corpse of the city – 'stuffed in closets, left until the stench / Wrenches the roof off, and explodes the bomb' (91) – dramatizes a topical crisis of racialized violence. This explosive revelation of the body presents violent consequences related to the repression of social problems. By speaking for the city, 'Vancouver' reveals the unspeakable. The speaker's method, however, is not that of the social worker: the annunciation of the Word is a mythical means of representing this revelation, this awakening of the city of the dead. This modernist 'mythical method' that forces the poem's closure sits uncomfortably with the leftist, didactic, agitational manner in this final stanza. The uncertain juxtaposition is perhaps indicative of a poet in transition, whose sense of social justice naturally leads her back to a 1930s leftist mannerism, but whose aesthetic disposition tends now toward the mythic modernism of her poetry in the 1950s. While the leftist manner of the poem resonates with the predominantly masculinist character of Livesay's poems of social critique in the 1930s, her transformation of this masculinist mode into a form of feminist critique demonstrates a significant turn in her poetry toward a feminist, gender-inflected mode of social protest. That Crawley published 'Vancouver' in *Contemporary Verse* attests not only to his implicit endorsement of her poem's feminist critique of an aggressive, masculinist social order but also to his consistent editorial support for so many women poets in Canada, Livesay among them.

If 'Vancouver' exposes Livesay's continuing negotiation with leftism, it also documents her concurrent development of modernist and feminist modes of expression. Throughout the 1940s, *Contemporary Verse* offered her a forum that enabled her to bridge her leftism of the 1930s and her modernism and emergent feminism of the 1950s. Even as she sought to develop a post-proletarian poetry for mass audiences, the magazine enabled her to work at locating some middle ground between 'poems for people' and 'poems for poets,' even if the results were not always successful. Without *Contemporary Verse*, Livesay could have found other editors and magazines – Birney and *Canadian Poetry Magazine*, for instance – at times sympathetic to her interests in cultivating a taste for poetry among mass audiences. Yet no other magazine so comprehensively and consistently represented the long transition in her poetry and poetics as *Contemporary Verse*.

After *Contemporary Verse*

As early as April 1945, Crawley had expressed his interest in giving up *Contemporary Verse*. In a letter to McLaren, he stated his editorial crisis: 'I am dissatisfied with what I am doing now with C[ontemporary] V[erse]. For some time I was able to hold my own with what I had already read but now this is getting faded and out of reach and no good' (n.d. [c. April 1945], FMP). Unable to keep up with reading the new 1940s poetry, Crawley sensed that his editorial tastes were falling behind those of other little-magazine editors. *Contemporary Verse*, he feared, might no longer be contemporary at all. Nevertheless, the founding committee (especially McLaren) urged him to persevere. By finally naming McLaren associate editor in the fall of 1950, Crawley not only received assistance to continue editing the magazine into its second decade but also made official what had been unofficial all along – that *Contemporary Verse* was a collaborative editorial production by himself and McLaren. When he finally decided to give up the magazine in the fall of 1952, McLaren initially resisted, but by early 1953 she acceded to making the fall-winter 1952 issue of *Contemporary Verse* the last. Writing in February 1953 to inform Livesay of the joint decision to terminate the magazine, Crawley updated his complaint of April 1945:

I have not been at all pleased with what I was able to do or did do in the past year and disappointed in the work I was getting, failing completely to fit in with much of the writing that gets into Contact [a Toronto-based little magazine, founded in January 1952 and edited by Raymond Souster] and seems to be the contemporary trend. Further than this the 'older writers' are not only doing very little or no work at all but do not seem to need what C[ontemporary] V[erse] once could do for them. (DLP-QU, box 3, file 11)

Livesay's reply was by no means conciliatory. Unlike the numerous letters Crawley received from contributors and subscribers lamenting the passing of *Contemporary Verse* (see McCullagh 48–9), her letter of 16 February 1953 was accusatory. First, she resented not having been consulted prior to McLaren's and Crawley's joint decision: 'I had sort of thought, having been so definitely a midwife, I might have been called in at the death.' Next she reproached Crawley's lack of commitment to the new poetry of the early 1950s and his nostalgia for the poetry of the early 1940s:

I am sad, but not to cry. Where there is no enthusiasm, poetry perishes. And I have felt strongly, this past year, that you have lost the fiery interest you once had. For this we are all probably to blame – we writers, that is. We move on and where we move doesn't perhaps interest you. I mean, you have to think of the publication and how it stands up; we think only of our own development: we have to have faith in ourselves and our direction. And your frequently expressed sense of disappointment – because work isn't the same as it was – does incline one to question: why should it be? How could it be? (DLP-QU, box 3, file 11)

Crawley was by no means alone among little-magazine editors of the early 1950s who sensed a decline from the heyday of the early 1940s, when *Contemporary Verse*, *Preview*, and *First Statement* first appeared on the scene of Canadian poetry. Sutherland and Souster both published articles in the early 1950s suggesting that a new era of Canadian poetry was beginning (see Souster; Sutherland, 'Past'). Given her questioning of Crawley, Livesay seems to have shared Sutherland's and Souster's belief in Canadian poetry's new directions in the early 1950s, rather than Crawley's nostalgia for the poetry of the early 1940s.

Yet during the 1950s, Livesay's poetry never appeared in Souster's *Contact*, or, after the February-March 1950 issue, in Sutherland's *North-*

ern Review. She may have had faith in herself but not in the direction of Souster's or Sutherland's magazines. Conversely, they may not have had faith in her new poetry of the early 1950s. No editorial correspondence between Souster and Livesay from the 1950s has survived, but the last extant letter from Sutherland to Livesay, dated 8 March 1951, is a rejection letter (Sutherland, *Letters* 181–2). Constrained by the loss of *Contemporary Verse* as an outlet for her poetry, Livesay had to rely on editors not always favourable to her submissions. Instead of publishing in a diversity of magazines as she had during the 1940s, she mostly appeared – after the disappearance of *Contemporary Verse* – in either the *Canadian Forum* or *Fiddlehead* throughout the balance of the 1950s. Unlike Marriott, Livesay did not give up publishing books and chapbooks, though she would not produce a full book of new poems during the 1950s, only two chapbooks, *Call My People Home* (1950) and *New Poems* (1955), and one retrospective collection, *Selected Poems of Dorothy Livesay 1926–1956* (1957). Following *Poems for People* in 1947, she let twenty years pass before releasing her next book of new poems, *The Unquiet Bed,* published by the Ryerson Press in 1967.

For Livesay, the demise of *Contemporary Verse* affected only one aspect of her experience of poetry culture. She had faith in herself and her own development via alternative means of publication. When she found herself in the mid-1950s without a local poetry-magazine culture, however, she might have reconsidered her criticism of Crawley's editorship and his nostalgia for a Canadian poetry culture of the 1940s. After her gravitation toward writing for radio as a means of mass communication failed to produce a reliable channel between her poetry and mass culture, Livesay discovered that she had partly followed Marriott's withdrawal from poetry-magazine culture in the early 1950s. Livesay did not withdraw as far as Marriott, but she nevertheless learned how the dissolution of *Contemporary Verse* in 1953 signalled the end of the local poetry-magazine culture that had supported her through the most distinguished phase of her career. Its absence eliminated the primary means through which she had reached her audience during the 1940s and early 1950s. The people for whom she had written in that period were not among an imagined mass culture but rather the people among her own poetry-magazine culture – the *Contemporary Verse* group and its audience. By 1951–2 she had annouced with obvious disillusionment that 'there was no mass audience' and that it was, in fact, 'the great twentieth century myth' (*Dorothy* 8; see also Tiessen 219–20). Having realized that her 'poems for people' could not reach their intended audience by means of book production and distribution and having attempted to disseminate poetry for mass consumption by means of radio, Livesay reconsidered her options in the early 1950s. Her *New Poems* of 1955, published by Jay Macpherson's Emblem Books, signalled her retreat from mass culture toward the specialized audience of 'poems for poets' and the medium of chapbooks produced by small presses. Rather than limit herself to one means of communication – book, chapbook, broadside, little magazine, academic journal, commercial periodical, newspaper, or radio – Livesay enlisted a multiplicity of means throughout the balance of her career to distribute her work to poetry's public. She proved as adaptable to changes brought about by the end of *Contemporary Verse* in the 1950s as she had to the collapse of *Masses* and *New Frontier* in the 1930s.

For Marriott, the discontinuation of *Contemporary Verse* severed her nearly two-decade-long relationship with poetry-magazine culture. Alongside Livesay, Marriott published her poetry in either the *Canadian Forum* or *Fiddlehead* throughout the 1950s. More important to her than to Livesay, Crawley's and McLaren's decision to suspend *Contemporary Verse* after February 1953 announced the end of a poetry-magazine culture that had officially originated in September 1941, but had unofficially commenced with the poetry group of the Victoria CAA and its first *Victoria Poetry Chapbook* in 1935. Marriott's participation in the formative decades of that poetry culture concluded with two events: her departure from *Canadian Poetry Magazine* in 1950 – as regional editor and contributor – followed by the cessation of *Contemporary Verse* in 1952–3. Detached from poetry-magazine culture, she subsequently disappeared from the Canadian poetry scene until the publication of her 1971 chapbook *Countries*. After the collapse of Vancouver-Victoria poetry-magazine culture, she resigned herself to writing sporadic 'magazine verse' until the 1970s. This verse may have been published in periodicals that circulated among a wider public than small-press chapbooks and books, but few readers seemed to notice.

Neither radio nor any other communication media could replace the function of that Vancouver-Victoria poetry-magazine culture from the mid-1930s through the early 1950s. Both the Victoria poetry group of the CAA and the *Contemporary Verse* group provided Marriott and Livesay with a community. Combined with their respective magazines, the communal function of these poetry groups established a place for women in modernist literary culture in Canada. Without these groups and without poetry magazines to publish their work, the isolation, invisibility, and even silence Livesay and Marriott experienced would likely have been exacerbated. Even for Page and Waddington, poets whose presence in Montreal little-magazine culture during the 1940s has been well-documented by scholars of Canadian literary modernism, *Contemporary Verse* provided an important outlet for their verse and a valuable source of editorial advice from both Crawley and McLaren. It offered them an alternative to the sometimes fractious Montreal little-magazine culture of the 1940s. If *Contemporary Verse* and *Canadian Poetry Magazine* were founded in the staid poetry-magazine tradition of *Poetry*, then the Montreal little-magazines *Preview* and *First Statement* were inheritors of the radical tradition of the *Little Review*. The Montreal little-magazine culture of the 1940s began in 1942 and reached its height by 1945; its decline after the merger of *Preview* and *First Statement* into *Northern Review* in 1945 and the mass resignation of key editorial members two years later resulted in the more frequent publication of Page, Waddington, and other poets associated with Montreal little magazines in *Contemporary Verse* throughout the latter half of the 1940s and into the early 1950s. Of that migration from the Montreal little magazines to *Contemporary Verse*, virtually nothing has been recorded in Canadian literary history.

3 Gendered Modernisms: Montreal Toronto Vancouver, 1941–1956

Now your least thought is the poor type on cheap newsprint.

P.K. Page, 'Elegy' (Hidden 1: 62)

Gender and Little-Magazine Cultures

Miriam Waddington's 1989 essay-memoir 'Apartment Seven' points to the largely unrealized potential for studies of gender in Canadian literary culture of the 1940s. Although the critical field has since shifted, her assessment is still pertinent to the study of women in little-magazine culture of that time: 'Gender has seldom, if ever, been studied or written about in relation to the literary life in Canada during the forties ... It would be interesting, all the same, to explore what part, if any, gender actually played in the development of the little magazines, in their selection of material and in their editing, and ultimately in the shaping of modern Canadian tastes and cultural attitudes'. (34–5n1). Waddington's gesture toward gender studies has since been followed up by Robert K. Martin, David Leahy, Justin D. Edwards, and Peter Dickinson, whose analyses of queer and leftist politics in Patrick Anderson's poetry of the 1940s have contributed to the past decade's criticism on the Montreal little magazines *Preview* and *First Statement*. Yet Waddington's own part in Canada's little-magazine culture of the 1940s has attracted minimal critical attention, even from those critics writing about her poetry from this period (Ricou, 'Into'; Panofsky). Recent feminist studies of Waddington (McLauchlan, '"I," "Unknown"' and 'Transformative') and of her contemporary P.K. Page (Relke, Killian, Paul, T. MacDonald, Swann) foreground the construction of gender in their poetry of the 1940s, but these readings disregard the historical contexts of the decade's little magazines. Brian Trehearne's *The Montreal Forties: Modernist Poetry in Transition* offers readings of gender in the modernist poetics of the period and its effects on Page's early poetry (43, 96–7), though her gendered poetics is not prominent in his narrative of the Montreal poets and their little magazines. Gender, in the decade or so following Waddington's pronouncement, has clearly entered the field of critical inquiry; its study in relation to modernist poetics and literary culture of the 1940s has so far exposed what Edwards calls the 'masculinist position' of the little magazine in Canada (67). Even among critics interested in a critique of the gendered discourses that circulate in and among Canada's modernist little magazines, the persistent identification of Canadian modernism as an exclusively masculinist phenomenon has occluded the emergent histories of women's modernism and the Montreal little magazines, including two of their most prominent women poets, Page and Waddington.

Waddington's push toward a gendered reading of Canadian modernism directs critical attention toward largely unopened areas of historical inquiry, namely, the contributions of women to Montreal little-magazine culture of the 1940s. Archival materials that document women's activities as poets and editors in this milieu are, however, far less abundant than those relevant to their contemporaries in Vancouver and Victoria. This scarcity should not deter the study of women's various roles – as poets, short-story writers, editors, critics, reviewers, typists, mimeographers – in Montreal during the 1942–5 period. Much has been recorded in articles, biographies, critical histories, and interviews about John Sutherland, Louis Dudek, Irving Layton, and *First Statement*; and, at least recently, as much published about Patrick Anderson, F.R. Scott, A.M. Klein, and *Preview*. Treatments of Page in the context of *Preview* have been few: there is no comprehensive study of her essays, short stories, and poetry published in that magazine (see Sutherland, 'P.K. Page'; Ringrose, '*Preview*'; Trehearne, *Montreal* 49–53). Nor has there been anything more than passing mention of Waddington, except in her own memoirs and criticism, in the context of *First Statement*.

Rather than duplicate another *Preview–First Statement* narrative of Montreal poetry culture, this chapter traverses the multiple cities and literary communities in which Page and Waddington were prominent contributors to Canadian little magazines between 1941 and 1956. This narrative imbricates the histories of three modernist little-magazine communities: the *Contemporary Verse* group (1941–53), the *Preview* group (1942–5), and the *First Statement* group (1942–5). By introducing *Contemporary Verse* into a history of two poets chiefly associated with *Preview* and *First Statement*, we may revisit this period of modern Canadian magazine culture without resorting to a reductive binaristic model of literary history.[1] After all, neither Page nor Waddington was restricted by allegiances to magazine groups. Both published more poems in *Contemporary Verse* than any of the members of its founding committee; they also appeared there more often than any other poet of the *Preview* and *First Statement* groups. In fact, Page was the poet most often published in the thirty-nine issues of *Contemporary Verse*; Waddington tied (with Anne Wilkinson) as its second most published poet. Beyond such statistics, however, Page and Waddington are figures through whom we may witness the communication and mobility among poetry communities of the 1940s and 1950s that have commonly been isolated or opposed in the literary-historical record, and through whom we may observe exchanges of and about modernist poetry among the *Preview*, *First Statement*, and *Contemporary Verse* groups.

I have divided this chapter into three sections: the first details Page's activities as an editorial member of the *Preview* group in Montreal, the second Waddington's involvement as a member of the *First Statement* writers' group in Toronto and interaction with the *First Statement* editorial group in Montreal, the third both poets' contributions to *Contemporary Verse*. From their debuts in the early issues of *Contemporary Verse* to their withdrawals from that magazine after joining the *Preview* and *First Statement* groups in 1942 and their returns to *Contemporary Verse* after the amalgamation of *Preview* and *First Statement* to form *Northern Review* in 1945, this literary-historical narrative follows the development of Page's and Waddington's poetry and poetics in relation to transitional events in modernist little-magazine culture during the 1940s and early 1950s.

These transitions have correlates in Page's and Waddington's biographies. Page's departure from Montreal for Victoria in the fall of 1944 and move to Ottawa to work at the NFB in the spring of 1946 coincided with the period of transition and amalgamation in Montreal – from *Preview* and *First Statement* to *Northern Review*. While she maintained her association with *Northern Review* as a regional editor in Victoria (1945–6) and in Ottawa (1946–7), her separation from the Montreal group began well before her resignation from the editorial board of *Northern Review* in 1947. And though Waddington had no editorial affiliation with *First Statement*, her departure from Toronto for Philadelphia in September 1944 to attend the University of Pennsylvania's School of Social Work initiated a transitional year during which she too distanced herself from Montreal little-magazine culture; even after her return to Canada and move from Toronto to Montreal in 1945, she took no active role among the Montreal groups. For Page and Waddington, the *Contemporary Verse* group provided a reliable source of personal and editorial advice through these years of transition. Even after the magazine's final issue in early 1953 and her move to to Australia later that year, Page continued her editorial relationship with Crawley and McLaren.

Given these broad historical and biographical contexts, we may begin to respond to Waddington's call for a gendered reading of Canadian modernist little-magazine culture of the mid-century. Her call recognizes the place of gender in the production of literary magazines, that is, in the selection and editing of material ('Apartment' 34–5n1). This acknowledgment of gender should, however, also account for women's roles in the physical production of the magazines, as we have already witnessed in the case of *Contemporary Verse*.

Page's part in the making of *Preview* deserves close attention, since it draws out connections among her and other women's roles in its physical production, feminized forms of labour, and her office poems in the magazine itself. Analysis of these office poems in their little-magazine context will help to trace her development of a gender-conscious poetry primarily through a modernist poetics of impersonality during her *Preview* period. This combination of gender consciousness and poetic impersonality re-emerges in Page's poetry of the late 1940s and early 1950s, as she increasingly counterweights a poetics of impersonality with a poetics of personality. Published in *Contemporary Verse*, her subjective, gender-conscious poetry and metapoetic critiques of impersonality from this post-*Preview* period invite a reconsideration of the *Contemporary Verse* group and its editors' effects on her poetry. After Page came in contact with the *Contemporary Verse* group, she too became a beneficiary of Crawley's 'unconscious' feminism and his advocacy of women's modernism. The extent to which he fostered an emergent women's modernism in an otherwise masculinist little-magazine culture can be measured not only by the amount of women's modernist poetry he published but also by the degree to which he (and his associate editor, McLaren) encouraged poets to write in a personal, subjective mode. Crawley's and McLaren's preference for a subjective, personalist poetics conflicted at times with Page's early objective, impersonalist manner; this division between the poet and her editors holds significant implications for readings of her gendered poetics and her participation in a women's modernism, particularly in light of recent feminist critiques of modernist impersonality as a masculinist poetics (see Killian 93). That Page developed her impersonalist style during her *Preview* years speaks to the correlation between her early modernism and its formation in a masculinist little-magazine culture; and given that the Crawley-McLaren influence on her modernism from the late 1940s to mid-1950s is marked by its subjectivist, gender-conscious turn and a self-critique of her impersonalist poetics, there is evidence to support the claim that her departure from a masculinist modernism was facilitated by the editors of *Contemporary Verse* and their 'unconscious' feminism. These determinist readings of gender in Page's modernist poetics would have to acknowledge that her early poetry's gender consciousness is present in its subjective and objective, personalist and impersonalist modes, however. To arrive at a more nuanced reading of her early poetics, then, we need to account for the 'unresolved contradiction' (to adapt a phrase from Marianne DeKoven [*Rich* 4]) between her gendered modernisms – that is, between her early objectivist, impersonalist poetics formed during her immersion in a masculinist little-magazine culture in Montreal and her later subjectivist, personalist, autocritical, gender-conscious poetics stimulated by her increased contact with the *Contemporary Verse* group.

Page's critique of both impersonality and gender in her poetry evolved into a crisis by the mid-1950s, followed by a decade of poetic silence. This crisis and subsequent silence between 1956 and 1967 has been the subject of ongoing critical speculation, most recently and comprehensively by Trehearne (see *Montreal* 41–105 passim). To his narrative of events leading to Page's mid-career silence, this chapter adds a supplemental history of the *Contemporary Verse* group and its complicity in her poetic crises. If Page's 'middle silence' (Trehearne, *Montreal* 45) remains enigmatic to critics and literary historians, it is in part owing to the fact that we have yet to account for the gendered contexts of her early poetry and the sociality of gender in modernist little magazines. Her prolonged negotiation with modernism's socially and aesthetically gendered discourses led to decisive consequences –

not only to her withdrawal from little-magazine culture and its gendered sites of literary production after 1956 but also to the necessary reformulation of her poetics during this post-1956 period. As a crisis in Page's modernism, this period is not a moment of rupture but rather the accumulated effect of her early poetry's oscillation between subjectivity and objectivity, between interiority and exteriority, between self-reflexivity and self-effacement, between a poetics of personality and one of impersonality, and between personation and impersonation. These unsynthesized dialectical pairs are emblematic of her early poetry's split between masculinist and feminist discursive positionings – its ambivalent gender consciousness – which is compounded by the gendered conditions of Canadian modernism and modernist little-magazine production.

Unlike Page, Waddington did not have direct access to the means of magazine production. She did not type stencils for the early mimeographed issues of *First Statement*, work that was done by Audrey Sutherland (née Aikman) (Fisher 5), or later typeset and print the magazine on the First Statement Press hand press, work chiefly carried out by Sutherland and Layton (note the gendered division of labour here – the woman typing stencils versus the men setting type); nor did Waddington take part in the magazine's editorial construction. Her role as a member of the *First Statement* group in Toronto subjected her to the editorial control of Sutherland and the *First Statement* group in Montreal. If gender played a role in her experience of *First Statement* and First Statement Press, it was in her subjection to the masculinist editorial practices of Sutherland, Layton, and Dudek. Not without a sense of irony, Waddington recollects that 'gender did not even exist ... or else it was completely submerged and invisible in our small circle. For my part, I accepted that men were top dog in this world' ('Apartment' 34n1). However, the invisibility of gender here does not signify its absence but rather the naturalization, and thereby dematerialization, of gender relations. Making gender visible will enable the analysis of its material part in the editorial handling of Waddington's poetry by Sutherland and the *First Statement* group. Their masculinist editorial manner in fact exacerbated Waddington's poetic crisis in 1943–5, as she grappled with problems of communicating human sympathy and social solidarity in the poems she published in *First Statement*. Less dramatic than Page's similar poetic crisis and subsequent withdrawal from little-magazine culture in the mid-1950s, her crisis in the mid-1940s was not signalled by a period of poetic inactivity but by her retreat from Montreal little-magazine culture. This retreat led to a decade-long gap between her first poetry collection, *Green World* (1945) – published by Sutherland's First Statement Press – and her next, *The Second Silence* (1955). Waddington's concurrent experiences with Crawley and the *Contemporary Verse* group in the early to mid-1940s will serve as a narrative in counterpoint to her trials with Sutherland and the *First Statement* group during the same period.

Because the periods of crisis in Waddington's and Page's early poetry were followed by their separations from little-magazine groups, I have taken these terminal events as end points in this chapter. Waddington's detachment from little-magazine culture takes place in the mid-1940s, Page's in the mid-1950s. Numerous poems published in *Preview*, *First Statement*, and *Contemporary Verse* but excluded from their respective volumes of the 1940s and 1950s offer insight into the accumulated self-questioning, self-criticism, and self-doubt that characterize these pivotal periods in their early careers. These are poems in which Waddington and Page articulated many of the most pressing concerns in their early development as modernists and the difficulties they experienced as women in the context of Canadian little-magazine culture at mid-century.

Page's *Preview*

Contemporary Verse and *Preview* were separately conceived in April 1941, months prior to the appearance of either in print. That same April, when the founding committee of *Contemporary Verse* gathered at Floris McLaren's house in Victoria (McLaren, 'Contemporary' 55–6), Patrick and Peggy Anderson produced their first little magazine in Montreal, *The Andersons* (Whitney, 'From Oxford' 34; Anderson, Introduction iii). By June the founding committee of the Victoria-Vancouver magazine had issued letters requesting submissions from poets across the country, and three of the founding editors of *Preview* – Patrick Anderson, F.R. Scott, and Margaret Day – had met to discuss the prospect of starting a magazine (Bentley and Gnarowski 95). During the fall months, Neufville Shaw and Bruce Ruddick joined the *Preview* group (Bentley and Gnarowski 95). The first issue of *Contemporary Verse* was published in September 1941, followed by *Preview* in March 1942. By April, Page had been introduced to Patrick Anderson and invited by him to join the *Preview* group. Anderson met Page through a mutual acquaintance in Montreal, but he may have already read her poems printed in the first two issues of *Contemporary Verse* (Bentley and Gnarowski 98). However he may have originally discovered her, she appeared as an editor on the masthead of the second, April 1942, issue of *Preview*.

If *Contemporary Verse* was designed in the image of the internationally renowned *Poetry*, *Preview* took after the production values of the virtually unknown *The Andersons*.[2] Neither *Contemporary Verse* nor *Preview* was a fine-press periodical; both were mimeographed from typed stencils. Pertinent to women's roles in modernist little-magazine culture, these production values embody feminized forms of labour. 'Two wives,' as Patrick Anderson recalled, 'Kit Shaw and Peggy Doernbach Anderson, were extremely important behind the scenes' (Introduction iii). Kit Shaw handled subscriptions and submissions through the first fifteen issues,[3] while Peggy Anderson managed production work for *Preview* from the first to the last issue.[4] Page and her employment in war offices proved indispensable to the physical production of *Preview*, as she had access to a heavy typewriter, which she used to cut the stencils for the magazine.[5] She also mentions doing the 'paste-up' of the July 1942 issue (Page to Scott, 18 July [1942], FRSP, reel H-1211), a job that Patrick Anderson singled out for derision in his August 1942 letter: 'I quite forgot to say that I thought the last issue of PREVIEW very disappointing typographically – I hope something can be done' (Anderson to Page, August 1942, PKPP, box 6, file 7). With the exception of Anderson himself, neither literary critics nor little-magazine historians have detailed the involvement of women in *Preview*'s physical production (see Anderson, Introduction and 'A Poet'). Like *Contemporary Verse*, *Preview* might never have appeared without the behind-the-scenes work of the group's women members. It could have existed otherwise as a Montreal writing group – analogous to the local poetry groups of the CAA – without producing any kind of publication; its 'Literary letter' (as Patrick Anderson dubbed *Preview* in the June 1942 issue ['Note']) might not, however, have materialized without the investment of time and skill by Peggy Anderson, Kit Shaw, and Page. Patrick Anderson saw fit in his editorial capacity to criticize the make-up but was unwilling (if not unable) to do anything to rectify it himself; he contributed content to *Preview* but not material labour toward its production. He may have declared himself a socialist, but at the same time he maintained gendered divisions of labour, for it was Peggy Anderson, herself an activist for the Labour Progressive Party, who frequently used the party's offices to mimeograph *Preview* (Ringrose, '*Preview*' 31; Anderson, *Search Me* 149).

Given Peggy Anderson's hand in the production of the prototype, *The Andersons*, it seems logical that it should have been the model and she one of the typists of *Preview*. If the first six issues of *Preview* appear crude, it is because the means of production available to its producers were those of the office – typewriter, mimeograph machine – not of the printing press. Certainly, *Preview*'s low production values prompted the editors to comment upon its presentation to the public. 'This is no magazine,' the first *Preview* editorial declares. 'It presents five Montreal writers who recently formed themselves into a group for the purpose of mutual discussion and criticism and who hope, through these selections, to try out their work before a larger public' (Anderson et al., 'Statement'). Three issues later, in June 1942, Patrick Anderson clarified its genre and its intended audience: 'PREVIEW is a private "Literary letter"' and 'in no sense a "magazine" on sale to the general public' ('Note' [1942]). *Preview* was not so much a 'private' letter as an 'open' one published for and disseminated to an audience of 80 to 100, perhaps 150, subscribers (McKnight 4; Bentley and Gnarowski 96). It was called a 'Literary letter' because the means of production available to the group necessitated that *Preview* appear (for its first six issues) as a mimeographed and stapled newsletter, not because the editors deliberately wanted to alienate the 'general public.'[6] A strict definition of *Preview* as a 'Literary letter' may not be vital to bibliographers of literary periodicals in Canada, but its production as such is crucial to our appreciation of the women responsible for its typing and mimeographing.

Page's role in the production of *Preview* situates her within the social and cultural history of women living and writing in Montreal during the war, particularly in the context of women's wartime labour. Her poetry from her *Preview* period often chronicles the social conditions of living, working, and writing in wartime Montreal from the perspective of a young woman; many of these poems were never published or, if published, not collected at the time. Although she had started writing such social poems as early as November 1941, when she first arrived in Montreal from Saint John, she published almost none before joining the *Preview* group in the spring of 1942. Her copybook of 1940–4, which contains fair-copy versions of her published and unpublished poems, chronicles the progress of her poetry toward social consciousness during these formative first months in Montreal in 1941–2 (see

PKPP, box 1, file 5). In *Preview* she found a place to publish her social poetry on a regular basis, not because she could find no other outlet (her first published war poem, 'Blackout,' appeared in the December 1941 issue of *Contemporary Verse*), but because the *Preview* group itself was intent upon producing a socially engaged modernist poetry. Her modernism resonated with the social consciousness of the group.

As a member of the *Preview* group, Page joined fellow poets who subscribed to an objective, modernist poetics of impersonality. Her copybook from the early 1940s, however, also contains several unpublished and uncollected poems in which she exhibits the subjective, personalist, self-reflexive style to which she returned after her withdrawal from the *Preview* group in the mid-1940s, notably those written prior to her contact with *Preview* but contemporaneous to her early publications in *Contemporary Verse*. Written after her move from Saint John to Montreal, her pre-*Preview* poems from late 1941 to early 1942 – all unpublished – not only record wartime conditions in Montreal but also work through problems in modernist poetics to which she attended throughout the 1940s and 1950s. This is especially true of her practice of a modernist poetics of impersonality. As early as November 1941, her nascent impersonalist poetry was inflected by gender consciousness. Several poems written during her first few months in Montreal are concerned with ideas of impersonality, sometimes in conjunction with reflections on the social conditions of urban alienation, sometimes in relation to the social construction of women's gender roles.[7] These pre-*Preview* poems employ personation both as a means of recording subjective impressions of impersonal phenomena and as a reflexive device for interrogating limitations of self-expression and communicating crises of subjectivity. These crises are not, however, restricted to her poetry of 1941–2: they anticipate the crises of subjectivity recorded in her poetry throughout the 1940s and 1950s.

During this pre-*Preview* period, Page not only adjusted her poetics and discovered new poetic subjects but also changed the way in which she composed her poems. From the summer of 1940 to the end of 1941, Page's copybook includes only handwritten poems. Beginning in January 1942, it contains only typewritten copies. Because only a few of the typewritten poems include manuscript corrections, it is apparent that these versions are likely fair copies and do not necessarily represent the full compositional process of early drafts and worksheets. Nevertheless, just prior to joining the *Preview* group and beginning its production work and coincident with her starting work in war offices, she incorporated the instrument of magazine production and office labour into her compositional practice. It is perhaps a commonplace to say that the typewriter introduced a depersonalized mode of writing into interpersonal communication, or that typewriting represents a 'disembodied impersonality' as opposed to 'handwriting's embodied human presence' (Olwell 48). Even so, the striking coincidence of Page's earliest experimentation with an impersonalist poetics and her simultaneous decision to shift from handwriting to typewriting deserves greater scrutiny.

Perhaps the most significant influence on her emergent impersonal-ist poetics was T.S. Eliot's *The Waste Land*, specifically the typist of 'The Fire Sermon,' whose 'automatic hand' (72) anticipates the depersonal-ization and automatism of Page's clerks, typists, and stenographers in her office poems of the early 1940s. We can be certain that she had read Eliot thoroughly by February 1942, immediately before she originally met with the *Preview* group. Her previously unpublished poem 'Diary' of that same month speaks ironically about digesting Eliot's poetry at the breakfast table:

> I should have brought my Eliot to breakfast
> and read of outworn disillusionment
> that found a sort of weary exaltation
> much later at the Anglo-Catholic font.
> I should have swallowed Wastelands with my porridge
> and Mr. Sweeney with my egg and bacon;
> the mood is definitely nineteen-twenty,
> T.S. was in my mind when I awakened.
> I lift my coffee spoon – at once remember
> his image that concerned a coffee spoon
> and though the hour is breakfast I become
> a paper figure leaning on the moon. (PKPP, box 1, file 5)

Unlike Eliot, Page does not conceal herself behind alternative person-alities such as Prufrock or Sweeney, nor does she disperse her per-sonae among fragments of quotation and allusion as in *The Waste Land*. Her persona's ironized recollection of Eliot is nevertheless occasioned by a mood of self-estrangement. Page estranges the diarist's 'I' from its quotidian breakfast routine. This effect lasts only for the instant of the closing surreal image, as the diarist quickly observes: 'The mood will pass. It has passed' (PKPP, box 1, file 5). While the grammatical – and, elsewhere in the poem, gendered female – first person shows no signs of disappearing in her imitation of Eliot, Page soon afterwards distanced herself from writing confessionalist poems such as 'Diary.' Approaching a modernist poetics of impersonality through tentative gestures of self-estrangement, she at once probed the limits of the self and located its poetic limitations.

Page attended her first *Preview* meeting in March 1942, just in time to help with the mail-out of the first issue.[8] Although we cannot know for certain which of her poems were written immediately afterward, there is a definite shift in her poetry following her introduction to the group. Entirely absent from the poems in her copybook prior to March–April 1942, the class consciousness and predominant impersonality of her poetry during this two-month period are signs of her early exposure to the poetry and poets of the *Preview* group. Her poetry of March–April 1942 is marked by an increased attention to class-specific subjects, often captured in impersonalist portraiture of isolated figures. Not surprisingly, Page's introduction to *Preview* in the spring of 1942 coincided with the publication of impersonalist social portraiture by other members of the group in the early issues. Many of her poems in *Preview* exhibit a pronounced social – if not socialist[9] – consciousness, especially in conjunction with civilian women's experiences on the home front.

Published in the July 1942 issue, 'The Stenographers' represents the realization of Page's early, mostly unpublished, experiments with an integrated poetics of impersonality, class consciousness, and gender consciousness. Among the many commentators on 'The Stenographers,' Laura Killian has noted 'the irony of choice of distance in this particular poem – the impersonal poetic treatment of impersonal labour practice' (91). While 'The Stenographers' impersonally chronicles the social and psychological conditions of urban alienation on the home front, the persona who appears in the final lines emerges as a credible witness to the suffering of female office workers. This act of self-inscription attempts to ascribe authenticity to the persona's account of the alienating effects of women's clerical labour. But one should not confuse this 'low-key personation' (Trehearne, *Montreal* 83) and 'impersonal, observing and distancing eye' (Killian 91) with self-expression. Unlike the majority of personae in Page's (mostly unpublished) poems from late 1941 to early 1942, the persona of 'The Stenographers' is neither self-reflexively constructed nor conspicuously gendered. From the persona's sympathetic representation of female office workers, we may infer a female persona, but nowhere in the poem is the persona's gender made explicit. Rather, it is revealed through a socialized gender coding that builds upon our expectation of gendered sympathies between the persona and a feminized labour force.

'The Stenographers' attracted immediate critical attention from her contemporaries. Writing of Page in the November 1942 issue of *First Statement*, Sutherland signalled the way in which 'The Stenographers' began to inflect readings of all her poetry from her *Preview* years: 'P.K. Page joined *Preview* after the appearance of the first issue, and she has been particularly influenced by their general policy ... As far as I know, everything that this writer has since produced has had some social implication. She has dealt with that section of society of which she has personal knowledge. She has been like a field worker for the magazine, making a special poetical report on the lives of stenographers' ('P.K. Page' 97). Sutherland's example of Page's poetical reports is 'Prediction without Crystal,' a poem which accompanies his article in *First Statement* and which contains no mention of stenographers. His assumption that a poem about 'girls' is also about 'stenographers' betrays an overdetermined autobiographical reading (though he does not mistake Page for one of her 'stenographers,' noting that she is not 'writing about herself' [96]). What Sutherland calls the 'general subject that [has] served her as a focal point for poetry' (97) presumably refers to the 'social implication' of her poems and not to the 'lives of stenographers.' In any case, his generalization was certainly premature, since the only office poem that she had published at the time was 'The Stenographers,' but his prescience is remarkable; given her composition and/or publication of numerous poems about women office workers over the next year.

It may seem unlikely that any of Page's other office poems from the 1940s could be read today as anything but context for a reading of 'The Stenographers.' In the absence of any other office poems in *As Ten as Twenty* (1946) and *The Metal and the Flower* (1954), it is perhaps inevitable that 'The Stenographers' should have gained canonical distinction. Of the other office poems she published in the early 1940s, the majority appeared in the year following the original publication of 'The Stenographers' in July 1942. Only 'The Stenographers' appeared in *As Ten as Twenty*; none of 'Typists,' 'Shipbuilding Office,' 'The Inarticulate,' 'Noon Hour,' or 'Offices' was collected until her 1974 retrospective volume *P.K. Page: Poems Selected and New*. In addition to these published office poems, Page's copybook from 1940–4 contains a number of unpublished poems documenting the lives of office workers. To retrace the trajectory of her office poems, which begins with 'The Stenographers,' we may recover and elaborate one of the definitive narratives of her *Preview* period. More than merely supplemental to 'The Stenographers,' her published and unpublished office poems from this July 1942 to October 1943 period develop a range of perspectives on a predominantly female sector of the wartime workforce. If 'The Stenographers' has been taken as a synecdoche for Page's office poems, its limited perspective cannot account for the subtle gradations of and hierarchies among office workers, whose occupations are often overlooked by historians of the war, especially those chroniclers of women's employment in industrial (and traditionally male) sectors of the workforce (see Pierson; Nash). Page was not herself concerned with the 'Rosie the Riveter' phenomenon and women's mobilization in war industries to compensate for shortages of male workers, but rather with the clerical and secretarial jobs of women workers in early to mid-twentieth-century offices and the feminization of their labour (see Lowe 255–62).

Page was employed in war offices – as a filing clerk, not as a stenographer. Her employment and skills as an office worker were nevertheless key to her work on the physical production of *Preview*. We need only note that 'The Stenographers' (July 1942), 'Typists' (February 1943), 'Shipbuilding Office' (August 1943), and 'Offices' (October 1943) all appeared in *Preview* to demonstrate that the means and conditions of the magazine's production were materially linked to the subject matter of her poetry. After all, the majority of her office poems from 1942–3 first appeared in *Preview*. Her poems do not have to refer to women doing the make-up, typing, and mimeographing of a little magazine for us to infer tacit connections between the representation in *Preview* of office work by women and the materiality of its production by women. Restored to the historical contexts of *Preview* and women's wartime office work, these poems become nuanced by details of Page's cultural and social milieu in Montreal during the early 1940s. Writing to F.R. Scott on 18 July 1942, she makes plain the correlation between her office work, the production of *Preview*, and the poems she published in that month's issue:

The reason I inflict my writing upon you is because my typewriter is at
the Shaws for Patsy to type the stencils. I feel lost without it – hardly
know how to hold a pen any more. I hope you smile upon the new issue.
It's difficult to know whether a thing's good or bad when you've mulled
over it for so long. But I think it stands up pretty well ... I've been turning
out practically nothing – in fact you will see almost my entire output in
this issue. I write a few lines a night and then scratch them out the next
night! I've been working terribly hard at the office – had two blissful
weeks of doing 2 jobs and 1 of doing 3, if you please. I honestly thought
I'd have to be put away. (FRSP, reel H-1211)

Page refers to yet another woman who volunteered to type the *Preview*
stencils, and the implication is evident: typing is, in this historical
context, the job of women.[10] Whether she is writing of her own labour,
that of women at the office, or that of women behind the scenes at
Preview, she documents the psychological and social conditions in
which her office poems of 1942–3 were written. As this July 1942 letter
attests, Page writes to Scott at the beginning of a period of reduced
productivity and creative frustration, a period during which she could
complete only two or three new poems a month – likely as a result of
her workload at the office and her responsibilities as an editor of
Preview.[11] The first of her office poems, 'The Stenographers,' appeared
in the same issue of *Preview* on which she had worked to finish the
'paste-up' the night before writing to Scott. Given the demands of the
office, it is not surprising that she should turn her workplace to poetic
account.

Page's poetic preoccupation with offices continued throughout the
late summer and fall months of 1942 and into early 1943, resulting in
an accumulation of unpublished poems about men and women
employed in various kinds of office work. Unpublished pieces such as
'The Office' (August 1942), 'For Michael' (September 1942), 'Janitor in
the Drafting Room' (September 1942), and 'Girl at Work' (c. early 1943)
appear at intervals in her copybook from this period.[12] Of these
unpublished poems, only 'The Office' appears to have been sent out –
first to *Partisan Review* and later to *Canadian Poetry Magazine* – and
rejected (PKPP, box 1, file 5). Its impersonal representation of office
work and stark juxtaposition of pastoral and urban imagery marks it
as a variation on 'The Stenographers,' with a focus instead on the
activities of a ledger-keeper and with the notable absence of any per-

sonation at all. In fact, the overwhelming majority of Page's office poems are written without the use of personation. There are notable exceptions, however, including 'The Stenographers.'

Her only unpublished office poem in which a persona figures prominently is a piece written for her brother Michael, who served as a midshipman in the North Atlantic during the Second World War (Orange 223). Titled simply 'For Michael' and dated September 1942, it is a rare personal poem from this period in which Page draws connections between her brother on the war front and herself on the home front:

> ... Look, there is blood
> in these factories where I work.
> There is blood on each tongue
> that licks an envelope
> or spits a 'yes sir.'
> These are your kind and close
> in the bulging little boat they crowd you.
> . . . .
> You are my doer, turning
> silver of your sinews
> like searchlights in a moth thick dark.
> Knee caps butter smooth as c[r]umpets slip you
> from bunk to bridge,
> while I spin corpses in my brain
> and ache from wounds
> in the battl[e]field of an office. (PKPP, box 1, file 5)

Earlier in the poem, the speaker's invocation of a 'brother' functions on a personal and political level, which configures the rhetoric of comradeship throughout the poem. Unlike the impersonal and distanced perspective of the speaker in 'The Stenographers,' 'For Michael' consistently gives a personal and intimate point of view that enables Page's articulation of empathy between persona and subject, office worker and seaman, home front and war front. The persona is self-conscious about this expression of empathy, citing it as a sign of weakness and asking, 'if I am sentimental / you be steel for my crumble' (PKPP, box 1, file 5). If, as Killian says of Page in particular and Suzanne Clark notes of women modernists in general, the sentimental is often viewed in the context of modernism as a feminine-coded discourse, then we might observe that the speaker's self-consciousness about her sentimentality exposes her femininity (Clark 2; Killian 87–90). 'For Michael' encodes the feminized gender of the speaker's personality in terms of her empathy and sentimentality.

Writing a prose report on war-office workers for a special issue of *Preview* in February 1943, Page characterizes the 'girls' in her office as 'people who think almost exclusively in terms of personalities ... They think of the war effort in terms of personalities, they think of their personal freedom in the same terms – both somehow arising from and connected with the boy-friend [in one of the services] and both, confusingly, seeming to pull in opposite directions ... Unfortunately there was no one to tell them that winning the war and attaining personal freedom are one and the same thing' ('Stenographers' 2). Page's feminization of the relationship between gender and personality is, in the context of her office poems, telling once we consider the feminized personae of 'The Stenographers' and 'For Michael.' If she believed that women war-office workers thought of their personal freedom in terms of the expression of personality and that their freedom was connected to a male figure at war, then we may want to consider how the transformation of the office into a battlefield – as in the opening lines of 'The Stenographers' and the closing lines of 'For Michael' – is a figurative correlation of the war front and the home front, how that correlation enables a female speaker's articulation of empathy with the war effort, and how that empathy allows for her expression of personality, itself an act of personal freedom.

But ironically, the majority of Page's office poems document women's inability to express their personality. Office workers are often represented as women either dispossessed of or alienated from language. The women 'seem to sense each others' anguish with the swift / sympathy of the deaf and dumb' in 'Typists' (*Hidden* 1: 103); the 'girl in gingham' types carbons of her emotions in 'her jargon,' the 'strange jargon of ships' in 'Shipbuilding Office' (*Hidden* 1: 104); the office 'girls who had held each other's hands like lovers' become estranged 'without speech' as 'no response or reply dotted the screaming i's / of their clamouring signatures' in 'The Petition' (*Hidden* 1: 106); and the office workers 'who cannot speak, / hammer all day at keys that do not print, and file their voices in the teeming vault' and practise instead 'the language of the deaf and dumb,' even though 'no one reads their hands' in 'The Inarticulate' (*Hidden* 1: 109). In all these poems, the alienation of these office workers is conveyed in terms of their dissociation from language and from one another, their lapses of personal and interpersonal communication. Language itself becomes impersonal, instrumental to the operation of offices, but alien to office workers and their social interaction. Page's office workers become emblems of a crisis of communication.

Her final office poem from her *Preview* period continues to present the same social conditions of alienation and depersonalization of language, but at the same time allows for the speaker's expression of personality. Published in the October 1943 issue of *Preview*, 'Offices' opens with a prominent declaration in the first person:

Oh, believe me, I have known offices –
young and old in them, both –
morning and evening;
felt the air
stamp faces into a mould;
office workers at desks
saying *go* to a typewriter
and *stop* to a cabinet. (*Hidden* 1: 100)

Trehearne has suggested that the opening line indicates 'a desire to claim ownership over the genre, and perhaps a defensiveness regarding her authority on the subject' (*Montreal* 354n53), a claim based on a perceived exchange of office poems between Page and Louis Dudek, whose poem also entitled 'Offices' appeared in the January 1943 issue of *First Statement*. Page's defensive gesture may owe something to Dudek's infringement on her poetic territory, but it seems as likely that if she were responding to the *First Statement* group on this matter, she would also counter Sutherland's criticism of her 'lives of stenographers' in his November 1942 article 'P.K. Page and *Preview*': 'as one feels that the emotion is overwrought and becomes subjective, so one feels that the phrasing is too overwhelming to be entirely true. There is lack of complete ease in the style and there is some emotional discomfort with the subject-matter' (97). While the objectivity and distance of the speaker from her subject in 'The Stenographers' confirms at least the latter part of Sutherland's criticism, the intimacy and empathy of Page's speaker in 'Offices' contests his claims against the emotional authenticity of her portraiture of office workers. As in 'The Stenographers,' however, the gender of the speaker in 'Offices' can only be inferred from the poem's detailed knowledge of women office workers, including the contents of their desk drawers and the dynamic of their smoke breaks in the washroom. 'Offices' is not so much a sympathetic portrait as a candid exposé, not a sentimental and empathetic lyric but a personal testimonial by a woman about women and offices. Its expression of personality lays claim to an intimate knowledge of women's experience and to a genre of socially committed poetry over which Page alone among her contemporaries could say she had gained mastery.[13] While neither the articulation of a specifically female subjectivity in her office poems nor the gendering of clerical labour is necessarily innovative, it would seem that Page's sustained attraction to the genre of office poems is unique among women modernist poets, whether in Canada or elsewhere.[14]

By the end of 1943, shortly after the publication of 'Offices,' the *Preview* group had started to show signs of fatigue. Having lost the services of the Shaws after the October 1943 issue, and with the Andersons occupied by editorial and production work on the leftist cultural magazine *En Masse* by early 1945, the group experienced in the departure of Page from Montreal in the fall of 1944 a significant problem regarding the physical production of *Preview*. In short, the magazine's regular pool of typists was otherwise and elsewhere occupied. Issues of *Preview* following Page's departure were typed on a new typewriter, one whose distinctive font matches the typewriter used by F.R. Scott; these late issues came out at irregular intervals, the final instalment in early 1945. The erratic publication of *Preview* throughout 1944 signalled that the group was in a period of disorganization and decline long before the merger with *First Statement*.[15] Although Page's departure was only one event contributing to the instability of the *Preview* group in 1944–5, it was a highly significant event when viewed in relation to her key role in the magazine's physical production. Without her clerical services, the remaining male members of the group were left to fend for themselves: Patrick Anderson, Scott, Ruddick, and Klein did not know offices the way Page knew them. Her contributions to *Preview* fell off significantly over the course of its final year. Probably as a consequence of her move to Victoria in the fall of 1944, she did not appear in the December 1944 issue. Since she had appeared in every issue of *Preview* since April 1942, her absence from the December 1944 issue proved to be a sign of the group's weakened state following her departure. During this final *Preview* year, Page submitted her poems to periodicals with larger audiences – instead of printing them in *Preview* first and then reprinting them elsewhere – and thus expanded her range of publications. That same year she not only published her prize-winning sequence of four poems in *Poetry* (Chicago) but also renewed her contacts with the *Contemporary Verse* group. This latter reconnection proved vital to Page during the period of transition within Montreal magazine culture from 1945 to 1947, a period during which her poetry itself underwent a major transition.

Waddington's *First Statement*

When *First Statement* first came out in August 1942, *Preview* had just completed the end of its original run of six issues and *Contemporary Verse* had been in operation for a full year. For its initial nine issues (August–December 1942), *First Statement* advertised itself as 'A Magazine for Young Canadian Writers.' With its January 1943 issue, the editors changed the subtitle to 'A National Literary Magazine.' Whether this change had an appreciable effect on the contents of the magazine is doubtful, though it did signal the editors' efforts during its first year to gain a national audience. As early as October 1942, *First Statement* had announced a merger with the single-issue little magazine *Western Free-Lance*, founded in Vancouver and edited by Geoffrey Ashe (Ashe, 'Editorial'). By February 1943 the Montreal-based editorial group had issued a proposal for the formation of *First Statement* groups in other Canadian cities (Sutherland, 'New Organization'). Interested authors were invited to contact the magazine's agents, Lois Darroch in Toronto or Ashe in Vancouver. By March 1943 progress had been made toward the organization of a group in Toronto: a report of its activities was promised for an upcoming issue (Sutherland, Editorial). The report from the Toronto *First Statement* group published in the 2 April 1943 issue included a list of its members: Miriam Waddington, Sybil Hutchinson, Patrick Waddington, and Lois Darroch (Sutherland, 'First Statement Groups').

The publication of Miriam Waddington's earliest poem in *First Statement* coincided with the original announcement of the *First Statement* groups in February 1943. According to her memoirs, she first met John Sutherland and others of the original *First Statement* group – Betty Sutherland and Louis Dudek – during a visit to Montreal in March 1943 (Introduction 7; 'Apartment' 30). Waddington's letter of 7 April 1943 to Dudek indicates that she returned to Montreal the following month to meet with John Sutherland and Dudek 'to discuss this whole matter of literary groups, what you do, how you function, etc.' (LDF, series 2, box 13, Waddington file). Both she and her husband had contributed short stories to *First Statement* as early as January 1943, and no doubt Sutherland had them in mind when he and the rest of the Montreal group proposed the creation of a Toronto *First Statement* group. But the Toronto group by no means fulfilled the Montreal group's lofty expectations:

> The chief concern of these proposed new groups would naturally be Canada and Canadian literature. It is not suggested that they form a patriotic organization, but that they assist in the development of a national consciousness. At regular meetings, papers will be presented on our modern writers, and a special emphasis will be placed on the writers of our past. Poets and prose-writers, either members of the group or members of the district, will attend meetings and read samples of their work. Selections from these, and from critical papers, will later be published in FIRST STATEMENT. A page will be given up to notices of the programmes and to accounts of the proceedings. (Sutherland, 'New Organization')

These groups appear to have been modelled after the local branches of the CAA, an organization that had, ironically, just come under fire in the December 1942 issue of *First Statement* (Sutherland, 'Production'). Sutherland was perhaps aware of this resemblance, given his suggestion that such a group should not be a 'patriotic organization,' but he seems unaware of the similarities between the practices of the CAA and its periodicals and the proposed activities of the *First Statement* groups.[16] Once the Toronto group did meet, however, its report, published in the 2 April 1943 issue (Sutherland, 'First Statement Groups'), revealed a far more informal gathering than the Montreal group had envisioned. The report itself consisted of little more than a restatement of Sutherland's 19 March 1943 editorial ('The Role of the Magazines') by Lois Darroch and an excerpt from a letter of criticism concerning the poetry of Page and Shaw in *Preview* by Patrick Waddington ('First Statement Opinions'). Unfortunately, Miriam Waddington's opinions were not recorded in the report, though it would seem from her letter of 7 April 1943 to Dudek that she was not entirely certain how she was supposed to contribute or how the group itself was intended to function. Although Sutherland reported plans for a second meeting of the

Toronto group ('First Statement Groups'), there was no further
mention of its or any other local group's activities in the pages of *First
Statement*.

Given the almost immediate disintegration of the Toronto group,
Miriam Waddington's contributions to *First Statement* cannot substan-
tively be attributed to its formation or influence. She published
almost as many poems in the magazine prior to the first meeting of
the Toronto group as she did after its disappearance. By her own
account, the extent of her relationship to *First Statement* amounted to
her personal rapport with Sutherland himself. Far more than her contributions to *First Statement* and *Preview*, Waddington documented
her relationship with Sutherland in her personal histories of Montreal
in the 1940s (see Introduction; 'Apartment'; 'John Sutherland').
Regrettably, their correspondence from the early 1940s is no longer
extant; so we cannot recover that immediate historical perspective.
But we can, fortunately, correlate her memoirs and her poems from
First Statement as a means of reconstructing the relationship between
poet and editor.

While all of Waddington's poems first published by Sutherland in
First Statement deserve some contextual consideration, a more detailed
and revealing picture of their editorial relationship can be developed
by specific readings of poems he excluded from her first collection,
Green World. This collection was part of the New Writers Series
launched by Sutherland's First Statement Press in 1945. She set down
her memory of his selections for *Green World* in the afterword to her
Collected Poems: 'When John Sutherland ... wrote to me in Philadelphia
that he would like to publish a collection of my poems, I was of course
pleased. I don't remember having much to do with putting the book
together. I was preoccupied with my courses [at the University of
Pennsylvania's School of Social Work] and my field work in the
Philadelphia Child Guidance Clinic' (412). If Waddington had made
the entire selection herself or in collaboration with Sutherland, there
would be little reason to question the circumstances of its making. But
the inclusion of less than half the poems that Sutherland had previously published in *First Statement* invites critical scrutiny.

By looking at those poems originally published in *First Statement* but
subsequently excluded from *Green World*, we may recover pieces of a
poetic narrative cast out in the editorial process. Sutherland's selection
of poems that foreground the speaker's social consciousness typically
represents the speaker's sympathy for others or self-reflexive situa-

tions in which the speaker's sympathy is under scrutiny. By omitting poems in which Waddington's speakers fail or refuse to demonstrate social sympathies, Sutherland elides the evident ambivalence in her poetry's social consciousness at this time. Even as it superficially ameliorates her profile as a socially conscious poet, his elision not only reduces the complexity of her social vision but also erases telling signs of a crisis in her early poetry. That ambivalence is nevertheless present in these early poems published in *First Statement*, even if it is attenuated in *Green World*.

Originally published in the February 1943 issue of *First Statement*, 'Social Worker' illustrates Waddington's recollection that 'at that time only half of [her] was a poet – the other half was a romantic middle-class social worker' (Introduction 7) and that her '1943 meeting with John Sutherland took place in a special context: after graduating from the [University of Toronto's] School of Social Work the year before, [she] had entered a new and exciting profession' ('Apartment' 33). Her speaker is not wholly 'romantic' in this chronicle of a social worker's passage by streetcar to 'slums in odd corners of cities.' The romantic half of the persona imagines her release from the social world and temporary escape to an imagined green world: she 'go[es] straight as the crow flies / Arrowing over the Don and its leafy mudlands, / Over the brickyards, over the scooped ravines, / The most direct route.' But she returns to the streetcar and her realist social-worker self in the final lines of the poem, addressing herself not to the families she visits in the city slums, but to those onlookers who witness her work: 'So do not wonder when I knock at battered doors / If my face is cold, busy with afterthoughts' ('Social Worker'). Here the social worker's address to onlookers in the street instead of her clients is indicative of her self-conscious impersonality: as she turns aside to deliver this final couplet, she dons the 'cold' mask of the social worker. Impaired by 'afterthoughts' or residual attachments to the green world, the social worker becomes deficient in showing sympathies for others in the social world, whether her clients at the door or passers-by in the street.[17]

By the time 'Indoors' appeared in the August 1943 issue of *First Statement*, the failure of sympathy in Waddington's social poetry had started to enter a critical stage. 'Indoors' portrays its speaker's utter alienation from the social world. Confined indoors, her impersonal speaker is wholly detached from the social dynamic of the domestic sphere. With an echo of Eliot's 'The Love Song of J. Alfred Prufrock'

(13), the speaker observes how the 'winter sky was cold' and 'The guests held forth in long debate / While the lamplight shone on the dark table / Like a soft tired operation.' Rather than contribute to the debate, the speaker ironically turns away and contemplates the loss of contact with the outside world:

One more day that I didn't see
The city move on its lighted wheels
And the toy trams with their small noise
Through the gothic vista of the arch
Framing old Saint Mary's. (*Collected* 361)

In counterpoint to the speaker amid the urban noise and jostle in 'Social Worker,' the speaker of 'Indoors' desires the city's aesthetic dynamism. Instead of a romanticized flight from the city to a pastoral green world, 'Indoors' figures the speaker's withdrawal into aesthetic contemplation of an imagined city. For Waddington, the green world need not be green at all; it is, as Berger says, 'a place into which the mind may withdraw for a variety of reasons, good and bad' (13). Even the speaker in 'Social Worker' returns from her pastoral green-world fantasy to knock on her clients' doors, however ambivalent her attitude toward her casework or how strained her sympathies toward her clients. Declining all contact and communication with the social world, the speaker of 'Indoors' seems incapable of human sympathy. This aestheticized city is, after all, devoid of people. While the religious imagery in the final lines may offer the faint prospect of aesthetic transcendence – and the redemption of the speaker from conditions of social, if not spiritual, alienation – there is little reason to believe that this aestheticization will ensure such fulfilment.

If Waddington's *First Statement* poems present a series of obstacles impeding her communication of human sympathy, her relationship to the magazine itself is indicative of the mutual failure of sympathies between herself and the *First Statement* group in Montreal. As a member of the *First Statement* group in Toronto, Waddington remained distant from the core group of Sutherland, Dudek, and Layton in Montreal. Although there is no evidence that she was ever hampered in her attempts to publish in *First Statement*, her poems were often punctured by the Montreal group's editorial and critical barbs. This was principally true of those poems first published in *First Statement* but subsequently omitted from *Green World*.

Appearing in the early March 1943 issue of *First Statement*, 'Now We
Steer' is a statement of political consciousness and poetics specific to
the wartime generation. Given its generational specificity, it is not surprising that the poem does not appear in either *The Second Silence*
(1955) or *The Season's Lovers* (1958); its exclusion from *Green World* is
less obviously motivated. It opens at the onset of the Second World
War, narrating a parable of political disillusionment among members
of the left:

> That was when
> The whole centre of my world wavered,
> The tenuous balance of revolution was upset by war,
> The cupboards of the future were all rifled,
> And I longed to be on a cold stone on that far island,
> With green to cover me up and blind me
> With trees growing out of my sealed eyes. (*Collected* 360)

Influenced by the political verse of the Auden generation, 'Now We
Steer' is a parable-poem in which the speaker imagines another green
world, a temporary 'place of withdrawal' (Berger 13) – that is, for leftists and fellow-travellers after the catastrophic events of 1939.
Waddington's homage to Auden and his circle follows thereafter:

> Since they
> Whose names were a white legend in our night
> Auden and Spender and Thomas Wolfe –
> Whose words poured through our blood like warm wine,
> Whose hands rang clear and warning bells
> Across the dark and troubled oceans of our youth –
> Whose names we conjured with, fire across our sky,
> A blessing and a curse together –
> They taught us to love at our own cost.
>
> One lesson we learned too well.
> *We must love one another or die.*

Quoting here from Auden's 'September 1, 1939,' the speaker invokes
the seminal poem of that generation's political disenchantment following the Nazi-Soviet non-aggression pact in August 1939 and the
outbreak of the Second World War in September. Waddington's

parable-poem does not close, however, with his pessimistic dictum; she is well aware of the Auden generation's retreat from the political left after 1939, observing that even 'though they have carried us no further / They are a golden compass pointing south / To a possible world, warm and good' (*Collected* 361). This optimistic turn is, in the end, the progressive political promise of a wartime generation, the 'we' of 'Now We Steer,' who may include Waddington and many of her contemporaries in the *First Statement* and *Preview* groups. We might read the poetics and politics of 'Now We Steer,' as a parable of the education and maturation of the wartime generation in relation to Waddington's report of her first encounter with Sutherland. 'At the time I met him,' she recalls, 'Thomas Wolfe was his favourite writer'; she also notes his reading of Auden and Spender (Introduction 8).

It is difficult to determine why Sutherland omitted 'Now We Steer' from *Green World*. His exclusion of a poem that, in effect, expresses solidarity with his own literary and leftist interests is a conspicuous rejection of Waddington's early sympathetic identification with him and *First Statement*. Among the possible influences on Sutherland's decision to exclude the poem, we might take Dudek's statement in the 2 April 1943 issue, immediately following the publication of 'Now We Steer' in March. There Dudek decries the faults of the *Preview* poets and offers a set of slogans for their edification, among them 'No poetry about poets and poetry' ('Geography' 3). Following so closely after the publication of 'Now We Steer,' Dudek's corrective must have registered with Waddington as a reprimand. Furthermore, Layton's poem 'The Modern Poet,' published in the same April 1943 issue, upbraids Waddington's invocation of Auden with his patronizing opening lines:

> Since Auden set the fashion,
> Our poets grow tame;
> They are quite without passion,
> They live without blame.
> Like a respectable dame.

The gendered inflection of Layton's caricature of Auden-generation poets must have struck Waddington as particularly, if not personally, offensive (see also Layton, 'Poetry'). In light of Dudek's and Layton's censures, Waddington must have wondered what the Montreal group could have wanted from her (and vice versa) when she joined the *First Statement* group in Toronto. While Patrick Waddington's criticism of

Layton (qtd. in Sutherland, 'First Statement Opinions') and Layton's riposte, published in the same issue, must have strained their personal relations, the added reproach of Miriam Waddington could have thrown the whole question of the Waddingtons' membership in the Toronto *First Statement* group into doubt. One might expect that Miriam Waddington arrived in Montreal in April 1943 with a number of pointed questions for Dudek and Layton. In any event, she seems to have heeded their criticisms, since she did not publish another poem about Auden or any other poet in *First Statement*. Nor did Sutherland publish 'Now We Steer' in *Green World*.

In view of Dudek's edict 'No poetry about poets and poetry,' Waddington's 'Two Poems,' published in the 19 March 1943 issue, also qualify as objects of his criticism. Both begin with a self-reflexive conceit comparing the speaker's beloved to a poem:

1
Your oh so gentle hands.
They are as pure and mobile as the lines of a poem.
They have all the cadences and wild changes
That ride my dreams at night ...
2
You
With your words and your desperate gestures
Are a violent punctuation to my life ... (*Collected* 360, 361)

Although it is not difficult to imagine why Sutherland passed over these two poems when putting together *Green World*, it is legitimate to ask why he, Dudek, and Layton agreed to publish her poems, if only to attack them in the next issue. This pattern, however, is not without precedent in *First Statement*: both Kay Smith and Page had published poems in early issues, accompanied by Sutherland's critical blasts (see 'A Criticism' and 'P.K. Page'). Added to Layton's 'The Modern Poet,' the gender specificity of this manner of masculinist *First Statement* criticism exposes its animus toward its own female authors. The magazine's questionable policy of public criticism of its own authors appears to have affected Waddington's contributions, since she did not publish another poem about poetry in subsequent issues. Here we can see how, in Waddington's words, she had 'accepted that men were top dog in this world' ('Apartment' 34n1), at least in terms of their editorial control over her poetry. Her call for a gendered reading of Cana-

dian modernist little-magazine culture clearly illuminates the significance of gender relations in her own dealings with the central male
figures in the *First Statement* group.

Possibly as a consequence of the blatantly masculinist editorial practices of Sutherland, Dudek, and Layton, Waddington temporarily suspended her contributions to *First Statement* following the appearance
of 'Indoors' in August 1943. Having decided to publish 'Indoors,'
Sutherland then proceeded to construct an editorial and critical apparatus in which her poem was subject to caricature. His August 1943
editorial declares, 'Of the several hundred manuscripts of verse that
we received as a mimeographed magazine, about eighty-five percent
were directly in the romantic tradition.' 'Indoors' might well be in the
modern 'romantic tradition' he derides. His September 1943 article
'The Role of Prufrock' attempts to sketch the archetypal figure of that
tradition. He gestures toward Waddington's persona in 'Indoors,'
writing of Prufrock as a modern poet-figure who 'grows unhappy and
falls victim to visions and self-romanticizing' (20). Just as his portrait
gives us Prufrock caught 'between an everyday personality and one
that is founded on romantic dreaming' (20), so Waddington depicts her
persona trapped in the quotidian and dreaming of the romanticized
city. Seizing upon her allusion to Prufrock and her predilection for
urban romanticism, Sutherland once more subjects Waddington to his
penchant for reproaching *First Statement*'s women poets.

Having published in *First Statement* on a consistent basis between
February and August 1943, Waddington did not contribute another
poem until the February 1944 issue. After the appearance of Sutherland's Prufrock essay in September 1943, this break with *First Statement* was predictable. At a time when Waddington herself was artic-
ulating problems of communicating sympathy for others, she must
have found little consolation in the consistently unsympathetic criticisms of Sutherland and the *First Statement* group. If we continue to
view her relationship with *First Statement* in light of her personal ties
to Sutherland, we may look to her memories of him at this time for
clues to explain her temporary withdrawal from the magazine after
the summer of 1943. Waddington's recollection of Sutherland in 1943
focuses on the projection and retraction of their interanimating
sympathies:

When I met John Sutherland in the spring of 1943 my emotional needs
were great. Our rapport was instantaneous and he seemed to be the one

person who would understand and respond to my literary and personal problems. That spring we began an intense daily correspondence about literature, love, life, and our hopes and ambitions. Undoubtedly I projected my own needs and problems on John and he did the same with me. Neither was prepared or able to face the reality of the other. By the end of that summer I had taken back my projection and realized that I would have to solve my own problems, literary, personal, and professional. ('Apartment' 33)

It would seem that Waddington had not only 'taken back' her projection but at the same time temporarily withdrawn further contributions to *First Statement*. This first period of withdrawal (August 1943 to February 1944), punctuated by a poem ('Sympathy') about projections and identifications, is symbolic of Waddington's psychological investment in Sutherland and his little magazine. Her next period of absence from *First Statement* (February to December 1944) following the publication of 'Sympathy' coincided with her decision to leave Toronto and her job at the Jewish Family Service and enrol at the University of Pennsylvania's School of Social Work in Philadelphia.

Her appearance in *First Statement* prior to her departure for Philadelphia revisits the problem of her speaker's sympathy, a problem she left unresolved six months earlier in 'Indoors.' Published in the February 1944 issue and later collected in *Green World*, 'Sympathy' presents a persona alert to psychological projection – in this case, the unconscious transfer of one's feelings to another person. It is telling that her persona in 'Sympathy' is the recipient of another man's projection: this had been, in effect, the predicament of Waddington herself in her relationship with Sutherland. In response to the man's projection, her persona communicates not in dialogue but through a self-reflexive internal monologue: 'I will answer with the round technique / That walls me from you; / Give your misfortunes; I'll remember mine' (*Collected* 5). The persona's sympathy is, then, internalized: there is no dialogic exchange, only the sympathetic reception of the other man's projection. 'So tell me your misfortunes, lay your plans,' the persona reiterates; 'I'm listening with one ear to my past' (6). Despite the persona's receptivity, the practice of impersonality ('the round technique') stands in the way of open dialogue; this manner of impersonal, yet sympathetic listening ends in communicative failure.

After 'Sympathy,' Waddington published her poems between February and December 1944 in magazines other than *First Statement*, many in early issues of *Direction*. None of her poems from this period appeared in *Green World*. Sutherland was certainly aware of *Direction* itself (he reviewed its first, November 1943, instalment in the March 1944 issue of *First Statement* [Rev. of *Direction*]); so it is likely that he would have seen Waddington's poems in its second and third issues, both undated but probably from early 1944.[18] Other Waddington poems from this ten-month period appeared in more prominent magazines such as *Contemporary Verse* and *Canadian Forum*, yet they too are absent from *Green World*. Since Sutherland assembled her collection on his own, and since he was out of regular contact with Waddington while she was living in Philadelphia and at the time he made his selections, it is easily conceivable that he was not fully aware of the extent of her poetry publications over the course of 1944. But because he included several of her most recent poems from her Philadelphia period after she had published 'In the Big City' in the December 1944–January 1945 issue of *First Statement*, we may surmise that he followed her publications more closely after December 1944.

Whatever the reasons for Sutherland's failure to collect any of Waddington's poems from the February–December 1944 period, he published some of the poems she sent to him after she moved to Philadelphia in the fall of 1944 in *First Statement* and/or later in *Green World*. It is particularly significant that he issued his offer to publish *Green World* immediately after her reappearance in *First Statement* in December 1944–January 1945.[19] Once he had made the offer, then, she must have kept him up to date on her most recent poems, whether already accepted elsewhere or submitted to him for publication in *First Statement*. Although she was not directly involved in the compilation process, she recalled 'sending Sutherland "Lullaby" and "Morning until Night," both of which were new and had their source in [her] Philadelphia experience' ('Afterword' 412), and both of which he included in *Green World*. She also must have sent him 'In the Big City,' written shortly after her arrival in Philadelphia and first published in the December 1944–January 1945 issue of *First Statement* and then in *Green World*. 'Lullaby,' her last poem published in *First Statement*, appeared in the April–May 1945 issue.

During the summer of 1945, Waddington returned from Philadelphia to Toronto and then immediately moved with her husband to Montreal. By the time she had settled in Montreal in July, the *Preview* group had accepted *First Statement*'s proposal to merge the two magazines and preliminary discussions about the new magazine (then called *Portage* but later *Northern Review*) were underway. In her 28 July 1945 letter to Livesay, Waddington noted the formation of the new magazine: 'here in montreal preview and [First Statement] have amalgamated to call themselves *portage* with a composite and unwieldy editorial board of eight – 4 from each group. i am still not in the group. and not sorry, because groups get very personal' (DLP-QU, box 5a, file 1). Writing to Livesay on 27 August 1945, Waddington commented further on her and her husband's relationship to the new little-magazine culture in Montreal: 'patrick [Anderson] wants us to contribute to *en masse* – so to help edit it. you know i cant help having a malicious little reservation – good enough for en masse but not good enough for portage sort of thing. but possibly other things are at stake and i may be being unfair about it. have you seen en masse? i will try and hunt you out a copy if you havent. it seemed to me to be dull, and had the disadvantage of being mimeographed' (DLP-QU, box 5a, file 1).

Waddington's reservations about the leftist cultural magazine *En Masse,* edited by Anderson and funded by the Labour Progressive Party in Montreal, were well founded, as it lasted for only four issues (March–October 1945). And given Anderson's attitude toward women's roles in the physical production of magazines, she may have been wise to his request that she help 'edit' *En Masse.* Having arrived in Montreal during a period of transition in that city's little-magazine culture, the Waddingtons remained outsiders to the *First Statement* and *Preview* groups. Updating Livesay on literary activities in Montreal and her recent rejection from the new *First Statement–Preview* magazine, Waddington announced her withdrawal from Montreal little-magazine culture: 're en masse. anderson asked me to be on the editorial board with honey. (on the new magazine [*Portage*] he rejects my poems with gall.) i went to one editorial meeting and felt unutterably depressed. it is worth while but somehow i hav[e]nt the heart to sit at meetings. dont know what's wrong with me. feel as if i must be holing in. Well, as forster says, after thirty one must close some doors if one wishes to grow in one's own true way' (DLP-QU, box 5a, file 1). As in her poetry of the early to mid-1940s, Waddington experienced a failure of sympathy in her relationship with Montreal little-magazine culture. Rather than seek social and cultural solidarity through little-magazine communities, she chose to 'close some doors.' Her falling out with the Montreal group was not limited to the formation of new magazines, though, as she told Livesay in her 11 November 1945 letter: 'I feel I have missed about 10 years of my life – rather slipped over them, and no longer find I have patience with many of the struggles and jokes of the young. Thinking mostly of John Sutherland and Irving Layton to whom a slight aura of bygone bohemia still clings' (DLP-QU, box 5a, file 1). Ultimately, her disillusionment with the Montreal magazines and lack of sympathy for their editorial members led her to a retreat into her self, into her social work, and into her domestic life.

Ironically, then, the publication of *Green World* in November 1945 signalled the end of Waddington's association with Montreal magazine culture. Her launch party at Sutherland's place was sparsely attended, emblematic of her outsider status among the former *First Statement* and *Preview* groups. 'John Sutherland had a small party for me,' she informed Livesay the next day, 'but he had been vague and casual in his invitations so that there were no "patrons" or prominent writers of the Montreal Group present'; though she would go on to note that F.R. Scott was in attendance and 'very kind' (Waddington to Livesay, 11 November 1945, DLP-QU, box 5a, file 1). Although we should not over-interpret Waddington's meagre reception by the Montreal poets at her launch, especially in view of Sutherland's ineptitude as a promoter of *Green World*, it was still a significant event in her shift away from Montreal magazine culture toward other venues and literary communities. Most telling of her detachment from the Montreal groups is the fact that she never published poems in either *En Masse* or *Northern Review*.

Waddington never again attached herself to a literary group, but her increased contributions to *Canadian Poetry Magazine* during Birney's editorship (1946–8)[20] and to *Contemporary Verse* after 1945 suggest her more intimate and enduring sympathies with poets and editors on the West Coast. With the disintegration of Montreal little-magazine culture after the mass resignation of editors from *Northern Review* in 1947, she found herself returning to the poetry magazines where she had first published in the early 1940s. Like Page, she benefited from Crawley's publication of her poetry in *Contemporary Verse* through the late 1940s and early 1950s. While *Contemporary Verse* offered Waddington a venue in which she overcame obstacles to her poetry's social consciousness after 1945, it provided Page with the primary forum in which she progressed toward her decade of silence after 1956.

Page, Waddington, and Their *Contemporary Verse*

As poets then uncertain of their place in Canada's emergent modernist little-magazine culture, Waddington and Page had cast about in the early 1940s in search of magazine editors and other poets. Both appeared in the early issues of *Contemporary Verse* – Page in the first (September 1941) and second (December 1941) issues, Waddington in the third (March 1942). Page had been introduced to Anne Marriott at the CAA convention in Sainte-Anne-de-Bellevue in 1940. Waddington had met Livesay in Toronto in the spring of 1941 (Waddington, 'Apartment' 21), probably not long after the founding committee of *Contemporary Verse* had initiated its plan for a new poetry magazine. Through these early personal contacts with the magazine's founders, Page and Waddington came to contribute to *Contemporary Verse*. After meeting the *Preview* and *First Statement* groups, however, both published far less frequently in *Contemporary Verse*. Aside from this interval of 1942–5, during which they established themselves in the Montreal little magazines, their poetry appeared on a fairly consistent basis in *Contemporary Verse*. Because critical and literary historical studies of their early poetry have largely focused on their activities in conjunction with the *Preview* and *First Statement* groups, we have yet to take into consideration their affiliations with Canada's West Coast little-magazine culture of the early 1940s to mid-1950s.

Page's earliest contact with *Contemporary Verse* had been through Marriott (via the CAA), not Crawley. In fact, her initial submission of five poems in the summer of 1941 is listed in her poetry notebook under the heading 'Anne,' probably because she sent the poems to Anne Marriott before the magazine had settled on a name (PKPP, box 1, file 4). From the group of poems Page sent to Marriott, Crawley selected 'The Crow' and 'Ecce Homo' for the September 1941 inaugural issue; he held 'Blackout' for the December issue. Of her poems submitted to *Contemporary Verse* but subsequently rejected by Crawley, 'Realization' is notable for its resonance with the subjective, personative verse she later contributed to the magazine following her *Preview* period. Preserved in her poetry notebook of 1939–41, it is itself undated but was probably written in late 1940 or early 1941. Its scrutiny of the 'personal' is remarkable, as is its self-reflexivity. Toward its close, the poem turns on itself, announcing the speaker's desire to retreat from 'the inside-out, no-corner spared, duster /of forgotten alley ways, / collection of memories: the swift pulse of the slow word.' The speaker realizes that this state of interiority is 'more personal – far more of me than my speech is.' Because the objectification of that state through metapoetic speech and personation provides only a superficial mask of impersonality, the speaker's attempt to 'escape the disclosure' exhibits anxieties about personalist modes of expression. In contrast to the impersonality and objectivity of 'The Crow' and 'Blackout,' 'Realization' problematizes its subjective, personative mode. With its inward gaze, the poem shares an exploration of subjective experience with 'Ecce Homo'; but unlike that poem as well, 'Realization' at once demonstrates the limitations that Page quickly recognized in the subjectivist mode and points the way to the objective, impersonalist style that soon predominated during her *Preview* period. That Crawley rejected 'Realization' is a telling instance of his preference for a subjectivist poetics and not for its metapoetic critique. Its rejection is even more significant in light of the fact that by March 1942 Page had joined the *Preview* group, where her early unpublished experiments with a subjective, personative poetics were displaced by an objective, impersonalist poetics. Rather than resolve the problems of her early subjectivist modernism, she repressed them behind impersonal masks.

None of Page's early poems in *Contemporary Verse* appeared in her 1946 collection *As Ten as Twenty*. By that time, Crawley's editorial tastes were not her only measure, though he had been among the earliest and most valued of her critics and correspondents when she started to submit to *Contemporary Verse*. Writing to him on 1 December 1941, she accepted his first offer of criticism: 'At the moment I am on my own in Montreal knowing practically no one who writes and having no critical eyes scan what I am writing and should welcome anything you have to say. More than anything in this world I would like to be a good poet' (ACP, box 1, file 20, item 10). Crawley's responses to Page's early letters have not been preserved, but we may infer from her replies that she appreciated his 'unbiased opinion' and praised his editorial standards: 'There has been too much kow-towing to personalities, lowering of standards and lack of discrimination shown in editorial policies before' (Page to Crawley, n.d. [c. January 1942], ACP, box 1, file 20, item 11). Presumably Page took no offence when Crawley did not publish the poems she enclosed with this letter ('I say "poems,"' she offered by way of caveat, 'but I fear they are a poor apology – and sent largely as a gesture'). Even though he chose not to publish her poems, he replied with critical admonishments and encouragements, as Page observes in her letter of 9 May 1942: 'How grand of you to write to me about the poems. You've no idea what a stimulating thing it has been – this contact with you, even across so many miles. It is doubly good to get praises from someone who is unafraid to damn' (ACP, box 1, file 20).

By the time Page was writing to thank Crawley for his criticism, however, she had joined the *Preview* group; her contact with him and *Contemporary Verse* predictably receded once she could rely on critical feedback from the editorial members of *Preview*. Together with her submission of new poems to *Contemporary Verse* on 20 October 1942, Page informed Crawley that she had herself turned critic and was publishing in that month's *Preview* 'a rather superficial summary-cum-criticism of the contemporary scene which touches briefly on Contemporary Verse' (n.d. [20 October 1942], ACP, box 1, file 20, item 9). I have already noted in the previous chapter the substance of Page's criticism of *Contemporary Verse* in her article 'Canadian Poetry 1942' and Crawley's response to *Preview* in the June 1942 issue of *Contemporary Verse* (see chapter 2: 85–6). Judging from Page's reply to Crawley in December 1942, his reception of her criticism of *Contemporary Verse* was 'generous' (n.d. [December 1942], ACP, box 1, file 20, item 8). As Crawley says of Page's article in his letter to Waddington on 13 November 1942, 'She is refreshing in her attack and manner ... At any rate she gives C[ontemporary] V[erse] credit of a BOO at the old writing and when I think of the ammunition from which it was made I am hap[p]y that it did get to be more than a sputt[e]ring PSSSS' (MWP, box 45, file 12). Just as Page praised Crawley for being 'unafraid to damn,' so he applauded her critical acumen and even commended her aggressive, masculinist 'attack' on *Contemporary Verse* and the 'pink tea pretties' of the CAA.

By the time Page submitted 'The Traveller' and 'The Sleeper' to *Contemporary Verse* on 20 October 1942, she had already sent the latter to *First Statement* in August and both to *Partisan Review* in September. With his acceptance of 'The Traveller,' Crawley returned 'The Sleeper,' which Page apologetically informed him had recently and, in view of her stern rebuke of Sutherland in 'Canadian Poetry 1942,' surprisingly been published in the November 1942 issue of *First Statement*. This pattern indicates that Page was at once attempting to expand her audience and no longer soliciting Crawley's criticism as she had before meeting the *Preview* group. Perhaps by way of excuse for not submitting any new poems, she told him in her letter of December 1942 that she had encountered difficulties writing: 'I find it more and more difficult to write – let alone do anything half way satisfying. Whether it's the times or the job or what, I don't know' (ACP, box 1, file 20, item 8). According to the log of submissions recorded in her poetry copybook of 1940–4, Page had suspended her submission of poems after 20 October 1942 until 23 January of the new year (PKPP, box 1, file 5).

Given her publication record in 1943, she also appears to have held off submission of poems to *Contemporary Verse*. In a letter to McLaren written just prior to the June 1943 issue, however, Crawley mentions that 'Pat [Page] has sent me some poems which she says she does not like but which I think are good and I would like to have them but if she is not insistent that they are used at once I would prefer to hold them against the [ne]xt issue but if you want some [m]ore for this issue let me know and I would put in one of hers' (n.d. [c. June 1943], FMP). Crawley goes on to talk about having Page for a visit, thus indicating that she had recently travelled to the West Coast and that her visits with him in Vancouver and McLaren in Victoria likely prompted the contribution of some new poems to *Contemporary Verse*. Although she submitted two poems ('Average' and 'Schizophrenic') just prior to the June 1943 issue, which were held for nearly a year before publication, Page did not publish in *Contemporary Verse* again until 'Round Trip' in the April 1945 issue. This contribution was her first in nearly two years – the first of a regular stream of poems she submitted to Crawley and McLaren between the mid-1940s and the early 1950s. This long-term return to *Contemporary Verse* coincided with her move from Montreal to Victoria in the fall of 1944, her separation from the *Preview* group, and the termination of *Preview* in early 1945.

After Page's debut in the fall of 1941, Waddington published groups of poems in *Contemporary Verse* on a regular basis between March 1942 and March 1943. Crawley received her first contributions in January 1942, just prior to the late release of the second issue. This batch of poems included 'The Bond,' 'Immigrant, Second Generation,' and 'Ladies,' all of which impressed Crawley and appeared in the March 1942 issue. As he had with Page, Crawley asked whether Waddington would mind if he suggested revisions and offered criticism of her poems (Crawley to Waddington, 14 January [1942], MWP, box 45, file 12). None of the poems included in her second submission impressed Crawley, prompting him to write her on 11 June 1942 to complain that, in comparison to 'The Bond' and 'Immigrant,' 'these MSS are anaemic' (MWP, box 45, file 12). Of the poems included in her third submission, 'Contemporary,' 'Shutters,' and 'Sorrow' appeared in the September 1942 issue; he asked for revisions to 'Uncertainties' (also among this batch), but she decided to publish it unchanged in the January 1943 issue of *Preview* (Crawley to Waddington,14 July [1942], MWP, box 45, file 12). Delays in the production of *Contemporary Verse* during the fall of 1942 compelled Crawley to return his cache of Waddington's poems on 13 November 1942, perhaps in accordance with her request, along with his apologies: 'I am sending back the MSS I have not used and hope the delay in return will not and has not been too inconveniencing or costly to y[ou]. I am pleased to hear of the acceptances of your work in other publications and my best wishes are with you for larger and grander fields' (MWP, box 45, file 12). Presumably Waddington had informed him of the acceptance of 'Investigator' and 'Ballet' by *Providence Journal* in Rhode Island, though his comments also anticipate her first appearances in *Preview* and *First Statement* and continued publication in the *Canadian Forum* and *Canadian Poetry Magazine*.

During the course of 1943, Waddington would indeed expand her audience through such diverse publications. With the exception of her appearance in *Providence Journal*, she had published only in *Contemporary Verse* in 1942. Crawley's response to her latest submission in his letter of 8 February 1943 suggests that she had been considering the need for 'larger and grander fields' for her poetry. While her 'I Love My Love with an S' and 'Proposal for Integration toward a Common End' appeared in the March 1943 issue of *Contemporary Verse*, she had other ideas for the magazine on her mind. Following on the heels of Livesay's proposals in the spring and summer of 1942 (see chapter 2: 111–12), Waddington's suggestion of a merger among the new little magazines was met with resistance from Crawley:

> It seems to me that the work the three new publications, C[ontemporary] V[erse], Preview and First Statement are doing is well worth while and the doing. But it does not seem that the time is ripe for a fusion of the three into a national magazine for the poetical and prose efforts of Canadian writers. That may come, indeed I look forward to such a magazine but think just now more is to be done by separate publications with their own individual slant and preferences. D[orothy] L[ivesay] disagrees with me in that in a voluable [sic] manner, but so far has failed to convince me. (MWP, box 45, file 12)

In concert with Livesay, Waddington disagreed with Crawley. She wrote to him after her spring 1943 visit to Montreal to inform him of the activities among the magazine groups, to which he replied on 15 June 1943:

I did so enjoy and chuckle at your pertinent observations on the groups of literati you ran into in Montreal. I had been wanting to know more of the First Statement lot other than what I could gather about them elsewhere and was greatly interest[ed] in what you told me. I like F[irst] S[tatement] and get a good deal of pleasure from the content and in making my own criticisms of the work most of which I find very wo[r]thwhile and interesting and thoroughly cheering, not in content, perhaps[,] but in showing what is being done by the younger writers and bringing to conviction almost my old [h]ope that something really worthy will come of the efforts to build a contemporary Canadian writing. (MWP, box 45, file 12)

We can only speculate on Waddington's report on the Montreal group, though we might suspect Crawley felt that she might balance her involvement in the Toronto *First Statement* group with assistance to *Contemporary Verse*. 'I cannot see that with the similar objects and in the less extensive field that C[ontemporary] V[erse] can in any way do more than help F[irst] S[tatement] and that we should not be able to go on workin[g] in our own ways to the common good,' Crawley observed in his 15 June 1943 letter to her; he then asked, 'would you represent CV in the east for us?' (MWP, box 45, file 12). Waddington must have replied in the negative, since she was never named a Toronto agent in the magazine, though she may have spread news of *Contemporary Verse* on an informal basis.

Crawley's conditional acceptance of Waddington's poems 'Prairie' and 'Fragments from Autobiography' in his 15 June 1943 letter was followed by a long delay in publication, partly as a result of his request for revisions to the former. Both eventually appeared in the April 1944 issue. Writing to Waddington on 15 December 1943, Crawley approved of the revised version of 'Prairie,' but added his disapproval of her most recent batch of poems: 'There is something in all the others that does not completely satisfy me and I find them uneven and [u]nfinished and bodiless' (MWP, box 45, file 12). She replied by sending copies of the first issue of *Direction*, perhaps adding that her poems would be appearing in the next issue (see Crawley to Waddington, 9 February [1944], MWP, box 45, file 12). Whether any of the poems that Crawley had deemed 'uneven and [u]nfinished and bodiless' were among those she published in *Direction* is uncertain. What is certain is that Waddington found other outlets for her current poems.

She published nothing else in *Contemporary Verse* before leaving for Philadelphia in the fall of 1944.

Waddington's period of withdrawal from *Contemporary Verse* (April 1944–January 1945) invites comparison with her ten-month absence from *First Statement* following the publication of 'Sympathy' (February–December 1944). On looking at her 'Fragments from Autobiography,' published in the April 1944 issue of *Contemporary Verse*, one recognizes the crises of subjectivity, sympathy, and social solidarity represented in her *First Statement* poetry of 1943–4. In the first section of 'Fragments,' her social-worker speaker contemplates the disparities between gender inequality under capitalism and the prospect of women's emancipation in the Soviet Union:

> I would have been a well-adjusted gal by now
> If I had been born in the Soviet Union.
> Driving a truck, a tractor or an aeroplane
> Captain of a tug-boat, first mate at least,
> Champion sniper, or cook for a guerrilla band,
> Who knows, maybe a writer of plays
> Sometime honored citizen of the republic,
> But certainly not this social worker
> Divided by double-guilt, public and private. (*Collected* 363)

Here the persona's ironies may undermine her political and gendered sympathies, but her social conscience still seizes her with socialist-feminist 'double-guilt.' Along with her speaker's declaration of socialist solidarity in 'Now We Steer' and her speakers' failures of sympathy in 'Social Worker' and 'Indoors,' her social worker's 'double-guilt' in 'Fragments' was suppressed by Sutherland in *Green World*.[21] The omission of 'Fragments' in particular is symbolic of Sutherland's masculinist editorial practices, highlighted by the exclusion of a poem in which her social-worker persona imagines a utopian (albeit ironized) socialist state of gender equality. Its publication in *Contemporary Verse* is, at the same time, symbolic of Crawley's editorial advocacy on behalf of so many women poets in Canada, Waddington among them.

Her only contact with *Contemporary Verse* after her move to Philadelphia was through Livesay. 'What can I do with the Crawleys,' she wrote to Livesay on 25 January 1945, 'when Alan owes me a letter? Is C[ontemporary] V[erse] still extant?' (DLP-QU, box 5a, file 1).

Waddington's three poems in the January 1945 issue – 'Problem,' 'Where,' and 'Circles' – were not sent to *Contemporary Verse* but directly to Livesay. Crawley wrote to Waddington on 1 February 1945 to inform her that he had received some of her poems from Livesay and to ask if he could include a selection in the immediately forthcoming, and behind-schedule, January issue (MWP, box 45, file 12). Following another lapse in correspondence, he contacted her on 2 July 1945 to complain of not hearing from her and to congratulate her on news of the forthcoming *Green World* (MWP, box 45, file 12). He ended his letter with a request for more poems, to which Waddington replied by sending 'adagio' and 'heart cast out' – both published in the October 1945 issue. Whatever minor rift that had arisen between Waddington and Crawley prior to her departure for Philadelphia had been bridged, thanks in part to Livesay's intervention on behalf of *Contemporary Verse*.

Though Crawley was a tough critic of Waddington's poetry in the early to mid-1940s, his rejection of some poems and requests for revisions of others did not ultimately deter her from contributing to *Contemporary Verse*. Following her break with Montreal little-magazine communities, Crawley's criticisms helped her to develop the sympathetic poetic sensibility he praised in his review of *Green World*, namely, her 'keen interest in people and deep compassion for their physical and mental ills' ("Editor's Notes" [Rev. of *Green World*] 18). If in the early 1940s she struggled to balance the urge to withdraw into subjective green worlds against the desire to communicate human sympathy, in the later 1940s and early 1950s she managed to coordinate these tendencies in a personalist mode of socially compassionate and humanitarian poetry. Her poetry of this period followed in the post-leftist, post-proletarian, social-modernist vein of Livesay's 'poems for people.' This progression in Waddington's poetry is evident in several sequences she published in *Contemporary Verse*: 'Three Poems for My Teacher' (April 1946), 'Three Poems to a Pupil' (fall 1948), and 'St. Antoine Street' (spring 1950). Along with the majority of her poems published in *Contemporary Verse* during the later 1940s and early 1950s, these sequences were later collected in *The Second Silence*.

Though the *First Statement* and *Contemporary Verse* groups held considerable sway over Waddington's poetry of the early to mid-1940s, it is too much of a stretch to suggest that after 1945 any *one* magazine, editor, or editorial collective exercised influence over the development of her poetry or poetics. Having absented herself from Montreal little-magazine culture by the mid-1940s, she continued to publish widely in Canadian and American periodicals, but by the time *The Second Silence* appeared in 1955, her audience seemed to have forgotten her. Her second volume received mediocre reviews from respected critics, including George Woodcock, Milton Wilson, and Northrop Frye.[22] Tepid critical reception of *The Second Silence* was accompanied by lacklustre sales, suggesting that her withdrawal from little-magazine culture had, in telling ways, an impact on her poetry and its readership.[23] In spite of her critics, Waddington persevered in writing, publishing, and collecting her poems through the mid-1950s and beyond.

Just as *Contemporary Verse* played a prominent role in Waddington's poetic development at mid-century, it allowed Page to expand the range of her poetry and poetics during the latter half of the 1940s and into the early 1950s. *Contemporary Verse* also offered her the support of a little-magazine community. While she held no official position in little-magazine culture after her resignation from *Northern Review* in 1947, her personal contact with the *Contemporary Verse* group more than compensated for the loss of the *Preview* group and Montreal magazine culture of the early 1940s. By the 1950s, *Contemporary Verse* provided her only outlet for publication; even after its termination in early 1953, she solicited editorial assistance from Crawley and McLaren.

After she moved from Montreal to live in Victoria in late 1944,[24] Page resumed regular contact with the *Contemporary Verse* group, especially with Crawley and McLaren. As a result of their close proximity, we might expect that little in the way of correspondence passed between them; none has survived. Instead of private exchanges of manuscripts and letters between Page and Crawley, the only record of their interaction from this period is in *Contemporary Verse* itself. Crawley's editorial relationship to Page entered the public forum of critical reviews, where he made plain his objections to her impersonalist poetics. His review of her poems in Ronald Hambleton's 1944 anthology *Unit of Five* is pointed: 'I think the selection of poems by P.K. Page is not the best that could be made. In too many of them there is too strong an impression of cold analytical detachment unwarmed by sympathetic understanding, so that the people of who [*sic*] she writes are lifeless and remembered only as the woman, the surgeon, they, them, he and she' ('Editor's Note' [1945] 15). Crawley's objection to the selection is telling: of her dozen poems, only one ('Cullen') had previously appeared in *Contemporary Verse*, while seven came from *Preview*.

Here the criticism and characterization of her impersonalist poetics is closely related to his disapproval of the selection in that 'Cullen' alone stands out from the mass of anonymous figures inhabiting her poems in *Unit of Five*. His review of *As Ten as Twenty* in the October 1946 number again takes issue with her impersonalist poetics: 'It is always the strange aspects of life which capture Miss Page, and her preoccupation with human behaviour, and intensification of ordinary gestures and mannerisms often produce a record only, from which no interpretation is made. She often avoids going below the surface of these aspects, and is content to be only a commentator detached and impersonal.' The review concludes with a gesture towards Page's future poems and poetics: 'In this book there is the promise that the writer will produce the rarest kind of poetry, the poetry which flowers out of experience, out of personality, into the immutable and absolute' ('Editor's Notes' [Rev. of *As Ten as Twenty*] 18).[25] Evidently, Crawley had forgotten her early anxieties about writing in a personalist mode.

Not until the summer 1948 issue did Page contribute to *Contemporary Verse* the kind of 'poetry which flowers out of experience, out of personality.' If her poetry from her *Preview* period in the early 1940s emphasized a poetics of impersonality, her poetry from the late 1940s shifted toward a poetics of personality. How much we may attribute this development to Crawley's criticism is unknown, though we can be sure that Page was aware of his reviews. Certainly, the gendered self-consciousness of her speaker in 'Meeting,' published in the summer 1948 issue of *Contemporary Verse*, responds to his critical desiderata. It is a self-reflexive poem about the gender of personality, the expression of a divided self:

> Still, in his sleeping head I am his love,
> still move like water in his dreams –
> a woman –
> who daily drown my sex
> to make it a swimmer.
> . . . .
> I live, unwilled, the way he moves me, speak
> in symbols fashioned from his symptoms, yet
> in him, I am more whole than in myself.

Here the divisions of gender collapse as masculine and feminine meet in a cohabited self. Page's persona is feminized, yet contained by a masculine body ('In head and heart / of him who held me, find me, / there I live') and discourse ('I see my figure through his eyes'). This is, then, the condition and conundrum of the female poet, particularly one who has practised a poetics of impersonality, occluding her self behind masks and excising her 'I.' 'Meeting' is her first self-reflexive exploration of the gendered construction of the self since her forays into a poetics of impersonality in the early 1940s. It is a transitional poem, a movement away from the impersonalist poetics of her Montreal period. Because it was left uncollected until the publication of *The Hidden Room* in 1997 (rpt. as 'Find Me' 2: 42), however, its self-reflexive interrogation of her poetics during this transitional period between the publication of *As Ten as Twenty* (1946) and *The Metal and the Flower* (1954) has gone unnoticed.

By the time 'Meeting' appeared in *Contemporary Verse*, Page had been living in Ottawa and working at the NFB for two years. During that time she resigned from the editorial board of *Northern Review*,[26] though she retained ties with the former *Preview* group. In late 1947 she wrote to Crawley about the mass resignation of 'the old Preview gang,' her personal exasperation with 'Sutherland and his works,' and her disagreement with his introduction to the anthology *Other Canadians* (n.d. [c. October–November 1947], ACP, box 1, file 20, item 16). Page's subsequent letters to Crawley document her attempts to consolidate the former *Preview* group against Sutherland and *Northern Review*: 'The chances are (slim as yet) that the exPreviewites will begin a new magazine come the New Year. In view of the fact that Sutherland has our subscriber's [*sic*] list & will not give it up we were wondering if you'd be generous & a lamb & let us have yours. Would you?' (n.d. [c. October–November 1947], ACP, box 1, file 20). In the meantime, Crawley and McLaren agreed to offer the *Contemporary Verse* list to the 'ex*Preview*ites,' but Page followed up with a letter on 11 January 1948 to decline their offer: 'Between us, I don't think we'll ever need the list ... A lot hinges on whether or not Here & Now is good. If it is we shall give it our support & and not try anything of our own' (ACP, box 1, file 20). The eventual disinclination among former *Preview* members to organize a new magazine and the demise of the Toronto-based magazine *here and now* in June 1949 after only four issues,[27] however, left Page disillusioned with the state of magazines in the Ottawa-Toronto-Montreal triangle.

Following the disappearance of *here and now*, Page channelled all her poems through Crawley, McLaren, and *Contemporary Verse*. Beginning with the spring 1950 issue, her contributions to the magazine oscillated between personal and impersonal, subjective and objective modes. Impersonalist poems from the spring 1950 issue such as 'Probationer' and 'The Map' are highly self-reflexive and seek to question a poetics of impersonality, especially its tenets of objectivity and anonymity. Others published in this issue – 'Summer' and 'The Verandah' – employ a subjective, personative mode appropriate to the pastoral lyric. Their pastoralism is not, as in the poems from Page's Montreal period, ironized or juxtaposed to conditions of urban alienation. Rather, they envision the pastoral topos that she had identified in her 1946 poem 'Subjective Eye' as 'the green world.' For Page, the green world is subjective space bounded by the circumference of the lyric self; it is, as is Waddington's green world, a 'place of withdrawal' (Berger 13). Just as Page's green world is imagined in 'Summer' in terms of her speaker's interiorization of a pastoral topos, so it is presented in 'The Verandah' in a similar manner:

> Each day as I awaken I see the sun
> spread like the ghost of gold-leaf on the verandah,
> . . . .
> an outside area supported by pillars
> which are not as bright but not as fragile as flowers
> and which are as everyday as a kitchen table
> but which are difficult to hold with the fingers
> being more inside the self than flowers or sun. (4)

This internalized, self-reflexive vision is, however, counterposed to its opposite in 'His Dream,' also published in the spring 1950 issue. 'His Dream' envisions the self externalized, where the dreamer projects his gaze, imposed upon a pastoral topos as a surrealistic 'coloured stare.' When his projection is resisted by a woman ('She stood beside him but refused to take / what she was offered, even with a choice' [*Hidden* 2: 43]), his dream vision is withdrawn. That resistance of the dreamer's projection is indicative of Page's aesthetic preference at the time: rather than project her self outward, she withdraws into her green world, the subjective 'I/eye' of the lyric self. The fact that it is a woman who refuses a male dreamer's projection is itself significant, particularly in view of a roughly contemporary poem such as 'Meeting,' in which the feminine self is 'unwilled' and subject to a masculine will.

Of the five poems Page contributed to this issue, 'The Verandah' and 'His Dream' were passed over when she put together *The Metal and the Flower*. However she assessed their faults in retrospect, 'His Dream' and 'The Verandah' nonetheless exhibit her oscillation in the early 1950s between a poetics of impersonality and a poetics of personality, between objective and subjective modes, and between gendered modernisms. We continue to witness this shifting back and forth among the poems she published in *Contemporary Verse* in 1951 and 1952. Of these poems, only 'Migration' and 'The Photograph,' published in the Summer 1951 issue, were omitted from *The Metal and the Flower*. Yet they too are typical of her alternating impersonalist ('Migration') and personalist ('The Photograph') tendencies. Also among these poems, 'Photos of a Salt Mine,' 'Portrait of Marina,' and 'The Event' are exemplary of the impersonalist portraiture included in *The Metal and the Flower*, while 'Incubus,' 'Poem,' and 'Elegy' are representative of the personalist verse present in the volume. In a letter to Page dated 4 January 1955, McLaren identified the cumulative effect of this vacillating pattern in the collection: 'We talked once about the arrangement of poems in a collection. It was absorbingly interesting to see the new poems and the ones I knew fit into a sort of pattern of ... sensibility ... a way of perceiving and feeling. The subjective and the objective all making a whole that is personal' (PKPP, box 8, file 16). Although McLaren's emphasis upon the personal in *The Metal and the Flower* effectively counterbalances Crawley's criticism of the impersonal in *As Ten as Twenty*, the assessment of Page's subjective–objective poetics as a 'whole' implies its synthesis rather than its evident schismatic condition. Given that the personal–impersonal balance shifted toward the impersonal after the publication of *The Metal and the Flower*, the disintegration of the 'whole' of her modernisms is far more apparent than its integration.

This subjective-objective dialectic of Page's impersonalist modernism manifests itself in the final two poems she published in the 1950s: the 'two Giovanni poems,' as McLaren called 'Giovanni and the Indians' and 'After Rain' (McLaren to Page, 19 April 1956, PKPP, box 8, file 16). Even though *Contemporary Verse* had folded just before her move to Australia in 1953, Page had asked if McLaren would still be willing to act as a kind of personal editor and agent, that is, to critique and send out poems for publication in North American periodicals. McLaren agreed to this arrangement in her letter of 26 March 1956, adding that she would also solicit Crawley's advice, and sent off her critique of Page's first batch of poems on 19 April. Page responded with revised versions of both Giovanni poems, among others, and another group of poems. 'The new poems interested me,' McLaren informed Page on 20 May 1956, 'because they are so utterly different from your work ... what I think of as your idiom and image' (PKPP, box 8, file 16; original ellipses). In her initial response to McLaren, Page expressed concern about what she perceived to be an idiomatic shift in contemporary poetry: 'I don't know what is at the root of this excessive uncertainty that has held me – Australia perhaps, and the current poetic idiom so different from my own' (n.d. [c. May 1956], PKPP, box 8, file 16). We may perceive Page's uncertainty concerning her own poetic idiom in the eclectic batches of poems she sent to McLaren. From these batches, McLaren selected a group with what she believed to be a coherent idiom – 'This Frieze of Birds,' 'When Bird-like, Air Surrounded,' 'The Glass Air,' 'Blowing,' 'Portrait,' and both Giovanni poems – and sent it simultaneously to the *Tamarack Review* and *Poetry*.[28] Of this group, only 'After Rain' and 'Giovanni and the Indians' were published; they appeared in *Poetry*'s November 1956 issue.

McLaren's decision to send Page's new poems to *Poetry* is, in itself, but a continuation of Crawley's editorial advice and practice and, in effect, a surrogate publication in the magazine that had once served as the model for *Contemporary Verse* (see chapter 2: 80–1). It is fitting that McLaren should have been the one to broker the publication of Page's last two poems prior to her decade of poetic silence after 1956 – that this editor who identified the objective-subjective 'whole' of Page's poetry and poetics should see her two Giovanni poems into print. Taken together, 'Giovanni' and 'After Rain' embody the objective-subjective dialectic in which Page's impersonalist poetry and poetics had been engaged since the early 1940s, when she first came into contact with the *Preview* and *Contemporary Verse* groups. Her Giovanni poems have since been separated by critics interested in 'After Rain' but not 'Giovanni'; this trend of critical attention to one but not the other has released the dialectical tension between the pair. In order to reanimate their representation of the subjective-objective dialectic in Page's impersonalist poetics, then, we might read the crisis of subjectivity in 'After Rain' in relation to the crisis of objectivity in 'Giovanni.'[29] Such a reading counters what McLaren calls the 'whole' of Page's modernist poetics and shifts toward an analysis of its disarticulated dialectic and terminal crises.

Both poems represent acute problems in her impersonalist poetics. 'After Rain' presents a poet-in-crisis as she withdraws into her subjective green world, unable to communicate or sympathize with her gardener, Giovanni, as he surveys the ruined garden (see Relke 26; Trehearne, *Montreal* 41). Oppositional responses to the garden set up a gendered dialectic between the male gardener, Giovanni, and the female poet-persona: his sentimental attachment to the garden is personal, her aesthetic detachment impersonal. This disturbing of modernism's normative gender binaries is significant to the poet-persona's intense gender consciousness, for her feminized impersonality is juxtaposed to the personality of a 'broken man' ('After Rain' 101). By projecting the personal and the sentimental onto her male gardener, the impersonal female poet-persona effectively witnesses the gender transference of her repressed personality. She opens with a catalogue of garden images, then pauses for a self-reflexive critique of such 'female whimsy': 'I see already that I lift the blind / upon a woman's bedroom of the mind' ('After Rain' 100). This 'self-chastisement,' as Page explained it to McLaren (n.d. [c. May 1956], PKPP, box 8, file 16), initiates the poem's gendered self-critique of her impersonalist poetics. This is followed by two more stanzas of garden imagery, punctuated by another self-critique: 'I suffer shame in all these images.' That 'recognition of the depersonalizing effects of such an impersonal aesthetic,' as Killian observes (97), announces the poet-persona's crisis of subjectivity. Even as she cultivates her image garden, the poet-persona observes that her shame is rooted in her inability to sympathize with Giovanni: 'I find his ache exists beyond my rim, / then almost weep to see a broken man / had satisfied my whim' ('After Rain' 101). That 'whim' is a verbal echo and reiteration of her 'female whimsy,' which she believes to be the cause of her shameful act of image-making and the source of her lack of sympathy.

Apparently Page's autocritical gestures failed to satisfy McLaren, since her objection to the repeated critique of 'female whimsy' in the poem prompted Page to excise the final stanza. According to McLaren, 'what is said in it is surely implied in what has gone before and it seems ... to drop in poetic level ... dangerously close to women's magazine emotion and thinking' (McLaren to Page, 19 April 1956, PKPP, box 8 file 16; original ellipses).[30] McLaren's masculinist criticism of 'After Rain' for its proximity to the implied sentimentality of women's magazines suggests 'the unacknowledged sentimentality of modernism itself' (Killian 93), in that modernism's repression of a sentimental, feminized discourse manifests itself in Page's poem as the disavowed femininity of her impersonal aesthetic. In following McLaren's advice, Page's temporary excision of the final stanza in 1956 eliminates the attempt at a closing rapprochement between her poet-persona's impersonalist poetics and Giovanni's sentimentality, a 'whole' in which she contemplates the integration of the sentimental and the aesthetic, the personal and the impersonal in the image of her 'heart a size / larger than seeing' (*Hidden* 2: 110). As it appears in *Poetry*, the poem closes without the final stanza's self-reflexive statement of a new poetics, but instead with an invocation: 'O choir him birds, and let him come to rest / within this beauty as one rests in love' ('After Rain' 101). No longer in a mood of self-chastisement the poet entreats the birds to communicate with Giovanni because she cannot. Ironically, then, her invocation of the birds reiterates her own crises of subjectivity, sympathy, and communication, and so anticipates the decline of her impersonalist modernism.

These crises are partly echoed in the opening lines of 'Giovanni and the Indians,' where the Indians 'call to pass the time with Giovanni / and speak an English none can understand.' Unlike 'After Rain,' 'Giovanni' does not sustain a metapoetic critique of the poet's apparent failures of sympathy and communication. We may, however, detect certain self-reflexive ironies in the difficult image-manner of the poem. Perhaps the Indians might ask of the poet whether hers is 'an English none can understand.' Page even chastized herself for what she called the poem's 'illegitimate obscurities' in response to McLaren's commentary in her letter of 19 April 1956: 'Giovanni and the Indians is (from this continent) a bright and strange (foreign) and objectively delightful painting. Being objective I feel that it is most necessary that it should be completely clear ... I can't help the feeling that the poem would be better if there were no groping whatever in that so-near-the-beginning verse ... if the picture were sharply clear and arresting to the uninformed and unready eye' ([c. May 1956], PKPP, box 8, file 16). McLaren's sense of the poem's objectivity demands that even the unfamiliar should appear familiar, that the poetic act of perception should, as she said of another of Page's Australian poems, create 'a fusion that will tie the familiar and the strange and convey it to the uninformed' (McLaren to Page, 20 May 1956, PKPP, box 8, file 16). What McLaren misses is the poem's enactment of defamiliarization, its communication of the sense of estrangement that the poet encounters upon seeing a new world. The foregrounding of 'foreign' imagery in 'Giovanni' indicates that the poet is detached from her gardener and the Indians, and that her objectivity in fact exposes her ethnocentric eye:

> Giovanni trims the weeping willow
> his ladder teetering in the yellow leaves.
>
> They make him teeter even when he's steady:
> their tatters blow and catch him through the trees;
> those scraps of colours flutter against stucco
> and flash like foreign birds;
>
> and eyes look out at eyes till Giovanni's
> are lowered swiftly – one among them is
> perhaps the Evil Eye. ('Giovanni' 101–2)

Such ethnocentric representation of the indigenous and the aboriginal suggests the poet's lack of sympathy with her environment – that is, her estrangement. The objectification of the Indians that closes the poem reinforces such a reading:

> One, on a cycle, like a ragged sail
> that luffs and sags, comes tacking up the hill.
> . . . .
> And one, his turban folded like a jug,
> and frocked, walks brittle on his blanco'd legs –
> a bantam cockerel. ('Giovanni' 102)

The depersonalized portraiture of the Indians is an effect of Page's impersonal poetics. Like the representation of Giovanni in 'After Rain,' the Indians exist only as aestheticized objects, subject to the impersonal poet's whim.

In contrast to the objective and impersonal poet, Giovanni possesses a means of communication with the Indians, a non-verbal expression of sympathy – an offering of flowers. The simplicity of his offering ('hyacinths, tulips, waterblue and yellow') undermines the complexity of the poet's impersonal image-manner. Similarly, Giovanni's verbal gesture that closes the poem may not be grammatically perfect, but it is an English all can understand, a declaration of human sympathy for and fraternal solidarity with the Indians: '"Good fellow" ... "Much good fellow"' ('Giovanni' 102). Giving him the last word, as it were,

Page calls into question the social functionality of impersonality and, instead, gestures toward the personal, speech-based idiom of Giovanni. As in 'After Rain,' Giovanni's personality is counterposed to the poet's impersonal aesthetic, thus introducing the dialectic between the personal and the impersonal in which the former's social engagement is juxtaposed to the latter's aesthetic detachment. In contrast to the crisis of subjectivity in 'After Rain,' the crisis of objectivity in 'Giovanni' is not explicitly gender-specific, although a feminist critique of modernist impersonality would identify the 'gender of impersonality' (Killian 86) with a normative masculinity. In this respect, the entirely male cast of 'Giovanni' and its gendered homosociality is consonant with its objective, impersonalist poetics. This gendered dialectic between Page's two Giovanni poems iterates the final impasse of her impersonalist modernism, for its subjective objective synthesis was never realized as the 'whole' that McLaren imagined.

Following the publication of the two Giovanni poems in November 1956, Page disappeared from print until the publication of *Cry Ararat!* in 1967. As early as July 1958, however, she attempted to enact the new poetics presented in the final stanza of the original and *Cry Ararat!* versions of 'After Rain':[31]

> And choir me too to keep my heart a size
> larger than seeing, unseduced by each
> bright glimpse of beauty striking like a bell,
> so that the whole may toll,
> its meaning shine
> clear of the myriad images that still –
> do what I will – encumber its pure line. (*Hidden* 2: 110)

In a draft of her unpublished poem of July 1958 entitled 'Could I Write a Poem Now?' Page restates the critique of her effusive image-manner. Recalling the poet's 'shame in all these images' in 'After Rain,' her poet-persona in 'Could I Write' confesses that 'the image derives / purely from guilt' (PKPP, box 3, file 17). In a revised version of the same poem, Page expands upon her ethics of the image, claiming that the image itself is

> ... a matter of guilt
> having believed
> (and pledged my troth)

art is the highest loyalty
and to let
a talent lie about unused
is to break faith. (PKPP, box 3, file 17)

As are so many of Page's self-reflexive poems about her poetics, 'Could I Write a Poem Now?' is most valuable for its insight into a period of crisis and transition. Its economic image-manner and phrasing indicate its attempt at the enactment of a new poetics. And unlike 'After Rain,' her image-making is neither profuse nor impersonal nor gender-conscious; she does not feel shame for 'female whimsy' or impersonalist aesthetics, but rather guilt for abandoning poetry altogether. This guilt may also indicate a degree of social consciousness, if only because the decision to 'break faith' entails a severing of social commitments and a retreat into the self; this anxiety about social obligations resonates with the crises of objectivity and subjectivity in Page's modernism and is perhaps amplified by her withdrawal from the social environment of little magazines. Because it was written at a time when she had removed herself from little-magazine culture, however, 'Could I Write' provides a counterpoint to the crises of her modernism and its gendered contexts, for her personal meditation on the artist's primary responsibilities to her art is no longer troubled by the gender of modernist aesthetics. Instead, the poet seeks to answer her conundrum: how do you write a poem about not writing poetry?

The result is the articulation of her poet-persona's crisis of faith: in order to create 'art,' she must forsake her faith in poetry. If, as the poem suggests, the creation of the poetic image is at once an expression of guilt and an act of faith, then 'Could I Write' is a private confession, a *mea culpa*. The source of the poet-persona's guilt and the true object of her faith are concealed until the final couplet, where her confessions regarding poetry and the poetic image are supplanted by an allusion to visual art: 'But how do you write a Chagall? / It boils down to that' (PKPP, box 3, file 17). As Page relates in her *Brazilian Journal*, she started working in visual media in June 1957 (59); her poem of July 1958 therefore acts as a segue from verbal to visual media. This painter's confession is, as she reflected upon a passage in her journal from this period, 'an attempt to understand [her] poetic silence, this translation into paint' (*Brazilian* 195). Where the poet of 1956 invokes the birds in 'After Rain' to communicate her aesthetics through a new poetics, the visual artist of 1958 calls upon the art of Marc Chagall to represent her aesthetics in a new medium. Her invocation of Chagall is, in the end, a declaration of faith in a religious and subjective art. As much as her summoning of Chagall's surrealism initiates her poetry's 'translation into paint,' it enables her to visualize alternatives to the repetition of the poetic crises of her modernism. Even as she identifies with the surrealism of a male artist, we can perceive the judicious selection of her painterly model in that Chagall's canvases are replete with fluid images of male-female couples and so offer her visual images of an integrated gendered aesthetic.

The reply to Page's question 'But how do you write a Chagall?' would have to wait nearly a decade until the publication of her title poem in *Cry Ararat! Poems New and Selected* (1967). The extent to which she achieved the synthesis of the objective-subjective 'whole' of her poetics in 'Cry Ararat!' is beyond the scope of this chapter, but it is enough to suggest that its 'focus of the total I' (*Hidden* 2: 186) envisions that integration (see Trehearne, *Montreal* 103–4). After the oscillation between objective and subjective modes prior to her period of silence, the formulation of a new poetics in 'Cry Ararat!' represents the resolution of crises in her modernism, most notably the dissolution of gendered oppositions in her early poetry and poetics. Given the correlations between Page's early modernism and the gendered contexts of modernist little-magazine culture, the dismantling of the period's gender binaries in her post-hiatus poetics is central to her formulation of a new poetics.

Her new poetics is, at least in part, an accumulated product of her affiliations with the *Preview* and *Contemporary Verse* groups. In particular, the editorial and critical interventions of Crawley and McLaren appear to have had a lasting impact on the advancement of Page's poetics, long after the demise of *Contemporary Verse*. It is fitting, then, that she should have singled out Crawley (and passed over other little-magazine editors) as one of the co-dedicatees of *Cry Ararat!* Her reference to Crawley acknowledges the importance of 1940s and early 1950s little-magazine culture to the development of Page's modernist poetry, some of which she collected for the first time in *Cry Ararat!* At the same time, his influence is acknowledged for its lasting impact on her poetics more than a decade after the demise of *Contemporary* Verse. It is equally telling that the second dedicatee should be her husband, Arthur Irwin. Following their marriage and his appointment as Canadian high commissioner to Australia in 1953, she left Canada and the little-magazine communities that had sustained her poetry through the 1940s and early 1950s. Though important to Page's biography and to the gendered contexts of her poetry, it is too reductive to conclude that her duties as a diplomat's wife were the primary determining factors in her decreased poetic creativity in the 1950s. In fact, her difficulties in putting together a manuscript of sufficient length for her second book had arisen several years prior to her departure from Canada; these years of poetic frustration during her Ottawa and Australia periods are well documented in her correspondence with editors Sybil Hutchison and Jack McClelland between April 1950 and July 1954 concerning *The Metal and the Flower* (see PKPP, box 15, file 9). *The Metal and the Flower* eventually appeared at the midpoint of a time of diminished productivity following the demise of *Contemporary Verse*, a four-year period during which she published nothing in periodicals and commenced her withdrawal from little-magazine culture. Coincident with news of her imminent move to Australia in early 1953, Page wrote to Crawley with her views on the end of *Contemporary Verse*: 'I cannot help but feel that a part of me dies with it. It has been of tremendous value & comfort to me & to many like me. But if it is to end, let it end' (ACP, box 1, file 20, item 22). It would appear that, indeed, a part of her had died with *Contemporary Verse*. Added to the aesthetic crises in her poetry of the mid-1950s, the collapse of that modernist little-magazine culture and its advancement of women's modernism in Canada heralded her decade of silence and transition to a new poetics in *Cry Ararat!*

While Page maintained contact with *Contemporary Verse*'s editors after 1952–3, Waddington sought alternative editors and venues for her poetry after the magazine ceased operation. Although *Contemporary Verse* had received all but one of her poems published in the 1950s prior to its final issue, Waddington did not seek or receive editorial advice from either Crawley or McLaren after her poems appeared in the winter-spring 1951–2 issue. She did not have the same personal attachments to the *Contemporary Verse* editors. Her withdrawal from little-magazine communities had taken place after the publication of *Green World* in 1945. Waddington's choice to distance herself from the Montreal magazine groups coincided with her decisions to raise her children and, at the same time, to teach and practise social work. These biographical circumstances could be adduced in a reading of the gendered contexts of her poetry after 1945, but they would tell us no more about her willed detachment from the personalities and masculinist editorial practices of Montreal little-magazine culture. The literary culture that gave Waddington a cold welcome when she published *The Second Silence* in 1955 was not the little-magazine culture she had known in 1945. Together with the folding of *Contemporary Verse* in 1952–3, the fall of *Northern Review* in 1956 signalled that modernist little-magazine culture in Canada had entered a period of transition. By 1956 Sutherland was dead, and with him went *Northern Review* and the last remnant of the little-magazine culture in which both Waddington and Page had found their first audience.

4 Editing Women: The Making of Little-Magazine Cultures, 1916–1947

They are all gone – like their little magazines.
And something has gone with them.

Norman Levine, 'We All Begin in a Little Magazine' (43)

Culture in the Making

Just as the early poetry and poetics of Livesay, Marriott, Page, and Waddington coincide with critical and transitional events in leftist and modernist magazine cultures, so the histories of other women editors of modern literary, arts, and cultural-interest magazines from the same period follow analogous narratives of crisis and transition. These 'other' little magazines and the 'other' women responsible for their editing participate equally in the making of a modern literary culture in Canada. Women's editorial construction of these magazines is informed by some common cultural discourses of the period: modernism, leftism, nationalism, internationalism, and feminism. These discursive formations are by no means isolated from one another: for any given magazine, one category of discourse may combine with another (or others) to define its compound cultural orientation. At times these cultural formations become unstable and enter into periods of decline and/or change, often coinciding with either the establishment or the termination of a magazine. Downturns in one magazine culture may prefigure the ascendancy of new magazines to fill a perceived void, or the inaccessibility of another magazine culture to a given constituency of authors may signal the need for change and the creation of new magazines. These general cultural trends apply as much to early- to mid-twentieth-century little magazines as to the commercial magazine and newspaper cultures from which many of the earliest women editors emerged, for the limitations of the mass-circulation newspaper and magazine necessitated the development of alternative means of publication. One of the distinctive features of the first three decades of women's editorial work on these periodicals is the interplay between a dominant commercial-magazine culture and an emergent little-magazine one; their histories are so closely intertwined that exclusive definition of modernist and leftist periodicals according to their anti-commercialism and avant-garde aesthetics misrepresents this formative period's actual characteristics. With an adjustment to the exclusivity of previous little-magazine historiography, we may begin to recover the emergent cultures of the women editors and their magazines from the first half of the twentieth century.

Some obvious reasons for the distortions of past scholarship may be attributed to the absence of a detailed map of Canadian print culture in the early to mid-twentieth century, an absence recently filled by the third volume of the *History of the Book in Canada*. English-Canadian cultural history has lacked a comprehensive account of magazine cultures from the early to mid-twentieth century. Histories of individual magazines, of isolated cultural and political groups, and of literary movements have produced a scattered record, but nothing close to a consolidated cultural history, particularly in the area of women magazine editors. Arranged as continuous narratives about lesser-known magazine editors that parallel and, on occasion, intersect with the literary histories of Livesay, Marriott, Page, and Waddington, the next two chapters gesture toward the integration of women poets and editors, and their publications and organizations into a cultural history. Where appropriate, then, I have noted poems by Page, Waddington, Livesay, and Marriott if they appear in little magazines edited or co-edited by women of this period: Flora MacDonald Denison of the *Sunset of Bon Echo* (1916–20), Florence Custance of the *Woman Worker* (1926–9), Mary Davidson of the *Twentieth Century* (1932–3), Hilda and Laura Ridley of the *Crucible* (1932–3), Eleanor Godfrey of the *Canadian Forum* (1935–47), Catherine Harmon of *here and now* (1947–9), Myra Lazechko-Haas of *Impression* (1950–1), Yvonne Agazarian of *pm magazine* (1951–52), Aileen Collins of *CIV/n* (1953–55), and Margaret Fairley of *New Frontiers* (1952–6). My intention in these chapters is not, however, so much to recover women's uncollected poems – though they receive brief mention – as to assemble the histories of women editors responsible for the selection of such poems in the contexts of English Canada's leftist and modernist little-magazine cultures.

For little magazines in Canada, the culminating cultural event of this period took place at mid-century: the Royal Commission on National Development in the Arts, Letters and Sciences (1949–51), also known as the Massey Commission, after its chairman, Vincent Massey. Though the Massey Commission has been at times mythologized as an institution that enabled the consolidation of Canadian cultural nationalism, its published *Report* of 1951 determined that Canada's literary culture was undergoing a 'crisis of orientation,' one attributed to competing views among those who valued the influences of other nations' literatures on Canadian authors and those who feared these influences as forces of cultural imperialism and/or colonialism (225). This 'crisis' at mid-century was by no means a recent phenomenon, for the history of early Canadian literature reveals the constant negotiation among colonialist and imperialist, as well as nationalist and internationalist, orientations. As Nick Mount notes, the crisis was so acute that many Canadian authors were motivated by economic necessity to move to the United States, predominantly to New York City, in the late nineteenth and early twentieth centuries (see Mount, 'Expatriate' and *When Canadian*). And as James Doyle remarks, the absence of modernist periodicals in early-twentieth-century Canada led to the export of an emergent Canadian modernism to Harriet Monroe and Jane Heap's Chicago-based little magazine *Poetry* (1912–), which served in the second and third decades of the century as a host to the poetry of the early Canadian imagists, among them women such as Louise Morey Bowman, Martha Ostenso, Florence Randal Livesay, and Constance Lindsay Skinner (see Doyle, 'Harriet'). For editors of early- to mid-twentieth-century little magazines, the 'crisis of orientation' extends from issues of cultural nationalism and internationalism to the economy of their periodicals, for the financial pressures of publication frequently necessitated the adaptation of mass-market advertising and marketing techniques to the context of non-commercial little-magazine production and dissemination.

As a consequence, the border between commercial and non-commercial periodicals was often highly permeable in the early period of Canadian little magazines (1916–47), so that an avant-garde cultural magazine would employ methods of mass-market advertising and promotional schemes more commonly associated with commercial mass-circulation magazines. While this open border, as Mark Morris-son observes, is characteristic of early American and British modernist little-magazine cultures (3–16), Canadian little-magazine editors and their historians have regularly attempted to defend against the incursion of commercialist phenomena into the field of avant-garde magazine cultures. Although the origins of the little magazine in Canada may be at times far more commercial and far less anti-commercial than later editors and literary historians have claimed, the history of repeated economic failure of little magazines in the period before the Massey Commission establishes a narrative that neither editors nor historians would likely contest. If, as the Massey *Report* suggests, modern Canadian literature moved toward a 'crisis of orientation' at mid-century, we should consider the disorienting effects of both economic and communicative problems experienced by earlier literary, arts, and cultural groups and their periodicals that anticipate the Massey Commission's findings. Among those magazines principally edited by women in the pre-commission era, such critical situations are prominent, though rarely (if ever) noted in our cultural histories.

These lacunae are conspicuous in the case of those cultural histories that foreground the Massey Commission. Maria Tippett's *Making Culture: English-Canadian Institutions and the Arts before the Massey Commission* (1990), for instance, ignores much of the activity associated with the emergence of modern literary magazines and magazine cultures. Her ambitious, yet inconsistent cultural history gives little more (often no more) than passing mention to the *Canadian Bookman*, the *Canadian Forum*, the *McGill Fortnightly Review*, the *Canadian Mercury*, *Masses*, *Canadian Poetry Magazine*, and *New Frontier*. But Tippett affords no space for *Contemporary Verse*, *Preview*, or *First Statement*, to name a few of the prominent little magazines of the period to which she attends. And though her study recognizes the importance of women as founders and members of 'art, literary, and dramatic societies and schools of music, art, dramatic expression, and elocution' and as 'private patrons' (103), she passes over those arts, literary, and cultural magazines with which women were affiliated and of which they were editors. Of those women 'making culture' in the literary-historical narrative I have compiled so far, only Livesay is recognized by Tippett as a contributor to *Masses* and *New Frontier* (31, 33). Nowhere in her narrative of Canadian culture before the founding of the Massey Commission does she identify women magazine editors. As a gesture toward women little-magazine editors who predate the Massey Commission – Flora MacDonald Denison, Florence Custance, Mary David-son, Hilda and Laura Ridley, and Eleanor Godfrey – the present chapter addresses their contributions to feminist, leftist, and modernist literary cultures in Canada. Following Tippett's historical orientation *toward* (but not *about*) the Massey Commission in her cultural history, their editorial work prepares the foundation for the history of the commission's cross-country public meetings, its reception of briefs from little-magazine groups, and its published report and recommendations for Canadian culture at mid-century.

Advertising 'Old Walt': Flora MacDonald Denison and the *Sunset of Bon Echo*

In 1912, when Harriet Monroe sought a motto to express *Poetry's* democratic, 'open-door' editorial policy, she seized upon the closing line of Walt Whitman's 'Ventures, on an Old Theme' (c. 1882): 'To have great poets, there must be great audiences, too' (1058). Just four years later, Flora MacDonald Denison turned to Whitman as the presiding spirit of her little magazine, the *Sunset of Bon Echo* (1916–20). As founder of the Whitman Club of Bon Echo, Denison also assumed the role of editor of its magazine, which she conducted under the pen name – 'Flora MacDonald' that she had adopted since her earliest publications in the 1890s (Gorham 211n7). Published at irregular intervals between March 1916 and May 1920, the *Sunset of Bon Echo* consists of only six issues, three of which appeared in 1916, followed by special issues in 1917 ('Souvenir Number'), 1919 ('Whitman Centennial'), and 1920 ('Whitman-Traubel Number'). Although Denison's contributions to Canadian little-magazine culture have been for the most part neglected, her role in Whitman studies has by no means gone unnoticed (see Greenland and Colombo; Kalnin; Lacombe, 'Songs' and 'Theosophy'; Lynch; McMullin; Savigny). By reclaiming her place in Canada's little-magazine history, however, we should assign her a more active role in the production of literary culture than literary critics and historians interested in her connections to Whitman and the Whitman fellowship have so far acknowledged.

While Denison is best known in Canada as an activist and journalist in the women's suffrage movement of the early twentieth century (see A. Williams; Gorham) and, to lesser degree, as the author of the novel *Mary Melville, the Psychic* (1900), a biographical, spiritualist novel based on the experiences of her sister, Mary, she is less often recognized for combining her social and political commitments to women's suffrage with her passions for Whitman and theosophy (see Cook 79–84; Gorham; Lacombe, 'Songs' and 'Theosophy'). When in 1906 she became secretary of the Dominion Women's Enfranchisement Association, she concurrently started to publish articles in the Toronto *Sunday World*, and by 1909 she was contributing a weekly column originally called 'Under the Pines' but later, in 1911, given a decidedly Whitmanesque title, 'The Open Road towards Democracy' (Gorham 56–7). As a member of the Canadian Suffrage Association (founded 1883) – which she served as leader from 1911 to 1914 and for which she provided headquarters in her Toronto home – Denison met with resistance from her fellow suffragists in Toronto when she joined Emmeline Pankhurst's militant suffragist Women's Social and Political Union (founded 1903) and was forced to resign her presidency (Gorham 62). By 1916 she turned her attention to the development of her recently acquired property on Mazinaw Lake, the present-day Bon Echo Provincial Park, to the creation of 'a combination summer hotel and avant-garde spiritual community' (Gorham 69) for her fellow Whitmanites and theosophists at Bon Echo, and to the publication of their prose and poetry in the *Sunset of Bon Echo*.

As with many little magazines in their early stages, the most frequent contributor to the *Sunset of Bon Echo* was its editor. The first issue opens with three editorial sketches ('Whitman,' 'Bon Echo,' and 'Flora MacDonald'), a compilation of fragmentary character sketches ('Short Stories'), a one-page sketch about an eccentric guest at Bon Echo ('Minnie'), an expository sketch about local native history ('Historical Sketch of the Indian Battle at Massanoga'), a reprint of Denison's column from *Sunday World* ('Vocational Training for Women'), an editorial manifesto ('Democracy'), a closing sketch about Bon Echo visitors and staff, and four miscellany pages with quotations, postcard-length sketches, and aphorisms interspersed throughout – all written (or compiled) by the editor herself. Other contributors are limited to the quotations on the miscellany pages, two poems (James G. Hughes's 'Harmony' and a reprint of Elizabeth Doten's 'The Chemistry of Character'), and an article about the Whitman Club of Bon Echo by Albert Ernest Stafford ('Crusts and Crumbs'), reprinted from *Sunday World*. Given the predominance of Denison herself and her Bon Echo resort in the first issue, I would concur with Michele Lacombe's description of the *Sunset of Bon Echo* as 'Flora's fanzine' ('Songs' 153) – though not without some qualification. As Lacombe writes of Denison's relationship to early twentieth-century print culture,

> For her and the international circle of mostly liberal suffrage and reform feminists who were her main cohort, the spiritualist press offered an accessible and appealing source of activism and authorship. Often denied access to post-secondary education, paying professions, the pulpit, the political platform and the mainstream press, they turned to what they perceived as the only radical forum (other than socialist organizations such as the Knights of Labor) that made sense and made room. Bon Echo came to stand for the wilderness equivalent of all of the above: a spiritual and educational centre, a source of income and meaningful work, a political alternative – in short, a 'free' space for women and woman-friendly progressives. ('Songs' 158–9)

For Denison, like other early-twentieth-century women 'denied agency symbolizing the status of a speaking subject' (Lacombe, 'Songs' 158), the *Sunset of Bon Echo* afforded the freedom to lay claim to a range of public voices – not just as a columnist for *Sunday World* but as the editor of and principal contributor to her own periodical. The profusion of different voices, genres, and prose styles that Denison adopts in the thirty-two pages of the magazine's first issue bespeaks a deliberate polyvocality, an orchestration of a capacious and multiply constituted self that befits the editor's devotion to the writings of Whitman. The predominant genre that Denison adopts is that of the sketch, a genre that lends itself to her spiritual investigation of different personalities, whether of those who visit or work at Bon Echo or of herself. Given the eclectic contents of the magazine and its emphasis on the character sketch, we may establish tentative links to the popularity of miscellanies and prose sketches among Victorian-era periodicals, but only with the provision that the multi-authored miscellany of the nineteenth century is here transformed into a predominantly single-authored little magazine whose interrogation of the self at times belies a distinctly modern – if not proto-modernist – preoccupation with interiority of the self, its splicing of multiple personalities, and its fragmentation. Consider, for instance, the editor's evident preoccupation with fragmented, accumulative expressive forms: the miscellany pages, the one- or two-sentence short stories, and the paratactic, anaphoric, staccato, single-sentence paragraph style of her autobiographical sketch in the first issue ('Flora MacDonald').

Denison's self-titled autobiographical sketch in the March 1916 issue addresses the multiple personalities that inhabit her as a speaking subject:

> It is difficult to write of myself.
>
> It would be impossible had I not met Whitman...
>
> I have been an interested tenant of Mrs. Denison's body and at times we differ so vastly in our reasoning and conclusions that I have come to believe she and I are two different personalities.
>
> However, as she is the one with whom I have grown and developed in the present life, I shall talk of her as of someone outside myself. (7)

It should be noted that this sketch appears after two others, 'Whitman' and 'Bon Echo,' thus situating the personality of the editor in relation to the personality of the poet (Whitman) and the locus (Bon Echo) that serves as the Whitman fellowship's spiritual retreat. Her self-portrait of what she calls 'two different personalities' (7) – her literary-spiritual self (Flora MacDonald) and her embodied self (Mrs Denison) – is deliberately juxtaposed to the two other portraits, for she regards both the poet and his spiritualized presence at Mazinaw Lake as constitutive of her personalities. For Denison to speak of herself, she embraces the accumulative, anaphoric style of Whitman's 'Song of Myself,' speaking through, as it were, the poet's literary form that she believes enables her self-expression. Yet Whitman is one among the many 'friends in the Spirit World' whom she names 'the personnel of the SUNSET': her sister, Mary Merrill; a 'Hindu prince' whose 'chief concern is the terrible wrongs brought about by unjust caste systems'; 'Sunset (for whom this little magazine is named),' an 'Indian Chief'; 'Crusts-and-Crumbs,' a weekly column written by Albert Ernest Stafford of the *Sunday World*; an 'Arab' whose 'swiftness of decision has helped'; and finally, 'Whitman makes the mystic seven complete.' 'Whitman,' she writes in conclusion of her eclectic catalogue and eccentric masthead, 'is the master guide' ('Flora MacDonald' 8). It is as if Whitman himself were called upon to serve as an honorary editor-in-chief of the magazine.

Before we begin to regard the *Sunset of Bon Echo* as Denison's 'Song of Myself,' however, it will be necessary to glance ahead to subsequent issues in which an increasing number of contributors begin to appear, no doubt as a consequence of the editor's dissemination of the first issue among her Whitman fellows. Other promotional activities also contributed to the growth of the magazine from its beginnings as essentially a one-woman venture. Writing in the June 1916 issue of her little magazine the *Forerunner* (1909–16) – concurrent with the serialization of the sequel to her utopian feminist novel *Herland* – Charlotte Perkins Gilman, who had already visited Bon Echo, plugged Denison's publishing and business ventures: 'The "Sunset of Bon Echo" is a little magazine, edited by one of Canada's ablest women, Flora MacDonald, and coming from one of the most beautiful places in a region famed for beauty – "Bon Echo" ... The magazine emanates the spirit of Walt Whitman, of the advancement of women, of social progress.' Denison not only reprinted Gilman's praise in the magazine's third issue (summer 1916) but also had promotional cards printed to advertise Bon Echo, which included the passage from the *Forerunner* (FMDP, box 1, file 13). Here we can begin to see how the little magazine, although a typical non-commercial organ of a literary society, was employed as an advertisement in the service of Bon Echo Inn. Its commercial function, then, was inseparable from its literary one, though the editor was careful to emphasize its non-commercial status as a little magazine in order to deflect attention from its tacitly commercial motives. 'Published every so often,' read an advertisement for the magazine first appearing in the second issue, 'according to our bank balance' (Denison, 'How'). Although the magazine contained no external advertisements and therefore attracted no advertising revenues, the inside front and back covers were devoted to advertisements for the inn and the magazine respectively, and the back cover of every issue included a map, train schedules, and other travel instructions to guide potential visitors to Bon Echo Inn. As one anonymous reader noted in 'Sayings Clipped from Sunset Letters,' 'The Sunset is too obviously an advertisement for Bon Echo.' Indeed, the *Sunset of Bon Echo* was, in effect, a literary travel brochure.

The literary contents of the magazine were, for the most part, limited to reprints of previously published poems and original poems by members of the fellowship on the subject of Whitman. In addition, excerpts from his oeuvre appeared throughout the magazine. Most of the poems about or dedicated to Whitman are written in obvious imitation of the accumulative, anaphoric, free-verse style of *Leaves of Grass*. While his poetry, as Alan Trachtenberg puts it, is a 'precipitant of the modern' (194), it would be misleading to describe poems written in imitation of Whitman and published in the *Sunset of Bon Echo* as definitively modernist. These early-twentieth-century Whitmanites admired the poet's distinctive and innovative style, upon which they modelled their own poetry, but their derivative manner bespeaks their hesitation to embrace an emergent North American modernism. For obvious reasons, they could not entertain a characteristically tendentious modernist break with the past, but they were disposed to articulate continuities between Whitman's poetry and that of the modernist avant-garde – as evidenced, for instance, by the program of the 1915 meeting of the international Whitman fellowship in New York, at which Reginald Wright Kauffmann delivered a lecture entitled 'The Imagists, the Vorticists – and Walt' (FMDP, box 1, file 9), and by a lecture ('An Artist's View of Whitman') delivered at the Toronto Central Reference Library by one of the members of the Group of Seven, J.E.H. MacDonald, who called Whitman's writing 'Modernist Art' and suggested that 'Whitman, of all writers, should be the patron saint of the modern artist' (qtd. in Davis 48).

Among contributors to the *Sunset of Bon Echo*, the practice of free verse is evident in certain poems not obviously modelled on Whitman, a practice that indicates the fellowship's tentative gestures toward literary modernism. For women poets published in the magazine, particularly those who wrote free verse, Whitman embodied a paternalistic figure whose authority provided legitimacy to their break with traditional poetic forms and social mores. Published in the third issue (summer 1916) under the pseudonym Ray Lewis (identified elsewhere in the magazine as Miss Ray Levinsky, a member of the Whitman Club of Bon Echo and author of *Songs of the Universe* [1915]), 'To Walt Whitman' expresses the conflicted situation of the woman Whitmanite poet:

They say I sing your songs;
I know that my tones
Are not as full, as round, as vibrant as yours;
Still I am glad that with my feeble voice
I have the courage to sing your melodies.
They shake their heads these critics, murmuring,
'It is a pity she follows Walt Whitman so closely';
And I in place of being dismayed
Pray that I may be enfolded in your strong thoughts,
Impregnated with your ideals,

And that my songs will so resemble yours
That all men hearing them will cry aloud,
'Walt Whitman is their father.'

Lewis's poem is at once typical of the fellowship's poetry in its direct
address to the dominant male poet, figured here as her poem's 'father,'
and exceptional in its divergence from the formal qualities of
Whitman's poetry. Her modernism is perhaps tempered by her willingness to 'follow' Whitman 'so closely,' yet the eroticization of her
relationship with him ('enfolded in your strong thoughts, / Impregnated with your ideals') appropriates his poetry's open sexuality as
the vehicle for the liberation of a woman's eroticism. Likely alluding to
the scandalous reputation of Whitman's poetry in early-twentieth-
century Toronto – his works 'were not available on the open shelves of
the public library, but could only be read after application and interview with the chief librarian' (Davis 48) – Lewis aligns her female
speaker's sexuality with that of a poet whose openness about sex
received public censure.

When Charlotte Perkins Gilman wrote of the *Sunset of Bon Echo* as
a magazine committed to 'the advancement of women' and 'social
progress,' she directed attention to its editor's activism on behalf of
women's suffrage and socialism. Although its irregular publication
after the first three issues of 1916 is characteristic of little-magazine
production, the reasons for the disruption are more remarkable. As
Denison writes in the 1919 issue after a year's hiatus, 'There was no
"Sunset," nor any Bon Echo story for 1917 because I was busy
helping to put New York State over the top for Suffrage that year'
('Mary the Indian' 10). Both the literary contributions and articles
published in the magazine directly and indirectly bolstered the cause
of women's suffrage, including Richard Le Gallienne's poem
'Woman and War' (summer 1916), reprinted from his volume *The
Silk-Hat Soldier and Other Poems in War Time* (1915), Charlotte Perkins
Gilman's poem 'Heroism' (April–May 1916), reprinted from her
volume *In This Our World* (3rd ed., 1898), and Denison's articles
'Vocational Training for Women' (March 1916), 'Democracy' (March
1916), and 'Mrs. Pankhurst – Premier Hearst' (April–May 1916). In
addition, the fellowship's Whitman-influenced poems in the magazine all advocated egalitarianism among the sexes, democracy, and
comradeship, likely inspired by one of the magazine's mottos, 'The
institution of the dear love of comrades,' taken from the 'Calamus'

sequence of *Leaves of Grass* (128) and reprinted at the head of the opening editorial pages.

The second of the magazine's mottos, 'Neither master nor servant am I,' a slight misquotation ('Neither a servant nor a master I' [211]) of Whitman's 'A Song for Occupations' in *Leaves of Grass*, appeared atop the magazine's editorial section. If the first motto repositions Whitman's ideal institution of comradeship in the context of early twentieth-century reform of legal institutions that enabled women's suffrage, the second introduces the poet's words into the context of a different but related kind of comradeship, that of socialism. Partly under the influence of Horace Traubel, who founded the Walt Whitman Fellowship International in 1894, who became one of Whitman's close companions during the poet's final years at Camden, New Jersey, and who during this period 'persistently urged a reluctant Whitman to admit that *Leaves of Grass* endorsed a socialist agenda' (Folsom 740), Denison not only represented in the magazine Traubel's and others' socialist interpretations of Whitman but also espoused her own sympathies for socialism in her articles, sketches, and editorials. In the editorial pages of the summer 1916 issue, she makes plain her class solidarity:

> I always feel a wave of humiliation when I hear 'The working class' spoken of in a supercilious way.
> 'She was only a poor working girl,' 'He was only a common workman.' As if we should not all belong to the working class, as if anyone has a right to enjoy and not to work in a world where no good thing can come except through work. ('Walt Whitman' 4)

Some of the more prominent socialist features of the magazine include boldface statements set off in text boxes, such as 'Not until we do away with the cursed wall that money builds between folks who ought to know each other, can we talk about a pure democracy' and, in the same issue, 'They tell me that Communism would be a failure. Do they think that our present social system is a success?' (April–May 1916: 4, 17). The editor's socialism extended to the everyday operations of the Bon Echo Inn, apparent in her depiction of the staff at the inn in her sketches ('Short Stories,' 'Who's Who at Bon Echo') and her frank critique of the wealthy and urbanite visitors at the resort ('Minnie,' 'Floppit'). Perhaps her most definitive endorsement of socialism and, in particular, of the socialist interpretation of Whitman is her dedication to Traubel of the 1920 final issue of the *Sunset of Bon Echo*, which recounts his visit to and death at Bon Echo in the summer of 1919 and contains numerous articles, poems, and letters in memoriam.

Among the main features of the 'Whitman-Traubel' commemorative issue are photographs and accounts of Denison and Traubel's joint dedication of a mile-long granite cliff on Lake Mazinaw in honour of Whitman's centenary. Stonemasons were commissioned to inscribe the following dedication in letters roughly two feet high:

OLD WALT

1819–1919

DEDICATED TO THE DEMOCRATIC IDEALS OF

WALT WHITMAN

BY

HORACE TRAUBEL AND FLORA MACDONALD

MY FOOTHOLD IS TENON'D AND MORTISED IN GRANITE

I LAUGH AT WHAT YOU CALL DISSOLUTION

AND I KNOW THE AMPLITUDE OF TIME

(FMDP, box 1)

If the *Sunset of Bon Echo* served as an advertisement for the Lake Mazinaw resort, the monument to Whitman ultimately transformed the site into a tourist attraction. The conversion of the granite cliff into a centenary monument to Whitman is not only an act of colonization, for the massive inscription 'overshadows the much older and much harder to see Algonquian pictographs on the Mazinaw rockface' (Lacombe, 'Songs' 155), but also an act of commercialization, for the cliff becomes the support for an immense 'Old Walt' billboard-style advertisement. Denison's and Traubel's acts of colonization of indigenous spiritual spaces and commercialization of the Canadian wilderness were unintentional, but nonetheless they bespeak their complicity in the permanent defacement of the granite cliff in the name of 'Old Walt' and in the interest of advertising both Whitman and the Bon Echo Inn. In this way, the monument to Whitman is the logical extension of a little magazine whose advertising motives were its raison d'être. While the magazine is an ephemeral means of advertisement for the Bon Echo Inn, the granite cliff is an enduring inscription of the editor and proprietor's participation in the tourism industry. After Denison's death in 1921, the *Sunset of Bon Echo* ceased publication, but the Bon Echo Inn continued to operate under the control of her son, the playwright Merrill Denison, though with diminished success and, by the 1930s, financial failure. One might wonder how extensively he advertised Bon Echo, for the loss of the *Sunset of Bon Echo* as an advertising medium surely deprived him of an effective means of communication with a perennial and devoted group of visitors among the Whitman fellowship.

Feminism on the Left: Florence Custance and the *Woman Worker*

While the socialist and suffragist contents of the *Sunset of Bon Echo* contributed to leftist-feminist movements of the early twentieth century, feminist little-magazine culture on the Canadian left marched ahead under a more militant banner by the mid-1920s. Fifty years prior to the formation of Canadian feminist 'literary magazines where women wrote for other women' in the 1970s (Godard, 'Women' 269) and contemporary with the rise of little magazines edited by men in Montreal and Halifax in the 1920s, Florence Custance founded the *Woman Worker* in Toronto in July 1926. Subtitled 'A Monthly Magazine for Working Women,' it was written by and for the members of the Canadian Federation of Women's Labor Leagues, a national working-class women's organization under the direction of the Communist Party of Canada (CPC). Histories of the *Woman Worker*, its editor, and the Women's Labor Leagues (WLLs) can be found in Joan Sangster's *Dreams of Equality* (1989) and in *The Woman Worker, 1926–29* (1999), an anthology of writings from the magazine, edited and introduced by Margaret Hobbs and Sangster. Chiefly concerned with the socio-political dimensions of Canadian women's history, these historical approaches consider literary content only as supplements to the *Woman Worker*'s articles, editorials, and correspondence columns. Admittedly, the magazine's literary contributors were often anonymous or identified by initials only; even among those men and women whose names appear in the magazine, none went on to make an impact on Canadian letters. Beyond their value as sociological and political source documents, though, these literary contributions were integral to the early formation of a proletarian feminist magazine culture in Canada.

Even the *Woman Worker*'s classification as a magazine has so far remained unsettled. References to the publication as a 'newspaper' (Sangster 28) and 'paper' (Sangster and Hobbs 8–12) have occluded its typical little-magazine format and at the same time exposed its origins in the CPC's newspaper, the *Worker*. Prior to editing the *Woman Worker*, Custance coordinated its prototype, the 'The Working Woman's Section' of the CPC paper (Sangster 28). At a transitional stage, the *Woman Worker* was first issued in mimeographed editions, before its premier printed number came out in July 1926. In recognition of this material aspect of magazine production, Custance opened her first editorial with a statement on the *Woman Worker*'s 'previous feeble mimeographed attempts' and outlined the economic 'means [by which] we have been able to get sufficient money together to pay for our first printed issue' ('Success' 32). Among other pressing issues of social and political concern among working-class women, the economy of magazine production took precedence in Custance's inaugural editorial address to the WLLs.

Her first editorial also made plain the *Woman Worker*'s antipathy to the commercialism of mass-market women's magazines and to the typical contents of women's pages in newspapers: 'It will be seen that our magazine will be quite unlike other magazines which are published for the benefit of women. It will not contain fashions and patterns, and we are leaving recipes for cooking to the cook book. We shall not print sickly love stories, we are leaving these to the other magazines. Instead, we shall devote our attention to things that are overlooked by the other magazines. Everything that will be printed in our magazine will deal with life, real life, not imaginations' ('Success' 33). One might expect from Custance's editorial that the *Woman Worker* published only documentary journalism, reportage, and reports and letters from local WLLs, though, as Sangster notes, she accepted a 'wide selection of fiction' (46) and, less regularly, poetry. Inflected by socialist idealism, 'real life' is invariably distorted in the *Woman Worker*'s literary pages. Literary realism in the *Woman Worker* typically edges toward socialist romanticism, especially in its poetry. This tendency is pronounced in the anonymous poem of January 1927 entitled 'Prostitutes,' whose portrait of a sex worker as capitalist victim and socialist martyr attends to those 'things ... overlooked' by commercial women's magazines, though in a manner idealized, moralized, sentimentalized, and remote from 'real life.' Even so, the literary-historical significance of its publication in the *Woman Worker* should not be missed, especially in view of the poetry published in other women's magazines and even in little magazines of the time. Custance's daring to publish a poem in 1927 with a prostitute first-person speaker is socially progressive and entirely unmatched by her editorial contemporaries in Canada.

In its only explicit editorial on literary matters, the *Woman Worker* highlighted the reactionary conservatism of another Canadian women's group, the National Council of Women, and its support for the government's ban on proletarian literature imported from the United States. The editorial in the April 1927 issue of the *Woman Worker* denounced the National Council of Women: 'these women, whose interests are bound up with the present order of things, can claim that anything which criticizes this order is "pernicious" and "demoralizing"' (Custance, 'War' 5). Documenting one of the main reasons for the establishment of the Canadian *Masses* five years later, the editorial went on to attack a recent censorship ruling on the American *New Masses*: 'Recently, a magazine called "New Masses" was declared "Unfit" by the Customs Department of the government. There is only one reason why such a magazine should be refused the privilege of the Canadian mails, and this is that it is "progressive." Unlike the Tabloid Press, "New Masses" is strictly educational' (5). As we have seen in the case of *Masses*, the *Woman Worker* was not itself subject to prosecution under Canadian censorship laws (see chapter 1: 33). In coming to the defence of *New Masses*, the *Woman Worker* demonstrated its solidarity with an international leftist magazine culture and its literary values. Custance's most definite gesture toward literary internationalism appeared in the September 1927 issue, in which she printed a page with selections from *The Sacco-Vanzetti Anthology of Verse* (1927), edited by Henry Harrison (Custance, 'Tribute'). At a time of reactionary conservatism, when American leftist literature could have been stopped at the Canadian border, Custance's publication of these poems in commemoration of the execution in August 1927 of Sacco and Vanzetti is a declaration of international solidarity and a defiance of repressive government legislation.

Just as *New Masses* in the United States was to a certain extent an educational forum for members of the John Reed Clubs, so the *Woman Worker* served a similar pedagogical function in Canada: its didacticism was intended to inform and instruct WLL members 'to champion the Protection of Womanhood, and the Cause of the Workers generally' (Custance, 'Success' 33). This didacticism was certainly evident in its literary content, particularly in those poems specifically addressed to working-class women: 'Wanted – Women M.P.'s / (Dedicated to Agnes M[a]cPhail, M.P.)' (August 1926) and 'A Word to Wage Slaves' (April 1929). The sex-worker speaker of 'Prostitutes,' however, aggressively targets the dominant classes as well as the repressive church and state institutions she deems responsible for her social and economic status. This tactic is typical of the leftist's tendentious, anti-capitalist manner; her leftist polemic focuses not on women's sexual oppression by men but on an economic critique of prostitution. 'This is not to say that it was seen as a form of work like any other,' Sangster and Hobbs caution, 'but rather prostitution was portrayed as an evil by-product of capitalist social relations' (160). Feminist issues in 'Prostitutes' are implicit yet marginal, edged out by its leftist priorities. Characteristic of literary leftism, and anticipating the communicative crises in Livesay's leftist poetry of the early 1930s, 'Prostitutes' never reached the social classes at which it aimed its socio-economic critique. As an educational forum, the *Woman Worker* and its literary content was limited in its audience to the female, working-class, and predominantly communist members of the WLLs.

Prefiguring the organizational and communicative problems encountered by later magazines of the Canadian left – *Masses*, *New Frontier*, and *New Frontiers* – the *Woman Worker* was constrained by its distribution among the WLLs. At the same time, the magazine could not have survived for almost three years without the WLLs' financial support; its economic base in the leagues anticipates the collectivist economies of non-commercial magazines on the Canadian left, supported by social, cultural, and political organizations. This organizational affiliation had a reciprocal effect on the magazine, since it also chiefly depended upon contributions from the WLLs. If the *Woman Worker* published poetry and fiction infrequently, it probably reflected the priorities among women activists in a labour organization: we need only recall, for example, Livesay's decline in literary production during her activist period in the early 1930s. And though the *Woman Worker* printed 'things that are overlooked by the other magazines,' the policy of publishing only writing about 'life, real life, not imaginations' may have staved off more literary contributions.

With the illness of Custance, reported in the October 1928 issue, followed by her death in July 1929, the *Woman Worker* lost its founding editor. The Toronto WLL continued the magazine in her absence for several months, but its final instalment was the April 1929 issue (Sangster 52). Having appeared monthly since July 1926, the *Woman Worker* far outstripped the erratic two-year print run of *Masses*, its successor in Canadian leftist magazine culture. Not until Fairley founded *New Frontiers* in 1952 did leftists in Canada produce a more enduring magazine.

Paper Kingdom in the Queen City: Mary Davidson and the *Twentieth Century*

Toronto in the 1930s witnessed the appearance and continuation of a number of left-oriented cultural magazines, including *Masses*, the *Canadian Forum*, and *New Frontier*. Edited and published in Toronto, these little magazines formed a distinct local magazine culture. While they have garnered significant attention in literary and cultural histories, another Toronto-based magazine of the period has gone completely unnoticed in the historical record. Leslie Bishop, an Oxford-educated expatriate, and his Canadian-born wife, Mary Davidson, founded the *Twentieth Century*, a short-lived literary-arts monthly that ran from November 1932 to November 1933. Davidson served as its editor, Bishop as its manager and co-editor; both contributed editorials, reviews, poems, and short stories to the magazine. Davidson likely handled the secretarial duties, and by the sixth issue (February 1933) Paul Ryley took over responsibilities for advertising. After the demise of the *Twentieth Century*, Bishop later wrote a thinly disguised autobiographical novel, *Paper Kingdom* (1936), a *roman à clef* about a fictional literary-arts magazine called the *New Conquest*, founded at the height of the Depression in the fictional city of Macgregor. If Bishop's novel is even a remotely reliable record of the *Twentieth Century*, it would appear that the only woman affiliated with the magazine was more or less employed in a limited clerical role. It is more likely, though, that in the novel Bishop has effaced Davidson's editorial role, since her regular editorial and literary contributions to the *Twentieth Century* indicate that hers was far more involved position than *Paper Kingdom* suggests. It is equally probable that Bishop and Davidson shared editorial responsibilities and that the editor figure in the novel is a composite of the *Twentieth Century*'s manager and editor. For the most part, Bishop's novel chronicles the shady deals that the editor makes with publishers, advertisers, and subscribers in order to bring out his magazine. Like the impoverished *New Conquest*, the *Twentieth Century* solicited copious amounts of advertising as the main source of revenue. The prominence of advertising in the *Twentieth Century* signalled its failed attempt at commercial viability in opposition to its non-commercial counterparts of Toronto's cultural left. For the manager and the editor of the *Twentieth Century*, the commercial capital of Toronto's Depression-era businesses fed into their conceptions of cultural modernity, articulated both in their editorials, reviews, poems, and short stories and in the advertising they printed in the magazine.

The collision of aesthetic and commercial, and by extension military, interests is immediately apparent in the selection of cover art for the magazine: a print (c. 1932) by British modernist C.R.W. Nevinson depicts a figure clearly modelled on Rodin's *Le Penseur* (1880) above the urban masses led by a flag-bearing revolutionary, with bayonets, cannon barrels, and a crane arm jutting up in the foreground and skyscrapers, ships, and a squadron of planes looming in the background. The print is contemporaneous with Nevinson's better-known painting of the same subject, entitled *The Twentieth Century* (1932–5), which he claimed represented 'the Clash between Thought, Mechanical Invention, Race Idolatry, and the Regimentation of Youth' (qtd. in Cohen 51). Taking its name from Nevinson's painting, the *Twentieth Century* presents the colossal figure of *Le Penseur* as the embodiment of the magazine's motive – 'to reflect the progress of Canadian Literature, Art, Music, and Drama and to present as much of the best scientific and economic thought as is essential to the intelligent understanding of the modern world' – declared in the inaugural editorial. At the same time, the Nevinson print reflects the editors' prescient warnings about the rise of fascism in Europe, the resurgence of economic conflict between nations, and the preparations for another global war. That Rodin's sculpture derives from his unfinished *La Porte d'Enfer* (*The Gates of Hell*) is apposite here: the turbulent modern city that surrounds the thinker figure on the cover of the *Twentieth Century* is analogous to that infernal, apocalyptic scene. Recalling his futurist period during the First World War, Nevinson's design is a typical wartime/interwar modernist urban scene: the thinker figure composes the still, sculptural centre amid the frenzied city in the machine age. This city may be any modern metropolis, but its localized association with Toronto – which was obviously not Nevinson's original intention – is implied by the inclusion of the magazine's postal address at the foot of the cover. Nevinson's universalized subject, the twentieth century, depicts an iconic site of urban modernity, whether Toronto or elsewhere. Like Eliot's, Woolf's, and Lewis's London, Joyce's Dublin, Baudelaire's Paris, Dos Passos's New York, and Klein's Montreal, the *Twentieth Century*'s Toronto is thus emblematized as a locus of cosmopolitan, interwar modernism.

Visual and textual icons of modernity are equally prevalent in the magazine's interior. A survey across issues should provide a representative montage of the various discourses of modernity that run through the advertising copy printed in the *Twentieth Century*. Publisher Sir Isaac Pitman and Sons ran an ad for its 'Art and Life' series with the headline 'Culture and Modernity' (November 1932), a religious magazine called the *New Outlook* hoped to attract the 'Modern-minded Man or Woman With More or Less Intelligence' (December 1932), the Boris Volkoff School of Dance defined itself as 'An Essentially Modern School' (December 1932), the Premier Vacuum Cleaner Company endeavoured 'To Help the 20th Century Woman' and 'To Give Women Greater Freedom' by insisting that 'No home is really modern without a Premier Spic-Span' (February 1933), Oldsmobile raced to 'set the style pace' with its 'completely modern cars' (March 1933), and freelance photographer Stephen Jones exhibited an example of his 'Modern Photography' in which he claimed to capture 'that fugitive moment between two expressions' (April 1933). This catalogue of advertising in the magazine indicates the rather blatant ways in which advertisers manipulated discourses of modernity as signifiers of technological, social, intellectual, and aesthetic progress. Typical of advertising copy of the period, the advertisements give prominence to the text: they deploy textual strategies of allurement, where verbal signifiers either stand alone or serve to explicate the modernity of visual icons.

This textual emphasis in the advertisements is replicated in a series of prose sketches signed 'The Gentleman with the Eyeglass,' a collection of impressionistic observations by a *flâneur* figure (Benjamin 156) that advertise the wares of Toronto merchants and artisans. Beginning with the early March 1933 issue, these sketches are laid out in the format of an advertisement, and each instalment catalogues high-end commodities available for purchase at select shops and studios in Toronto. The anonymous 'Gentleman' is, in all probability, none other than the manager and co-editor of the *Twentieth Century*, Leslie Bishop. His creation of the Gentleman with the Eyeglass as a persona, a distinct personality whose aesthetic disposition leads him into what Marx and later Walter Benjamin call the 'phantasmagoria' of commodity culture (Marx 83; Benjamin 156), is backed by editorials Bishop and his co-editor, Davidson, contributed to the magazine.

Their joint defence of personality against the depersonalizing conditions of urbanization, industrialization, and mechanization serves to critique the consequences of modernization and their impact upon the individual. In an unsigned editorial for the third issue (December 1932) entitled 'What's the Use,' the co-editors lament the loss of personality in an age of impersonality: 'It has become difficult in these days of crowds and machines, – of industries that swallow humans each morning and pour them forth each night, of roaring cars and buses and jumping lighted words, of sudden recognitions and sudden forgettings, to realize what those old writers meant when they spoke of "Man" ... The breakdown of Man could only mean, for humans, the end of the world' (2). To a later issue (March 1933), Davidson contributed a short story ('Geneva Evans') and Bishop a poem ('Expatriate'); both texts place emphasis upon individual personalities, Davidson's short story through an interior monologue in a stream-of-consciousness style and Bishop's poem through a confessional free-verse lyric. Geneva Evans in Davidson's story meditates upon her solitary life as an unmarried woman of thirty-three and imagines the scene of her own funeral, and the persona in Bishop's poem contemplates his expatriate life, 'Experienced alone, / Unreal and laughable / Both to my fathers and my pallbearers.' The solemnity with which both Davidson and Bishop approach these isolated figures and their deaths is continuous with their apocalyptic considerations of the death of personality: the utter alienation of the individual in the modern world is, in their view, a symptom of the breakdown, even the annihilation, of human existence. Bishop's poem 'Children of Darkness' (April 1933) speaks further to the consequences of alienated social relations within an impersonal mass culture, where those who 'live in secret / So that they may touch each other / And remain unknown, / Speak to each other without revealing / What they think' he condemns because 'They are the breeders of war – / The public eruption en masse / Of ugly fears.' Witnessing Bishop's critical attitudes toward alienated individuals and the public unrest that allegedly ensues from their failure of communication, we may recall the individual thinker set above the thronged, revolutionary masses on the cover of the *Twentieth Century*. Is the thinker an icon of modern, urban alienation, or is he the artist or intellectual who transcends the 'ugly fears' of the masses?

Bishop's ambivalence toward the 'public eruption' of collectivist social action, the Gentleman with the Eyeglass's consumerist predilection for high culture, and the editors' joint advocacy for the individual intellectual and artist constitute the *Twentieth Century*'s definite dissent

from leftist social and political organizations affiliated with contemporary magazines in Toronto, such as the *Canadian Forum* and *Masses*.
While Davidson, in a review of E.J. Pratt's *Many Moods* (1932), employs
a masculinist discourse in praising his poetry's and the nation's 'viril-
ity' that is typical of both leftists and nationalists of the period, her
romanticist portrait of labour and its relationship to modern Canadian
poetry would have likely failed to satisfy the realist appetites of the
editors, readers, and writers of the *Forum* and *Masses*. 'Canada is not a
country for retired nature-lovers to praise,' Davidson writes. 'She is
a country, as yet, of hewers of wood and drawers of water and her
poetry must have the strength of her workers' (23). There are, however, no labourers or labour-oriented poets represented in any of the
poems or short stories published in the *Twentieth Century*. Davidson's
passing invocation of leftist discourse is more an imitation of the style
of reviews and poems published in the *Forum* and *Masses* than a
genuine call for workers' poetry. In this respect, we may be justified in
calling into question the *Twentieth Century*'s affiliations with leftist
magazine culture, for the editors seem attracted to the spectacle of
socialism and its increasing fashionability among artists and intellectuals of the early 1930s, but perhaps only as a stylish way of marketing their magazine. As Bishop's portrait of the magazine's socialism in
Paper Kingdom attests, 'the scarlet cover of the first number' caught the
eye of authorities in a city that 'was, in truth, being thoroughly
menaced by more or less imaginary Communists and extremely real
policemen' (171, 170). As much as its provocative cover and occasional
pro-socialist articles may have attracted the *unwanted* attention of 'real
policemen,' the *Twentieth Century* may have equally *wanted* to employ
the spectacle of the 'red menace' as an advertising ploy to gain a
foothold among leftist artists and intellectuals.

However one regards their methods of self-promotion, Bishop and
Davidson deserve credit for publishing the work of an international
cast of notable authors, including essays by British bookseller and
publisher Basil Blackwell ('Children and Reading' [December 1932]),
philosopher Bertram Russell ('The Influence of Technique on Politics'
[April 1933]), Macmillan of Canada publisher Hugh Eayrs ('Publishing
Books in Canada' [April 1933]), and Group of Seven artist Arthur
Lismer ('Art in Canada,' a series of thirteen essays [November
1932–November 1933]), a short story by Leo Kennedy ('Death Comes
to the Undertaker'), and poems by E.J. Pratt ('Two Sonnets' [Novem-
ber 1932]). Still, most of the fiction and poetry in the magazine was

written by the editors themselves. Bishop and Davidson were typical little-magazine editors and aspiring authors, a young and ambitious literary couple who created the *Twentieth Century* as a public forum for their own modernist poetry and fiction. Given that they actually made a point of paying their contributors, which few little magazines could manage, it would seem in some ways a wise decision to have published so much of their own work, but in other ways it emphasizes the financial folly of a magazine whose editors unwisely decided to expand its size – likely to increase advertising revenues – at a time when the global economy was suffering through its *annus terribilis* in 1933.

Predictably, when Bishop published *Paper Kingdom* in 1936, the managing editor of the *Canadian Forum*, Eleanor Godfrey, reviewed his novel unfavourably and observed that the fate of the *Twentieth Century* should not be 'unfamiliar to anyone who has watched the birth and early death of similar ventures, undertaken as a rule without even a shoestring' (30). At the height of the Depression in 1932–3, the *Twentieth Century* relied on a commercial culture in Toronto whose existence was itself increasingly under threat and consequently less and less inclined to invest dwindling advertising budgets in a limited-circulation literary-arts magazine. During its single year of operation, the *Twentieth Century* and its advertisers capitalized on discourses of modernity; but with the continuing global economic crisis throughout the 1930s, the hardened promise of modernity's actual progress and success under a capitalist system must have seemed more and more like Marx's vision of that historical conjuncture when all that is solid melts into air. Rather than fall in with Toronto's active communist-socialist magazine culture, the *Twentieth Century* collapsed in a state of financial crisis after a one-year run. The expatriate *flâneur* Bishop fell down and lost his paper crown, and his editor Davidson came tumbling after.

In the Making: The Ridleys and the *Crucible*

Around the same time as the Toronto PAC was making arrangements for the launch of *Masses*, the first issue of the *Crucible* appeared in March 1932. If only by name, the *Crucible* connotes the revolutionary and experimental intent of its leftist and modernist contemporaries. Like *Masses*'s emergence out of a discussion group convened in 1928, the *Crucible* evolved out of the Writers' Craft Club (WCC), founded in

1925. The WCC's approximately twenty members were drawn from across Canada, and its 'official organ' was circulated in manuscript form between 1925 and 1932 ('Old Friends'; Ridley and Ridley, 'Open').[1] Unlike the national organizations of the PAC and the CAA, formed of local branches, the WCC and the *Crucible* brought together individual authors, rather than arts or literary collectives, into a national body. Among its Toronto members were the founding editors of the *Crucible*, sisters Hilda and Laura Ridley. In addition to the Ridleys, who served as managing editors, the *Crucible* enlisted an editorial committee, originally including members from Manitoba, Ontario, Quebec, and Nova Scotia and later expanded east and west to New Brunswick, Saskatchewan, Alberta, and British Columbia, overseas to England, and south of the border to Maine and Florida. Although international in its editorial membership, the *Crucible* remained committed to Canadian cultural nationalism; its patriotic contributors tended to 'paint the native maple' as often as its CAA contemporaries (Scott, 'Canadian').

Launched with the subtitle 'A Quarterly Dedicated to Canadian Literature in the Making,' the *Crucible* advertised itself as a nationalist publication. Emblematic of its national organization, the magazine's early covers were emblazoned with the crests of the nine provinces. Given the origins of both the WCC and the *Crucible*, the design and marketing of the magazine as a nationalist print organ are signs of its historical relationship to earlier Canadian magazine cultures. Its opening editorial in March 1932 lays claim to a nationalist heritage, tracing the genealogy of the magazine back to 1925: 'when one of its editors was reading manuscripts for *The Canadian Magazine*, she was impressed by the excellent quality of much of the material submitted that, through lack of space or other considerations, could not be published' (Ridley and Ridley, 'Open'). That reader was Hilda Ridley. Her distinction as a reader for the *Canadian Magazine* served to establish the *Crucible* as a periodical with respectable affiliations. Borrowing on the cultural capital of the *Canadian Magazine* (1893–1939), she lent to her magazine dedicated to Canadian literature the history of a popular general-interest periodical devoted to the development of a national cultural consciousness since the 1890s.

Although Hilda Ridley gives only a vague account of her responsibilities as a reader for the *Canadian Magazine*, her experience with the magazine may well have provided an informal apprenticeship for her editorial work on the *Crucible*. Most important, her apprenticeship with a commercial magazine taught her the value of having a business plan. In a May 1932 form distributed to prospective members of the *Crucble* editorial board, she listed two necessary qualifications: '1. Literary ability, and a fearless, independent attitude of mind. 2. Sufficient business ability and interest in the development of the magazine' (Letter to A. Ellis Jones, 24 May 1932, CLCF, Correspondence from other organizations file). Both literary and business abilities were, therefore, deemed of equal importance to the *Crucible*'s success. Editors were required to secure 'three subscriptions (or the equivalent of $3 a quarter),' and this income was 'applied to the ALL IMPORTANT PRINTING FUND.' Proceeds from any additional subscriptions and any advertisements solicited by editors were shared on the basis of a 50 per cent commission. In addition to the modest financial advantages offered to members of the editorial board, they were guaranteed recognition on the masthead and given rights 'to pass judgment on the contents of the magazine, to suggest material, and to make contributions to each issue.' Demonstrating her business savvy, Ridley appended to the form two pages of favourable comments about the March 1932 issue drawn from recently published reviews (in the *Mail and Empire*, the *Globe*, the *Saint John Times-Globe*, the *Montreal Daily Star*, and the *Regina Leader*) and correspondence from independent authors, officers of local branches of the CAA, the president of the Canadian Literature Club of Toronto, the provincial librarian and archivist of British Columbia, and fellow members of the WCC. Just as advertising and subscription revenues were crucial to the business interests of the *Crucible*, so self-advertising helped to promote the magazine's literary interests by demonstrating its appeal to a diverse and nationally dispersed group of readers, subscribers, contributors, and potential editorial board members. By taking the commercially oriented model of the *Canadian Magazine* and transposing it to a cooperative literary culture, Hilda Ridley effectively established a viable business plan for her non-commercial magazine.

She also brought to the *Crucible* her modest reputation as a literary journalist and regular contribtor to nationally circulated commercial magazines. As a writer for the *Canadian Magazine* in the early 1920s, she had contributed nine features entitled 'Great Friendships,' a series that chronicles the personal relationships among British and American eighteenth- and nineteenth-century literary figures. Published in monthly instalments between October 1922 and July 1923, these vignettes about famous authors anticipate by three decades the biography for which Ridley is best known, *The Story of L.M. Montgomery* (1956). This three-decade interval bears witness to the emergence of Hilda Ridley's national consciousness as literary biographer, moving from writing lives of eminent British and American authors to the life of a popular Canadian author. Her involvement as a reader and writer for the *Canadian Magazine* inevitably played a formative role in her espousal of a cultural-nationalist ideology.

Coincident with her literary journalism for the *Canadian Magazine*, Hilda Ridley contributed features about women to *Saturday Night*. For twelve years she was a member of the 'contributing staff' of *Saturday Night* ('Hilda'); prior to her employment on its staff, she was, 'successively, associate editor of two women's magazines' (Robinson). Between October 1922 and October 1929, she published seventeen articles in the women's section of *Saturday Night* about distinguished women living in or visiting Canada. To these portraits she added numerous scholarly articles about Canadian women, which appeared in the *Dalhousie Review* between April 1926 and July 1946. Ridley published a pamphlet called *A Synopsis of Woman Suffrage in Canada* in 1933 and a small collection of essays largely derived from her *Dalhousie Review* and *Saturday Night* articles, entitled *The Post-War Woman*, in 1941. These publications about the lives of women in Canada make plain her gender consciousness and its overlap with her nationalist interests. Given her writings as a historian of modern women in Canada, it is fitting that Hilda Ridley should now be recognized (albeit belatedly) as one of the first woman editors of a modern literary magazine in Canada. Her journalism and scholarship from the 1920s, 1930s, and 1940s present a range of perspectives on the modern woman, her social, political, cultural, and economic interests, and her involvement in literary activities. In her roles as editor, journalist, and scholar, Ridley is herself the embodiment of the modern woman who figures prominently in her articles from this period.

Though on occasion she also published poetry, Hilda Ridley was outflanked on this front by her sister and co-editor, if only in sheer output of verse. In 1943 the Crucible Press, the magazine's imprint, issued Laura Ridley's *Christmas Eve and Other Poems*, one in a series entitled the Carillon Poetry Chapbooks. Hilda Ridley did not publish a collection of her own poems, either with the Crucible Press or elsewhere. But both Ridley sisters contributed poems to the first Crucible Press publication, *A New Canadian Anthology* (1938), co-edited by Alan Creighton and Hilda Ridley. That the anthology was co-edited by only one of the

Ridley sisters speaks to the division of editorial labour on the *Crucible* itself. According to H.T.D. Robinson's brief history of the *Crucible*, Hilda Ridley alone founded the WCC and the *Crucible*; Laura Ridley primarily attended to the advertising end of the magazine. The Ridleys were similarly divided in their poetic sensibilities, as their respective contributions to the Crucible Press anthology attest. Counterposed to Hilda Ridley's impersonal political sonnet 'Sir Wilfrid Laurier,' Laura Ridley's quatrains in 'Beauty' and 'Late Spring in Canada' manifest a subjective, lyrical manner devoid of such topical content. Laura Ridley's verse is, according to her sister's generalization, typical of 'the poetry produced by women ... [in] that it is nearly always intensely subjective – concerned with intimate emotions evoked by the contemplation of nature, or introspective to a tortuous degree' (*Post-War* 10). Both poets, however, are equally nationalist in their choice of Canadian subjects and conservative in their use of conventional closed forms. These tendencies in terms of form and content are predominant not only in the selections for the magazine but also in the Crucible anthology. Just as the appellation 'new' is a misnomer for the anthology, so the connotation 'experimental' is, if restricted to the magazine's poetry and its editors' poetics, misrepresentative of the *Crucible*.

If the Ridleys' inaugural editorial of March 1932 declared the *Crucible*'s nationalism, it also proclaimed the magazine's modernism: 'The very word "Crucible" suggests that the function of our magazine is experimental ... The writers we shall especially welcome are those who are making an honest endeavour to express their real selves – and those who are in the process of "becoming"' (Ridley and Ridley, 'Open'). The editors continued in this progressive idiom, echoing their modernist little-magazine counterparts in their critique of commercial magazines:

> Most of our periodicals cater necessarily to the public at large, its current tastes, fads, and needs, and writers who contribute to them must keep this fact constantly in mind. Their editors are in their places to see that they do so, and to say to would-be contributors who do not conform, 'You shall not pass.'
>
> It is evident that the writer with an original slant whose work does not fit into the existing scheme of things, runs the risk of failing to impress himself, and his message, esthetic, dynamic, or premonitory, is lost, – or he conforms, and the public is presented, not with the real man, but with a caricature.

With such an editorial position, the Ridleys' ambivalence about commercial magazine culture is evident. Granted that Hilda Ridley founded the WCC and the *Crucible* after determining that many of the submissions she was reading for the *Canadian Magazine* went unpublished because of 'lack of space or other considerations,' the first *Crucible* editorial at once capitalizes on the *Canadian Magazine*'s reputation as a mass-culture periodical and launches a critique of its commercialism. The WCC and the privately circulated version of the *Crucible* emerged shortly after changes in the *Canadian Magazine*'s format in May 1924 moved it away from its origins as a general-interest journal of 'Politics, Science, Art and Literature' toward a mass-market periodical in the style of *Saturday Night*. Where poetry had once been the subject of features in the *Canadian Magazine*, it was relegated to a decorative role after the implementation of a new editorial mandate in that month ('Larger' 19). It would seem, then, that this transition in the *Canadian Magazine* precipitated the formation of the *Crucible* as an alternative to commercial magazines.

That Hilda Ridley had been a reader for the *Canadian Magazine* and a 'contributing staff member' of *Saturday Night* adds authority and conviction to the *Crucible*'s critique of such commercial magazines and its editor's experimentation with alternative means of publication ('Hilda'). With an idealism characteristic of socialist economists of the time, the Ridleys even envisioned their printed magazine not as a commercial product on sale to the general public but as a cooperative venture supported by writers themselves: 'Co-operation, we hope, is to be the keynote of our changing economic system, and we want it to be the keynote of our own undertaking' (Ridley and Ridley, 'Open'). Although the *Crucible* may not have been experimental in terms of its poets' or its editors' poetics, its cooperative means of production and circulation among the members of the WCC between 1925 and 1932 was itself a cultural experiment that succeeded in securing sufficient national interest and economic resources for the publication of the *Crucible* as a printed magazine from March 1932 to April–May 1943.

Among those who were 'making an honest endeavour to express their real selves ... in the process of "becoming"' in the *Crucible* were younger women poets such as Anne Marriott and P.K. Page. Marriott's second published poem, 'Strangers,' appeared in the Christmas 1933 issue, a poem that may have been solicited by the Victoria member of the *Crucible* editorial committee, M. Eugenie Perry. After her introduction to the Victoria poetry group of the CAA in 1934, Marriott did not publish again in the *Crucible* until 1940. Between the fall of 1940 and the spring of 1942, she submitted two more poems, 'I Cannot Write –' (autumn–Christmas 1940) and 'Resurrection' (spring 1941). None of these poems appeared in the poetry collections of her early period. Similarly, neither Page's 'Light and Shade' (Christmas 1938) nor her 'Safety' (Christmas–New Year 1940), published in the *Crucible*, appeared in her poetry collections of the 1940s. All these early uncollected poems may have contributed to the process of Marriott and Page 'becoming' poets, their coming to lyric expression of their 'real selves,' but their exposure to new little-magazine groups in Victoria, Vancouver, and Montreal during the early 1940s propelled them, as we have seen in previous chapters, toward a modernist poetics of impersonality.

The Ridleys once more made overtures toward modernist poetry and poetics in their winter 1936 editorial (Ridley and Ridley, 'Word'). They later ran advertisements beginning in the Christmas–New Year 1940 issue in which Alan Creighton, Hilda Ridley's co-editor for the Crucible Press's *A New Canadian Anthology* (1938), offered the magazine's contributors editorial services to help 'modernize' their poetry (Creighton, 'Modernize'). Yet the discrepancy between such editorial gestures and advertising in the magazine and the actual selection of poems indicates a contradiction between intention and action on the part of the *Crucible*'s editors.[2] Its advocacy of modernism in poetry either amounted to an empty gesture or, if genuine, ended in failure. Like other modernist poets who ignored the *Crucible*, Marriott, once she became involved with the *Contemporary Verse* group, and Page, once she joined the *Preview* group, found no occasion to contribute to the *Crucible*.

According to the editorial in the February–March 1943 issue, the *Crucible* was in fact suspended for a two-year period after the spring 1941 issue. In the interim, Hilda Ridley had moved to Ottawa 'due to the war' and resigned her position as managing editor, which was taken over by John S. Crosbie of Halifax (Crosbie). She remained an Ottawa-area regional editor for the last two issues of the new *Crucible*. Its abrupt reception by John Sutherland was a telling sign that Canadian magazine culture had changed its guard during the *Crucible*'s two-year hiatus. Sutherland's review in the 19 March 1943 issue of *First Statement* notes that the new *Crucible* 'has become streamlined and adjusted to meet popular taste as far as possible,' and that it 'puts the stamp on its own badness, and claims with the old gall that it is

"attaining recognition for Canadian writers"' ('Crucible's Standard').
The wartime generation's assessment of the *Crucible* must have
alarmed Hilda Ridley, whose expressed intention as its founder had
been to counteract the detrimental effect of 'popular taste' on poetry
published in commercial magazines. According to Sutherland, the new
Crucible had succumbed to commercial magazine design, where
poetry merely serves a decorative function: 'Set in niches between
prose are a series of pieces [of poetry] intended to entertain the reader
for a passing moment.' While Sutherland's caricature of the new *Crucible* is typical of his polemical style, his sharp assessment must have
resonated with that of the magazine's readership, since the April–May
1943 issue was its last. The *Crucible*'s experiment in non-commercial
magazine production had been superseded by the wartime generation's modernist little magazines. For the *Crucible*, this transition in
little-magazine culture coincided with its decline and the ascendancy
of the modernist magazines.

After the demise of the *Crucible*, Hilda Ridley published an article in
the July 1944 issue of the *Dalhousie Review* on the subject of the contemporary writer and his or her relationship to commercial and non-
commercial magazine cultures. 'The Literary Aspirant' is, in some
ways, her lament for the passing of the *Crucible* and, in others, her
advocacy for a non-commercial magazine culture. Addressing the
hypothetical figure of an aspiring young writer who refuses to
conform to the strictures of the commercial press, she describes the
non-commercial magazines available to the writer for publication:

> A few 'quality' magazines servive [*sic*], but these serve the interests of a
> cultured minority. Contributors are carefully selected, and they are often
> the members of a privileged staff. Year after year, we witness the rise and
> demise of small, independent magazines whose editors declare that they
> have but one desire – to discover original talent. Sometimes, in turning
> the pages of these derelicts of a decade or so ago, one is impressed by the
> rare quality of a poem, so flawless in execution and so vital in substance
> that one marvels ... Surely the names of such writers must have become
> well known. But no! – the signatures evoke no recognition. These creators
> of vital beauty are 'to fame unknown,' – and the world is poorer, perhaps,
> because they were effectually silenced. (181)

Taking Katherine Mansfield as an instance of the exemplary 'literary
aspirant,' Ridley sketches the story of Mansfield's dependence for

early publication on a little magazine called the *Blue Review* (May–July 1913), edited by her husband, John Middleton Murry, and on another called *Signature* (October–November 1915), edited by Murry, D.H. Lawrence, and Mansfield herself.[3] After the demise of these little magazines, Mansfield apparently had no place to publish her writing until in 1919 Murry became an editor of the *Athenaeum*, the prestigious London periodical where she published her short stories and gained the notice of book publishers (Ridley, 'Literary' 181–2). 'Such an experience,' Ridley submits, 'offers an eloquent plea for the existence of small, privately printed journals, edited with vision' (182). While she is aware that the crux of her story about Mansfield is that she found her audience and earned her literary reputation only after securing her place in a prominent commercial periodical, Ridley insists upon the value of 'small, short-lived publications, edited by youthful enthusiasts,' such as those in which Mansfield started off. Although she never mentions her own editorial history, Ridley makes a tacit case for the value of publications such as the *Crucible* and editors such as herself and her sister, aligning these with such modernist little magazines as the *Blue Review* and *Signature* and such editors as Mansfield and Murry. That Hilda Ridley should look to Mansfield and England for a success story might indicate the degree of her disillusionment with Canadian literature and little-magazine culture, which had yet to produce a modernist of Mansfield's calibre. But even though she had just experienced the collapse of the *Crucible* and its unfavourable reception among Canada's emergent modernists, Ridley could still appreciate the value of modernist little-magazine cultures to Canadian literature in the making.

Taking Care of Business: Eleanor Godfrey and the *Canadian Forum*

Despite her position as managing editor of the *Canadian Forum* (1920–2000) for two terms, 1935–7 and 1939–47, Eleanor Godfrey has received scant attention in histories and memoirs of the magazine. Her historically undervalued managerial position on the *Forum* editorial board exemplifies the chronic marginalization of women's editorial labour in Canadian cultural history. J.L. Granatstein and Peter Stevens neither mention her in their preface to *Forum: Canadian Life and Letters, 1920–70* (1972) nor select anything of hers for inclusion in this anthology of writings from the *Forum*. Neither Sandra Djwa in her article

'The *Canadian Forum*: Literary Catalyst' nor Margaret Prang in her essay 'F.H.U. of *The Canadian Forum*' refer to Godfrey. Rose Potvin in *Passion and Conviction: The Letters of Graham Spry*, Djwa in *The Politics of the Imagination: A Life of F.R. Scott*, and Elspeth Cameron in *Earle Birney: A Life* neglect to name the *Forum*'s managing editor during Spry's tenure as editor and publisher of the *Forum* (July 1935–May 1936), during Scott's tenure as a *Forum* contributing editor (July 1935–September 1936, March–September 1939) and fellow member of its editorial board (October 1936–February 1939), and during Birney's tenure as its literary editor (December 1936–November 1940). Of the retrospectives collected in the *Forum*'s fiftieth-anniversary issue, Godfrey rates only two passing glances (Frye, 'Rear'; Horn, 'Forum'). Only Carlton McNaught in 'Volume Thirty: In Retrospect,' Ann Stephenson Cowan in '*The Canadian Forum* 1929–1950: An Historical Study in Canadian Literary Theory and Practice,' Michiel Horn in *The League for Social Reconstruction: Intellectual Origins of the Democratic Left in Canada 1930–1942* (131, 165), and Birney in *Spreading Time* (28–9) call attention to Godfrey's activities on the editorial board of the *Forum*. These usually brief citations, however, are unequal to her central role in the management of the magazine through the end of the Depression and the war years and to her written contributions that addressed issues of commercialism, feminism, modernism, and nationalism in literature and literary-magazine culture.

Soon after its formation, Godfrey joined the 'New Group' of the *Forum*, an editorial collective established after Graham Spry purchased the magazine from its former editor and owner, Stephen Cartwright, in July 1935. She was named the new managing editor on the masthead of the November issue. Headed by Spry, the 'New Group' declared its intentions in the July editorial: 'The principle of free controversy will be adhered to by the new group and it is hoped that the Forum will be looked upon as a journal in which advanced thought may be expressed without the odious blue-penciling that reduces most attempts at originality to a uniform pattern of maudlin commercialism' (Spry et al.). Having expressed its anti-commercialism, the group proudly noted its reduction in the cost of production, thereby referring obliquely to the *Forum*'s recent acquisition of a second-hand press (Horn, *League* 129). Even though Spry had obtained the press in order to reduce printing costs, the *Forum* quickly fell into financial trouble. He then appealed to his colleagues in the League for Social Reconstruction (LSR) for assistance; by May 1936 the league had assumed control of the *Forum*. As the LSR national secretary, Helen Marsh, announced in a postscript to the minutes of the 1936 national convention: 'The Forum, an excellent monthly to which all LSR members should be subscribers, is now the official organ of the LSR, and as such will consistently express its views' (qtd. in Horn, *League* 130–1).

From December 1935 to May 1936, editorial positions were divided among the board members: Frank H. Underhill (politics), H.J. Davis (literature), G.M.A. Grube (book reviews), and Pegi Nicol (art). These editorial assignments were not distinguished as such on the masthead after June 1936, except for the position of managing editor. Given this division of editorial labour, we may well suspect that Godfrey had little to do with the literary affairs of the magazine. From Horn's history of the LSR, we might also be led to believe that Godfrey was a minor player on the editorial board of the *Forum*; his first of only two references to her managerial activities is a quotation of her 19 March 1940 remark on the *Forum*'s troubled financial situation. Godfrey presumably had a great deal more to contribute than platitudes ('It is a pity the Forum is such a money sponge' [qtd. in Horn, *League* 165]). Carleton McNaught is more generous to Godfrey in a series of articles published on the occasion of the *Forum*'s thirtieth anniversary; in the third of these, he notes her appointment as managing editor, details her responsibilities, 'which at that time involved the onerous duty of planning each issue, organizing material, and looking after make-up,' and commends her for sustaining the *Forum* through the war years (58). Birney also recognizes Godfrey's editorial and production work and, further, indicates that she did in fact play a role in the literary composition of the magazine: 'Poetry ... because it was generally shorter than anything else, had sometimes to be treated as filler. When seven or eight of us sat around Eleanor Godfrey's diningroom table, making up the dummy far into the night, there would be a cry from her or from Mark Farrell, the business manager, for something between ten-to-fifteen lines to fill out a column' (*Spreading* 29). Birney, as literary editor, was therefore subject to the everyday, material concerns of magazine production, which Godfrey handled – like so many other women involved in little-magazine culture of the 1920s, 1930s, and 1940s. Cowan, given the advantage of private interviews with former *Forum* editors in 1973, composes the most complete biographical portrait of Godfrey available: a composite record and study of her interactions with other members of the *Forum* board of editors, her responsibilities as managing editor, and her critical responses as a reviewer. But because of the scope of Cowan's history of the *Forum*'s first three decades, her portrait of Godfrey is necessarily cropped, though still valuable for its representation of a dynamic editorial figure among the more often chronicled men and women of the *Forum*.

Though historians have been inattentive to Godfrey, the *Forum*'s readers, correspondents, and contributors during the Second World War could not have missed her on the masthead. For fear of persecution by authorities and employers, the *Forum* board of editors removed their names from the masthead after the October 1939 issue (Horn, *League* 165). Only Godfrey, who resumed her position as managing editor in November 1939,[4] and L.A. Morris, as business manager, remained on the masthead for the duration of the war; they were joined by assistant editor (and former Crucible anthology co-editor) Alan Creighton in June 1943. While other board members carried out their editorial duties anonymously, Godfrey stood alone in her exposure to public scrutiny.

Although the *Forum* was never subjected to censorship after the implementation of the War Measures Act and the Defence of Canada Regulations, Godfrey was attacked on another front. At least one *Forum* reader took extreme exception to her editorship. In his letter to the editor published in the January 1940 'Correspondence' section, Ian MacPherson of Vancouver objected not only to Godfrey but to all women involved in the production of magazines:

> Had I known that the editor of The Forum was a woman I would not have sent anything. Magazines have fallen on evil days. Most of the copy readers are women. And behold what trash they give us – sloppy stories full of slang and 'wise-cracks' – most of them written for American publications and refused, probably not reaching the high editorial standards of Gotham. See last issue of Maclean's. Fifty years ago there were good magazines publishing things of literary merit ... today – well let us not contemplate it. (original ellipsis)

MacPherson's expression of anger toward the wartime magazine industry, in which women were becoming even more frequently employed as men were conscripted for war duty, manifests an alarming misogyny. His implicit feminization of the popular style found in such commercial magazines as *Maclean's* is linked both to the women he alleges are responsible for the editing of magazine copy and to the change he perceives in editorial values. Published in the previous,

December 1939, issue, Godfrey's own short story 'The Samaritans' is a prime example of the 'slang and "wise-cracks"' to which her disgruntled reader objects. No doubt he had her story in mind when he penned his letter to the editor.

Reading the brief biographies of the New Group on the back cover of the November 1935 issue, one learns that Godfrey 'writes book reviews and general criticisms. Is a literary jack-of-all trades' ('New Group'). Godfrey had published her first feature-length book review in the August 1935 issue, just prior to joining the Forum's New Group. With her review article on Sinclair Lewis's Selected Short Stories, she offered the first of her regular book reviews to Forum readers. Opening with a hard-nosed critique of Lewis and his publishers, she immediately proved herself the kind of writer that Spry was interested in having on the staff of a publication opposed to the literary values of commercial magazines. She skewered Lewis's collection for its commercialism: 'it must be explained that these exercises in commonplace are reprinted from a number of smooth paper family journals; but this scarcely serves as a recommendation' ('Sinclair' 333). In calling attention to literature intended for a popular audience, Godfrey presumed such readers to be less discriminating than those of the Forum; her elitism betrays her predictable bias toward a non-commercial magazine culture represented by the Forum and its editors' literary values, chiefly modernist in aesthetics and left-wing in politics. Unfortunately for the Forum's New Group, its readers were not so plentiful that it could afford to alienate the general public. Consequently, Godfrey continued to review books – novels, short-story collections, and popular biographies – whose audience may have held little regard for the social and political aims of the LSR, the CCF, or any other progressive movement supported by the Forum's editors. Because Godfrey was not among its primary editorialists, her written contribution to the Forum was restricted mainly to book reviews and review articles.

Godfrey wrote and reviewed only prose. Poetry she left for her Forum colleagues: Grube, Northrop Frye, Birney, and Creighton, among others. The sheer quantity of reviews that she published in the Forum prevents a comprehensive survey of her contributions. Nor, admittedly, are the books she reviews always relevant to the study of modernist and leftist women poets and magazine editors. Some of her reviews stand out, though, for their shrewd commentaries on magazine publishing and modernist magazine culture. Perhaps indicative of her experience as a managing editor, they exhibit an acute awareness of the economics of magazine production. This economic interest, prevalent in her first review, reappeared in later reviews of the 1930s and 1940s.

Neither named as a *Forum* editorialist during her tenure on its board nor vocal in terms of defining its editorial policy, Godfrey nonetheless voiced definite opinions on magazine culture – or as much as could be expected in the confines of her reviews. Among her earliest reviews, her September 1936 commentary on Leslie Bishop's novel *Paper Kingdom* exposes it as a *roman à clef* about a Toronto literary-arts magazine during the Depression. 'The novel is concerned,' she writes, 'with the efforts of an irresponsible young man to establish an incoherent literary magazine, The New Conquest, in Macgregor' (30). Godfrey goes on to note that Bishop had spent a few years in Toronto as the manager and publisher of the *Twentieth Century*. Her dismissive attitude toward Bishop and his foundered magazine is somewhat overstated; she writes from the perspective of a managing editor with significantly more experience than herself and with far more secure financial backing than that of the *Forum* in the mid-1930s. Even with the recent injection of support from the LSR, the *Forum* was running on little more than a shoestring budget itself at the time of Godfrey's review. Her tacit objection to the *Twentieth Century* is that it aspired to be a commercial magazine without the financial resources to do so; her satisfaction with the *Canadian Forum* may have been that it survived because it always stayed within its meagre means of production and circulation, never hazarding gains and losses in the commercial-magazine market. Without access to public funding, the *Canadian Forum* and the *Twentieth Century* represented two different magazine economies: the former backed by the LSR (and later by a private fund), the latter dependent on advertising revenues.

Godfrey is no more sympathetic to non-commercial, modernist little magazines. Reviewing *American Writing 1943: The Anthology and Yearbook of the American Non-Commercial Magazine*, edited by Alan Swallow, she disparages the desire 'to present in accessible form and to the editor's best critical ability the finest creative writing which appears in the "little" or non-commercial little magazines of America' (Swallow 7; qtd. in Godfrey, Rev. of *American Writing*). In Godfrey's view, literary standards should transcend the economic means available to little-magazine editors: 'Good writing is good writing and no matter how arbitrary the anthologist's other bases for selection may be he should at least be governed by the kind of writing and not where it appears. It is possible that the best writing, especially of an experimental nature, is found in the non-commercial magazines but this certainly cannot be proved by excluding the commercial magazines from consideration.' To be fair, one should note that in his introduction Swallow refutes the notion that the 'literary production which is to be called "great" is the exclusive property of the "little" magazines,' but maintains that 'the larger proportion of it which appears in magazines at all does appear in those magazines' (12). He contends that because their circulation is so limited, little magazines cannot hope to attract a wide enough subscription base to stay solvent and that his anthology is another means of promoting American little magazines and reaching untapped markets (14–15). Yet Godfrey is unmoved by Swallow's appeals, disputing the validity of his categorization of the non-commercial magazine: 'Because commercial poetry simply does not exist in the same sense that commercial prose fiction does, the editor is drawing on substantially the same sources for the anthology as he would without his non-commercial magazine restriction.' Of course 'commercial poetry' does exist: it is the 'magazine verse,' as Sutherland says ('Anne' 101), that fills out the columns of such periodicals as *Saturday Night*, *Chatelaine*, and the *Saturday Evening Post*. Godfrey seems to have forgotten her own criticisms of the commercial values in mass-market magazines.

Even as she expressed reservations about the distinction between commercial and non-commercial magazines, the *Forum* helped to promote non-commercial modernist literary magazines in Canada. Reviews of *Contemporary Verse*, *First Statement*, and *Direction* appeared in the *Forum* on a regular basis from 1941 to 1944.[5] Although she never reviewed any of the magazines herself, Godfrey was by no means oblivious to the spirited dialogues among these groups. According to Cowan, the *Forum* 'was often a clearing house for the arguments raging between little magazines of opposing views' and 'served as a neutral area for arguments between members of opposing groups' (7, 15). Citing the infamous native-cosmopolitan debate of the 1940s chronicled by literary historians, she points to a sequence of exchanges among Frye, Livesay, Margaret Avison, Patrick Anderson, A.J.M. Smith, and W.W.E. Ross that appeared in the form of reviews, articles, poems, and letters to the editor in the *Forum* (18–22). Public acrimony among Canadian modernists dotted the pages of the *Forum* between December 1943 and July 1945. Yet the private correspondence among the key figures in the debate represents a period of reconciliation and transition in modernist literary culture. Extant archival evidence indicates that Godfrey herself may have favoured the 'native' side of the debate, though the complexity of relations among various personalities and the freedom of opinion among reviewers and correspondents should discourage assured conclusions (see Godfrey to Livesay, 7 June 1944, DLP-QU, box 2, file 17). As managing editor, she oversaw the *Forum*'s impartial role in this critical negotiation between competing discourses of nationalism and internationalism in Canadian modernist literary culture. While Godfrey may have held strong opinions about any given magazine, poet, or magazine group, the *Forum* policy of withholding such editorial statements allowed literary rivals to air their grievances in the magazine's public space and, ultimately, come to terms of agreement in closed forums. Rather than voice an opinion in the native-cosmopolitan debate, Godfrey and the *Forum* editorial board helped to facilitate the negotiation between nationalist and internationalist cultural discourses that converged in Canadian modernist literary culture of the 1940s and 1950s. That convergence was effected in the transition of modernist magazine culture in Montreal and the merger of the *Preview* and *First Statement* groups in 1945.[6]

The *Forum* itself had undergone transition over the course of Godfrey's editorship, beginning with the New Group of the 1930s. Despite her marginalization in *Forum* histories, her managerial and production work was vital to the magazine's continuation through the Depression and the Second World War, the most trying years of the *Forum*'s life. Having joined the board at a time of economic uncertainty and editorial reorganization in the mid-1930s, Godfrey contributed to the *Forum*'s stabilization by holding her post as managing editor over a decade during which the magazine established itself as a cultural institution. When she resigned in February 1947 ('To Our Readers'), modernist little-magazine culture in Canada had similarly reached a point of stability: the Montreal magazines had joined to form *Northern Review*, Birney was editing *Canadian Poetry Magazine*, *Contemporary Verse* was still thriving, and new magazines were in the making.

5 Guardians of the Avant-garde: Modernism, Anti-modernism, and the Massey Commission

It is popularly believed that the editor of a little magazine would scornfully reject an offer of government aid. It might be worthwhile to give him the chance.

Edward McCourt, 'Canadian Letters' (82)

Commissioning the Avant-Garde

The Royal Commission on National Development in the Arts, Letters and Sciences (1949–51) – the Massey Commission – witnessed Canadian literary modernism's transition from an emergent to a dominant cultural formation. For Canada's mid-century little magazines, the public hearings and publications surrounding this event signalled their recognition by the state as emissaries of an official Canadian literary culture. The Massey Commission's desire for 'universalism' found its literary model in modernism's mediation between apparently antagonistic nationalist and internationalist cultural discourses (*Report* 226; Berland 22). At the same time, its universalist notion of a national literature and its interpellation of the literary avant-garde were met with significant resistance from modernists and anti-modernists alike.

As Philip Massolin reports in *Canadian Intellectuals, the Tory Tradition, and the Challenge of Modernity, 1939–1970* (2001), the Massey Commission brought together intellectuals to deliberate over the pernicious effects of modernization and mass culture. The intellectual bent of these 'critics of modernity,' Massolin argues, was emphatically anti-modernist (9). These anti-modernist tendencies are outlined in Paul

Litt's *The Muses, the Masses, and the Massey Commission* (1992): 'Cultural modernism could not serve the political and social ends that the commissioners demanded of high culture ... A variety of marginal and discordant voices were drowning out the harmonious ideal of a wholistic Western culture. These trends were clear enough during the Massey Commission's existence. Its indifference to them again reflected the relative insignificance of the artist, and especially avant-garde artists, among its supporters' (253). In dialogue with the commissioners' anti-modernism, however, are the voices of cultural modernism documented not only in briefs submitted by little-magazine editors such as Alan Crawley and Dorothy Livesay of *Contemporary Verse*, John Sutherland of *Northern Review* and First Statement Press, and Paul Arthur and Catherine Harmon of *here and now*[1] but also in transcripts of the public hearings. Far from apathetic to cultural modernism or avant-garde writers and editors, the Massey Commission entertained their appeals for financial assistance in their defence of Canadian literature against the influence of American mass-culture magazines imported into Canada and the loss of Canadian literature exported to the United States for publication in commercial magazines. Both the Massey *Report*'s qualified endorsement of these briefs and its own defence of a national literature endeavoured to protect the non-commercial values of Canada's modernist literary culture against the commercial values of American mass culture. Even though, as Massolin and Litt contend, the Massey Commission represented a contingent of anti-modernist intellectuals, its report sought to calibrate the literary culture of Canada's modernist avant-garde with its critique of modernity and mass culture.

Litt's analysis of English Canadian magazines and their responses to cultural issues during the tenure of the commission and after the publication of its *Report* is restricted to *Maclean's*, *Saturday Night*, and the *Canadian Forum*, with references to others by name only. None of the Canadian literary magazines in circulation at the time enters his cultural history. While Litt also calls attention to the demography of Canadian cultural organizations, noting that it is 'an inarguable fact that women dominated the local cultural associations across the country' (34), he fails to correlate this observation with an analysis of briefs submitted by such groups to the Massey Commission. To his credit, he does incorporate into his findings the briefs from the local and national arms of the CAA, whose membership represented a typical predominance of women in cultural bodies of the period (106,

171, 172). And though he also entertains the views of such groups as the Canadian Writers' Committee (which included Birney, Scott, Livesay, and Page, among others) and the Fiddlehead Poetry Society (which was represented by Fred Cogswell), Litt rationalizes what he perceives to be the commission's diffidence toward such groups. Rather than contest the commission's views, he perpetuates indifference by not attending to the voices of cultural modernism represented in briefs submitted by little-magazine groups and the transcriptions of their public hearings.

In contrast to Litt's assertion that the Massey Commission believed modernism and cultural nationalism to be incompatible, Jody Berland's article 'Nationalism and the Modernist Legacy: Dialogues with Innis' (2000) focuses on what she calls 'the formative coalition between nationalism and modernism which arose in Canada in the 1950s' (15). She argues that the Massey Commission's nationwide hearings in 1949–50, the publication of its *Report* in 1951, and the founding of the Canada Council in 1957 brought cultural modernism to the forefront of national culture: 'These events placed modernist art discourse – nationalist in their rhetorical claims but international(ist) in aesthetic strategies and terms of reference – at the centre of the country's new official culture. Modernism thereby served the apparently antagonistic but actually complementary goals of nationalism and internationalism which motivated and defined Canada as an emergent nation in the postwar period' (22). Berland's thesis is consistent with the Massey *Report*'s section on literature and Edward McCourt's supplemental report on literature in *Royal Commission Studies* (1951). In Berland's view, modernism mediated between nationalist and internationalist cultural discourses. Even as the Massey Commission sought to reconcile these discourses through its advocacy of what Berland calls a 'nationalist modernism' (28), its findings ultimately exhibited the conditions of social fragmentation, disorientation, and dislocation symptomatic of cultural modernity. Rather than heralding the emergence of an autonomous national literature, then, the Massey Commission's record of literary modernism identified a state of cultural homelessness for the modernist writer. In the words of the Massey *Report*, 'if our writers are uncertain of the road ahead, their uncertainty, it seems, is derived from the general confusion in a society with no fixed values and no generally accepted standards' (226).

Contrary to the cultural-nationalist myths that still haunt the Massey Commission, its *Report* actually determined that 'Canada has not yet established a national literature' (225). Its findings document a critical moment in Canadian literature, a crisis predicated upon the absence of a coherent national culture. Instead of a national literature, the Massey Commission was presented with evidence of a multiplicity of literatures, a heterogeneity of literary discourses and cultures. As noted in the previous chapter, its *Report* declared that Canada's literary culture was in the midst of a 'crisis of orientation' (225), which saw proponents of cultural nationalism and internationalism engaged in heated debates about the threat of American cultural imperialism and the state of Canadian literature's neocolonialism. These oppositional orientations correspond to the two sides of the infamous native-cosmopolitan debate among Canadian literary modernists of the 1940s. Trying to avoid taking a side, the Massey *Report* regretted that the Canadian author 'has not yet reached that level of universalism which would permit his work to awaken echoes outside of our country as well as within it' (226). This attempt to remain neutral in fact reveals the Massey Commission's tacit bias toward an internationalist or cosmopolitan modernism, a cultural discourse that prizes 'universalism.' At the same time, the Massey *Report*'s support for a national literature accords with those writers and editors who argued on behalf of a so-called native modernism. Modernism's negotiation between the cosmopolitan and nativist camps orients, in Berland's terms, the competing discourses of a 'nationalist modernism.' In this respect, the Massey *Report* actively participated in one of the defining narratives of literary modernism in English Canada.

The Massey Commission's support for cultural modernism was confirmed in Edward McCourt's 1951 supplemental report 'Canadian Letters,' in which he advocates giving financial assistance to avant-garde magazines (81). Collected in *Royal Commission Studies*, his report draws particular attention to the modernist little magazines of the 1940s:

The little magazine is, in nearly all countries, defiantly *avant-garde*; it is precocious, revolutionary, often snobbish. But, significantly, it has fostered a large number of genuinely creative artists, particularly poets. In Canada the little magazine, nearly always the publication of a small, irritatingly self-assured, and genuinely talented group, has for obvious reasons an unusually short and troubled life. But many of our best poets and some of our best prose writers have made their first appearance in the pages – frequently mimeographed – of *Preview, First Statement, Contemporary Verse, Northern Review, Here and Now*, etc. (81–2)

While his report rates their literary value highly and recommends subsidies to alleviate their chronic financial crises, McCourt's conclusions about these magazines somewhat distort the evidence of the briefs submitted to the Massey Commission. His contention that the little magazine editor would rebuff any offer of government assistance (82; see epigraph) reiterates a masculinist stereotype of the belligerent little magazine. While this stereotype preserves the myth of the avant-garde's autonomy, it bears little relation to the economic situation of non-commercial magazines that was detailed in briefs submitted by the editors of *Contemporary Verse*, *Fiddlehead*, *Northern Review*, and *here and now*. Judging by *here and now*, whose Massey Commission brief we will revisit, the avant-garde magazine of that period was not necessarily indisposed to the idea of accepting government support. In the case of *CIV/n*, however, McCourt's characterization of the little-magazine's indifference to government aid proved well founded: its editors deplored the Massey Commission's plans for a subsidized national culture and promoted its magazine as an international avant-garde literary organ supported by an international reading public. Its defence of an autonomous avant-garde counters the cultural discourse sanctioned by the Massey Commission, the compound discursive formation that Berland calls 'nationalist modernism' (28). Other variations on Berland's modernist-nationalist thesis to which we will turn include 1950s periodicals such as *pm magazine* and *Impression*, both of which were founded in the years immediately after the Massey Commission.

Building upon Berland's analysis of the Massey *Report*, we may begin to examine the ways in which modernism's tendency toward aesthetic autonomy finds its correlative in the Massey Commission's concern for Canada's cultural autonomy. According to Berland, 'The connection between the arts and national defence – between autonomous art and an autonomous nation – was a fundamental component of postwar reconstruction and continued to lay the foundation for cultural policy' (22). Implicit in her correlation of aesthetic and national autonomy is the cultural concept of the avant-garde, especially its derivation from a militaristic discourse. Though uncited, her claim is certainly based in part on the pairing of national culture and national defence in the Massey *Report*: 'Our military defences must be made secure; but our cultural defences equally demand attention; the two cannot be separated' (275). The attractiveness of little magazines to the Massey Commission may be partly attributed to their alignment with the avant-garde, particularly in light of its militaristic significations and its anti-commercialism. As Renato Poggioli puts it, the little magazine is 'an independent and isolated military unit, completely and sharply detached from the public' (23; see also Hoffman et al. 3–4). Summarizing briefs submitted by author organizations and non-commercial magazine groups, the Massey Commission recorded 'the efforts of those literary groups belonging to various schools of thought which strive to defend Canadian literature against the deluge of the less worthy American publications.' These writers and magazine editors submitted that American popular magazines 'threaten our national values, corrupt our literary taste and endanger the livelihood of our writers' (Report 225). Among women editors of non-commercial magazines, the protest against the literary values of commercial periodicals was unanimous, whether voiced in terms of aesthetic or of national autonomy.

The briefs submitted to the Massey Commission by Canadian modernist little-magazine editors attest to their desire for wider publicity and not, as Poggioli claims, their detachment from the public. As John Sutherland writes on behalf of *Northern Review*, 'the so-called "little magazines" have exerted an influence out of proportion to the small impression they have been able to make on the general public ... Resisting the commercialization of literary taste, such magazines have provided an eventual entrance to public attention for many deserving writers.' During his Massey Commission hearing, Sutherland called attention to two Toronto-based little magazines, *here and now* and *Reading* (1946), whose editors had attempted to compete with commercial magazines by employing mass-market advertising and mass distribution. 'They have tried to turn the best contemporary writing into a promotional venture,' Sutherland sneered, and then added that both magazines had folded after only a few issues (RC, vol. 19, brief 208, reel 19). Sutherland's ridicule of little magazines that engaged techniques of self-promotion and publicity speaks to the ways in which masculinist modernists regarded a feminized mass culture as a threat to the integrity of little-magazine culture. That one of the two magazines he selects for disparagement was co-edited by a woman (Catherine Harmon of *here and now*) is perhaps incidental but just as likely symptomatic of Sutherland's persistent disdain toward a commercial magazine culture that he explicitly identified with women and women's poetry ('Anne').

Conversely, in his submission to the Massey Commission, Alan Crawley of *Contemporary Verse* lamented that 'vast sections of the public are shut off from poetry' and anticipated the commissioners' interests in fostering a national literature when he stated that 'There is a growing realization that the pressures, tensions, and relationships of our complex industrial society can often be best comprehended through the poet['s] uncanny eye' (RC, vol. 17, brief 176, reel 16). Neither Sutherland nor Crawley desired the transformation of the little magazine into a mass-communication medium. For Crawley, the most promising mechanism for the promotion of modernist poetry among the general public was not through structural changes to the economy of the little magazine but through public-school pedagogy, public poetry recitations, and increased collaboration with CBC radio. While Sutherland regarded 'promotional ventures' as a menace to little-magazine culture, Crawley held no such qualms about alternative means of generating modernist publicity, though he wisely aimed to maintain the limited scale of the little magazine as a cultural formation in which he, as an editor, could sustain his extensive correspondence with contributors and, in doing so, continue to foster Canadian modernist poetry in general – and, as the pages of *Contemporary Verse* attest, women's modernist poetry in particular.

The obverse of the Massey Commission's attraction to cultural modernism was articulated by the leftist cultural wing of the Labour Progressive Party (LPP). Opposed to the advocacy of cultural modernism or avant-gardism, the LPP Cultural Commission contested the findings of the Massey Commission and disseminated its views in its own cultural-interest magazine, *New Frontiers* (1952–6). Edited by Margaret Fairley, *New Frontiers* represents a leftist cultural lobby whose radical policies promoted a people's culture as the only legitimate and democratic expression of Canadian nationalism. Unlike the internationalism of leftist and Popular Front magazine cultures of the 1930s, cultural leftism in Canada during the Cold War was predominantly nationalist in character and, in reaction to anti-communism and cultural imperialism from the United States, anti-American. Fairley stood among the leaders of the cultural left and promoters of a nationalist leftism in mid-century Canada. Her published responses to the Massey Commission, in particular, will provide material for reflection on the emergence of leftist magazine cultures in the first half of the twentieth century and especially women's participation in their making. After all, the sources of her radicalism in Canadian little-magazine culture actually extend back to the late 1910s, when she was a contributor to the University of Toronto student magazine, the *Rebel* (1917–20), the precursor to the *Canadian Forum*.

One of the striking disparities between the pre- and post-commission eras of little magazines is that the earlier period of little magazine production (1916–47) saw a greater degree of flexibility in the orientation of certain little magazines toward commercial culture, but the later period (1947–56) developed a modernist-leftist magazine culture more strictly non-commercial – and, in the cases of *CIV/n* and *New Frontiers*, anti-commercial. Given that alternative cultural formations, as Raymond Williams notes, typically bear traces of the dominant cultures coextensive with emergent cultures (*Marxism* 124–5), it follows that the early little magazine should on occasion wear some markings of the mass-market periodical. The anti-commercialism of the post-commission-era little magazine thus marks the period's tendency toward *oppositional* cultural formations, primarily motivated by a critique of the dominant national culture advocated by the Massey Commission and by a critique of the commission's invocation of modernism as the nation's dominant cultural formation.

Her Yellow Book: Catherine Harmon and *here and now*

Just as Eleanor Godfrey's resignation from the *Canadian Forum* was announced in early 1947, Catherine Harmon and Paul Arthur were making plans to found and co-edit a new literary-arts magazine based in Toronto. Among Canada's women magazine editors at mid-century, Harmon holds a position of distinction in the literary-historical record. Though the entire run of *here and now* consists of only four issues (December 1947–June 1949), little-magazine historians Ken Norris and Bruce Whiteman and bibliographer David McKnight have devoted a respectable amount of attention both to the magazine and to Harmon's co-editorship. As well, Birney's memoir *Spreading Time* is particularly valuable for its record of Harmon and *here and now*, as is their extant correspondence, on which he bases his recollections (see EBP, box 11, folder 18). Wynne Francis's entry on literary magazines in English in the latest edition of the *Oxford Companion to Canadian Literature* unfortunately indicates only that *here and now*'s designer and editor was Paul Arthur and that the magazine lasted for only three issues (Francis, 'Literary' 666). Francis is correct in identifying Arthur as the designer and editor, but he was by no means the *only* editor. Harmon is listed as the editor on the masthead of all four issues, Arthur as the managing editor. Although *here and now*'s editorials were written primarily by Arthur, they were signed by 'the editor'; these were actually collaborative compositions that emerged out of joint editorial discussions between the two co-editors.[2] They were aided by a number of successive editors: Alan Brown and Anne Wilkinson as literary editors, Robert Hall and Paul Duval as art editors, Carrol T. Coates as American editor, and Jean Mallinson, Tom Mallinson, and Belle Pomer as assistant editors. Only Harmon and Arthur were affiliated with the magazine for all four issues.

Harmon and Arthur's collaboration on *here and now* produced an avant-garde arts magazine, a publication distinguished for its cultural internationalism and nationalism, a periodical without precedent in Canada for its aestheticist design and editorial values and its editors' simultaneous commitment 'to unearth, encourage and project the truly native in our [Canadian] literature and art' (Prospectus, n.d. [1947], Ralph Gustafson Papers, Harmon file, item 2). *here and now*'s rapid ascendancy and decline is exemplary of the crisis in Canadian modernist magazine culture at mid-century: its avant-garde aesthetic disposition, international consciousness, and national orientation might have appeared to be the ideal vehicle for the Massey Commission's professed cultural values. Yet it lacked the economic means to continue production beyond its fourth issue in June 1949.

Of those who have written about *here and now*, Birney, Norris, Whiteman, McKnight, and Francis all foreground and comment upon its expensive production values. In fact, Dudek's only references to *here and now* in his July 1958 article on Canada's little magazines slight its editors' 'very expensive venture' and 'extravagant' magazine ('Role' 210, 211). In contrast to the inexpensive production values of its contemporaries, the multicolour printing, glossy art reproductions, and elaborate typographic design of *here and now* reveal the influence of both aestheticism – particularly that of *fin de siècle* little magazines – and William Morris's Arts and Crafts movement upon a modernist little magazine in Canada. On the whole, the twentieth-century avant-garde little magazine owes much to the late-nineteenth-century American and British progenitors of the genre; this kind of international context and lineage sets *here and now* apart from its Canadian predecessors and contemporaries. *here and now* exploits the historical value of an established avant-garde magazine culture in order to create for itself a kind of cultural distinction in Canada's modernist milieu of the late 1940s.

As co-editors, Arthur and Harmon impressed a distinctive editorial stamp on *here and now*. They intended to produce a Canadian modernist arts magazine in line with aestheticist magazines of the 1890s and Morris's Kelmscott Press (1890–6). That aestheticism and modernism should coincide in *here and now* is, as Trehearne has shown in the case of early twentieth-century Canadian poetry, typical of the development of literary modernism in Canada (see *Aestheticism* 1–21). With its faint visual allusion to Aubrey Beardsley's signature design, the first issue of *here and now* appeared in a yellow cover, often associated with the aestheticist periodical the *Yellow Book* (1894–7). Even *here and now*'s reproductions of etchings by Joan Miró, paintings by David Milne, illustrations by Jean Cocteau, drawings and paintings by Alfred Pellan, and sculpture by E.B. Cox suggest the example of the *Yellow Book* in reproducing the original work of contemporary avant-garde artists. As *here and now*'s designer, Arthur traced his genealogy of influence in his article 'In Silk and Scarlet Walks Many a Harlot,' published in the January 1949 issue, where he advocated the aesthetics of typography and book production:

> Suffering from all the ill effects of having become a puff of air, [typography] has dissolved into an inconsequential vacuum. For books are not like pots and pans, purely functional objects. They are too much weighted with the aesthetic. And the aesthetic, as everyone knows, is an 'imponderable,' meaningless, another puff of air. Yet surely the question is resolved very simply. Eric Gill stated an immutable truth when, like Carlyle, Ruskin, and William Morris, he said that the beauty one attaches to any well-made object whatever is the only indication that it *is* well-made. (17; original italics)

The invocation of a nineteenth-century canon – Carlyle, Ruskin, Morris – reveals the intellectual foundation of Arthur's principles of magazine design and production. His article on typographic aesthetics was accompanied in the same issue by H.A. Nieboer's article on the history of industrial design, featuring Morris's Arts and Crafts movement ('History and Industrial Design'), and was anticipated in the first issue by A.B. Garrow's article on British book and periodical design of the 1860s ('The Golden Age of English Illustration'). The December 1947 and June 1948 editorials prefigure Arthur's 'Silk and Scarlet' article; both employ the language of the Arts and Crafts movement, especially that of Morris's writings on book design, typography, and production. The first editorial closes with the expectation that 'readers will also see in our pages an attempt to reform the typographical manners of this country' and an expression of 'regret that in this issue we have not an essay on typography (as in the future we expect to have)' and of 'hope that this production will prove an essay in typography of a different sort.' The second disparages the 'utilitarian doctrine ... within arts, crafts and industries,' where the 'printer was once a guiding spirit and an artist as well as the actual engineer of the printed book' but now like 'a worm caught in a lawn-mower, this complete identity of the printer has been chopped up by the advance of the industrial revolution's whirling machinery' (4). All these articles and editorials contributed to *here and now*'s *fin de siècle* orientation, which was clearly not limited to slavish imitation of the *Yellow Book* or of any other late nineteenth-century periodical, but rather incorporated into the editorial values and practice of its co-editors.

In line with Arthur's design, the inaugural editorial of December 1947 traced *here and now*'s preferred heritage back to an era of late-nineteenth-century aestheticism:

> At the present time there are, in England and in the United States, a number of excellent Little Magazines which play a very considerable part in the culture of these countries. Ever since the nineties of the last century, they have, with varying degrees of popularity, presented the greatest writers and artists of the time. That Canada has played a small part in this movement is a result less of its being a 'young country' than of a preconceived notion that Canada does not possess enough *avant-garde* writers and artists to warrant such publications. With the exception of *Canadian Poetry Magazine* and *Contemporary Verse*, two poetry magazines of a very high order, which have for many years been attempting to disprove this, there is no publication whose primary aim it is to provide an outlet for the wide variety of Canadian Art that we know does exist.

Having invoked the 1890s as a decade of origin for little magazines, the editors in their reference here to the emergence of the modern avant-garde in *fin de siècle* aestheticism gesture toward the foundation of a Canadian avant-garde through its little-magazine culture. Yet neither Canadian poetry magazine to which the editors point is really avant-gardist – not in the manner of early twentieth-century periodicals such as Wyndham Lewis's *Blast* (1914), Margaret Anderson and Jane Heap's *Little Review* (1914–29), or Eugene and Maria Jolas's *transition* (1927–38). As I have already shown in an earlier chapter, the Canadian magazines named in the editorial bear closer affinities to the modernism of Harriet Monroe's *Poetry* (1912–). *here and now*, however, can legitimately claim ideological and aesthetic kinship with British avant-garde periodicals and print cultures of the later nineteenth century. With its commitment to a national culture and an international aesthetic, *here and now* attempts to consolidate a native-cosmopolitan (or nationalist-internationalist) cultural discourse and thereby capitalize on a current public debate among modernist authors and editors conducted in the pages of the *Canadian Forum*, *First Statement*, *Preview*, and *Northern Review*.

The editors' strategic allocation of *Contemporary Verse* and *Canadian Poetry Magazine* to a 'high order' of magazines also effectively extended an invitation to the *Contemporary Verse* group and the CAA to support *here and now*. *Contemporary Verse* ran advertisements in all four issues, and Crawley even offered manuscripts in his possession for publication in *here and now*.[3] Former editor E.J. Pratt returned *here and now*'s compliment to *Canadian Poetry Magazine* with his salutation 'A Greeting,' and then editor Birney answered with a poem ('Prairie Counterpoint'), both published in the inaugural issue of *here and now*. Birney's association with *here and now* resumed in the January 1949 issue, where the editors agreed to publish extracts from his 15 November 1948 letter to CAA bursar Philip Child, in which he made public the reasons for his resignation as editor of *Canadian Poetry Magazine* ('Age'). With this gesture, the editors must have been conscious that, as a consequence, they inevitably and irreparably severed relations with both the CAA and its poetry magazine. In fact, the publication of the Birney letter seems to have been carefully calculated insofar as its appearance coincided with the formation of the Canadian Writers' Committee (CWC), a CAA rival organization whose ad hoc steering committee in Toronto was located in the *here and now* office and whose unofficial magazine was, while it lasted, *here and now* (Birney, *Spreading* 137–8).

Conspicuous in its absence from *here and now*'s higher order of Canadian magazines, *Northern Review* had recently suffered from the controversy over Sutherland's editorial conduct and the concomitant exodus of editors from the magazine after the August–September 1947 issue. The timing of the resignation of the former members of *Preview* from the editorial board of *Northern Review* and the emergence of *here and now*, as noted in the previous chapter, is more than a historical coincidence. Rather than found a rival to *Northern Review*, the former editors of *Preview* were content, as Page put it, to give *here and now* their support, if it continued to fulfil the promise of the first issue (Page to Crawley, 11 January 1948, ACP, box 1, file 20). Page, Anderson, and Klein all contributed poetry and/or prose to *here and now*. Page's interest in the magazine can be traced back to a letter of 19 November 1947, which indicates that she had already made an earlier inquiry about *here and now* and submitted some work (Harmon to Page, PKPP, box 16, file 5). Her short story 'The Neighbour' and her poem 'Sleepers' appeared in the first issue (December 1947), her poems 'Portrait' (retitled 'Paranoid' in *The Metal and the Flower*) in the second issue (May 1948), and 'The Age of Ice' in the fourth issue (June 1949). For Page, her informal commitment to *here and now* may also be linked to her association with the CWC; she had been enlisted as a committee member and consultant on the CWC brief submitted to the Massey Commission.[4]

True to its genre, the *here and now* brief submitted to the Massey Commission amounted to little more than a precis of the editorials. Dated 16 May 1949, the brief itself was signed by Arthur, Harmon, and their new business manager, Langford Dixon. By the time *here and now* met with the commissioners in Toronto in November 1949, however, Arthur and Harmon had moved to England, leaving the magazine's business affairs to Dixon; though he had just joined the magazine with the fourth issue, he spoke to the Massey Commission on behalf of *here and now*. Anne Wilkinson, who had been enlisted as a reader for the magazine in February 1949 and named literary editor in the fourth issue, was visiting Arthur and Harmon in England at the time of the commission's Toronto hearings (Wilkinson 34, 48–59). Prior to their departure, Arthur and Harmon had brought out the fourth issue (June 1949) and compiled a fifth (which Whiteman notes was 'devoted to the short story in Canada,' but never made it into print ['*Here*' 78]). The brief that they submitted to the Massey Commission before leaving for England was composed around the time that the editors were discussing the editorial for the June 1949 issue. Indicative of *here and now*'s ongoing concerns, it echoes not only the current editorial but also an earlier editorial of May 1948, both of which comment on the loss of Canadian authors to magazines in the United States or to commercial magazines: 'It is constantly being brought to the attention of the editors of HERE AND NOW that young authors are being forced either to remove to the United States or to have the major portion of their work published there for lack of proper remuneration here. Another alternative is that these same authors turn to writing exclusively for the 'pulp' magazines because serious writing is not a profitable profession. In this way Canada is losing its literary heritage piecemeal' (RC, vol. 19, brief 225, reel 12). The editors' proposed solution to this crisis entailed the establishment of 'a fund similar to that set up by the Rockefeller Foundation on behalf of two comparable magazines in the United States: *Kenyon Review* and *Sewanee Review.*' Distant from the aestheticist periodical to which *here and now* had once traced its origins, the *Kenyon Review* (1939–), edited by John Crowe Ransom, and the *Sewanee Review* (1892–), edited by Allen Tate, represented the kind of modern American literary quarterlies that *here and now* could expect members of the Massey Commission to appreciate as models for a Canadian counterpart. Even so, *here and now* justified the proposal for the creation of its own fund in terms reminiscent of aestheticist principles of the autonomy of art and the artist, concluding that 'it would enable writers of merit to continue in their endeavours without resorting to the complete debasement of their art' (RC, vol. 19, brief 225, reel 12).

To its brief, *here and now* attached a plan for the distribution of a $4,900 fund among its contributors over the period of one year. No part of the fund was marked for payment of printer's bills or office rent, staff, and supplies.[5] Even though the brief claimed that 'writers of Canada have responded to the magazine in a fashion hitherto unequaled, contributing generously of their work without remuneration,' and that '[t]he magazine has in its files the work of, or promises of work from, nearly every writer of competence in the Dominion,' Dixon admitted, after questioning by the commissioners, that 'we are not saying that all the material is of a calibre that we would like to get' and that without 'real money to pay the authors, you cannot get the top material.' But it would be a mistake to conflate *here and now* with commercial magazines: its aestheticist orientation is reconfirmed during the commission hearing by Dixon's admiration of the 'quality of taste' and 'quality of art' in a Montreal School of Art and Design periodical and by his prepared statement, in which he advances 'the premise that art begins with self[-]expression which is moulded by the playwright, the composer, and the poet into something of beauty' (RC, vol. 19, brief 225, reel 12).

Given the specificity of *here and now*'s brief, it seems that Harmon, Arthur, and Dixon expected immediate results from their appeal to Massey Commission. The magazine's troubled financial situation certainly required an expedient remedy. After publishing issue four in

June 1949, *here and now* owed its printer $2,700 (Whiteman, 'Here' 78). Without additional sources of patronage, it could not maintain its editors' aestheticist principles of magazine production and consequently was forced to halt publication within a year of its submission to the Massey Commission. While both editors compiled material for a fifth issue and Harmon continued to work on a sixth after moving to England (Whiteman, 'Here' 78), the editorial in the fourth issue had already hinted that the continuation of *here and now* was doubtful: 'With regard to the Little Magazines, the invariable seed-beds for the best work of our time, they hardly exist. Admittedly their numerousness in the United States is rather appalling, but surely we deserve more than we have. Or do we, really? Costs are again colossal and the proper distribution throughout such a gigantic territory is veritably impossible: all of which is very disheartening for the editors and for the interested public' ('here'). Aestheticism, as a principle of magazine design and production, demanded patronage. What *here and now* required was not a fund for the payment of contributors but a patron to cover basic printing and distribution costs. Although Wilkinson's invitation to join the magazine as literary editor in early 1949 does not appear to have been motivated by a need to solicit new patrons for *here and now* – at least she never mentions offering financial assistance to the magazine in her extant correspondence or in her journals – several years later she became a major patron of Canadian culture in helping to found, edit, and finance the *Tamarack Review* (1956–82) during its early years. From the start, *here and now* had relied upon the generosity of such patrons, including Massey himself; but in the end its desire for aesthetic value exceeded the resources of those patrons who, as the editors acknowledged in the dedication to the first issue, supported a magazine 'published in the interests of Canadian culture' (n.p.). In this respect, one could even characterize the decline of *here and now* as a kind of decadent corollary to its initial period of aesthetic intensity. The editors' pursuit of beauty in the aesthetics of the arts magazine had, in a manner typical of the aesthete, exhausted itself in the process of making culture.

Making Her *Impression*: Myra Lazechko-Haas's New Canadianism

Just months after the demise of *here and now*, Myra Lazechko-Haas laid out the groundwork for another national arts magazine. Based in Winnipeg, *Impression* first appeared in the spring of 1950 under the editorship of Lazechko-Haas, assisted by John Bryant and George Nasir. For the first three issues, the masthead also listed a contingent of editorial board members. According to David McKnight's bibliography of Canadian little magazines, *Impression* was the only new magazine founded in Canada between 1949 and 1951 (24). Like *here and now*, it started with fanfare but lasted for only four issues, its final instalment issued in the spring of 1952. But where *here and now* published many of our most prominent modernist authors, *Impression* devoted its pages chiefly to the early work of emergent authors: Phyllis Webb, George Nasir, and James Reaney, among others. As a corollary, *Impression* has received no more than mention by name, and its editor is not even acknowledged in the published record (Norris, *Little* 55; Dudek, 'Role' 210). McKnight's brief annotation on *Impression* is the only literary-historical document in which Lazechko-Haas has been given credit for her editorship. *Impression* is distinctive among Canadian arts magazines of the period for its representation of an immigrant literary culture; its 'nationalist ambitions may not have been achieved,' as McKnight notes (24), but its editor's articulation of Canadianism as the core of a people's culture gives voice to a 'nationalist modernism' among immigrant cultural groups otherwise assimilated into the Massey Commission's conception of a bilingual and bicultural Canada (Berland 28; Litt 113–14).

Impression's editor was not a neophyte when she founded the magazine in the spring of 1950. The biographical note to her 1952 poetry chapbook, *Viewpoint*, informs us that she had been engaged in a number of editorial roles: 'Mrs. Myra Lazechko-Haas' name is familiar and prominent in Ukrainian-Canadian circles, and her articles and poems have appeared in a wide number of Canadian and American newspapers as well as periodicals of Ukrainian descent ... A graduate of Berkeley University, California, she is now literary editor of *Opinion* (Winnipeg), *New Canadian Poetry Column* (Toronto) as well as editor of *Impression* (Winnipeg)' (inside cover). As the literary editor of *Opinion* (1945–55?), the official newsletter of the Ukrainian Canadian Veterans' Association, Lazechko-Haas worked out of a Winnipeg-based immigrant culture.[6] Her opening editorial for *Impression* thus situates the magazine in relation to the local literary community, its cultural groups, and its other periodicals such as *Opinion*:

Canada, specifically Winnipeg, is in dire need of newspapers, literary journals and magazines, capable of bringing into the public light, the artistic efforts of our many diversified talents ... There are ... the occasional magazines of Icelandic, Ukrainian and Jewish descent, which do splendid work and encourage the splendid work of others. But their following is necessarily limited. The only magazine or newspaper in Winnipeg to actively enforce some measure or force of pure Canadianism in the printed word today, is 'The Manitoban,' and this is run almost exclusively by the student body and University staff.

Having outlined the local cultural contexts, Lazechko-Haas then expands upon her plans for the magazine's dissemination to a national audience and her concept of Canadianism:

Impression is, mainly, a journal for the Arts. It is an independent magazine whose sole aim is to instigate, encourage and make known, the latent as well as the developed talents of young Canada; to investigate the talents of all Canadians of various racial differences; to bring together under the common denominator of the mutual arts, these peoples; to sublimate these peoples into a whole, rounded sum – Canadianism! (2)

Lazechko-Haas's emphasis on youth recalls a similar intention in the early issues of First Statement. But where Sutherland's 'Magazine for Young Canadian Writers' aims to strike a discordant modernist and nationalist 'fighting mag' pose, Lazechko-Haas's magazine seeks to develop a Canadian youth magazine culture whose nationalism is based upon harmony, not dissonance. Her editorial manner is antithetical to Sutherland's polemical attacks on Preview, Canadian Poetry Magazine, and the Crucible. Local periodicals whose readership consists of immigrant communities receive her praises rather than her reproaches; her support of such ventures was reciprocated, as she demonstrates in the first issue by publishing a supportive letter from one H.F. Danielson, editor of the Icelandic Canadian.

Lazechko-Haas's concept of Canadianism is related, but not identical, to the discourses of multiculturalism in current theoretical lexicons. Extrapolating from a liberal editorial policy of inclusiveness for the 'mutual arts,' she articulates a multicultural, liberalist approach to the representation of 'racial differences.' Images of the arts as a 'whole, rounded,' or as a 'common denominator' and of artistic expression as the sublimation of difference, however, may in fact connote the cultural practice of assimilation. Her metaphor of sublimation suggests the transmutation of difference into the sameness of Canadianism, if only in the arts. The hypothesis and expected outcome of this cultural experiment are by no means well defined, though clearly distinct from contemporary articulations of Canadian cultural nationalism. Lazechko-Haas's orientation toward a people's culture indicates a crucial distinction from a national culture – or what Litt calls the 'liberal humanist nationalism' mandated by the Massey Commission as an official culture.[7]

Published in the spring 1951 issue, Lazechko-Haas's next editorial offers her own artistic expression of a people's culture. Opening it with a poem of her own, she presents a catalogue of the people's means of communication through their manual labour:

> speak to me not in the tongue of trees and valleys,
> the primary alphabets of hills and prairies,
> teach me instead, the syllables of tractor,
> of drill press, smelting ladle, motivated
> by human hands
> . . . .
> I have outgrown
> the stumbling speech of soil, the rhetoric of rivers
> teach me the living language of people, my people,
> and I will spell out Canada for you. (45)

Lazcheko-Haas's rhetorical manner is remarkably similar to that of Livesay's social and political poetry of the 1930s; their common proletarian subject also suggests a thematic link between the two poets. (One could compare, for instance, Lazechko-Haas's 'living language of people' to Livesay's 'Invitation to Silence,' or the former's Canadianism to the latter's vision of the 'people' in 'Canada to the Soviet Union' [*Right Hand* 72].) The proletarian idiom of the poem is typical of the verse circulated in labour and farm papers of the early to mid-century, chiefly published by and distributed in immigrant communities. With its version of Canadianism, Lazechko-Haas's poem repudiates the pastoralism typical of the so-called Maple Leaf poets and the literary fashion of nineteenth- and early-twentieth-century boosterism. Instead, she correlates the language of people's labour in immigrant communities and the discourse of modernist progress. This idealized vision of modernity embodies the tenets of an agrarian utopianism. Lazechko-Haas's understanding of modernism and modernity is antithetical to the social and economic conditions of modernity that foster a modernist poetry preoccupied by urban alienation and industrial mechanization. Rather, her Canadianism integrates a utopian approach to modernity, a modernist poetics of language, and a nationalist conception of social, cultural, and economic forces. As she writes in the prose section of the editorial, 'In us is the human bridge to cultural and economic understanding between ourselves and the outside world' (45).

The magazine appeared at approximately six-month intervals for the first three issues, but the fourth and final issue of *Impression* did not come out until a year after the spring 1951 issue. No doubt the editors had experienced difficulties raising funds to cover printing costs. In the second issue, Lazechko-Haas compiled a page of responses from readers and advertisers and excerpts from positive and negative reviews, entitled 'Court of Comment.' Its final anonymous 'witness' delivered a prophetic testimony: 'Come back and see me about my three dollar advertisement when your circulation is 5,000. We can't afford to gamble right now on your indefinite magazine.' Given subscriptions at $1.00 for one year or single issues for 35¢, one suspects that advertisements generated most of the magazine's revenue. Circulation figures for *Impression* are not available, but if the readership of its contemporaries is taken as evidence, we may conclude that circulation never reached a level satisfactory to advertisers, and consequently, the magazine never managed to obtain sufficient revenues to keep it afloat.

Concurrently with the final issue of *Impression* in the spring of 1952, Lazechko-Haas shifted her attention to the composition of her poetry chapbook, *Viewpoint*. Published in the Ryerson Press series in early 1952, it includes two of her poems first printed in *Impression*: 'After This' from the first issue (spring 1950) and 'Selkirk Avenue' from the second (autumn 1950). The collection received moderate praise from B.K. Sandwell, editor of *Saturday Night*. His review of 17 May 1952 situated Lazechko-Haas as a writer 'well-known to the Ukrainian part of the population' and noted her 'rich fertility of figuration,' deploying an agricultural image that connoted and reiterated her ethnic background (33). Sandwell must have been impressed by her, since he published her photograph beside the omnibus review, which also covered three other titles in the Ryerson Poetry Chapbook series: *The Searching Image* by Louis Dudek, *It Was a Plane* by Tom Farley, and *Mint and Willow* by Ruth Cleaves Hazelton. The publicity afforded by the *Saturday Night* review did not translate into recognition by a national reading public: Lazechko-Haas may have been well known to readers of Ukrainian periodicals, but she moved for only a brief period beyond that immigrant audience into a national arts culture – as editor, poet, and reviewer in *Impression* and as author of *Viewpoint*. Once *Impression* faded after the spring 1952 issue, so too did her prospects of national recognition as a modernist poet in Canada.

Though short-lived, Lazechko-Haas's contributions to little-magazine culture should not be underestimated: her editorial and poetic vision of a national people's culture offered Canada an alternative to the official national culture advocated by the Massey Commission. The collapse of *Impression* not only signalled the lack of economic support for little-magazine culture in Canada but also exemplified the critical failure of the commission to comprehend multiculturalism in the arts. Had Lazechko-Haas had the financial backing available to magazines affiliated with political organizations, *Impression* might have sustained a national people's magazine culture without the restrictions of authorship or audience placed upon periodicals such as its leftist contemporary, *New Frontiers*.

Art in Small Print: Yvonne Agazarian and *pm magazine*

During the year-long interval between the penultimate and final issues of *Impression*, Yvonne Agazarian headed an editorial group intent upon founding an arts magazine in Vancouver. With Agazarian as its editor, *pm magazine* arrived on the Vancouver arts scene in November 1951. Its appearance trailed the release in June that year of the Massey *Report*, which had given brief notice of the non-commercial magazine in its section on the press and periodical literature:

> A final word should be said about the non-profit periodical, the little magazine which, published by a small and confident group of talented people, not infrequently has given encouragement to genuinely creative writers, to poets in particular. Its literary and other criticisms are severe but usually well-informed, written brilliantly and without restraint. These small and generally short-lived magazines which attract few readers and as a consequence no advertisers, play a most important part in the cultural life of our country; their precarious life, their premature extinction and their courageous reappearance are no doubt all essential to our slow growth as a cultivated community. (65)

The commission's assessment of non-commercial magazines advocates a kind of cultural Darwinism: its figurative language of extinction and organic metaphors of regeneration support its recommendation not to interfere in the natural life of the little magazine. The editors of non-commercial periodicals did not all share the same non-interventionist perspective on Canadian magazine culture. Just as *here and now* gratefully acknowledged the support of patrons, so too *pm magazine* gave thanks to its private supporters, including Dr Norman MacKenzie, president of the University of British Columbia and former member of the Massey Commission (Agazarian, Editorial [1952] 2). The 'premature extinction' of *pm magazine* after only three issues highlighted the problem of overspecialization among non-commercial magazines intended for a local rather than a national audience; its regionalism foregrounded a critical gap in the Massey Commission's mandate in that a national culture may in fact be composed of a multiplicity of local cultural groups.[8]

Unlike *here and now* and *Impression*, *pm* was not concerned with the cultivation of a national arts culture. Its arts calendar was limited to Vancouver events; its patrons and advertisers were for the most part local, as were its contributors of articles, poems, and short stories. The local emphasis of the magazine likely dissuaded prominent authors from contributing their work. *pm*'s most notable literary contributor was Phyllis Webb, who had graduated from the University of British Columbia in 1949 and moved to Montreal in 1950 (Butling, *Seeing* 130); she even offered to distribute subscription forms for *pm* in Montreal (Webb to Agazarian, 27 December 1951, PMMP, box 1, file 2). The third and final issue included one of her early poems, 'Is Our Distress,' later collected in *Trio* (1954), a Contact Press anthology of poems by Eli Mandel, Gael Turnbull, and Webb herself. Of the local Vancouver literati, Ethel Wilson opted for a financial contribution to *pm* rather than a literary one (Agazarian, Editorial [1952] 2); Livesay offered a review but no poems.

As a Vancouver arts monthly – of visual art, film, music, theatre, ballet, fiction, and poetry – *pm* differentiated itself from its local literary counterpart, *Contemporary Verse*. Production values (offset printing, tricolour and black-and-white art reproduction) also distinguished *pm* from the mimeographed *Contemporary Verse*. Page's evaluation of the first issue in a letter to Crawley about *pm* perfectly captures the stark disparity between its aesthetic and literary values:

'What do you think of P.M. & how long do you give it? I thought the first issue pretty bad in the writing line. In fact, awful. But I liked the courage of so many [lino-]cuts' (Page to Crawley, n.d., ACP, box 1, file 20). The positive elements of her response to *pm*, especially its design aesthetic, reflect the early design and print work of Robert R. Reid, an innovative typographer, printer, and graphic designer (McKnight 26). Page's admiration for *pm*'s visual art and design did not, though, compel her (or others of her calibre) to submit poems to the new magazine in order to raise its literary profile.

Agazarian's opening editorial offers a rather abstracted view of *pm*, in that she employs the figure of typographic design as a conceit to represent the magazine's aesthetic principles. In brief, her self-reflexive editorial suggests that 'art' and 'ART' represent two extreme perspectives on the 'arts': 'Remove art from the small print of life and put it into capitals and it becomes the barrier between the half of us who don't understand and the other half who do. Look through the wrong end of a telescope and the capitals suddenly become familiar. They diminish into that piece of music you hum, that story you remember, or that painting you want to see again.' Presumably, *pm* could represent the point of view of the reversed telescope: just as upper-case 'ART' becomes lower-case 'art,' so, by analogy, 'PM' becomes 'pm.' The typographic analogy is somewhat harder to sustain after the opening exposition: 'But where did ART go? – the impetus that is behind hundreds of books, meetings, exhibitions and shows? Basically the change of perspective does not alter art, however capitalised, at all. It merely shows two extremes of the same thing, one a part of living, the other a development of one slice of living until it becomes as specialized as atom-splitting. No focus can alter either art or its value.'

Agazarian commits *pm* to a view of 'ART,' but admits that its readers may only see 'art': 'If at first you judge what you see as art in small print we will abide by your judgement, in the hope that subsequent issues will convince you, or re-enforce your conviction, that art is an important part of living. Then voluntarily you may decide to set it in the capitals it deserves' (Editorial [1951]). Insofar as its audience may prefer to read 'ART' as 'art,' so the editor intends 'to present a view of the arts' as part of 'the small print of life' so that the reader may eventually be inclined to accept 'ART' as integral to everyday experience. For Agazarian, the generic everydayness of the magazine (which is also implied by *pm*'s title) lends itself to the project of integrating art into life. The notion that it is the reader him or herself who must decide to set 'art in ... capitals' is indicative of a democratic view of art – that is, an everyday art that Agazarian had hoped to promote through the monthly publication of *pm*.[9]

As much as she practised the democratic editorial principle of keeping *pm* open to younger writers, she could hardly deny the value of publishing the work of older, accomplished writers. Enlisting Livesay as a reviewer in the February 1952 issue, Agazarian invited a dissonant voice into *pm*'s back pages. Reviewing the special Canadian issues of *Arena*, a New Zealand magazine guest-edited by John Sutherland, and of *Poetry Commonwealth*, a British magazine guest-edited by Earle Birney, Livesay delivers an incisive assessment of each editor's approach: 'Admittedly, it is a hard thing to be an anthologist! Either you let your own tastes take you any whichway, as Birney does; or you try and be catholic, judicial and representative, like Sutherland. The first method encourages new talent, sets a new name in print. But one poem by an unknown writer, with no published work behind him, is scarcely giving accurate measure to the reader abroad' (62). Livesay makes plain her preference for Sutherland's anthological construction of 'a bird's eye view of Canadian poetry from its beginning to the present' (62). Given her decision to review for *pm*, her criticism of the method adopted by Birney is rather ironic in that she thereby attacks one of the mandates of Agazarian's magazine, as Agazarian states in the editorial to the same issue: 'Our aim is to give young artists and writers a medium of expression' (Editorial [1952]). Perhaps accustomed to Crawley's editorial inclination to represent longer poems and groups of poems by individual authors in *Contemporary Verse*, Livesay finds the representation of a poet by a single poem insufficient. Because of the broad representation of the arts in *pm*, each issue could print only one or at most two poems. While Agazarian stood by *pm*'s policy of publishing younger and unknown writers for its three issues, she did not have the opportunity to experiment with Livesay's views and publish larger groups of poems or longer poems in future issues.

We should not conflate the views of a contributor with those of *pm*'s editor, but Agazarian published only a single article about the Massey Commission, one that confirmed the commissioners' view of the cultural Darwinism that inexorably haunts the life of the little magazine. Published in the second issue, Rene Boux's article 'A Note on Theatre and the Massey Report' echoes the commissioners' assessment of little magazines: 'Neither the commissioners nor any of the contributors [to

Royal Commission Studies] suggest that true culture is anything but an organic growth, and the Report eschews any suggestion that the federal government present Canadians with a large beribboned gift-box of custom designed luxuries … Let us distrust any sort of direct state patronage of the arts when the artists are not in a strong enough position' (49, 50). In the third and final issue of February 1952, Agazarian implemented a plan to put the magazine in a stronger position. She announced the growth of *pm*'s circulation from five hundred to two thousand, together with a plea for 'the capital for further expansion' in order to attract advertising revenues, and a request for assistance 'to handle our growing organization' (Editorial [1952]). Increases in *pm*'s print run and plans to expand further still indicate its editor's efforts to compete for a larger share of the periodical market. But if Agazarian's claim that *pm* 'will not be talking advertising language until five or ten thousand' is not an exaggeration, then *pm* could hardly have reached its target market by advertising itself as 'B.C.'s only arts magazine' (Editorial [1952]). Having obtained start-up funding from the local Community Arts Council of Vancouver, *pm* could legitimately expect to serve a local market, and it had managed to balance its books up until the third issue (Editorial [1951]); but without the resources of a Canada Council and without attracting major advertisers or charging advertising rates on a national scale, it could never expect to secure a share in a national periodical market. As Boux put it in his article, 'What a dream world the Massey Report created, full of modest but exciting treasures!' (48). Had the 'dream world' of Canada Council funding materialized in time for Agazarian and *pm*, it might have allowed her to complete the magazine's expansion plans, to attract literary contributions from established poets such as Page and Livesay, and to help launch the careers of still more emergent modernists such as Phyllis Webb. With the collapse of *pm* after February 1952, it fell into the category of 'premature extinction' that the Massey Commission had identified as the defining trait of the little magazine.

'Not a one man job': Aileen Collins and *CIV/n*

'Let us distrust any sort of direct state patronage of the arts' is a declaration that could have found its way into Montreal's *CIV/n* instead of Vancouver's *pm*. *CIV/n* lends credibility to McCourt's conjecture in 'Canadian Letters' that the editor of a little magazine 'would scornfully reject the offer of government aid' (82). *CIV/n*'s first 'editorial' was, in effect, a critique of the Massey *Report* and its proposals for government subsidies for the development of Canadian culture. This 'editorial' was, in fact, an advertisement for Irving Layton's *Love the Conqueror Worm*, published by Contact Press: 'We are asking readers of this magazine to order a copy of this book. This is not a paid advertisement. We are not welshing or quoting the Massey Report. The way to support Canadian literature is to buy and read the work of our best writers' ('Love'). Who are meant by 'we'? If the reference is to Contact Press, then 'we' represents Raymond Souster, Louis Dudek, and Layton himself. If it is *CIV/n*, then 'we' stands for Aileen Collins, Jackie Gallagher, Stanley (Buddy) Rozynski, and Wanda Staniszewska (later Rozynski). Or, better yet, 'we' includes both groups. From the start, the *CIV/n* group extended its collective to include Dudek and Layton, both of whom accepted advisory roles: they attended editorial meetings and read submissions, but neither appeared on the masthead. With the exception of Souster, then, this extended group comprised the 'we' of *CIV/n*'s first editorial-advertisement. In any case, the advertisement makes plain the resistance of a number of Canadian poets, editors, and artists to cultural policies outlined in the Massey *Report*. Instead of opening with a typically tendentious little-magazine manifesto, *CIV/n* employed advertising as an aggressive avant-garde editorial discourse.[10] These are not the same techniques of mass advertising, marketing, or distribution tested by the Toronto-based little magazines *here and now* and *Reading* in the 1940s: *CIV/n*'s advertisement of Layton's poetry is not directed to a mass audience but to the limited readership of the little magazine. Its explicit anti-commercialism parodies the economy of mass marketing and advertising strategies, and its resistance to the governmentalization of culture in Canada is typical of the avant-garde's desire for aesthetic and economic autonomy.

Edited by Collins, *CIV/n* was conceived in Montreal in 1952, and its first issue appeared in January 1953. Like *here and now*, it published a range of established and emergent North American modernist poets of the time: Waddington, Dudek, Layton, Souster, Scott, Smith, Wilkinson, Webb, Ralph Gustafson, Leonard Cohen, Eli Mandel, D.G. Jones, Charles Olson, Cid Corman, and Robert Creeley, among others. Probably because of this impressive list of North American contributors, *CIV/n* has garnered significant literary-historical attention. Histories and memoirs particular to the magazine have been written by Dudek ('Making'), Norris ('Significance'); *Little* 63–8), Francis ('Dramatic'), and Collins (Introduction). Biographical studies of Dudek (Davey

17–18) and of Layton (Cameron, *Irving* 204–6) also bear witness to their advisory roles among the *CIV/n* group. Given her primary position as the magazine's editor, Collins's role in these histories, memoirs, and biographies requires recasting.

Because of its cryptic signature, the starting point for historical narratives about *CIV/n* has always been the name of the magazine itself. By way of explication, the *CIV/n* masthead offers a gloss below the title: 'civilization is not a one man job.' The source of both *CIV/n*'s title and its gloss, as Dudek reveals in his memoir 'The Making of *CIV/n*' (1965), is an unidentified letter by Ezra Pound. (In his annotations to *Dk/ Some Letters of Ezra Pound* [1974], Dudek notes that the name *CIV/n* originated in 'one of Pound's laconic sayings' [103], making no mention of a letter.) Placed in quotation marks, the gloss is itself suggestive of Pound's practice of unattributed quotation, notably in the *Cantos* but also generally as an idiosyncratic notational practice in poems and correspondence. Commentators have often noted Pound's influence on *CIV/n*, especially through his correspondence with Dudek (c. 1949–55). As a consequence, Collins's activities as an editor have been sidetracked by critics and historians exclusively interested in the Dudek-Pound correspondence; this tendency has also bypassed potential inquiry into Pound's influence on Collins. There is no evidence to suggest that Pound was ever in correspondence with Collins. Nevertheless, her editorial decisions to publish excerpts from Pound's prose writings, essays about Pound, and her own editorial about his views on 'Kulchur' in *CIV/n* indicate an intellectual influence deserving of consideration.

In her 1983 memoir about *CIV/n*, Collins carefully distances herself from any direct association with Pound. Recalling the selection of a name for the magazine, she refers to Dudek's 'high enthusiasm for Ezra Pound' and suggestion of 'CIV/n, from Pound's off-hand statement in a letter,' but she attributes no agency to herself as part of the process: 'This name struck us as perfect for our intentions. So CIV/n it was' (Introduction 8). In reporting Stanley (Buddy) Rozynski's retrospective view of *CIV/n*, she again disassociates herself from Pound: 'Central to our work, Buddy believes, were the ideas of Ezra Pound, especially the motto we had adopted as our title' (Introduction 10–11). Nowhere in her memoir does Collins indicate any direct association between Pound or his ideas and herself. In light of Pound's self-confessed antisemitism (and his self-condemnation), her historical revisionism is understandable: she detaches herself from Pound himself, though not from his influence on *CIV/n*. In this respect, her retrospective handling of Pound is somewhat representative of her indirect contact with him through his correspondence with Dudek.

All communication between Pound and *CIV/n* was channelled through Dudek. One could even say that Pound's relationship to *CIV/n* bears a residual resemblance to his transatlantic correspondence and editorial affiliations with Harriet Monroe and Alice Corbin Henderson of *Poetry* and Margaret Anderson and Jane Heap of the *Little Review*. Pound's attempts to manoeuvre *CIV/n* are tinged with his nostalgia for a modernist little-magazine culture of the 1910s and 1920s. His correspondence with Dudek is scattered with references to *Poetry* and the *Little Review*. In a letter of April 1950, for instance, Pound writes to Dudek about the 'difference between Harriet's Poetry and Little Review,' concluding that 'the L. R. did NOT try to putt [*sic*] writing on mantelpiece' (Dudek, *Dk/* 19). Pound's distinction may be debatable, but if one were to choose between the two, the eventual model for *CIV/n* would have to be the avant-garde *Little Review*. If his caricature of *Poetry* is any indication, the admiration Pound still held for the *Little Review* was based as much on its editors' willingness to engage in polemic as on the poetry, fiction, and criticism they published in the magazine. Any contemporary little magazine, according to Pound, should carry out a polemical agenda.

As part of their correspondence, Dudek sent copies of Canadian literary magazines – *Northern Review*, *Contact*, and *CIV/n* – on which Pound passed swift judgment. Disappointed by the second issue of *CIV/n*, for example, he chastised Dudek in a letter of April 1953: 'surely among all you bright young things yu [*sic*] OUGHT to be able to find the makings of at least one pl polemical writer ... Immediate NEED, 1953, of polemical writers/ in eras of ease. decadent 90s etc.' (Dudek, *Dk/* 101). Dudek, in his annotations to this letter in *Dk/*, clarifies his and others' resistance to Pound's polemical program: 'The magazine [*CIV/n*] was in fact extremely 'polemical,' but Pound only recognized as rightly polemical and 'useful' those magazines which parroted his little program to the letter ... We were very much for Pound, but we could not possibly serve him in the way he wanted. In fact, *CIV/n* had its own ego-personalities, and a very locally-focused Canadian program, so that it could not be entirely subordinated to Pound's internationalist ideas' (103). *CIV/n* was never granted Pound's unconditional (or even conditional) approval. After receiving the fourth issue in December 1953 – which contained a pamphlet reprinted at Pound's request,

Dudek's review of *The Translations of Ezra Pound* and article 'Why Is Ezra Pound Being Held in St. Elizabeth's Hospital, Washington, D.C.,' a translation of Camillio Pellizzi's article 'Ezra Pound: A Difficult Man' from the Italian newspaper *Il Tempo*, and excerpts of letters in support of his release – Pound broke off communication with Dudek and *CIV/n* (Dudek, *Dk/* 107).

Resuming correspondence with Dudek in December 1954, Pound acknowledged his continued receipt of *CIV/n* and thereafter offered laconic commentaries on the magazine. In a letter of 21 April 1955 he inquired about Collins: 'who is the CIV/N female. No civilization without civic sense. which I can't recall hitting HIGH in Civ/n. tell me more about the gal's Anschauung [outlook]' (Dudek, *Dk/* 111). Apart from identifying Collins as the editor of *CIV/n*, Dudek provides no annotation on her editorial ideas or 'outlook.' Pound's query probably stemmed from Collins's editorial in the fifth issue, published in March 1954:

> Culture ... is the main topic to-day, for CBC radio talks, letters to *Saturday Night*, etc, etc, etc. ... Now, to me, it doesn't matter half a damn whether we ever achieve a 'Canadian Culture' – or not. Nothing will be done until we start concentrating on producing *poetry* without qualifications as to nation. But a poet in Canada is forced to write with maple syrup on birch bark ... The kind of poetry we want will be a vital representation of what things are, done in strong language (if necessary) or any language, but it will rouse the reader to see just what the world around him is like ... For Kulchur's sake, at least, let's have a lot of bad *good* poetry in future, instead of more *good* bad poetry – and let the dead-head critics hold their peace until the call of the last moose. ('Canadian'; original emphasis)

Collins's adoption of Pound's vernacular neologism 'Kulchur' and advocacy for poetry as its primary vehicle may allude to his *Guide to Kulchur* (1938): 'Man gittin' Kulchur had better try poetry first. If he can't get it there he won't get it anyhow' (122). For Pound, 'Kulchur' signifies no less than the history of a civilization, 'the perception of a whole age, of a whole congeries and sequence of causes' (*Guide* 136). The shift from 'Canadian Culture' to a Poundian 'Kulchur' in the space of Collins's editorial is itself indicative of a continued resistance among the *CIV/n* group to the popular articulation of cultural nationalism. As in the magazine's advertisement-cum-editorial of January 1953, Collins's March 1954 editorial targets the idea of a national culture as represented in the Massey *Report* and circulated through popular print and radio media. Given her rejection of a 'protected and insured' Canadianism and defence of an international 'Kulchur' ('Canadian'), Collins likely would have concurred with some of Pound's exclamatory comments in his letters to Dudek, especially those delivered in reaction to the national orientation of little-magazine cultures in Canada: 'naturally to HELL with Canadian or any other parochial pt/ of view' and '[h]ell No/ git yr/ eye off Canada/ and onto internat/ criteria/' (Dudek, *Dk*/ 88, 89). If we read Pound's April 1955 letter of inquiry as a diffident response to Collins's March 1954 editorial (which it probably is, since she contributed no editorials to subsequent issues), his correlation of what he calls her 'civic sense' and what he deems to be the mediocre level of 'civilization' in the magazine is a clear sign of his disapproval – both of *CIV/n* and of its editor. While her editorial was primarily directed at a national Canadian audience (a 'parochial pt/ of view,' according to Pound), Collins published in the same issue poems by Creeley; translations from the Provençal of Arnaut Daniel and from the French of Rilke and Verlaine; reviews of Woolf and of Creeley, Olson, and Paul Blackburn; and excerpts from Pound's *ABC of Reading* (1934) and *The Letters of Ezra Pound 1907–41* (1951). Subsequent issues displayed its editors' continued maintenance of an international literary profile. Contrary to Pound's assessment, then, Collins edited *CIV/n* with an eye on international criteria, contributors, and literary-magazine culture.

Pound's question, 'who is the *CIV/n* female?' is one too rarely considered by literary historians.[11] In his history of the magazine, Norris diminishes Collins's role to that of an adjunct: 'Despite Dudek's contention that he and Layton tried to stay in the background, their presence was very much felt ... The production work and distribution were handled by Aileen Collins and the Rozynskis, but much of the energy expressed in the magazine stems from Layton and Dudek, and particularly from Dudek' (*Little* 63–4). Reiterating Norris's narrative, Francis has similarly suggested, 'The truly "antithetical" individuals involved with *CIV/n* were Louis Dudek and Irving Layton, and the "real dramatic story" of this magazine derives from the tensions between them' ('Dramatic' 90). Both Norris and Francis thus dispute Dudek's retrospective forward to the *Index to CIV/n*: 'There was always a tactful solicitude on the part of Layton and myself not to interfere with the editorial freedom of the actual editors. We read poetry before a group at Layton's house, enjoying free comments and debate over the poems, but we made no decisions and left the final choice of what was to go in the magazine up to the Editor' ('Making' 230). In her memoir of *CIV/n*, Collins also emphasizes the collaborative nature of the editorial and production work on the magazine. In a letter of 15 August 1954, however, she wrote to Dudek about Layton's interference with *CIV/n*, as he was wanting 'Smith and Scott to be asked to be contributing editors' and Dudek, Layton, and Robert Currie to be 'listed as associate editors,' and 'saying that you can't have unknowns listed in editorial capacity in the magazine any more – because now we have important names in it and the civ/n will increase and people *must* know who really run it, hence, inspire confidence. Staniszewska, Collins, Rozynski – who ever heard of those three wierdies?' With Dudek away from Montreal, Layton seems to have thought himself a Pound – in the manner of Pound's editorial infiltration of Harriet Shaw Weaver's *New Freewoman* (1913) – and attempted to renovate *CIV/n*. Collins's concluding remarks in her letter to Dudek about Layton make plain her anger toward him and his failed takeover bid: 'I am just about ready to pull out – but will see this issue through – Layton is an overpowering son of a, and is also crazy now for names and a policy to cater to said names. Maybe I'm being too sensitive and 'childish' about it – but I feel strongly – why does he want to be publicly ass/d with the editorial staff now? – it is quite obvious and if we wants [sic] it that way, I am not staying as editor to do the typing and send out the mail – ' (LDF, series 2, Collins file). Having invested in a new electric typewriter (which, incidentally, she thought to name 'Ezra') and abandoned mimeograph for print, Collins soon found the costs of printing as overwhelming as Layton's directives (Collins to Dudek, 15 August 1954, LDF, series 2, Collins file).[12] In the end, though, it was not Layton but the lack of a sufficient economic base that brought about the demise of *CIV/n* – a direct and unfortunate result of Collins's decision in the summer of 1954 'to venture into print' (Collins, Introduction 9). While others would rather have the more sensational figures of Layton and Dudek dominate the history of *CIV/n*, Collins herself deserves final recognition for her central role in its editing and its physical production – and, ultimately, in its downfall.

Because the only advertisements carried in *CIV/n* were those of other little magazines or of recent publications from small presses, Collins and the Rozynskis 'paid the costs of the magazine – several hundred dollars before the project ended' (Dudek, 'Making' 231).[13] Whatever the exact circumstances of the decline of *CIV/n*, its editors' intention to engage with an international little-magazine culture was nevertheless accomplished in the later issues. Like the opening editorial-advertisement in the first issue, the advertisements on the back cover of the seventh and final issue, entitled 'CIV/n in Canada / and Abroad,' served as a kind of editorial. This self-advertisement quoted the *Globe and Mail*'s assessment of *CIV/n* as '"the latest poetic purgings" in Montreal' and, in contrast, noted the magazine's enthusiastic reception by a Spanish quarterly called *Quadernos*, the publication of a long article on 'recent Canadian poetry' (presumably on *CIV/n* poets) in the Rome newspaper *Il Secolo d'Italia*, and the dedication of a special New Canadian Poetry issue of the British magazine *Artisan* to 'the Contact-CIV/n poets' (Layton, Dudek, Souster, Webb, and Mandel, among others) ('CIV/n in Canada'). Despite the breadth of its international contacts (it was also listed in James Boyer May's *Trace* magazine, a kind of little-magazine directory), *CIV/n* ended up with a large mailing list of issues 'sent out free of charge to a galaxy of Canadian and American writers' and a small subscribers' list of 'about 100' (Collins, Introduction 8, 9). Though they conferred distinction upon *CIV/n*, these international contacts did not translate into capital to cover the basic production costs for a printed magazine with a limited circulation. Without a grant, a patron, or an organization to underwrite their expenses, the editors of *CIV/n* could not afford to sustain the magazine beyond its final two printed issues. Yet Collins and her fellow editors remained indifferent to the Massey Commission's promise of subsidies for Canadian culture. Rather than write editorials to solicit government aid, *CIV/n* continued through its final issue in early 1955 to run advertisements for little magazines and small-press books and thereby encourage its readers to support both Canadian and international literary culture through the purchase of such publications.

A People's Culture: Margaret Fairley and *New Frontiers*

Even as *CIV/n* contested the Massey *Report* and promoted an international literary avant-garde, cultural leftists likewise opposed the findings of the Massey Commission, but at the same time deplored cultural internationalism and avant-garde art. Canada's cultural leftists and modernists were fellow critics of the Massey Commission but otherwise irreconcilable. When news of the forthcoming leftist cultural magazine *New Frontiers* had started to circulate in Toronto literary circles by the end of July 1951, it mobilized an oppositional modernist literary-magazine culture. In his letter to Dudek dated 6 October 1951, Souster wrote of the Labour Progressive Party's plans to launch *New Frontiers* and of his own scheme to release a new magazine at the same time: 'Biggest factor is the forthcoming publication of the L. P. P. called *New Frontiers*. This will leave no other literary mag in Toronto, and I think that just isn't good enough. There must be some other publication, even if it's only a token gesture. Therefore we plan to bring out the first issue of a mimeographed magazine of verse to be called *Contact* in February.' Adding that 'MAKE IT NEW is our unofficial slogan,' Souster aligned *Contact* with Pound's modernist dictum – and perhaps, if one takes into consideration his anti-communist politics and internationalist cultural agenda, alluded to an ally in opposition to the leftist nationalism of the LPP's cultural arm (Souster qtd. in Gnarowski, *Contact* 4). A preliminary report on the LPP's proposed cultural magazine had been circulated at the Second National Cultural Conference of the LPP, held in Toronto, 12–13 May 1951 (MFP, box 2, file 13). Souster had probably received word of the prospectus and dummy of *New Frontiers* prepared and distributed by the LPP Cultural Commission during the summer and fall of 1951. Opposition to *New Frontiers* seems to have been shared not only by Souster but also among contemporary modernist poets and fellow veterans of Canadian modernist little-magazine cultures of the 1930s and 1940s. None of Canada's prominent modernist poets of the early to mid-1950s would be published in *New Frontiers*.

Edited by Margaret Fairley, the magazine first appeared in January 1952 (Doyle, 'Margaret' 86). Fairley was well aware of the current modernist poets in Canada, including Kennedy, Souster, Klein, Livesay, Scott, James Wreford, Anderson, and Waddington, all of whom she named in 'Our Cultural Heritage,' published as the lead article in the first issue of *New Frontiers*. Rather than refer to them as immediate contemporaries, however, she situated them in the earlier social, economic, and political contexts of the Depression, the Spanish Civil War, and the Second World War: 'Writing in the *Canadian Forum*, and elsewhere, they showed that the life around them was their life, and the energy of their work expressed the response to life of the men who fought back. Where are they now? Is no fighting back needed today?' (1). As the editor of *Spirit of Canadian Democracy: A Collection of Canadian Writings from Beginnings to Present Day* (1945), Fairley had anthologized poems by Waddington ('Partisans,'

'Summer on My Street'), Page ('Foreigner'), and Livesay ('West Coast'), among other modernist poets of the 1940s. She had even submitted a preliminary list of selections to Livesay, asking for suggestions of poems (other than Livesay's own) for inclusion in the anthology (Fairley to Livesay, 27 October 1944, DLP-QU, box 1, file 1, item 13). While, as an anthologist in the early to mid-1940s, she could take her pick among numerous social and/or political poems written by Waddington, Page, Livesay, and others, Fairley did not have the same plenitude available to her as an editor of *New Frontiers* in the early to mid-1950s.

Her literary and political life has been well sketched in articles by David Kimmel and James Doyle, but the story of Fairley's editorial work still remains in outline – that is, a general biographical and historical narrative to which the present study adds detail about her editorships in Canadian leftist magazine cultures. *New Frontiers* naturally tends to dominate this narrative not only as a highlight of her editorial career but also as a resuscitation of a leftist magazine culture dormant in Canada since the fall of its forerunner and namesake, *New Frontier*, in October 1937. The planning of *New Frontiers* in the months concurrent with the release of the Massey Commission's *Report* in 1951 and the launch of the magazine in January 1952 make Fairley's editorials and articles in response to the commission's findings significant cultural documents. Both Kimmel (47–8) and Doyle ('Margaret' 86–7) have devoted attention to her articles and editorials about the Massey Commission in *New Frontiers*. But apart from a nod to the numerous editorials and articles about the commission in the 'left-leaning' *Canadian Forum* (232) and record of the commissioners' refusal to entertain partisan political groups such as the CCF (46–7), Litt's history of the origins, conduct, and reception of the commission and its *Report* omits all reference to leftist cultural organizations and periodicals such as the LPP and *New Frontiers*. This omission is emblematic of *New Frontiers's* reception in Canadian cultural history: except in studies of leftist figures, groups, and publications, the LPP's cultural magazine of the 1950s has been left out of the historical record, especially that of Canadian literary culture at mid-century. Because the majority of studies about English Canadian literary cultures of the 1950s have focused on the development of modernism, Canada's contemporary leftist and anti-modernist literary culture – as represented by magazines such as *New Frontiers* – has so far remained outside the prevailing critical narrative of the period.

If, however, a leftist magazine such as *New Frontiers* is recontextual-ized in relation to its modernist contemporaries, then the history of Canadian magazine culture can accommodate the heated conversa-tions between leftists and modernists in the 1950s. This agonistic rela-tionship reactivates the leftist-modernist dynamic operative in cultural magazines of the 1930s such as *Masses* and *New Frontier*. Just as Livesay's poetry and prose in *Masses* and *New Frontier* often denigrate modernism in the 1930s, so Fairley's involvement with the LPP's Cul-tural Commission and *New Frontiers* promotes an analogous anti-mod-ernist agenda in the 1950s. One crucial distinction, however, is the transition from the internationalism of those leftist and Popular Front cultural magazines of the 1930s to the nationalism of Canadian leftist magazine culture of the 1950s.

Fairley's association with Canadian periodicals began in Toronto with the University College student magazine the *Rebel* (1917–19), which was superseded in 1920 by the *Canadian Forum*; she contributed to both magazines 'articles and reviews that were informed by moder-ate feminism, Fabian socialism and pacifism' throughout the late 1910s, 1920s, and early 1930s (Doyle, 'Margaret' 79). From January 1929 to October 1930, Fairley was an associate editor of the *Forum*. During her editorship, she contributed only one piece of writing, a review article about Virginia Woolf published in the March 1930 issue. Commenting on *Orlando* (1928) and *A Room of One's Own* (1929), Fairley praised Woolf's modernist prose style and handling of the 'woman-artist' as an historical feminist figure ('Virginia' 204); this interest in feminist literature stems from Fairley's commitments to political feminism and activism in the late 1910s and early 1920s, artic-ulated in such early articles as 'The Women's Party' (1918) and 'Domestic Discontent' (1920). These feminist political interests antici-pate her involvement in communist politics by the mid-1930s.

Though she did not follow Livesay's leftist tendencies of the early 1930s and turn anti-bourgeois feminist, Fairley became a member of the Communist Party of Great Britain after moving to England in 1932 and upon her return to Canada in 1936, a member of the Communist Party of Canada (CPC) (Kimmel 36). From November 1936 to October 1937, she contributed to *New Frontier* book reviews, review articles, and even a drawing of the Scottish nationalist and communist poet Hugh Mac-Diarmid. Having re-established herself in Canadian periodical culture through her publications in *New Frontier*, she was appointed book-review editor of the progressive weekly paper the *Canadian Tribune* in the early 1940s, a position she held throughout the war (Doyle, 'Margaret' 83–4). Unlike Livesay, Fairley did not distance herself from the CPC after 1939; she remained with the party (and its 'unofficial' paper, the *Tribune*) through its underground war years (1939–42) and its re-emergence as the LPP in 1943.

After the war, she became a member of the LPP Cultural Commission, founded by Stanley Ryerson in April 1947 (*The L.P.P. and the Arts: A Discussion Bulletin* [n.d.] [1], MFP, box 2, file 13). As a result of her work on the commission, Fairley was appointed editor of *New Frontiers*. Among the first tasks of the commission was a 'study of the background and structure of the Canadian Arts Council' (CAC), an independent administrative body consisting of sixteen national arts groups, whose original May 1944 brief to the House of Commons Special Committee on Reconstruction and Re-establishment called for the creation of a government-sponsored arts administration, among numerous other items of cultural concern (*LPP Cultural Bulletin* [June 1948], MFP, box 1, file 13).[14] Though the LPP's cultural arm did not gain affiliation with the CAC, the party's support of the council's initiatives led to the LPP's subsequent demands for the implementation of the CAC's government-appointed successor, the Canada Council, whose formation was recommended by the Massey Commission in 1951. Among those LPP Cultural Commission members who kept a careful watch on the Massey *Report*, Fairley remained sceptical of the government's intentions. Her lead article in the first issue of *New Frontiers* takes a scalpel to the Massey *Report*, a document to which she returned in her winter 1954 editorial ('The Canada Council'), written in response to Prime Minister Louis St-Laurent's announcement in October 1953 of the government's plan to form the Canada Council.

Fairley used her positions as a representative of the LPP Cultural Commission and editor of *New Frontiers* to promote the cause of a progressive Canadian people's culture, one to which she believed the Massey *Report* and its conception of a national culture stood in opposition. In her January 1952 article 'Our Cultural Heritage,' she offers a useful delineation of the terms 'culture in general ... and progressive Canadian culture in particular': 'our progressive culture is the energetic expression of our life of social struggle, directed to positive, creative, fruitful ends. It is a culture which seeks to record, adorn and change the real life of men in our country. Such culture is opposed to violence in a corrupted world; it is opposed to the negative self-pity of introspective poets, and the escape from reality of abstract artists; it is opposed to the Massey–External Affairs–U.S. State Department culture which would close our eyes to what is happening in half the world, and fix our attention on brutality and murder' (2). Fairley's melodramatic description of oppositional cultures alludes to the second section of the Massey *Report*, where the commissioners correlate national culture and national defence, declaring their inseparability (275). For Fairley, this connection between militarism and culture signals the antithesis to the peaceful and democratic people's culture to which *New Frontiers* pledged itself in its inaugural editorial ('For a Canadian'). Anti-Americanism and anti-militarism are pervasive in the Cold War cultural discourse of *New Frontiers*, foregrounded in the opening editorial, where blatant derogations such as 'the degenerate products of U.S. commercialism' and 'the war-fostering U.S. culture' make plain what Fairley fears in the 'Massey–External Affairs–U.S. State Department culture' ('For a Canadian'; 'Our Cultural'). *New Frontiers*'s anti-modernism is equally pronounced. Her characterization of contemporary modernist poetry and art betrays an antipathy toward modernist modes of subjectivism and non-representational abstraction. Given the turn toward subjectivist modes in modernist poetry of the 1950s – not only in the poetry of Livesay, Marriott, Page, and Waddington, but more generally in Canada, the United States, and Britain – the fact that none of the prominent modernist poets of the day published in *New Frontiers* is hardly surprising.

The logic that enables Fairley to draw links between modernist aesthetic practices and what she calls 'Massey–External Affairs–U.S. State Department culture' may seem dubious, but it derives from her advocacy of an indigenous national culture, a Canadian people's culture. In Fairley's view, literary modernism in Canada is another product of American cultural imperialism. The Massey *Report* mistakenly focuses on the underdevelopment of a contemporary modernist literature, she claims, rather than properly celebrating Canada's literary heritage. Her main objection to the Massey *Report* is, then, that it neglects to report on 'the content of Canadian culture' and instead 'focus[es] the attention on what is not there' ('Our Cultural' 1). Writing of Canadian Mohawk poet E. Pauline Johnson (Tekahionwake), for instance, Fairley makes plain her aversion to literary modernism as a 'cosmopolitan' cultural import and her preference for a native – Canadian and aboriginal – literature: 'It is not difficult to see why she is cold-shouldered by the clique of poets and novelists who are more at home with the cosmopolitan writers of the United States and Britain than with the people of Canada. There are a number of Canadian verse-writers who choose to stand aloof from their country, and write as if suspended in mid-air over no-man's land' ('Pauline' 43). In her editorials and articles in *New Frontiers*, then, Fairley challenges the question posed in the Massey *Report* – 'Is it true, then, that we are a people without a literature?' – and its conclusion: 'all our informants agree that Canada has not yet established a national literature' (222, 225). She disputes the commission's conclusions, arguing that the 'level of universalism' to which the *Report* would have the Canadian author aspire is not the measure of a national literature (226). Universalism is, in this instance, another term for the 'cosmopolitanism' of those American and British modernist authors whose influence is, according to Fairley and *New Frontiers*, the bane of a national people's culture and literature.

While most would dismiss her choice of Canada's greatest poet, Fairley championed the communist poet Joe Wallace above any Canadian modernist of the period: 'At the present time there are men and women in Canada bursting to speak their minds. Some of them are hampered by lack of training and lack of craft. But in different fields some are leading the way; and others are striving through self-education and mutual criticism to overcome their difficulties. In poetry J.S. Wallace writes about and for the people. He expresses the struggles and hopes of the working class in language clear and moving. In emotional power he is the finest poet Canada has yet produced' ('Our Cultural' 6). The import of Fairley's canonization of Wallace is that, in her estimation, Canada had in fact produced a national literature, even if, in view of the findings of the Massey *Report*, it was unrecognized by the legislators of Canadian culture. In its negative assessment of Canadian literature in the 1950s, the Massey *Report* recalls Ruth McKenzie's and Livesay's pessimistic conclusions about the absence of a Canadian proletarian literature in the 1930s (McKenzie 49; Livesay, *Right Hand* 230; see chapter 1: 29–31). According to Fairley, there was a national literature, the democratic and patriotic expression of a people's culture, which had already developed in Canada. So instead of lamenting the lack of a national literature, she asked of the Massey Commission: 'Why not examine more carefully what is there, find out its worth, and discover why, if such is the case, it has been hidden?' ('Our Cultural' 1). *New Frontiers* was thus designed as the means to uncover, discover, and recover a Canadian people's literature: for established contemporaries (Wallace, Kenneth Leslie, Wilson MacDonald), for newcomers (Milton Acorn, George Ryga), and for canonical and non-canonical authors in reprint (Johnson, Norman Bethune, Isabella Valancy Crawford), among others.

New Frontiers outdistanced the combined runs of *Masses* (1932–4) and *New Frontier* (1936–7), but its sixteenth and final issue appeared at the end of a four-year campaign in the summer of 1956. The minutes and memoranda from the LPP Cultural Commission meetings corroborate Doyle's determination that the 'main reasons for the disappearance of *New Frontiers* were economic' ('Margaret' 88). Both the January 1956 memorandum on *New Frontiers* and Fairley's report at the 12 January 1956 meeting of the commission indicate that the magazine faced other obstacles as well, one of which involved the recruitment of editorial board members from Montreal, Winnipeg, and Vancouver to assist the Toronto members. No doubt it was hoped that these local groups – analogous to the Women's Labor Leagues, Progressive Arts Clubs, and New Frontier Clubs affiliated with the *Woman Worker*, *Masses*, and *New Frontier* – could help to increase the distribution and readership of *New Frontiers* across Canada. Plans for a pocket-size format intended to boost circulation and for a reduction in printing and paper costs were implemented in time for the spring 1956 issue, and an appeal was made at that time for subscription renewals and donations. However, as Charles Simms, chairman of the LPP Cultural Commission, predicted in his comments on Fairley's January report and the memorandum on *New Frontiers*, 'There is a growing feeling that the objective situation in the country does not lend itself to the sustaining of a cultural magazine like this' (MFP, box 1, file 13). Simms's prediction, followed by the publication in English of Khrushchev's revelation and denunciation of Stalin's crimes in spring 1956, ensured the end of *New Frontiers*. In his post-mortem on *New Frontiers*, Doyle is incisive in his anatomy of the magazine's failings: 'The non-Communist literary establishment ignored it, most book and periodical dealers boycotted it, and the relatively small number of party members interested enough in cultural matters to subscribe fell far short of what was needed to break even' ('Margaret' 88). Just as the Hitler-Stalin pact of 1939 had thrown the CPC into disarray and prompted members such as Livesay to withdraw from political life, so too the impact of Khrushchev's speech proved devastating to the LPP and its already weakened cultural arm.

On 15 October 1947 Fairley delivered a lecture in which she reiterated a lesson that she might well have learned from the failures of *Masses* and *New Frontier*: 'our own progressive periodicals ... reach only the limited number who for the most part are already on the right track' (qtd. in Kimmel 53). After 1956, there was little hope that the LPP could reach out to a people disillusioned by the confession of Stalin's reign of terror, let alone promote its own cultural magazine. Since the demise of *New Frontiers* in the summer of 1956, the CPC has produced several successors: *Marxist Quarterly*, *Horizons*, and *Communist Viewpoint* (Kimmel and Kealey 254). All these leftist periodicals reinforce Fairley's lesson of October 1947, since none has reached beyond the limited and insular audience of the already converted to realize the promise of a people's culture in Canada.

Granting Culture

Ranging from the nationalism and failed modernism of Hilda and Laura Ridley's *Crucible* to the leftism, anti-modernism, and failed nationalism of Fairley's *New Frontiers*, the histories of women editors and their making of little magazines form a series of critical and transitional events. These events in women's editing of literary, arts, and cultural magazines often correspond to analogous (though not necessarily contemporaneous) moments in the histories of leftist and modernist women poets, particularly those who were also magazine editors and/or members of little-magazine groups. Always shadowing these poets and editors were matters endemic to the business of little-magazine production: the chronic financial, organizational, and communicative problems of the non-commercial literary, arts, and cultural magazine.

Chief among the stumbling blocks encountered by women little-magazine editors were the economic obstacles related to the cost of magazine production and distribution, which usually signalled the end of a given magazine's existence. Such economic difficulties were inevitably related to the problem of securing a sufficient audience to guarantee the continuation of these non-commercial magazines. For some magazines, the means of continuance was found after 1957 through granting agencies such as the Canada Council and provincial and civic arts councils. *here and now* had already obtained support from a forerunner to the Canada Council, the Canada Foundation (est. May 1945), whose founder, Walter Herbert, contributed financial assistance and an appeal on behalf of the magazine to the June 1948 second issue.[15] *pm magazine* had similarly solicited funding from the Community Arts Council of Vancouver (est. October 1946). These small grants-in-aid could not, however, support either magazine for any extended period of time. Without sustainable funding, such non-commercial magazines became part of a continuous cycle of economic crisis, failure, and transition to another magazine. Having set up its own sustaining fund in the late 1930s, the *Canadian Forum* proved an exception to this economic cycle; its survival to the end of the twentieth century was, in large part, owing to the foresight of its editorial board in its second decade. Other magazines without access to private money looked to public funding administered by the Canada Council in the post-1957 period. For those magazines founded prior to 1957, though, the pattern of insolvency and collapse became entrenched in non-commercial magazine culture, perpetuating a historical narrative of cultural growth and extinction. This is not to suggest that the Canada Council could possibly have redeemed all non-commercial magazines from this cycle of cultural Darwinism. The founding document of the Canada Council – the Massey *Report* – may not have proposed subsidies for non-commercial magazines, but McCourt's supplemental report and recommendation, as we have seen, anticipated the Canada Council's policy of offering grants-in-aid to non-commercial magazines. Had these grants been available to such promising editors as Catherine Harmon and Myra Lazechko-Haas, the histories of their magazines probably would have been substantially longer. Given the continued founding of non-commercial literary, arts, and cultural magazines by women after 1957 – with or without funding from the Canada Council – we do well to attend to those women whose editing and publishing of such ephemeral periodicals opened the way for contemporary women editors making their own literary culture.

Conclusion

In Transition

After 1957 the number of little magazines in Canada increased dramatically. The transition to a Canada Council era in the production of literary, arts, and cultural magazines also enabled the continuation of magazines from the pre-council era, including the *Canadian Forum* (1920–2000), *Fiddlehead* (1945–), the *Tamarack Review* (1956–82), and *Quarry* (1952–). Of these magazines, however, only *Quarry* was ever edited by a woman, though not until Gail Fox took over the editorship in 1976; she was succeeded by Bronwen Wallace (1978–81). The decade that witnessed the appearance of *here and now*, *Impression*, *pm magazine*, *New Frontiers*, and *CIV/n* (1947–56) remains one of the most productive periods for women editors of Canadian little magazines. As the number of little magazines in circulation increased after 1957, the percentage of women editors affiliated with these magazines actually dropped.[1] While this statistic does not discriminate between funded and unfunded little magazines, it does suggest a motive for the emergence of a distinct feminist literary-magazine culture in an era of little-magazine proliferation. Since increasing numbers of men had taken up editing little magazines after 1957, it is not surprising that Canadian women in the 1970s perceived the need to band together to found and edit their own magazines for the publication of women's writing. Just as editors of earlier generations often established their modernist or left-oriented magazines at moments of cultural crisis, so too the editors of feminist literary magazines took collective action during a period of men's ascendancy – if only in number – in Canadian little-magazine culture after 1957.

The feminist literary magazines of this period first appeared during a transitional decade in the 1970s and 1980s, one that witnessed the creation of *CV/II* (now *Contemporary Verse 2* or *CV2*) (1975–), *Fireweed* (1978–), *Room of One's Own* (1975–), and *Tessera* (1984–). Compared to the poor survival rate among magazines founded and/or edited by women from the pre–Canada Council period, the high survival rate among contemporary feminist literary magazines indicates the degree to which their existence has been facilitated by funding from the Canada Council and other (provincial and civic) public sources of funding for the arts. The chronic insolvency characteristic of pre-1957 magazines may have abated for the most prominent feminist literary magazines, but this amelioration should not lead one to conclude that the Canada Council itself alleviated the problem of women gaining access to the means of magazine production or to miss the point that a male-dominant magazine culture precipitated a crisis for women writers and a decade of transition during which their feminist literary-magazine culture emerged. While it is not possible to survey here the ongoing editorial and literary contributions of women involved with these magazines, it will be useful to outline the relationship between an earlier generation of little magazines founded and edited by women (1916–56) and the production of feminist literary magazines by contemporary women's writing and editorial collectives.

The need for this kind of transgenerational narrative becomes immediately apparent with the appearance of a feminist literary history such as Barbara Godard's 'Women of Letters (Reprise)' in *Collaboration in the Feminine: Writings on Women and Culture from* Tessera (1994). 'For a number of generations in Canada,' Godard observes, 'young men have seized the means of production to found little magazines and publish their own work.' She goes on to trace a genealogy of magazines founded and/or edited by men since the turn of the nineteenth century, itself a masculinist history, which finally leads to 'literary magazines where women wrote for other women' in the 1970s (269). Her historical narrative accounts for none of the women who edited little magazines prior to the 1970s, suggesting that the advent of feminist periodicals in the 1970s constitutes a rupture in Canada's literary-historical narrative. This perspective can only perpetuate the literary-historical representation of Canadian modernist and leftist little-magazine cultures as masculinist. Rather than accept Godard's view of feminist literary magazines founded in the 1970s as phenomena isolated from previous generations of periodicals founded and edited by women, we might consider the circulation of feminist discourses in earlier literary periodicals studied here as constitutive elements in the later formation of a late twentieth-century feminist literary culture. Feminist literary magazines founded by women for the publication of women authors may not have appeared in Canada until the 1970s – since Godard's emphasis on 'literary' magazines excludes the feminist *Woman Worker* – but the history of periodicals in this country repeatedly records instances since the mid-nineteenth century where women have taken control of the means of literary-magazine production. Citing Gwendolyn Davies's essay ('"Dearer"') on pre-Confederation literary women, collected in *Gynotexts/Gynocritiques* (1987), Godard attests to the histories of women writing for periodicals, yet she neglects the fact that some of the women about whom Davies writes were themselves editors of literary periodicals. Instead of acknowledging these women as editors and foremothers, Godard reads their history as a cautionary tale for contemporary literary women: 'the lesson Gwen Davies has drawn from the past is that the vast body of writing by women in Canada from the eighteenth and nineteenth century appeared in periodical form and, when it has not disintegrated with the paper it was published on, has rarely been taken into account by literary historians charting the periods and genres of literary production in Canada' (265). Despite its erasure of the histories of Canadian women as magazine editors, Godard's assessment of the feminist project of recovery undertaken by Davies speaks eloquently to the necessity for studies of literary women in both the nineteenth and twentieth centuries, including Godard's own history of *Tessera*.

In Godard, it appears, the myth of Canadian modernism and its little magazines as masculinist phenomena has not yet been displaced by an alternative literary-historical narrative; it is a myth that is recentred in her history of *Tessera*, not decentred.[2] That history elides the little-magazine origins of at least one leading feminist literary magazine in Canada. Among the 'literary magazines where women wrote for other women' to which Godard alludes, *CV2* attests to profound continuities between Canada's contemporary feminist literary-magazine culture and its little-magazine culture of the early to mid-twentieth century. At the time Dorothy Livesay founded *CV/II* in 1975, it was a literary magazine edited by a woman and soliciting women's writing, but not yet a feminist literary magazine. *CV2*'s transition from Livesay's editorship (1975–7) to its first women's editorial collective (1984–) provides a case study in the historical connections between the feminist literary magazine and the little magazines founded and/or edited by women in Canada. *CV2* is, to the present day, a standing tribute to her pioneering work on little magazines in the 1930s, 1940s, and 1950s. Her historical span between magazine cultures has been recognized by editors of feminist literary magazines through the publication of the Dorothy Livesay special issues of *Room of One's Own* (1979) and *CV2* (1999). Livesay's enduring significance for contemporary literary women may be attributed in part to the ways in which her modernism and feminism have bridged gaps between generations and literary cultures. Her early political radicalism has also continued to appeal to feminist historians, literary critics, writers, and editors, particularly those involved in feminist editorial collectives such as *CV2*. A history of the beginnings of this magazine, leading from Livesay's editorship to its takeover by a women's editorial collective and transition to a feminist literary magazine, will serve as an apt conclusion to this narrative of her own and other women's contributions to the formation of little-magazine cultures in Canada.

'A Putting Down of Roots': Livesay and *CV/II*

Among the Canadian literary magazines established by women in the post-1957 period, *CV/II* is distinguished from its contemporaries by its ties to Livesay.[3] During her tenure as its founding editor from May 1975 to September 1977, she not only drew upon her experiences with Canadian little magazines of the 1930s, 1940s, and 1950s but also documented these experiences in her own articles, interviews, and editorials in *CV/II*. Livesay herself employed the magazine as a literary-historical archive, a repository for the cultural discourses communicated through her poetry and editorial work since the early 1930s. Cultural modernism and leftism coexist for her in *CV/II*, inflected by her various nationalist, internationalist, and regionalist interests and by her feminism. Through *CV/II*, she recovered some of the histories of little-magazine cultures with which she had been involved for extended periods from 1932 to 1952–3; this recuperative strategy lends itself to my own rearticulation of the histories of modernism and the cultural left developed throughout the present study.

For her first editorial, 'A Putting Down of Roots,' Livesay announced that *CV/II* would function not just as another poetry magazine but as a critical forum for 'perspectives' and 'retrospectives' on Canadian poetry: 'The main body of our magazine will consist of book reviews, review articles, taped interviews concerning "Perspectives." It will contain, as well, "Retrospectives" dealing with poetry and poetic criticism of the past (especially in areas which we feel have been neglected by our literary historians).' That *CV/II* should *not* serve primarily as a venue for contemporary poetry Livesay justified on grounds that 'in 1975 "the times is different"': the proliferation of small presses and little magazines in the 1960s and early 1970s had obviated the need for another Canadian poets' corner. Yet she distinguished her new quarterly from academic journals of the period such as *Canadian Literature* (1959–) or *Essays on Canadian Writing* (1974–) by situating *CV/II* in a genealogy specific to her own editorial experience: the little magazine. Notably, in her editorial, Livesay uses the term 'magazine,' – but not *little* magazine. Instead of being a little magazine – limited in size, circulation, financial resources, and duration – *CV/II* could imitate the style of a little magazine but at the same time appeal to a more extensive literary and academic audience and secure funding from cultural institutions (including St John's College at the University of Manitoba and the Canada Council). Livesay founded *CV/II* in recognition of a multiplicity of cultural discourses and institutions, an amalgam representing the diversity of poetry and poetry criticism advanced in the mid-1970s. She was particularly careful not to cut it from its modernist little-magazine origins, though, as she took a graft from *Contemporary Verse: A Canadian Quarterly* in 'putting down roots' for *CV/II: A Quarterly of Canadian Poetry Criticism*. Even as she refers to *CV/II* as a 'magazine,' the subtitle itself makes an ancillary allusion to the little 'quarterly,' *Contemporary Verse*.

The times were indeed different when the progenitor of *CV/II* came into being, as Livesay recalls in her May 1975 editorial: '*Contemporary Verse* was the name of a poetry quarterly published in Vancouver from 1941 to 1952 – years of drought for the publishing of poetry in Canada.' Putting into practice her own editorial mandate, she attempts to redress the literary-historical neglect of *Contemporary Verse* and to restore it to the forefront of Canada's little magazines of the 1940s. Her editorial 'retrospective' on the publishing 'drought' in Canadian poetry intimates that *Contemporary Verse* was founded at a time of cultural crisis. Compared to the hundred or so little magazines founded in the 1970s alone, the dozen or so little magazines established in the 1940s corroborate Livesay's impressions (see McKnight). Surveying Canada's little magazines of the 1940s, she regards a literary culture consisting of isolated regional publications. She proposes the integration of regions in *CV/II*: 'We would like to have criticism from all the regions, about all the regions. For regionalism is the putting down of roots' (2). For Livesay, the work of the little magazines of the 1940s had marked out the regional frontiers of modern poetry, and 'the work of criticism' could represent the settlement, the cultivation, and 'the growth into maturity of the arts in Canada'; this developmental model is, however, predicated upon the belief that a national quarterly of poetry and poetry criticism could unite Canadian poets and critics. Though she acknowledges the Canadian poetry criticism contributed to academic journals, she derides such 'reports in the elitist quarterlies (with a few honourable exceptions)' and rebukes such criticism for tending 'to concentrate on books published within our "golden triangle"' (Montreal–Toronto–Ottawa). Here Livesay's recollection of little-magazine culture of the 1940s carries over into her outlook on Canadian literary culture of the mid-1970s. She redefines her perception of geographical fault lines among modernist little magazines and poets of the 1940s, categorizing *CV/II* as a 'grass roots,' regionalist, western quarterly in opposition to 'elitist,' cosmopolitan, eastern quarterlies. These fault lines are mapped onto a new context – not among poetry magazines but among quarterlies of poetry criticism. For *CV/II* shares with *Contemporary Verse* a 'western,' regional affiliation, but likewise mandates a national interest in Canadian poetry.

The genealogy Livesay traces – from *Contemporary Verse* to *CV/II*, from poetry quarterly to quarterly of poetry criticism – signifies far more than the passing on of a name and a tradition to the next generation. Between the lines of her comments in 'A Putting Down of Roots' the complex genealogical sources of her editorial practice emerge. Livesay neither alludes to her role as a member of the founding committee for *Contemporary Verse* (except to say that she and McLaren 'gave [Crawley] support through letter writing and contributions') nor mentions her earlier involvement as a member of the editorial board of *New Frontier*. Even so, her roots in both of these magazines anchor her editorial outlook for *CV/II*.

Albeit nearly forty years after the April 1936 inaugural issue of *New Frontier*, Livesay's May 1975 editorial addresses many of the same issues concerning provincialism, social disengagement, and unity of action raised in the first *New Frontier* editorial.[4] Granted 'the times is different,' but the social and cultural concerns and the calls for change remain constant. Although signed by Livesay alone, her editorial is written on behalf of the *CV/II* collective and responds to 'a sense of community.' She is more inclusive and more precise than the *New Frontier* group in her appeal to include issues of class, ethnicity, gender, language, and region under the *CV/II* banner: 'The poetry we want to praise and to print must have the authority of experience and action from all levels of society: the deprived, the enslaved, the sheltered, the brainwashed; as well as the fat, sleek, jaded. It must spring from all ethnic (and immigrant) sources, whose roots will nourish us. Where necessary, as with the literature of Quebec, we must translate and expound. And especially from all parts of the country we would like to explore the true feelings of women.'

During her editorial tenure, Livesay started to fulfil her goal of inclusiveness by publishing special-interest numbers of *CV/II*: 'Special Issue: Women Poets' (fall 1975), 'The Thirties' (May 1976), 'Canadian Indian Poetry and the Folk Tradition' (August 1976), 'A Special International Issue' (December 1976), and 'Manitoba Poets and Poetry' (spring 1977). Also in the interests of inclusiveness, she organized a national editorial network for *CV/II*: 'We are centred here [in Winnipeg, Manitoba], but we are setting up a network of regional scouts from Prince Edward Island to Vancouver Island: first, so that critics may come to know the work of poets better; and second, as added impetus for the fast-developing interest in Canadian writing in the high schools and universities.' This network of regional 'scouts' or editors was similar in organization to the local branches of the Progressive Arts Clubs and the New Frontier Clubs – and, beyond Livesay's history, to the *Crucible*'s Writers' Craft Club and the *First Statement* groups. Where *New Frontier* had hoped to reach a general Canadian public, *CV/II* was more specialized and institutionalized in its intentions: to inform an audience of poets, critics, teachers, and professors already interested in Canadian poetry and poetry criticism. Of course, the actual audience of *New Frontier* had not been so general as the Canadian public either; its own specialized audience comprised a limited group of leftists and fellow-travellers among intellectuals, writers, and artists in Canada in the 1930s.

Livesay's retrospective turn to the 1930s in *CV/II* came about in the 'Perspective' piece in the first issue, 'How I Began,' which contained 'selections from an interview with Joe Wallace, veteran Canadian labour journalist, poet and humanitarian ... conducted by Allan Safarik and Dorothy Livesay: January 1975 in Vancouver, B.C.' (35). Even the title of the Wallace interview serves as a kind of vicarious retrospective on Livesay's beginnings as a leftist activist. In the interview, she recalls when she first met Wallace in Montreal in the 1930s, at a time when he, like herself, was contributing poetry and articles to *Masses*. The interview, like Livesay's editorial, is 'putting down of roots.' As both a perspective on Wallace's literary activities in the 1970s and a retrospective on his and other Marxists' literary and political activities in the 1930s and 1940s, the interview documents one of those areas that Livesay believed to have been neglected by social and cultural historians. Even the 'Retrospective' article in the following special issue on women poets reflects Livesay's interests in renewing her leftist vision from the 1930s. Her headnote to Kenneth J. Hughes's article ('Democratic Vision of "Malcolm's Katie"') sets his Marxist reading in the context of a feminist act of historical revision and reclamation: 'Emphasis in this issue on women poets makes it fitting that we print an article on a neglected aspect of the work of Isabella Valancy Crawford' (38). 'A Special International Issue,' which appeared in December 1976, also embodies the internationalist concerns espoused in *New Frontier* in the 1930s. Of particular interest is Livesay's interview with Hugh MacDiarmid in that issue, which demonstrates her wide knowledge of communist politics and Marxist theory. Taken together, the 'Perspective' on Wallace, the 'Retrospective' on Crawford, and the interview with MacDiarmid represent Livesay's entwined ideological positionings in the 1930s and in the 1970s – at once leftist and feminist.

The *CV/II* May 1976 special issue, 'The Thirties,' headlined retrospective pieces by two veterans of *New Frontier*: Livesay ('Canadian Poetry and the Spanish Civil War') and Leo Kennedy ('A Poet's Memoirs'). As Livesay mentions in her article, Kennedy was 'one of the contributing editors to the magazine founded in April 1936, *New Frontier*' (14). In calling attention to Kennedy's June 1936 article in *New Frontier*, 'Direction for Canadian Poets,' she praises his 'setting up critical standards which he was the first to follow' ('Canadian' 14). Kennedy's article speaks to the social responsibility of Canadian poets: 'It is my thesis that the function of poetry is to interpret the social scene faithfully; *to interpret especially the progressive forces in modern life which alone stand for cultural survival*' (22; original italics). Four decades later Livesay refers to poetry of the same orientation in her May 1975 *CV/II* editorial: 'The aim of poetry, which has the potential of surviving fashions and fads, is to illuminate the world and mankind's task within it' ('Putting'). The complementary purpose of poetry criticism, as she envisioned it in putting together 'The Thirties' issue, is to ensure that such poetry survives for even forty years in our cultural memory. Collectively, Livesay, in her article 'Canadian Poetry and the Spanish Civil War,' Kennedy, in his memoir and review of the special Raymond Knister issue of the *Journal of Canadian Fiction* ('A Poet's Memoirs'), and Roy St. George Stubbs, in his review of the 1975 reissue of Kennedy's 1933 collection, *The Shrouding*, contribute to the preservation of 1930s culture for contemporary audiences. Cultural memory depends, though, on the interests of contemporary culture. Robert Enright's 'Reflections and Expectations' editorial of August 1976 therefore underscores the relationship between perspectives and retrospectives on the past and *CV/II*'s situation in the present: 'The "Thirties Issue" was an attempt to combine a traditional poetic with a more modern one, to look back at where we have been and ahead to where we might proceed.'

Just as *CV/II* provided the forum for Livesay to generate critical awareness of her own and others' contributions to the cultural left in the 1930s, it also gave her the opportunity to pay homage to Crawley and the *Contemporary Verse* group of the 1940s and early 1950s.[5] At certain moments in 'A Putting Down of Roots,' she even echoes Crawley's editorial policies. Like Crawley, Livesay adopts a policy of openness toward poetry. What he calls 'poetry that is sincere in thought and expression and contemporary in theme' ('Editor's Note' [1942] 3) she names 'poetry – whatever its genre – that expresses our craving for confrontation with the real, with direct, day-to-day living' ('Putting'). (Livesay's demand for social realism, though, is more typically her own criterion than a reflection of Crawley's request for sincerity and contemporaneity.) In terms of poetry criticism, her scepticism toward avant-garde poetics resonates with his diffidence toward the current 'literary trend': 'Thus, we need to challenge, in terms that are cogent, apropos, and informed, the writings of our avant-garde experimentalists, so that we may profit by what extends the bounds of poetry, and not be held back by sentimental revisitations of the scandals and astonishments of the past' (Livesay, 'Putting'). To be 'contemporary in theme and treatment and technique,' to reiterate Crawley's poetic criteria, is not licence to what Livesay terms 'metaphysical, linguistic, and absurdist strivings' or 'gamesmanship with pun and counterpun, a glittering skill in mounting maps of montage' ('Putting'). She may want to be liberal, but her bias against poetry that generates an anti-referential free play of signifiers is unequivocal; she is not so much rearguard as cautious in her advocacy of the contemporary poet's progress. Livesay's editorial policy is aimed at the advancement of multiple constituencies, including poets of the avant-garde.

One of the effects of Crawley's editorial policies was his strong representation of women poets in *Contemporary Verse*. In his memory Livesay's 'Rememberings' article of fall 1975 serves as an important retrospective in the context of the 'Women Poets: Special Issue' of *CV/II*: 'Alan Crawley has been so closely associated with poets, especially women poets, over the past forty years that none of us, perhaps, can write of him with detachment' (2). As editor of *Contemporary Verse*, Crawley had anticipated her offer to women poets in her first *CV/II* editorial: 'from all parts of the country we would like to explore the true feelings of women. Many women poets today are either looking into mirrors or speaking from behind masks' ('Putting'). In the eight issues of *CV/II* edited by Livesay, the number of male and female poets is roughly even. (S.G. Buri calls attention to this statistical fact in his editorial to the 'Women Poets' issue: 'CVII would like to strike a balance fairly soon based on gender, not for political reasons, but because it is a fact of Canadian poetry's life.') However, the number of critics and reviewers published during Livesay's editorship is weighted toward men – approximately four men to one woman. (Buri takes note of this gender imbalance in the same editorial: 'I hope we shall have more women critics.') Women poets and critics are represented in less than one-third of the reviews, articles, and interviews carried by *CV/II* during these first two years. It should be noted, however, that Livesay's *CV/II* was, as Butling says of *Contemporary Verse*, not a 'women's magazine.' Statistics on the representation of region, class, race, ethnicity, and region in *CV/II* could substantiate different interpretations. According to Livesay's original objectives for the magazine, women were but one constituency, albeit privileged, that she wished to represent in the demographic of *CV/II*.

Unlike Crawley's decision to terminate his editorship of *Contemporary Verse*, Livesay's resignation from *CV/II* obviously did not signal the end of the magazine. Published in the January 1978 issue, her final editorial opens with a reversal of her May 1975 position on 'surviving fashions and fads': 'Fashions in clothes change, fashions in painting and poetry change. And so, in the course of things, editors change' ('On the Way'). Rather than invest in the illusion of permanence she so desired in founding *CV/II*, Livesay admits that magazines are sites of cultural impermanence, always subject to change. With her resignation in September 1977, she left open the possibility for an editorial transformation of *CV/II*.

Almost a decade after Livesay's 'Women Poets' special issue in 1975, gender returned to the foreground of *CV/II*'s editorial concerns. In 1984 Pamela Banting, Di Brandt, Jane Casey, and Jan Horner announced yet another transformation of *CV/II*: '[The conference] *Women and Words* focused our frustrations and our energies and we began to think seriously about forming an editorial collective.' These four women of *CV/II* assumed editorial responsibility for what the four women on the founding committee of *Contemporary Verse* had started more than four decades earlier. In her editorial for the newly designed, newly named *CV II* (later *CV2*), Pamela Banting offered her retrospective on the gender distribution among the editors and publishers of *Contemporary Verse* and *CV/II*: 'Vol. 1, No. 1, of *Contemporary Verse: A Canadian Quarterly* was published in September 1941 ... Four women conceived of the magazine and elected a man ... to edit it ... At the launch of *CV/II* in 1975 the editor was a woman, Dorothy Livesay, and the three assistant editors were men ... At this juncture, all the editors are female, and we operate as an editorial collective ... Dorothy Livesay remains the publisher, and we have a tradition to draw on, to scribble on' ('blurred' 5, 6, 7).

To this genealogy, I would preface *New Frontier*, a Popular Front magazine with a socialist ideology and organized around the idea of the editorial collective. As an ideal (though, as we have seen in the first chapter, in reality imbalanced) democratic editorial prototype, *New Frontier* embodied what the four women editors of *CV II* might have imagined in 1984 when they 'were talking about men and women in dialogue, reinterpreting Dorothy Livesay's original vision for a national poetry magazine.' The democratic model of *Contemporary Verse*, whereby four women elect a man to edit the magazine, is by no means an adequate template. The feminist model of *CV/II*, whereby Livesay takes over Crawley's position as editor with male assistants, is also flawed because it reproduces a hierarchical, even patriarchal, editorial structure. The takeover of *CV II* from Robert Foster by the women's editorial collective in 1984 was, in theory and in practice, an act of deconstruction: a tradition of hierarchical editorial power was dismantled, and an editorial collective founded. This editorial takeover signals yet another moment of transition in the history of women and little magazines in Canada, the transition to a women's literary-magazine culture. No longer styled or organized in imitation of

the little magazines of the 1930s and 1940s, *CV II* evolved thereafter
into a feminist literary magazine.

Contrary to Godard's version of feminist literary-magazine history,
CV2 has not forgotten its little-magazine origins. Livesay's historical
recovery of her own little-magazine activities through the 'perspective'
and 'retrospective' pieces she published during the two years of her
editorship rooted the magazine in the histories of modernist and leftist
little-magazine cultures. These histories are not, as Godard would
have it, exclusively masculinist. They are, at least in part, the histories
of literary women that the *CV2* editorial collective commemorated in
1999 by publishing a special Livesay issue. These histories are, rather,
the intertwined narratives of modernist and leftist women poets and
little-magazine editors that I have recovered and compiled in this
account.

1957 and After

None of the other magazines founded and/or edited by women
between 1916 and 1956 has been re-established at a later date. Nor did
any other women magazine editors from that period found new magazines in subsequent decades. During the 1970s, Dorothy Livesay, P.K.
Page, and Miriam Waddington did return to editing, but not to editing
magazines. Livesay and Page both tried their hands at editing anthologies of poetry (see Livesay's *40 Women Poets of Canada* [1971] and
Woman's Eye: 12 B.C. Poets [1974] and Page's *To Say the Least: Canadian
Poets from A to Z* [1979]). Waddington edited John Sutherland's *Essays,
Controversies, Poems* (1972) and *The Collected Poems of A.M. Klein* (1974).
And Livesay, Anne Marriott, Page, and Waddington, of course, continued to publish new and retrospective collections of poetry throughout
the latter half of the twentieth century.[6]

There is scant evidence of literary activity among the rest of the
magazine editors after the demise of their respective publications.
Except for Hilda Ridley, who published a biography of Lucy Maud
Montgomery in 1956, the output of these women was sharply attenuated after the early to mid-1950s. Catherine Harmon published a
handful of poems in *Fiddlehead* and the *Canadian Forum* in the summer
of 1959, but nothing more came of her brief venture into poetry. After
a promising debut chapbook in 1952, Myra Lazechko-Haas seems to
have stopped publishing her poetry – at least in periodicals outside the
Ukrainian Canadian community. As the editor (with the assistance of

Simon Dardick) of *CIV/n: A Literary Magazine of the 50's* (1983), Aileen Collins renewed critical and literary-historical interest in the magazine she had founded; she has since edited and introduced Louis Dudek's *In Defence of Art: Critical Essays and Reviews* (1988) and his *1941 Diary* (1996). Margaret Fairley continued to write articles for the successor to *New Frontiers*, the Marxist quarterly *Horizons*: 'Roots of Patriotism in English Speaking Canada before Confederation' (1963), 'Moral Responsibility of the Communist' (1966), and 'The Cultural Worker's Responsibility to the People' (1968). Of Mary Davidson, Laura Ridley, Eleanor Godfrey, and Yvonne Agazarian, not a trace of literary or editorial activity is evident in the years after their departure from Canadian magazine culture. New evidence may surface to contradict these findings, but searches through currently available indexes and bibliographies have turned up nothing to suggest their ongoing activity.

Unlike the long careers of poets such as Livesay, Page, Marriott, and Waddington, those of little-magazine editors last only as long as their ephemeral periodicals. Because many of the little magazines edited by women between 1916 and 1956 folded after short runs, and because all but one (Hilda Ridley) of these women seem to have ended their literary and/or editorial careers along with their magazines, women little-magazine editors have fared poorly in Canadian literary history. Fairley's long career has attracted the attention of several historians, and to a lesser extent, Flora MacDonald Denison, Florence Custance, Harmon, Godfrey, and Collins have gained some recognition, but Davidson, the Ridleys, Agazarian, and Lazechko-Haas have been invisible to Canadian literary history. Certainly, the rarity of copies of little magazines such as the *Sunset of Bon Echo*, the *Woman Worker*, the *Twentieth Century*, the *Crucible*, *pm magazine*, and *Impression* has hindered research on their editors. The scarcity of archival documents related to women little-magazine editors has likewise hampered research in the field. Histories of these women may always remain incomplete for lack of resources, yet even partial histories are better than their exclusion from narratives about the literary cultures they helped to develop through their little magazines.

Women poets who contributed to leftist and modernist little magazines have of course fared much better in literary history. Livesay, Marriott, Page, and Waddington responded to and recovered from the poetic crises of their little-magazine years in different ways. While Marriott and Page lapsed into periods of silence, Livesay and Waddington continued to write and collect their poems through the

1950s, 1960s, and thereafter. All four poets returned to their early poetry in retrospective collections, recovering for later generations the modernist and/or leftist poems of their little-magazine years. The publication of Waddington's *Collected Poems* in 1986, the release of Page's two-volume *The Hidden Room: Collected Poems* in 1997 and *Planet Earth: Poems Selected and New* in 2002, and the reissue of Livesay's *The Self-Completing Tree: Selected Poems* in 1999 represent their publishers' continued commitment to Canadian women's poetry from the 1920s through the 1950s and, presumably, their readers' abiding interest. Both Waddington's and Page's collections have reprinted previously uncollected poems. If the response to Livesay's *Collected Poems: The Two Seasons* in 1972 and *Right Hand Left Hand* in 1977 is any measure of the effect that the reprinting of previously uncollected poems can have on a poet's critical reception, the literary-historical narratives we have constructed around Page and Waddington will likely require revision. In Livesay's case, her oeuvre has been augmented once more with my own recovery of additional pieces in *Archive for Our Times: Previously Uncollected and Unpublished Poems of Dorothy Livesay* in 1998. It is, however, probably still too soon to judge whether or not these poems will induce substantial change in critical and literary-historical narratives. Compared to Page, Waddington, and Livesay, Marriott has not sustained a consistent following among critics and literary historians. With *The Circular Coast: Poems New and Selected* (1981) long out of print and her poetry now rarely anthologized, it is difficult to imagine a renaissance in Marriott criticism, though Marilyn Rose's recent essay collected in *The Canadian Modernists Meet* (2005) is a promising sign of renewed interest. Perhaps a collected (or even a complete) volume will appear in future years to spark interest in a poet whose early success has not been matched by a sustained record of criticism.

Access to little magazines probably represents the major obstacle to the advancement of research in the field. *Preview* was reproduced in a facsimile edition in 1980. The text of *CIV/n* was issued in book form in 1983. An anthology of material from the *Woman Worker* was compiled in 1999. *Masses*, *New Frontier*, and *First Statement* are available on microfilm. The *Canadian Forum* is easily the most accessible among these magazines. Plans for a facsimile edition of *Contemporary Verse* were made in the early 1970s but scuttled once Crawley determined that the collection might infringe upon authors' copyright; it is, however, available in bound copies at Library and Archives Canada and in special collections across the country. Projects such as the Canadian Institute for Historical Microreproductions (CIHM) have made a selection of pre-1900 Canadian periodicals readily available for scholarly research on microfiche; but CIHM has not yet reached the 1920s and after. Were full runs of little magazines such as the *Sunset of Bon Echo*, the *Woman Worker*, the *Twentieth Century*, the *Crucible*, *Contemporary Verse*, *here and now*, *pm magazine*, and *Impression* more widely available in reproduction,[7] the literary-historical investigation of women little-magazine editors could be undertaken by a greater number of scholars and their work more often taught to students of Canadian literature and history. The problem of access is equally true of poetry published in these little magazines but never collected; it is obviously more pronounced in the case of poems never published and only available in archives. Having drawn attention to little magazines edited by women and to previously uncollected and unpublished poems written by women, I expect the need for further critical and editorial projects designed to retrieve and recontextualize these materials should be apparent. Otherwise we may continue to reproduce literary-historical narratives based on oeuvres circumscribed by editors, publishers, and the poets themselves, but not necessarily representative of the poetry and poetics at a particular historical moment.

Continued editorial and historical reconstructions of little-magazine cultures between 1916 and 1956 and of women's modernist and leftist poetry will be essential to remaking literary-historical narratives of that period. By documenting women poets' editorial activities and memberships in writers' groups, I have sought to restore their poetry to the historical circumstances of little-magazine cultures and to the actual practices of little-magazine editing and production. At the same time, I have attempted to read their poetry in the immediate context of its publication in little magazines or in relation to its rejection by little-magazine editors, by publishers, and by the poets themselves. These poems left out of books or chapbooks and consequently from literary history have provided the textual resources for alternative literary-historical narratives about Canadian women's modernist and leftist poetry. It should be evident that I have not undertaken a survey of Canadian women's poetry published in little magazines between 1916 and 1956. Rather than sweep through the period with a broad overview, I have recorded literary-historical minutiae and recontextualized these findings. This strategy has proven useful to a project of exposing masculinist editorial practices and recovering histories of women's editorial labour in the context of Canadian little magazines.

With the knowledge of particular editorial practices and decisions, we may begin to understand with greater precision the ways in which cultural phenomena as capacious as literary modernism and leftism have been constructed by Canadian women poets and little-magazine editors. That knowledge will enable further literary-historical reconstructions written in a manner strange to the narratives we have known, yet written in order to reclaim the histories of women and little magazines in Canada.

Notes

Introduction

1 For studies specific to women little-magazine editors and modernism, see
   Jayne E. Marek's review of the literature and bibliography of articles,
   books, theses, and dissertations in *Women Editing Modernism: 'Little' Magazines and Literary History*. See also M. Jones; Morrisson; and McKible. A
   Canadian adjunct to Anglo-American modernist studies, Doyle's essay
   'Harriet Monroe's *Poetry* and Canadian Poetry' (1989) addresses Canadians published in the American little magazine *Poetry: A Magazine of Verse*
   (1912–).
2 See Benstock; Huyssen; DeKoven, *Rich and Strange* and 'Modernism and
   Gender'; Clark; Rabinowitz; B. Scott; Felski, *Gender*; Gilbert and Gubar;
   Rado; Ardis and Lewis.

1 Invitation to Silence

1 Peter Stevens's information about the terms of publication for *Green
   Pitcher* is taken from the correspondence series between Livesay and
   Hugh Eayrs of Macmillan dated 5 March 1928 to 15 August 1928 (MA,
   box 114, file 3). Correspondence concerning the publication of *Signpost* is
   no longer extant. Another correspondence series, between Livesay and
   G.E. Rogers of Macmillan and dated 1 April to 2 June 1936, indicates that
   she had submitted to Macmillan a poetry collection entitled 'The Outrider and Other Poems' circa March 1936. Macmillan agreed to publish
   the collection on terms similar to those for *Green Pitcher*, an offer that
   suggests they had reached a comparable agreement for the printing costs
   of *Signpost*. According to Rogers's letter of 25 April, Livesay's proposed

collection was forty-four pages in length. Her reply of 25 May requested the return of her collection so that she could 'shorten the ms. somewhat.' She asked for a deadline for submitting the collection for publication in the fall of 1936. Rogers gave her one of 30 June, but we may surmise that Livesay must subsequently have changed her mind about publishing her collection with Macmillan (MA, box 114, file 4).

2 Ellen Elliott's letter of 14 April 1942 mentions Livesay's submission of another collection to Macmillan (DLP-QU, box 1, file 1).

3 In a subsequent letter to Pierce, dated 16 August 1943, Livesay alludes to an offer from the recently founded First Statement Press to bring out her collection in the fall of 1943, but adds that she is willing to wait for Ryerson to release *Day and Night* in the spring of 1944 (LPP, box 9, file 16, item 45). No correspondence between John Sutherland of First Statement Press and Livesay has survived to corroborate her claim.

4 In *Journey with My Selves: A Memoir 1909–1963*, Livesay recalls that in Toronto in 1932–3 she 'was in the writers' group chaired by Ed Cecil-Smith' (81); she was secretary of the Montreal PAC in 1933–4 (a letter, dated 16 January 1934 and published in *Right Hand Left Hand*, from the Montreal PAC, is signed by 'D. Livesay, Secretary' [83]); she was chair of the Vancouver PAC in 1936 (an incomplete carbon bearing the minutes of a PAC meeting dated 15 June 1936 names Livesay among other members of the executive committee; see DLC-UM, box 15, file 3).

5 The June 1932 issue of *Masses* features on its 'Criticism and Self-Criticism' page a linocut print that depicts a worker hoisting a flag emblazoned with the slogan 'Proletcult' ([14]). For more detailed discussion of the history of the Soviet cultural organizations in the 1920s and 1930s, see Murphy 21–35.

6 According to Ryan, *Masses* 'had national circulation in the principal Canadian cities and in some smaller ones.' 'Our sales were modest,' he says, 'but we obviously created some interest' (qtd. in Gordon Ryan 27).

7 See Livesay, *Right Hand* (115) for her explanation of the use of pseudonyms to conceal her leftist activism from her father, J.F.B. Livesay.

8 *Masses* later published a series of editorials attacking the *Canadian Forum*. See 'The Canadian Forum'; 'Canadian Forum'; 'Canadian Forum – The General Articles'; and 'The Forum Editorials.'

9 See Livesay's letter to the editor of *Collected Poems*, Laura Damania of McGraw-Hill Ryerson, dated 22 June 1972: 'It['ls strange after feeling so frustrated last evening about the inclusion of "Testament" amongst The Thirties galleys (now sent back to you), today an answer came. A young socialist in Fredericton sent me a poem of mine he liked from the Thir-

ties. I have no recollection of writing it, but I'm sure it's mine.' The poem to which Livesay refers is clearly 'A Girl Sees It!'; she adds a note at the bottom of the letter requesting that 'Testament' be pulled from the collection and replaced with the retitled 'In Green Solariums' (DLC-UM, box 51, file 3).

10 For a corroboration of this reading of Livesay's socialist feminism, see Gingell (3).

11 Biographically speaking, the newspaper image evokes Livesay's familial connections to the industry. Livesay's father, J.F.B. Livesay, was general manager of the Canadian Press.

12 Doyle suggests that M. Granite may be 'a pseudonym for Oscar Ryan, who also wrote as "Martin Stone"' (*Progressive* 97).

13 This definition of socialist realism was widely adopted after the collapse of the Russian Association of Proletarian Writers in April 1932 and the subsequent abandonment of its limited definition of proletarian literature. The formation of the All-Russian Union of Soviet Writers in October 1932 was accompanied by the official acceptance and definition of socialist realism as 'the faithful description of life in all its aspects, with the victorious principle of the forces of the socialist revolution' (qtd. in Murphy 145). In his article, Cecil-Smith reproduces definitions of socialist realism from Lunacharsky's article 'Problems of Style in Socialist Art' (1933) and his speech to the second plenary session of the Organization Committee of the All-Russian Union of Soviet Writers (1933).

14 For a history of Livesay's social work and its relationship to her poetry and poetics, see Moffatt 46–68.

15 Autobiographically speaking, 'Growing Up' fits perfectly in the 'Montreal 1933–1934' section of *Right Hand Left Hand*. According to the date on Livesay's worksheet, however, the poem was composed on 13 September 1934, two months after her return to Toronto. Likewise, her worksheet for 'Twenty Years After' is dated August 1934 (DLC-UM, box 80, file 4).

16 An early version of this poem, entitled 'Case History I,' is dated October 1933 (DLC-UM, box 80, file 4).

17 Whether or not this poem was written immediately after the events or several years later to commemorate the death of Zynchuk is uncertain. The surviving typescript of the poem, the copy text for the poem as it appears in *Right Hand Left Hand*, is undated. The poem may have been revised in 1936 for publication in the *Worker*.

18 The typescript of 'Rain in April' appears among a selection of poems entitled 'Down and Out Series,' which Livesay retrospectively dated 1934–5 (DLC-UM, box 80, file 4).

19 'Repeal,' which is undated, may have been written while Livesay was
living in Montreal. Her reference in the poem to the incarceration of CPC
secretary Tim Buck in October 1932 offers one clue to its earliest possible
date of composition; another piece of evidence is her later notation on the
typescript, '1934 or whenever the 8 were jailed' (DLC-UM, box 80, file 4).
(The '4' of 1934 is written over a '5,' indicating Livesay's uncertainty as to
the exact date of composition.) The Kingston Eight – the imprisoned
members of the CPC who were the subject of the PAC's performance in
December 1933 of *Eight Men Speak* – served over two years in prison.
'Repeal' could have been written at any time between their conviction in
October 1932 and their release over two years later.

20 'Broadcast from Berlin' and 'Canada to the Soviet Union' contain lines
duplicated in the mass chant 'Struggle' and the poem 'Montreal: 1933.'
This duplication may help to explain why 'Montreal: 1933' but not
'Canada to the Soviet Union' was included in *Collected Poems* and why
'Struggle' but not 'Broadcast from Berlin' was collected in *Right Hand Left
Hand*.

21 See Livesay's recollection of her conversation in 1934 with Louis Kon, a
Russian immigrant and activist for the Friends of the Soviet Union, in
Right Hand Left Hand: '"Why aren't you writing poems? You have the
lyric gift and you are wasting yourself writing propaganda?" "But my
poem Nick Zynchuk is not just propaganda!" ... I told him I did not want
to write lyric poetry anymore. All that was finished. My guide was
Lenin' (101).

22 Given Livesay's close working relationship with Cecil-Smith while he
was the chair and she a member of the Toronto PAC writers' group, we
may look to his 'Propaganda and Art' article for affirmation of such an
aesthetic principle. Cecil-Smith quoted the following passage from
Anatole Lunacharsky's 1933 speech to the Organization Committee of the
All-Russian Union of Soviet Writers: 'One of the most important variations of this mastery of reality by art is socialist romanticism which can
fancy the future and picture utopias that may provide scientific socialism
with an excellent form of the essentially realistic dream which Lenin
regarded as a necessary element of a general revolutionary outlook'
(Cecil-Smith 11).

23 In a passage from *Right Hand Left Hand* that angered her former communist friends, Livesay recanted and at the same time rationalized her
youthful participation in the CPC: 'I learned a great deal about Communist tactics of penetration and camouflage; but I was too committed to be
shocked. It was only years later that the false actions and fractional

tactics were revealed to me in their real light. This did not cause me to hate the communists, or to red-bait; rather I was disgusted with myself for having been so duped. But I believe I let myself be duped because no one else except the communists seemed to be concerned about the plight of our people, nor to be aware of the threat of Hitler and war' (74).

24 Remonstrations against Livesay's overstatement concerning the absence of radical poets in North America contemporaneous with the MacSpaunday group in Britain have already been made convincingly by Irr (215); there is no need to add to her list of North American candidates.

25 W.E. Collin had already written about 'The Outrider' (still unpublished at the time) in his chapter on Livesay in *The White Savannahs* (1936; see 161–6). When it was published in 1943, an editorial note informed the reader that the poem, 'hitherto unpublished, was written in 1935. It was discussed at length by W.E. Collin in his "White Savannahs"' (Livesay, 'Outrider' 18).

26 Candida Rifkind identifies another fugitive poem from this 1934–5 period, 'For a Young Communist,' which was published in the 6 July 1935 issue of the *Young Worker*, a CPC newspaper that appeared from 1924 to 1936 ('Labours' 53–4). Its experimentation with a heavily accented two-beat line clearly anticipates the marked machine-like rhythms of 'Day and Night.'

27 For more on the 1936 CAA convention, see Colman; and Livesay, 'Livesayings.'

28 There are tentative parallels to be found in the ways that Canadian performances of international agitprop plays, such as Clifford Odets's *Waiting for Lefty* (1935), were often adapted to address the contexts of local labour struggles (see Bray; Filewod; Rifkind, 'Modernism's'). This is not to suggest that Livesay merely rewrote versions of the Auden generation's poems for localized Canadian audiences but to acknowledge a common tendency among writers on the left during the 1930s.

29 Writing to Livesay on 16 July 1937, Jocelyn Moore noted that Leo Kennedy wanted to print sections of 'The Outrider' in an upcoming issue of *New Frontier* (DLC-UM, box 64, file 36). No further mention of the poem is made in the extant *New Frontier* correspondence.

30 An untitled typescript of 'In Praise of Evening' is so numbered in roman numerals, indicating its former inclusion in a sequence (DLC-UM, box 80, file 5).

31 As chair of the Vancouver NFC, Livesay approached Lawson in the spring of 1936 with a proposal for the merger of *New Frontier* and the *Canadian Forum*. Lawson's guarded response in his letter of 6 May 1937 to

Livesay not only makes clear the impossibility of a merger on his terms but also speaks to problems of organization among left-wing groups in the Popular Front: 'The basis of unity would be the exclusion of Trotskyites and putting two or three of our people on the Forum board. We couldn't as I see it do anything about the united front policies for the time being, but that should be no reason for delaying the merger if it can be effected' (*Right Hand* 237).

32 Cf. Eliot: 'the poet has, not a "personality" to express, but a particular medium, which is only a medium and not a personality' ('Tradition' 42).

33 Although separate from the PAC, the Vancouver NFC had been officially affiliated with the local PAC since July 1936 (DLC-QU, box 15, file 3).

34 These clubs were first proposed to the national readership in the 'Between Ourselves' column of March 1937. The proposal for the NFC was occasioned by managing editor Lawson's 'tour of Western Canada, with the object of building our circulation in the western cities. He will visit Saskatoon, Edmonton, Calgary, Vancouver, Victoria, Regina and Winnipeg. New Frontier clubs, organizations of individuals interested in our magazine and willing to help increase its influence, have been set up in Vancouver, Montreal, and Toronto.'

35 For more on the financial situation of the *Canadian Forum*, see chapter 4. See also Carr 43–4.

2 Marginal Modernisms

1 As early as December 1936, McLaren and Ferne were seeking alternative venues for their own poetry, both having interviewed Hugh Eayrs of Macmillan about bringing out an anthology of the strongest poets from the Victoria poetry group and about publishing individual collections of their own (Perry to Edgar, 28 December 1936, MEPP, box 5, file 23).

2 This coexistence of conservative and modernist poets in the same publication attests to the representativeness of *Canadian Poetry Magazine* as a forum for the nation's poetry culture in transition. Indeed, closer scrutiny of the first volumes of *Poetry* would also reveal a magazine – where late-Romantic, late-Victorian, and Georgian verse was often printed alongside that of the Imagists – not unlike *Canadian Poetry Magazine* during Pratt's editorship (1936–43).

3 Pratt's January 1936 editorial contrasts the non-commercial poetry magazine with the 'popular journals and academic reviews,' where 'the general position for verse contributions was in the backyard of the peri-

odicals' – that is, in deference to 'the far greater marketability of short stories, sketches, and articles' and 'public consumption' ('Foreword' 5).

4 See also Livesay's letter of 9 June 1941 to A.J.M. Smith, in which she solicits poems for the as yet unnamed poetry quarterly: 'Apropos of the Chicago "Poetry" a B.C. Group represented there are [sic] anxious to continue the good work, hoping thereby to set a higher standard for Canadian poetry than has been evident heretofor' (AJMSP-UT, box 1). Klein and Smith had themselves published in *Poetry* and would be aware of the import of Livesay's comparison.

5 As Brown's biographer notes in *E.K. Brown: A Study in Conflict*, 'Pratt was his collaborator, although his name did not appear with Brown's on the editorial page' (Groening 64). Given Pratt's editorial hand, the Canadian number of *Poetry* bears a certain relation to its Canadian counterpart, *Canadian Poetry Magazine*.

6 In the 'News Notes' section at the back of the issue, *Poetry* editor George Dillon emphasized the significance of the issue to both Canadian contributors and American readers: 'It has been assumed, by editors and readers in general, that the work of Canadian writers would make itself known in this country through the usual publishing channels; that it would be as readily available for publication as the work of European writers. For various reasons, however, this has not been the case. New poets are "discovered" almost simultaneously here and in England, their careers are fostered by magazines and book publishers in both countries, but there is no comparable interchange between the United States and Canada' (57).

7 While she attempts to distance herself from the earlier magazine by calling attention to her mother, Florence Randal Livesay, a traditional versifier of the kind most often published in the Philadephia-based magazine, Dorothy Livesay had herself submitted a group of poems for publication in *Contemporary Verse* in 1927. In his 7 December 1927 letter, Benjamin Musser of *Contemporary Verse* wrote to Livesay to accept her poem 'Sympathy' (published in *Green Pitcher*) and to reject two others (DLP-QU, box 2, file 24).

8 During the First World War, Crawley was working as a lawyer in London when he came across Harold Monro's Poetry Bookshop, a meeting place for contemporary British poets, where they would give recitations of their poems and where Crawley would find volumes of the Georgian poets Davies, Hodgson, and de la Mare, as well as the war poets Brooke, Owen, Sassoon, and Edward Thomas (Livesay, Foreword ix–x).

9 Appealing to the modern poet's desire to communicate with as wide an audience as possible, Monroe selected a quotation from Whitman – 'To have great poets there must be great audiences too' – as the democratic motto emblazoned upon the cover of *Poetry*.

10 By the mid-1930s, when Crawley had established relations with members of the Victoria poetry group, he could count a number of modern British poets of the 1930s among his reading repertoire. When making arrangements to give a poetry reading in February 1935 to the Victoria CAA, he proposed Sassoon's *The Road to Ruin*, and on another occasion, he suggested the addition of Auden, Spender, and Day Lewis (Crawley to Perry, 30 January 1935, MEPP, box 2, file 7). See also note 12.

11 The society, whose honorary members included Bliss Carman, Charles G.D. Roberts, and Lorne Pierce, was founded in October 1916. One of its proudest achievements was its role in influencing Pierce to commence the Ryerson Press Poetry Chapbooks series, inspired by the press's publication of president Fewster's chapbook *Three Poems* in 1925. For an anecdotal history of the VPS, see *The Vancouver Poetry Society 1916–1946: A Book of Days*.

12 The range of Crawley's influence on the poetry groups of Victoria and Vancouver is evident in the description of his preparations for the 1939 VPS reading and talk: 'As the two high spots and big pieces of the talk I am saying [Auden's] Spain, the last thing, and in the middle somewhere almost all of the Lament of Lorca. Then three poems of Archibald MacLeish, and [t]hree of Louis MacNeice; [f]or Canadians L[eo] Kennedy's Circling Eagles and Words for a Resurrection and Pratt[']s Erosion and Dorothy Livesay has made me very proud and happy by promising to let me say a new one of hers not yet published which she read to me the other af[t]ernoon. Jean wants me to give also Lorca's Presciosa which she likes and I may do so. Then I have four from the W[ar] P[oetry] A[nthology] writers, and several odd ones of British writers' (Crawley to McLaren [1939], FMP).

13 As Victoria branch president Perry reported to CAA president Pelham Edgar in her letter of 28 December 1936, 'Our Year-book gives the impression that [Crawley] chose all the poems in the collection. But I am sure some of them give him acute pain. When he sent in his report, Doris [Ferne] and Floris [McLaren] and I were horrified to find he had chosen three for each of us and for Anne [Marriott], and only one for everyone else ... As the three of us were on the committee of arrangement, we were in a quandary; but got out of it by adding an extra poem to his choice for

most of the older members, or the juniors whose work seemed in our opinion to merit it' (MEPP, box 5, file 23).

14 As he reflected in a letter to Livesay, 'I would be no earthly good as associate editor and would be nothing and I think the whole standard and value of a magazine is in the character and likings of the sole editor' (n.d. [c. August 1946], DLP-QU, box 3, file 7). He expressed similar sentiments in a letter of August 1946 to McLaren: 'I said [to Birney] I did not think I could work satisfactorily as an associate as I thought a magazine lost a lot unles[s] it were under one pers[o]n[']s sole editorial management and that I thought this was shown in some of the numbers of Poetry Chicago' (FMP).

15 Page's private retraction of her remarks on *Contemporary Verse* in a letter to Crawley is worth noting for the record: 'I no sooner saw it in print than I wanted to disown it – send out letters to everyone saying "there has been a mistake." Actually I still agree on the whole with what I said but it was so condensed that it seemed distorted. And the fact that I was a Previewer and a would-be poet seemed to make it worse – as if I were setting myself above everyone else, which I was *not* doing' (Page to Crawley [1942], ACP, box 1, file 20, item 8).

16 Butling's statistics refer only to British Columbia little magazines. As I noted in the introduction, the percentage of women poets published in the *Crucible* and *Canadian Poetry Magazine* was significantly higher.

17 Ryerson Press had accepted the poem by January 1939 and published it in its chapbook series in February, and Livesay herself had reviewed it on 23 February 1939 in the Victoria *Daily Times*, before she saw fit in her 'Open Letter' to assail the Canadian publishing industry on Marriott's behalf for not publishing the poem (see Marriott to Norma MacRostie, 2 February–3 March 1939; LPP, box 7, file 6, items 73, 75–6).

18 On the contrary, in the winter 1947–8 issue, Crawley refers to an anonymous young poet whom he had recently read in a little magazine sent to him, who argued that 'Canadian poetry which boomed considerably during the war has again gone on the skids,' and that 'what we need is more simplification of style and meaning, less borrowing from all the British poets … less feminine poetry.' ('Notes' 18–19). Crawley voices his disapproval of the use of 'feminine' as a derogatory term: 'If the word "feminine" is used as a definition of a quality of poetry it is surely outdated and has an offensive application.' 'If it is not used in this way,' that is, if it implies that too many women poets haved appeared in print since

the end of the war, 'the word is less applicable, as is shown by the work in books and magazines' ('Notes' 19).

19 See also 'Prairie Graveyard,' published in the April 1941 issue of *Poetry* (rpt. in Marriott, *Circular* 43).

20 The impetus to publish *Calling Adventurers!* may have come from McLaren. As Marriott recorded in a list consisting of comments she had received from friends and fellow writers in Victoria, McLaren recommended that Marriott 'get it published somewhere, like [Archibald] M[a]cLeish's 'Fall of the City'' (AMP, box 16, file 2).

21 Prefacing a 1942 reading from *Calling Adventurers!* over CJOR radio in Vancouver, Marriott commented on the limitations and advantages of radio as a broadcast medium: 'In radio, the writer of poetry is presented with a marvelous new medium of making his work take on vitality, and of presenting it to an audience of a size that no book of poetry would be very likely to reach ... Writing poetry for radio has of course its particular problems – one of them is the need for simplicity. Long tangled up phrases and complicated words just won't go over the air' (AMP, box 15, file 9).

22 In March 1945, when Marriott contacted Ryerson about the sales of *Calling Adventurers!* and *Salt Marsh*, Pierce noted in the margin of her letter that 63 of 250 total copies of the former and 327 of 500 of the latter were still in stock (LPP, box 12, file 7, item 59).

23 Birney, like many of her contemporaries, assumed Marriott's intimate knowledge of the prairies on the basis of *The Wind Our Enemy*. She made certain to disabuse him of this assumption in her letter of acceptance on 21 August 1946: 'I never knew anyone there who *did* write, that I can remember, though I'll see if memory can be forced to yield anything up' (EBP, box 14, file 25; original emphasis).

24 Birney misremembered the events leading up to his resignation when he wrote in his memoirs of *Canadian Poetry Magazine* that in the summer of 1947 he had received a note from Marriott 'resigning from the editorial board by reason of marriage and removal to the wilds of Prince George' (*Spreading* 107).

25 Marriott mentioned the talk in her letter of fall 1946 to Birney, complaining of the NFB that 'generally the people are pretty uninterested in poetry – when Alan Crawley spoke here last month in spite of signs on the bulletin boards and so forth, if it hadn't been for a solid back-log of the despised CAA, the hall would have been more than half empty' (EBP, box 14, file 25). However ironically she intends Birney to read her

distaste for the CAA, Marriott nonetheless lets slip her discontent with poetry communities in Ottawa.

26 The deeper biographical context of this poem may refer to Marriott's first engagement, later broken off. M. Eugenie Perry, in her letter of 14 May 1944 to Edgar, mentions Marriott's recent engagement (MEPP, box 5, file 23). Marriott herself, in a letter of 8 June 1944 to Pierce, also mentions her engagement and attaches a manuscript of sonnets written by her fiancé, H. Wakefield Maunsell of Calgary (LPP, box 11, file 1, item 113). She later met Gerald McLellan, whom she married in Ottawa in 1947.

27 The list includes twelve poems – 'Country Sunday,' 'Pussy Willows from a Train,' 'The Riel Road,' 'New Season,' 'How Most Imperfect,' 'The Rideau,' 'For Friends Far Away,' 'Poetry Mountain Valley,' 'Seeing Him,' 'Waiting Room Spring,' 'Old Maid,' and 'Ottawa Payday' – left incomplete with a note indicating the possible addition of 'new poems.'

28 In a letter to McLaren about the publication of *The Wind Our Enemy* in the Ryerson series, Crawley's perception of the chapbooks is instructive in this regard: 'these Ryerson Chapbooks have been rather a thorn in the side of the newspapers and reviewers and they dislike doing much with them, I expect the "girls" who have written the others that have been brought out take sadly and vituperatively to any serious criticism. I have liked the poem so much that I am sorry that the stupidity of its handling is not to make it more widely read. I thought at first that its publication in this forum was a good thing for it and for Ann[e] but now I am inclined to believe that it is not so, it is too good to be in the company of the others in the forum and may suffer greatly from the association' ([1939], FMP).

29 In an example of his editorial practice of encouraging poets to attempt publication in *Poetry*, Crawley wrote to Livesay on 20 February 1942 about her poem 'Serenade for Strings': 'Sorry about your luck with Poetry certainly I think the poem good enough and if you want to let me have it will be delighted' (DLP-QU, box 3, file 3). The poem appeared in the September 1942 issue of *Contemporary Verse*. There are numerous other instances when Crawley published Livesay's poems after she had received rejections from other editors.

30 For analysis of reportage as a species of leftist prose in general and Livesay's prose reportage in particular, see Carr 180–1, 184–5.

31 See her *Regression* 11–42 and '"Mapping"' for Sherrill Grace's studies of the influence of expressionist aesthetics on Canadian modernism. Setting the context for the arrival of expressionism in Canadian visual art, she

not only notes the expressionist influence on Lawren Harris's paintings in the 1910s and early 1920s but also cites Charles Comfort's defence of expressionism in his 1931 article 'The Painter and His Model' (*Regression* 24–5). As noted above, Livesay was familiar with Comfort's murals from the West End Community Centre in Vancouver in the late 1930s (*Journey* 158). But even if she was exposed to expressionist motifs in murals by Comfort or if his murals were influential on her conception of 'Motif,' there is little more than circumstantial evidence to corroborate such a claim. 'There is less evidence of Expressionism in any modernist Canadian poet [than in novelists or painters],' Grace cautions, 'although *expressionistic tendencies* are apparent in some poems by Bertram Brooker, Lawren Harris, F.R. Scott, and Dorothy Livesay' (*Regression* 248n5; emphasis added).

32 For another example of Livesay's transitional poetry and her postwar return to the self, see 'V-J Day / Improvisations on an Old Theme,' published in the October 1945 issue of *En Masse* (1–2).

33 Prior to its publication in *Contemporary Verse*, Livesay had submitted 'Call My People Home' to B.K. Sandwell at *Saturday Night* and Hayden Carruth at *Poetry*. Both editors returned the poem, claiming its length exceeded their means (see Sandwell to Livesay, n.d., DLP-QU, box 1, file 1; and Carruth to Livesay, 26 May 1949, DLP-QU, box 2, file 25).

3 Gendered Modernisms

1 This is the subject of Trehearne's recent correctives to previous scholarship on Montreal little magazines of the 1940s, including articles by Louis Dudek, Michael Gnarowski, and Wynne Francis, indexes by Don Precosky and Neil Fisher, biographies by Elspeth Cameron and Sandra Djwa, Waddington's introduction to her edition of John Sutherland's *Essays, Controversies and Poems*, and Ken Norris's *The Little Magazine in Canada*. Trehearne argues for more affinities than disparities among the Montreal poets and little-magazine editors of the 1940s. See his 'Critical' and *Montreal*.

Earlier attempts to expose the *Preview–First Statement* binary as a fallacy include literary histories from the perspectives of either *Preview* or *First Statement*: originally, in a rarely cited master's thesis entitled '*Preview*: Anatomy of a Group' (1969) by Christopher Xerxes Ringrose, and more recently, in the introduction to *The Letters of John Sutherland, 1942–1956* (1992) by Bruce Whiteman. Ringrose is usually noted for his 1970 article 'Patrick Anderson and His Critics,' much of which is taken directly from his thesis. He admirably downplays what he calls the 'melodrama' of the *Preview–First Statement* rivalry (in reference to Francis's 1962 article 'Montreal Poets of the Forties') and provisionally attempts to reconstruct the social and political conditions in Montreal during the Second World War and personal tensions within the group that impinged upon the production of *Preview* ('Patrick Anderson' 16; '*Preview*' 20). Without merely reiterating the misinformation provided by critics and literary historians writing from the perspective of *First Statement*, Whiteman scrupulously details some of the extant correspondence among the *Preview* and *First Statement* editors, confirming some stories and refuting others about the conflicted relations between the two groups.

2 Patrick Anderson makes note of *Preview*'s predecessor in his introduction to the facsimile edition: 'The format of the first six issues of *Preview*, about six folio mimeographed sheets with a printed title in either red or blue, owed much to an almost totally forgotten "literary letter" presented by my American wife and myself to some thirty friends in April, 1941. This was *The Andersons*, of which there was no more than a single issue' (Introduction iii). See also Whitney, 'First Person': 'Peggy had typed it ... and [Patrick] wrote the content and ran off the copies at [Selwyn House] school' (where he was employed as an English master) (90).

3 Both Kit Shaw and her husband would relinquish their positions in the group prior to the October 1943 issue, though extant correspondence indicates that Neufville Shaw continued with the group in a casual capacity. See Neufville Shaw to Miriam Waddington, 16 March 1944, MWP, box 34, *Preview* file; see also Shaw to Dorothy Livesay, 16 March 1944, DLP-QU, box 2, file 17. Kit Shaw's marginal position in relation to the editorial members of the *Preview* group is recorded in Patrick Anderson's letter of 18 November 1942 to her, the only extant document in which she figures so prominently and occupies a central position in the group. He addresses her 'as someone in the PREVIEW group' and goes on to apologize for his recent animosity toward her and, afterward, to refute her '"sexual" or "Freudian," or alternat[iv]ely "up in the clouds" theory' concerning his poetry (FRSP, reel H-1211). Evidently, she too participated in group discussions of the work published in *Preview*.

4 See Anderson, *Search Me* 149. See also Anderson's letter to A.J.M. Smith: 'I feel quite bitter about Preview's attitude toward Peggy. She spent hours and hours mimeographing the magazine, carrying paper etc. and actually called most of the meetings. She never got a word of thanks' (PAP, box 1, Correspondence 1945 file [n.d., c. 1946–7]). Patricia Whitney

excerpts a longer passage from this letter and notes: 'This holograph letter is written on *Northern Review* stationery and is undated' ('From Oxford' 48n41).

5 I would like to thank P.K. Page for answering my queries, in conversation and in a letter (9 August 2000), about her roles in the physical production of *Preview*.

6 After sending out a questionnaire with the sixth issue in August 1942, the editors decided to change the periodical's format from a single-stapled newsletter mimeographed on *Preview* letterhead to a side-stapled magazine with mimeographed content pages and printed covers. Although replies to its questionnaire are not extant, the *Preview* group's subsequent investment in higher production values was most likely a result of feedback from current subscribers.

7 See 'Impressions,' 'Let no nice woman ...,' 'Diary,' and 'Train Ride' (PKPP, box 1, file 5).

8 Thanks to Page's biographer, Sandra Djwa, for sharing and comparing notes on Page's first months in Montreal and the timing of her introduction to the *Preview* group.

9 However, as Page says of the *Preview* group in a letter of 9 May (1942) to Alan Crawley, 'It is a strange group to be associated with – especially as I am the only non-political member' (ACP, box 1, file 20).

10 Page mentions the collaborative nature of *Preview*'s production at the head of the letter, saying, 'We did the paste-up last night.' One might guess that 'we' refers to the Shaws and Bruce Ruddick (the Andersons were, as Patrick's August 1942 letter to Page indicates, vacationing that summer in Baie-Saint-Paul; PKPP, box 6, file 7).

11 Having completed an average of fourteen poems every month since she arrived in Montreal in October 1941, she would experience a gradual decline in production after joining the *Preview* group in April 1942, composing seven new poems in April and nine in May, but only two in June and July and three in August. The trend would continue through to the end of the year: she would write eighteen more poems in the next four months.

12 Together with these unpublished poems in her copybook of 1940–4 are such published poems as 'Noon Hour' (c. early 1943), 'The Petition' (c. early 1943), and 'Typists' (February 1943).

13 For an earlier, Marxist version of a poem in this genre, see Weiss. See also Livesay, 'Depression Suite,' part iii ('I sit and hammer melodies ...'), in *Collected Poems* 87.

14 As illustrated by the case studies of 'typewriter literature' (206) included

in Friedrich Kittler's *Gramaphone, Film, Typewriter* and the essays collected in Leah Price and Pamela Thurschwell's *Literary Secretaries/Secretarial Culture*, the related sub-genres of typewriter and office literature were dominated by men in the late nineteenth and early twentieth centuries. According to Kittler, '1889 is generally considered the year zero of typewriter literature, ... the year in which Conan Doyle first published *A Case of Identity*' (206), which was followed most notably by Bram Stoker's *Dracula* (1897), Grant Allen's *The Type-Writer* Girl (1897), and John Kendrick Bangs's *The Enchanted Typewriter* (1899).

15 As early as December 1943, the group had issued an insert in the magazine entitled 'The PREVIEW Fund,' in which it outlined its financial situation: 'The production of all little magazines is hazardous and many, too many of them, fold up within a month or two of their first appearance. They are the dragonflies of the literary world. Our case is somewhat different for we are an inexpensive, modest but tenacious insect. We can resort to the cocoon of the clique or the caterpillar stage of limited circulation. But to make ourselves heard, to multiply, to take the nuptial flight – for this we need money. Not a great deal. But some. We need your nickels for our gold, upon your quarters and dollars our irridiscence [*sic*] depends' (Anderson, 'PREVIEW' n. pag.). The group set a goal of one hundred dollars as its target. A reminder about sending contributions to the *Preview* fund appeared in the February 1944 issue (Anderson, 'Note'); no subsequent issues contain notices about the fund. How the group planned to invest the money from the fund is unknown; it is possible that it hoped to be able to afford to have the magazine printed instead of mimeographed. The *First Statement* group had recently obtained a printing press and had started to issue a printed magazine in August 1943; it had announced the *First Statement* fund in the 13 March 1943 issue in order to raise money to purchase the press (Sutherland, 'Role of the Magazines' 1–2).

16 Geoffrey Ashe, the *First Statement* agent in Vancouver, reported in his letter of 2 March 1943 to Sutherland that he had in fact attended a CAA branch meeting on 26 February 1943 to canvas subscriptions and support for the magazine. Ashe's follow-up letter to Dudek on 8 April 1943 mentions the possibility of setting up a Vancouver *First Statement* group, but promises little: 'If you knew the nature of the Vancouver literary public you would realize, better than I can convey myself, how little is to be expected even when the group is formed' (LDF, series 2, box 6, Ashe file). One suspects that Ashe's pitch to members of the Vancouver CAA may have sounded too much like the same organization

with a different name, but without the financial resources or national reputation.

17 According to Harry Berger Jr, such poems illuminate the constitutive ambiguity of the green world: 'It appears first as exemplary or appealing and lures us away from the evil or confusion of everyday life ... Those who wish to remain, who cannot or will not be discharged, are presented as in some way deficient. Thus the second quality of the green world is that it is ambiguous ... In its positive aspects it provides a temporary haven for recreation or clarification, experiment or relief; in its negative aspects it projects the urge of the paralysed will to give up, escape, work magic, abolish time and flux and the intrusive reality of other minds' (36). See also Frye, Rev. of *Green World* for an anatomy of Waddington's green-world symbolism.

18 In 'Miriam [Dworkin] Waddington: An Annotated Bibliography,' Ricou has dated the second and third issues of *Direction* October and December 1944 respectively (300–1). This cannot be the case, since these dates correspond to the fifth and sixth issues. While issue one is dated 20 November 1943, issues two through four are undated.

19 See Waddington to Livesay, 24 January 1945: 'Dee – you heard about the F[irst] S[tatement] project of chap books (to be financed by FS). So far Layton and Souster are slated. They invited me, and I am vacillating. I want to get my stuff published but don['t]t have too much faith in my prospective editors ... would that compromise one[']s integrity? In a way, maybe yes. What do you think of me issued under FS sponsorship? Somehow I feel I deserve better, but maybe I am conceited?' (DLP-QU, box 5a, file 1; original ellipsis). As early as 1943, Waddington had submitted to the Ryerson Press a collection entitled 'Canadian Summer,' which was subsequently declined and returned (see Lorne Pierce to Waddington, 11 November 1943, MWP, box 35, file 21); she received another rejection slip from Ryerson in early 1945 (see Pierce to Waddington, 16 February 1945, MWP, box 35, file 21). After this latter rejection, we may expect that Waddington then decided to accept Sutherland's offer.

20 Patrick Waddington was Montreal regional editor for *Canadian Poetry Magazine* during Birney's editorship.

21 Of the thirteen poems Waddington published in *Contemporary Verse* before the launch of *Green World* in November 1945, only four were selected by Sutherland for this first collection. Of the next fifteen published in *Contemporary Verse* previous to *The Second Silence* in 1955, twelve were chosen by Waddington herself for this second collection.

22 See Frye, 'Letters'; Wilson; Woodcock, 'Recent.' For Waddington's immediate reply to Wilson, see her letter in the December 1955 *Canadian Forum*.

23 See Waddington to Pierce, 7 June 1956 to 25 November 1957. Waddington had sent another full-length manuscript to Pierce in 1956. He attributed his hesitation to publish another collection of hers to the poor sales of *The Second Silence*. As of 25 November 1957, Ryerson still had 256 of the 500 copies in stock. Waddington eventually agreed to purchase 100 copies for herself. Writing to Pierce on 5 September 1957, she assessed the situation: 'I realize the difficulties involved in publishing books of poetry and the lack of financial gain that is attached to such ventures. I have no answer to that problem either, except to say that if my next book received favorable reviews it may help to sell the first book' (MWP, box 35, file 21):

24 During her Victoria period, Page not only published a dozen poems in Hambleton's anthology *Unit of Five* in November 1944 but also assembled and submitted a poetry manuscript to Macmillan in the early fall of 1945. After withdrawing the collection from Macmillan, she sent it to Ryerson in December that year. This manuscript, originally called 'The Untouched Hills,' was published by Ryerson under the title *As Ten as Twenty* in September 1946. See Ellen Elliott of Macmillan to Page, 11 October 1945; see also Pierce to Page, 5 December 1945, PKPP, box 17, file 8.

25 Ironically, Crawley's criticism of the 'detached and impersonal' accompanies five new poems by Page – 'Morning, Noon and Night,' 'Sailor,' 'Virgin,' 'Piece for a Formal Garden,' and 'Squatters, 1946' – in which she persists in the practice of an impersonalist poetics. Crawley not only accepted these poems for the October 1946 issue but later honoured them with the Bertram Warr Memorial Award for the best group of poems published in *Contemporary Verse* that year (Crawley, 'Bertram').

26 Although Page's official letter of resignation was published in the October–November 1947 issue of *Northern Review*, she had in fact submitted her resignation to Sutherland in a personal letter dated 23 August. There she expands upon the reasons for her resignation: 'I, as you may know, have for some time been unhappy about the way the magazine was being operated. Having covered a considerable part of Canada in the last year I have some idea of how people react to it. I think that had we been attempting to do a job of creating ill-will we could not have done much better. I wrote to you about this when I was in Victoria, suggesting that some measure of courtesy was necessary. Also I have agreed less and less with opinions expressed in your critical articles and as there is

nothing in the magazine explaining that the opinions are those of the reviewer himself – the whole board, whether regional editors or otherwise is automatically implicated. I am no longer prepared to be implicated and would be glad if you would remove my name from any further issues' (ILP, box 15, Page file).

27 For a full discussion of *here and now*, see chapter 5: 226–33.

28 For typescript versions of the poems in this group, see AJMSP-TU, 78–007, box 1, file 6.

29 In keeping with the historical basis of my argument, all passages will be quoted from the 1956 versions of 'After Rain' and 'Giovanni,' as published in *Poetry*.

30 For another account of McLaren's suggested revisions to the early version of 'After Rain,' see Trehearne, *Montreal* 101. Page in fact accepted McLaren's recommendations – not only to retitle the poem (originally called 'Kitchen Garden') but also to omit the final stanza. See also Page's reply to McLaren: 'It seems so slight, but then so does everything I do. And the Kitchen Garden poem was of course, self-chastisement for just this. The title and last verse were further chastisement, and whereas legitimate enough, hardly legitimate in that context, so I have acted on your advice, and made another small deletion' (n.d. [c. May 1956], PKPP, box 8, file 16). A copy of the revised version, without the final stanza, can be found in AJMSP-TU, 78–007, box 1, file 6; it was submitted by McLaren to the *Tamarack Review* (for which Smith was an advisory editor) but withdrawn once it was accepted by *Poetry*, to which it had been simultaneously sent. The truncated version appeared in the November 1956 issue of *Poetry*. McLaren's assessment of the final stanza was corroborated by Crawley in his letter of 6 May 1956 to Page: 'I listened quite absorbed and content with the two Giovanni poems. The first reading ... struck me deeply and when it ended I was for a moment unaware that it was over and at the second reading the last two stanzas came as new to me, the earlier ones were so right that they held strong against the last two which I feel are weaker and might, God I say "might" only be a weakening effect. The line beginning "Choir ... me" starts a verse I thought weak and could be improved or cut off, but I would hate to lose the fine strong last line of this stanza' (PKPP, box 6, file 43).

31 The original version of 'After Rain,' entitled 'Kitchen Garden,' has not survived in typescript. I am assuming that the final stanza as it appears in *Cry Ararat!* is by and large the same as that in the version Page sent to McLaren in April 1956. Given the changes of wording and phrasing

made between the *Poetry* and *Cry Ararat!* versions, however, others were likely introduced in the final stanza as well.

4 Editing Women

1 An undated WCC membership form preserved in the Broadsides Collection in the Baldwin Room at the Toronto Reference Library indicates that the 'manuscript CRUCIBLE, copies of which circulate among groups composed of 6 to 10 members,' continued for some time after the appearance of the printed magazine. I am grateful to Heather Murray for bringing this membership form, along with other *Crucible*-related correspondence in the Canadian Literature Club Fonds, to my attention.
2 Also published in the Christmas–New Year 1940 issue, Creighton's article 'Pioneering in Poetry' gives extended attention to modern poetic themes (industrialization, mechanization, commerce). For another reading of these 'modernist' *Crucible* editorials and articles as well as their failed application, see Thompson, 'Emphatically' 94–101.
3 The *Blue Review* superseded a quarterly entitled *Rhythm*, edited by Murry, Mansfield, and Michael T. Sandler between the summer of 1911 and March 1913 (Hoffman et al. 243, 240). For a note on *Signature*, see Hoffman et al. 248.
4 Even during the two-year period when she was replaced as the *Forum*'s managing editor (July 1937–October 1939), Godfrey remained a member of the board of editors and continued to be a contributor.
5 See Frye, Rev. of *Contemporary Verse* (December 1941); Birney, Rev. of *Contemporary Verse* (April 1942); Creighton, Rev. of *Contemporary Verse* (September 1944); Frye, Rev. of *First Statement* (November 1942); Frye, Rev. of *Direction* (March 1943).
6 Plans for the formation of a new literary magazine had been proposed as early as July 1944. A preliminary meeting of the Federation of Canadian Writers (FCW), an organization proposed as an alternative to the CAA, was held in May or early June 1944 (see Dorothy Livesay to Earle Birney, 7 June 1944, EBP, box 13, file 23; and A.J.M. Smith to Livesay, 24 June 1944, DLP-QU, box 5, file 15, item 2). The provisional executive committee of the FCW included Anderson, Klein, and Shaw of the *Preview* group and Layton and Dudek of the *First Statement* group. Others in attendance at the original FCW meeting were Audrey Aikman and John Sutherland of the *First Statement* group, Scott and Ruddick of the *Preview* group, and Smith. Among the suggestions raised at the FCW's preliminary meeting was a proposal to 'consider the creation of a national literary magazine,

perhaps through the amalgamation of existing magazines' ('A Proposal
for a Federation of Canadian Writers,' 29 July 1944, DLP-QU, box 1, file 1,
item 11). Although the FCW itself never moved beyond the planning
stage, its proposal for a national magazine would eventually take the
form of *Northern Review*, whose founding editorial board chiefly consisted of members of the provisional executive committee of the FCW
and others from the *First Statement* and *Preview* groups in attendance at
the meeting.

5 Guardians of the Avant-garde

1 See RC, vol. 17, brief 176, reel 16 (Crawley); RC, vol. 32, brief 420, reel 19
   (Livesay et al.); RC, vol. 19, brief 208, reel 19 (Sutherland); RC, vol. 19,
   brief 225, reel 12 (Harmon et al.).
2 Thanks to Catherine Harmon and Paul Arthur for recalling their collaborations on *here and now*'s editorials. I spoke with the two co-editors in
   separate telephone conversations on 1 March 2001.
3 See Harmon to Crawley, 18 October 1948, AWP, box 4, file 9.
4 An early draft of the CWC brief and Page's commentary on it have survived. Her undated letter to Sybil Hutchison (c. September 1949) has
   been transcribed and preserved along with the draft in the Birney Papers.
   Of particular note in the draft is a passage on the little magazine: 'The
   gap between the non-paying or poorly paying magazines which publish
   serious literary work – the so-called "little" magazines (such as Contemporary Verse, Northern Review, and Here and Now) and the university
   quarterlies – and the commercial magazines is great, and there are in
   Canada as yet no magazines between these two poles such as provide
   markets for writers of a great many types in the United States.' Page's
   response is pointed: 'The "little magazines." Nothing in the world could
   sound more pitiful to the uninitiated than that term. I think we would do
   better to express the *idea* of the "little m[a]gs" and I shall hunt up, if I
   can, the book THE LITTLE MAGAZINE, written by two Americans to see if
   they have any good points on the subject. Certainly, it must be made
   clear to the boys on the Commission that it is the "little mags" that first
   published the Lawrences, the Eliots (let's skip the Pounds to avoid
   another Saturday Review controversy). And that seems to be about the
   extent of my thought on the subject' (EBP, box 11, file 67; original emphasis). All references to little magazines were excised from the final version
   of the brief.
5 The following figures are listed for a projected one-year run of four

issues: short stories (fifteen at an average of $100 each, total $1500); critical essays (ten at an average of $100 each, total $1000); poetry (2000 lines
at $1 a line – minimum $10 per poem, total $2000); reviews, book notices,
etc. (total $400) (RC, vol. 19, brief 225, reel 12).

6 I have not been able to track down *New Canadian Poetry Column*, but the
title suggests that it may have been a poetry supplement with contributions from New Canadians.

7 Litt's analysis of the commission on this point of contention is trenchant:
'Massey and others were willing to accept the integration of ethnic cultures into a distinctive Canadian culture, but the idea of an ethnic mosaic
had yet to be translated from an emerging demographic trend into an
acknowledged good. Thus each of the two constituent elements of liberalist humanist nationalism imposed constraints upon the other. Nationalism limited liberalism just as liberalism qualified nationalism' (113–14).
For a telling portrait of the Massey Commission's handing of multiculturalism, see the Ukrainian Canadian Committee brief and transcript of
its presentation to the commission (RC, vol. 31, brief 401, reel 18).

8 See the brief submitted to the Massey Commission by R.R. Arkell and
G.C. Andrew of the Community Arts Council of Vancouver for its
request for federal recognition and support for the development of
regional cultural groups (RC, vol. 16, brief 161; reel 9).

9 Though by no means as explicit as *here and now*'s editorials, Agazarian's
statement of aesthetic principles is also reminiscent of Morris's reform of
typographic, printing, and design practice. Collaboration with Reid as
the printer and typographer of *pm* more than likely influenced her thinking in the field of aesthetics and design. Her ideas of the usefulness of
art, of art as inseparable from living – these are aesthetic principles fundamental to Morris's Arts and Crafts movement, particularly his practice
of the so-called lesser arts, which included typography, printing, and
book design.

10 For a study of language usage in scientific, literary, and advertising discourse, see D.G. Jones's article 'The Question of Language Prostitution,'
published in the fourth issue.

11 Although Collins would never comment on her gendered position as
editor of the magazine, her contributions indicate that she was certainly
aware of the representation of gender and its politics. Her poem 'Renewal,'
published in the third issue of *CIV/n*, articulated a consciousness, a politics,
and a poetics stripped of all that is stereotypically feminine:

Toss your frustrations on the nearest chair,
Place your neuroses neatly on a shelf,

> Wash out your inhibitions and hang them up to dry.
> Yes, dearie, you can sleep now,
>   unclothed, free.
> Tomorrow you will be bitter, satirical, even gay,
> No bloody gorgons chasing through the intestines of a giraffe,
> No thundering herds of centaurs pounding through the brain.
> Brush aside now the maggots that gnaw
> Heart, hope, ambition;
> Sink into a sleep where all is sane, logical, safe.
> Its bright, alive, lurid and loathsome
>   nightmares:
> Where loudness of voice, power, not intelligence
> Or justice dominate;
> Stenches rise from unaired
> Minds rancid with petty fears, conventions, cowering
> Before all newness, clean thinking. (67–8)

Just as Collins calls for vital and experiential poetry in her editorial, so her poem bears the same stamp.

12 In a letter of 24 August 1954 to Dudek, Layton defended his actions: 'Of course I agree with you that A/C stays on as editor. But, pray, when did I say different? I don't know who's twisting your ear: the plain fact is that I have no more aspiration than your modest self to be conspicuously laid out on the masthead. For me it was and is entirely a matter of responsibility – call me a crank, but I do like to do my sniping in broad daylight. I thought that since we were responsible for what goes into the trash heap we were under no obligation to own up to the deed. If however as you point out A/C is free to pick and choose among our respective opinions then we exist only in an advisory capacity and the final responsibility rests with her. That rests my soul, and I am content' (LDF, series 1, box 8, Layton file).

13 Extant correspondence indicates that Robert Currie, together with Collins, invested in an electric typewriter with a print-quality typeface (see Currie and Collins to Dudek, 7 August 1954, and Currie to Dudek, 5 September 1954, LDF, series 1, box 4, Currie file) – presumably the same typewriter that Collins remembers selling to settle debts for the printing of the sixth issue (Introduction 9). Plans were made at that time to have the magazine printed in England. Though doing so would have been less expensive than laying out the magazine themselves in Montreal, printing costs were so much higher than those for mimeographing that the two printed issues of CIV/n (nos. 6 and 7) would be the last. In a letter of 10

July 1955, Currie wrote to Dudek about the fact that he had not 'asked AC about CIV/n 8 yet,' and in a later (undated) letter he reported that she had made '[n]o mention of CIV/n' (LDF, series 1, box 4, Currie file). Letters from Currie to Dudek indicate that the end of the magazine may have been as much caught up in personal affairs as it was in the magazine's troubled financial affairs (see Currie to Dudek, 10 July 1955, LDF, series 1, box 4, Currie file).

14 For a more comprehensive analysis of the CAC and its brief, see Tippett 171–6.

15 For a concise history of Herbert and his activities with the Canada Foundation, see Tippett 177–81. See also Herbert's appeal in the June 1948 issue of *here and now*.

Conclusion

1 According to David McKnight's bibliography, of those little magazines founded between 1941 and 1956, 11 of 23 (47 per cent) had at least one woman editor; for those little magazines established between 1957 and 1980, the ratio decreases to 65 of 177 (36 per cent).

2 Godard's own women-centred narrative of Canadian modernism, entitled 'Ex-centriques, Eccentric, Avant-Garde: Women and Modernism in the Literatures of Canada,' appeared in the inaugural *Tessera* issue (1984); this overview of women's writing from Mère Marie de l'Incarnation to Nicole Brossard deals primarily with prose and considers only those texts that incorporate 'the language innovations necessary in order to enter Modernist writing' (62). 'An account of the importance of women in the advent of Canadian Modernism,' Godard claims, 'will of necessity result in a decentring of the existing tradition which has denied the presence of modernism before 1960' (63). And though her examples – Elizabeth Smart, Sheila Watson, Thérèse Tardif, and Gabrielle Roy – amply demonstrate the presence of Canadian women modernists prior to 1960, her failure to take account of the modernist poetry of Louise Morey Bowman and Livesay in the 1920s and 1930s or that of Page, Waddington, and Marriott in the 1940s indicates how far her history is out of alignment.

3 An earlier and longer version of this section appeared in the Livesay special issue of *Contemporary Verse 2*. See Irvine, 'Dorothy.'

4 See Irvine, 'Dorothy' 67–8 for an expanded reading of this *New Frontier* editorial.

5 See also McLaren,'For the Record.' Written in response to the May 1975 editorial in *CV/II*, McLaren's 'feedback' letter recalls the production work

on *Contemporary Verse* conducted by herself, Marriott, and Ferne in Victoria.

6 Page still publishes collections of poetry; she has recently written a cycle of renga, *And Once More Saw the Stars: Four Poems for Two Voices* (2001), in collaboration with Philip Stratford, released a new volume of selected poems, *Planet Earth* (2002), and issued a memoir in verse, *Hand Luggage* (2006).

7 If Alan V. Miller's The Sunset of Bon Echo Web page, which includes facsimile reproductions of the magazine, is any indication of the current interest in Canadian little-magazine digitization, then perhaps others of these early magazines may be made available in digital format in the not too distant future. See http://www.ryerson.ca/~a7miller/ index.html.

Works Cited

Archival Sources

Patrick Anderson Papers. MG 30 D177. Library and Archives Canada.
Earle Birney Papers. MC 49. Thomas Fisher Rare Book Library, U of Toronto.
Broadsides Collection. Baldwin Room, Toronto Reference Library.
Canadian Literature Club Fonds. S 83. Baldwin Room, Toronto Reference Library.
Alan Crawley Papers. A. Arch 2010. Queen's U. Archives, Kathleen Ryan Hall.
Flora MacDonald Denison Papers. Thomas Fisher Rare Book Library, U of Toronto.
Louis Dudek Fonds. Library and Archives Canada.
Margaret Fairley Papers. MC 83. Thomas Fisher Rare Book Library, U of Toronto.
Ralph Gustafson Papers. MSS. 6/2 A.62. Special Collections, U of Saskatchewan Libraries.
A.M. Klein Papers. MG 30 D 167. Library and Archives Canada.
Irving Layton Papers. Special Collections, Vanier Library, Concordia U.
Dorothy Livesay Collection. MSS. 73. Dept. of Archives and Special Collections, Elizabeth Dafoe Library, U of Manitoba.
Dorothy Livesay Papers. A. Arch. 2024. Queen's U. Archives, Kathleen Ryan Hall.
Macmillan Archives. William Ready Division of Archives and Research Collections, McMaster U. Library.
Anne Marriott Papers. Special Collections, U of British Columbia Libraries.
Floris McLaren Papers. Private collection, Victoria, BC.
P.K. Page Papers. MG 30 D 311. Library and Archives Canada.

M. Eugenie Perry Papers. MS 697. Provincial Archives of British Columbia.

Lorne Pierce Papers. A. Arch. 2001a. Queen's U. Archives, Kathleen Ryan Hall.

PM Magazine Papers. Special Collections, U of British Columbia Libraries.

Royal Commission on National Development in the Arts, Letters and Sciences, briefs and submissions. Microfilm. Toronto: Micromedia, 1972.

F.R. Scott Papers. MG 30 D211. Library and Archives Canada.

A.J.M. Smith Papers. 78–007. Trent U. Archives.

A.J.M. Smith Papers. MC 15. Thomas Fisher Rare Book Library, U of Toronto.

Miriam Waddington Papers. MG 31 D54. Library and Archives Canada.

Anne Wilkinson Papers. MC 29. Thomas Fisher Rare Book Library, U of Toronto.

Published and Other Sources

Aaron, Daniel. *Writers on the Left*. 1961. New York: Avon, 1965.

Agazarian, Yvonne. Editorial. *pm magazine* 1.1 (1951): 8.

– Editorial. *pm magazine* 1.3 (1952): 2.

Anderson, Patrick. Editorial. *Preview* 6 (1942): 1.

– Introduction. *Preview*. Facsim. ed. Millwood, NY: Kraus, 1980. iii–v.

– 'Note.' *Preview* 4 (1942): 1.

– 'Note.' *Preview* 18 (1944): 10.

– 'A Poet Past and Future.' *Canadian Literature* 56 (1973): 7–21.

– 'The PREVIEW Fund.' Insert. *Preview* 17 (1943).

– *Search Me: Autobiography – The Black Country – Canada and Spain*. London: Chatto and Windus, 1957.

Anderson, Patrick, et al. 'Statement.' *Preview* 1 (1942): 1.

Ardis, Ann L., and Leslie W. Lewis, eds. *Women's Experience of Modernity, 1875–1945*. Baltimore and London: Johns Hopkins UP, 2003.

Arthur, Paul. 'In Silk and Scarlet Walks Many a Harlot.' *here and now* 3 (1949): 17–22.

Arthur, Paul, and Catherine Harmon. Editorial. *here and now* 1 (1947): 6.

– Editorial. *here and now* 2 (1948): 4–5.

– 'here and now Criticism Issue.' Editorial. *here and now* 4 (1949): 5–6.

Ashe, Geoffrey. 'Editorial: Intended Especially for B.C. Readers.' *First Statement* 1.5 (1942): 1.

Bailey, Anne Geddes. 'Re-visioning Documentary Readings of Anne Marriott's *The Wind Our Enemy*.' *Canadian Poetry: Studies, Documents, Reviews* 31 (1992): 55–67.

Banting, Pamela. 'blurred mirrors and the archaeology of masks.' Editorial. *CV II* 9.2 (1985): 5–7.

Banting, Pamela, et al. Editorial. *CV II* 9.1 (1984): 4.

Barthes, Roland. *Mythologies*. 1957. Abr. ed. Trans. Annette Lavers. London: J. Cape, 1972.

Benjamin, Walter. 'Paris, Capital of the 19th Century.' 1935. *Reflections*. Ed. Peter Demetz. Trans. Edmund Jephcott. New York: Schocken, 1986. 146–62.

Benstock, Shari. *Women of the Left Bank: Paris, 1900–1940*. Austin: U of Texas P, 1986.

Bentley, D.M.R. *The Gay Grey Moose: Essays on the Ecologies and Mythologies of Canadian Poetry, 1690–1990*. Ottawa: U of Ottawa P, 1992.

Bentley, D.M.R., and Michael Gnarowski, eds. 'Four of the Former *Preview* Editors: A Discussion.' In 'Three Documents from F.R. Scott's Personal Papers.' *Canadian Poetry: Studies, Documents, Reviews* 4 (1979): 93–119.

Berger, Harry, Jr. *Second World and Green World: Studies in Renaissance Fiction-Making*. Berkeley: U of California P, 1988.

Berland, Jody. 'Nationalism and the Modernist Legacy: Dialogues with Innis.' *Capital Culture: A Reader on Modernist Legacies, State Institutions, and the Value(s) of Art*. Ed. Jody Berland and Shelley Hornstein. Montreal: McGill-Queen's UP, 2000. 14–38.

Betcherman, Lita-Rose. *The Swastika and the Maple Leaf: Fascist Movements in Canada in the Thirties*. Toronto: Fitzhenry, 1975.

'Between Ourselves.' Editorial. *New Frontier* 1.11 (1937): 31.

Birney, Earle. 'Age Shall Not Wither Thee.' Letter to Philip Child, 15 November 1948. *here and now* 3 (1949): 86–7.

– Editorial. *Canadian Poetry Magazine* 10.1 (1946): 5–6.

– 'Has Poetry a Future in Canada?' *Manitoba Arts Review* 5.1 (1946): 7–15. Rpt. in Birney, *Spreading* 1: 69–77.

– Rev. of *Contemporary Verse*. *Canadian Forum* 22.255 (1942): 29.

– *Spreading Time: Remarks on Canadian Writing and Writers*. Vol. 1. Montreal: Véhicule, 1980.

Bishop, Leslie. 'Children of Darkness.' *Twentieth Century* 1.9 ([Apr.] 1933): 13.

– 'Expatriate.' *Twentieth Century* 1.7 ([Mar.] 1933): 25.

– *Paper Kingdom*. London and Toronto: W. Heinemann, 1936.

Boux, Rene. 'A Note on Theatre and the Massey Report.' *pm magazine* 1.2 (1951–2): 48–50.

Boylan, Charles Robert. 'The Social and Lyric Voices of Dorothy Livesay.' MA thesis, U of British Columbia, 1969.

Bray, Bonita. 'Against All Odds: The Progressive Arts Club's Production of *Waiting for Lefty*.' *Journal of Canadian Studies* 25.3 (1990): 106–22.

Brown, E.K. 'The Development of Canadian Poetry, 1880–1940.' *Poetry* 58.1 (1941): 34–47.

Buri, S.G. 'Some Facts of Poetry's Life.' Editorial. *CV/II* 1.2 (1975): 4.

Butling, Pauline. "Hall of Fame Blocks Women' Re/Righting Literary History: Women and B.C. Little Magazines.' *Open Letter* 7th ser., 8 (1990): 60–76.

– *Seeing in the Dark: The Poetry of Phyllis Webb*. Waterloo: Wilfrid Laurier UP, 1997.

Cameron, Elspeth. *Earle Birney: A Life*. Toronto: Viking, 1994.

– *Irving Layton: A Portrait*. Toronto: Stoddart, 1985.

'The Canadian Forum.' Editorial. *Masses* 2.9 (1933): 5.

'Canadian Forum.' Editorial. *Masses* 2.10 (1933): 7.

'Canadian Forum – The General Articles.' Editorial. *Masses* 2.11 (1934): 5–6.

Carr, Graham. 'English-Canadian Literary Culture in the Modernist Milieu, 1920–40.' Diss. U of Maine at Orono, 1983.

Cecil-Smith, Ed. 'Let's Have More Discussion ...' *Masses* 2.12 (1934): 7, 16.

– 'Propaganda and Art.' *Masses* 2.11 (1934): 10–11.

'Censored!' Editorial. *New Masses* 1.3 (1926): 3.

'Civil War in Spain.' Editorial. *New Frontier* 1.5 (1936): 3.

'CIV/n in Canada/and Abroad.' Advertisement. *CIV/n* 7 (1955): [28]. Rpt. in Collins, *CIV/n* 226.

Clark, Suzanne. *Sentimental Modernism: Women Writers and the Revolution of the Word*. Bloomington: Indiana UP, 1991.

Cohen, David. 'The Rising City: Urban Themes in the Art and Writings of C.R.W. Nevinson.' *C.R.W. Nevinson: The Twentieth Century*. Ed. Johnathan Black, David Cohen, Gordon Cooke, and Richard Ingleby. London: Merrell Holberton and the Imperial War Museum, 1999. 39–53.

Collin, W.E. 'Drought on the Prairies.' Rev. of *The Wind Our Enemy*, by Anne Marriott. *Poetry* 58.1 (1941): 53–7.

– *The White Savannahs*. 1936. Toronto: U of Toronto P, 1975.

Collins, Aileen. 'Canadian Culture.' Editorial. *CIV/n* 5 (1954): 1. Rpt. in Collins, ed. 129.

– ed. *CIV/n: A Literary Magazine of the 50's*. Montreal: Véhicule, 1983.

– Introduction. Collins, ed. 7–11.

– 'Renewal.' *CIV/n* 3 (1953): 5. Rpt. in Collins, *CIV/n* 67–8.

Colman, Mary Elizabeth. 'Our Proletarian Verse.' *Canadian Author* 14 (1936): 12.

'Constance Fairbanks Piers.' Biographical note. *A New Canadian Anthology*. Ed. Alan Creighton and Hilda Ridley. Toronto: Crucible P, 1938. 153.

Cook, Ramsay. *The Regenerators: Social Criticism in Late Victoria English Canada*. Toronto: U of Toronto P, 1985.

Cooley, Dennis. 'Dorothy Livesay's Political Poetry.' *The Vernacular Muse: The Eye and Ear in Contemporary Literature*. Winnipeg: Turnstone, 1987. 223–75.

Cowan, Ann Stephenson. '*The Canadian Forum* 1920–1950: An Historical Study in Canadian Literary Theory and Practice.' MA thesis, Carleton U, 1974.

Crawley, Alan. 'About "Call My People Home."' Editorial. *Contemporary Verse* 28 (1949): 23.

– 'Bertram Warr Award.' Editorial. *Contemporary Verse* 20 (1947): 18.

– 'Dorothy Livesay.' *Leading Canadian Poets*. Ed. W.P. Percival. Toronto: Ryerson, 1948. 117–24.

– 'Editor's Note.' Editorial. *Contemporary Verse* 4 (1942): 3–4.

– 'Editor's Note.' Rev. of *Unit of Five*, ed. Ronald Hambleton. *Contemporary Verse* 12 (1945): 14–16.

– 'Editor's Notes.' Rev. of *As Ten as Twenty*, by P.K. Page. *Contemporary Verse* 19 (1946): 16–18.

– 'Editor's Notes.' Rev. of *Green World*, by Miriam Waddington, *Now Is Time*, by Earle Birney, and *When We Are Young*, by Raymond Souster. *Contemporary Verse* 17 (1946): 17–19.

– 'Foreword.' Editorial. *Contemporary Verse* 1.1 (1941): 2.

– 'Notes and Observation.' *Contemporary Verse* 23 (1947–8): 18–22.

– 'Two Reviews.' Rev. of *Poems for People*, by Dorothy Livesay, and *Other Canadians*, ed. John Sutherland. *Contemporary Verse* 21 (1947): 15–19.

Creighton, Alan. 'Modernize Your Poetry Technique.' Advertisement. *Crucible* 6.2 (1940): 29.

– 'Pioneering in Poetry.' *Crucible* 6.2 (1940): 5–6.

– Rev. of *Contemporary Verse*. *Canadian Forum* 24.284 (1944): 142–3.

Creighton, Alan, and Hilda Ridley, eds. *A New Canadian Anthology*. Toronto: Crucible Press, 1938.

'Criticism and Self-Criticism.' *Masses* 1.3 (1932): [14].

Crosbie, John S. 'The Last Page.' Editorial. *Crucible* 9.1 (1943): n. pag.

'Cultural Reaction Continues.' Editorial. *Masses* 1.10 (1933): 3.

'Cultural Reaction in Germany.' Editorial. *Masses* 1.8 (1933): [1–2].

Custance, Florence. 'Success to the "Woman Worker."' Editorial. *Woman Worker* 1.1 (1926): 17–18. Rpt. in Sangster and Hobbs 32–3.

– comp. 'Tribute in Verse.' *Woman Worker* 2.3 (1927): 6.

– 'War Is Declared on "Demoralizing Literature."' Editorial. *Woman Worker* 1.10 (1927): 5–6. Rpt. in Sangster and Hobbs 120–1.

Danielson, H.F. Letter. *Impression* 1.1 (1950): 16.

Davey, Frank. *Louis Dudek and Raymond Souster*. Vancouver: Douglas and McIntyre, 1980.

Davidson, Mary. 'Geneva Evans.' *Twentieth Century* 1.7 ([Mar.] 1933): 9–12.

– 'Turn Over a New Leaf.' Rev. of *Many Moods*, by E.J. Pratt. *Twentieth Century* 1.3 (1932): 23–5.

[Davidson, Mary, and Leslie Bishop]. Editorial. *Twentieth Century* 1.1 (Nov. 1932): 2.

– 'What's the Use.' Editorial. *Twentieth Century* 1.3 (Dec. 1932): 2–3.

Davies, Gwendolyn. '"Dearer than His Dog": Literary Women in Pre-Confederation Nova Scotia.' *Gynocritics/Gynocritiques: Feminist Approaches to Canadian and Quebec Women's Writing*. Ed. Barbara Godard. Toronto: ECW, 1987. 111–29. Rpt. in Davies, *Studies* 71–87.

– ed. *Myth and Milieu: Atlantic Literature and Culture 1918–1939*. Fredericton: Acadiensis P, 1993.

– *Studies in Maritime Literary History, 1760–1930*. Fredericton: Acadiensis P, 1991.

Davis, Ann. *The Logic of Ecstasy: Canadian Mystical Painting, 1920-1940*. Toronto: U of Toronto P, 1992.

Deacon, William Arthur. *Dear Bill: The Correspondence of William Arthur Deacon*. Ed. John Lennox and Michele Lacombe. Toronto: U of Toronto P, 1988.

DeKoven, Marianne. 'Modernism and Gender.' *The Cambridge Companion to Modernism*. Ed. Michael Levenson. Cambridge: Cambridge UP, 1999. 174–93.

– *Rich and Strange: Gender, History, Modernism*. Princeton: Princeton UP, 1991.

Denison, Flora MacDonald. 'Bon Echo.' *Sunset of Bon Echo* 1.1 (Mar. 1916): 5–6.

– 'Democracy.' *Sunset of Bon Echo* 1.1 (Mar. 1916): 26.

– 'Floppit.' *Sunset of Bon Echo* 1.4 (1917): 15–17.

– 'Flora MacDonald.' *Sunset of Bon Echo* 1.1 (Mar. 1916): 7–9.

– 'Historical Sketch of the Indian Battle at Massanoga.' *Sunset of Bon Echo* 1.1 (Mar. 1916): 20–1.

– 'How Do You Like 'The Sunset' of Bon Echo?' Advertisement. *Sunset of Bon Echo* 1.2 (Apr.–May 1916): n. pag.

– 'Mary the Indian.' *Sunset of Bon Echo* 1.5 (1919): 10–12.

– 'Minnie.' *Sunset of Bon Echo* 1.1 (Mar. 1916): 19.

– 'Mrs. Pankhurst – Premier Hearst.' *Sunset of Bon Echo* 1.2 (Apr.–May 1916): 9–11.

– comp. 'Sayings Clipped from Sunset Letters.' *Sunset of Bon Echo* 1.2 (Apr.–May 1916): 33.

– 'Short Stories.' *Sunset of Bon Echo* 1.1 (Mar. 1916): 16–18.

– 'Vocational Training for Women.' *Sunday World* 15 Feb. 1914. Rpt. in *Sunset of Bon Echo* 1.1 (Mar. 1916): 22–5.

– 'Walt Whitman Centuries Past – 1819–1892 – Centuries to Come.' *Sunset of Bon Echo* 1.3 (summer 1916): 3–5.

- 'Whitman.' *Sunset of Bon Echo* 1.1 (Mar. 1916): 3–4.
- 'Who's Who at Bon Echo.' *Sunset of Bon Echo* 1.1 (Mar. 1916): 29–31.

Denning, Michael. *The Cultural Front: The Laboring of American Culture in the Twentieth Century*. New York and London: Verso, 1996.

Dickinson, Peter. *Here Is Queer: Nationalisms, Sexualities, and the Literatures of Canada*. Toronto: U of Toronto P, 1999.

Dillon, George. 'News Notes.' Editorial. *Poetry* 58.1 (1941): 57–8.

Djwa, Sandra. 'The *Canadian Forum*: Literary Catalyst.' *Studies in Canadian Literature* 1 (1976): 7–25.
- *The Politics of the Imagination: A Life of F.R. Scott*. Toronto: Douglas, 1987.

Dowson, Jane. Introduction. *Women's Poetry of the 1930s: A Critical Anthology*. Ed. Jane Dowson. New York : Routledge, 1995. 1–28.

Doyle, James. 'Harriet Monroe's *Poetry* and Canadian Poetry.' *Canadian Poetry: Studies, Documents, Reviews* 25 (1989): 38–48.
- 'Literary Magazines and the Cosmopolitan/Nationalism Debate in Canada.' *Context North America: Canadian/U.S. Literary Relations*. Ed. Camille R. La Bossière. Ottawa: U of Ottawa P, 1994. 97–105.
- 'Margaret Fairley and the Canadian Literary Tradition.' *Canadian Literature* 147 (1995): 77–92.
- *Progressive Heritage: The Evolution of a Politically Radical Literary Tradition in Canada*. Waterloo, ON: Wilfrid Laurier UP, 2002.

Dudek, Louis, ed. *Dk/ Some Letters of Ezra Pound*. Montreal: DC, 1974.
- 'Geography, Politics and Poetry.' *First Statement* 1.16 (1943): 2–3.
- Introduction. Gnarowski, ed. 230–1.
- 'The Making of CIV/n.' Gnarowski, *Index*. Rpt. in Collins, *CIV/n* 230–1.
- 'The Role of Little Magazines in Canada.' Dudek and Gnarowski 205–12.

Dudek, Louis, and Michael Gnarowski, eds. *The Making of Modern Poetry in Canada: Essential Articles on Contemporary Canadian Poetry in English*. Toronto: Ryerson, 1967.

Editorial. *New Frontier* 1.1 (1936): 1.

Edwards, Justin D. 'Engendering Modern Canadian Poetry: *Preview, First Statement*, and the Disclosure of Patrick Anderson's Homosexuality.' *Essays on Canadian Writing* 62 (1997): 65–84.

Eliot, T.S. 'The Love Song of J. Alfred Prufrock.' *Collected Poems 1909–1962*. London: Faber, 1974. 13–17.
- *Selected Prose of T.S. Eliot*. Ed. Frank Kermode. London: Faber, 1975.
- 'Tradition and the Individual Talent.' 1919. Rpt. in Eliot, *Selected Prose* 37–44.
- '*Ulysses*, Order, and Myth.' 1923. Rpt. in Eliot, *Selected Prose* 175–8.
- 'The Waste Land.' Eliot, *Collected* 61–86.

Endres, Robin. Introduction. *Eight Men Speak and Other Plays from the Canadian Workers' Theatre*. Ed. Richard Wright and Robin Endres. Toronto: New Hogtown, 1976. xi–xxxvi.

Enright, Robert. 'Reflections and Expectations.' Editorial. *CV/II* 2.3 (1976): 2.

Fairley, Margaret. 'The Canada Council.' Editorial. *New Frontiers* 3.4 (1954): 1–2.

– 'Domestic Discontent.' *Canadian Forum* 1.2 (1920): 44–5.

– 'Our Cultural Heritage.' *New Frontiers* 1.1 (1952): 1–7.

– 'Pauline Johnson.' *New Frontiers* 3.2 (1954): 43–5.

– ed. *Spirit of Canadian Democracy: A Collection of Canadian Writings from the Beginnings to the Present Day*. Toronto: Progress, 1945.

– 'Virginia Woolf.' *Canadian Forum* 10.114 (1930): 203–4.

– 'The Women's Party.' *Rebel* 3.1 (1918): 27–9.

Felski, Rita. Afterword. Ardis and Lewis 290–9.

– *The Gender of Modernity*. Cambridge and London: Harvard UP, 1995.

Filewod, Alan. '"A Qualified Workers Theatre Art": *Waiting for Lefty* and the (Re)Formation of Popular Front Theatres.' *Essays in Theatre* 17.2 (1999): 111–28.

Fisher, Neil. *First Statement, 1942–1945: An Assessment and an Index*. Ottawa: Golden Dog, 1974.

Foley, Barbara. *Radical Representations: Politics and Form in U.S. Proletarian Fiction, 1929–1941*. Durham: Duke UP, 1993.

Folsom, Ed. 'Traubel, Horace L. (1858–1919).' *Walt Whitman: An Encyclopedia*. Ed. J.R. LeMaster and Donald D. Kummings. New York and London: Garland, 1998. 740–2.

'For a Canadian People's Culture in a World at Peace.' *New Frontiers* 1.1 (1952): n. pag.

'The Forum Editorials.' Editorial. *Masses* 2.9 (1933): 5–7.

Francis, Wynne. 'A Dramatic Story Missed.' Rev. of *Northern Review 1945–1956: A History and an Index*, by Hilda Vaneste, and *CIV/n: A Literary Magazine of the 50's*, ed. Aileen Collins. *Canadian Poetry: Studies, Documents, Reviews* 15 (1984): 84–93.

– 'Literary Magazines in English 3. The Forties to the Sixties.' *Oxford Companion to Canadian Literature*. 2nd ed. Ed. Eugene Benson and William Toye. Toronto: Oxford UP, 1997. 664–6.

– 'Literary Underground: Little Magazines in Canada.' *Canadian Literature* 34 (1967): 63–70.

– 'Montreal Poets of the Forties.' *Canadian Literature* 14 (1962): 21–34.

Frye, Northrop. 'Letters in Canada: 1955. Poetry.' *University of Toronto Quarterly* 25 (1956): 296–7. Rpt. in *The Bush Garden: Essays on the Canadian Imagination*. Toronto: Anansi, 1971. 50–2.

– 'Rear View Crystal Ball.' *Canadian Forum* 50.1 (1970): 54–5.
– Rev. of *Contemporary Verse*. *Canadian Forum* 21.250 (1941): 283.
– Rev. of *Direction*. *Canadian Forum* 23.278 (1944): 287.
– Rev. of *First Statement*. *Canadian Forum* 22.262 (1942): 253.
– Rev. of *Green World*, by Miriam Waddington. *Canadian Forum* 26 (1946): 141–2.
Gerson, Carole. 'Anthologies and the Canon of Early Canadian Women Writers.' McMullen 55–76.
– 'The Literary Culture of Atlantic Women between the Wars.' Davies, *Myth* 62–70.
Gilbert, James Burkhart. *Writers and Partisans: A History of Literary Radicalism in America*. New York: John Wiley, 1968.
Gilbert, Sandra M., and Susan Gubar. *No Man's Land: The Place of the Woman Writer in the Twentieth Century*. 3 vols. New Haven: Yale UP, 1988–94.
Gilman, Charlotte Perkins. Rev. of the *Sunset of Bon Echo*. *Forerunner* 7 (June 1916). Rpt. in *Sunset of Bon Echo* 1.3 (summer 1916): 2.
Gingell, Susan. 'Claiming Positive Semantic Space for Women: The Poetry of Dorothy Livesay.' *Essays on Canadian Writing* 74 (2001): 1–25.
Gnarowski, Michael. *Contact, 1952–1954: Notes on the History and Background of the Periodical and an Index*. Montreal: Delta, 1966.
– ed. *Index to CIV/n*. 1965. Rpt. in Collins, *CIV/n* 229–47.
– 'The Role of "Little Magazines" in the Development of Poetry in English in Montreal.' Dudek and Gnarowski 212–22.
Godard, Barbara. 'Ex-centriques, Eccentric, Avant-Garde: Women and Modernism in the Literatures of Canada.' *Tessera* issue. *Room of One's Own* 8.4 (1984): 57–75.
– 'Women of Letters (Reprise).' *Collaboration in the Feminine: Writings on Women and Culture from Tessera*. Toronto: Second Story, 1994. 258–306.
Godfrey, Eleanor. Rev. of *American Writing – 1943*, ed. Alan Swallow, *Three Tales* by Gustave Flaubert, trans. Arthur McDowell, and *The Literary Fallacy*, by Bernard DeVoto. *Canadian Forum* 24.287 (1944): 213.
– Rev. of *Paper Kingdom*, by Leslie Bishop. *Canadian Forum* 16.188 (1936): 30–1.
– 'The Samaritans.' *Canadian Forum* 19.227 (1939): 290–1.
– 'Sinclair Lewis.' Rev. of *Selected Short Stories*, by Sinclair Lewis. *Canadian Forum* 15.175 (1936): 333–4.
Gordon Ryan, Toby. *Stage Left: Canadian Theatre in the Thirties*. Toronto: CTR, 1981.
Gorham, Deborah. 'Flora MacDonald Denison: Canadian Feminist.' *A Not Unreasonable Claim: Women and Reform in Canada, 1880s–1920s*. Ed. Linda Kealey. Toronto: Women's Press, 1979. 47–70.

Grace, Sherrill. '"Mapping Inner Space": Canada's Northern Expressionism.' *The Canadian North: Essays in Culture and Literature*. Ed. Jørn Carlsen and Bengt Streijffert. The Nordic Association for Canadian Studies Text Series. Vol. 5. Lund, Sweden: The Nordic Association for Canadian Studies, 1989. 61–71.

– *Regression and Apocalypse: Studies in North American Literary Expressionism*. Toronto: U of Toronto P, 1989.

Granatstein, J.L., and Peter Stevens. Preface. *Forum: Canadian Life and Letters 1920–70: Selections from the* Canadian Forum. Toronto: U of Toronto P, 1972. xiii–xv.

Granite, M. 'On Canadian Poetry.' *Masses* 1.4–5 (1932): [9].

Greenland, Cyril, and John Robert Colombo, eds. *Walt Whitman's Canada*. Willowdale, ON: Hounslow P, 1993.

Groening, Laura Smyth. *E.K. Brown: A Study in Conflict*. Toronto: U of Toronto P, 1993.

Hambleton, Ronald, ed. *Unit of Five*. Toronto: Ryerson, 1944.

Harrington, Lyn. *Syllables of Recorded Time: The Story of the Canadian Authors Association 1921–1981*. Toronto: Simon, 1981.

Herbert, Walter B. '[HERE AND NOW ...].' *here and now* 2 (1948): [3].

'Hilda M. Ridley.' *A New Canadian Anthology*. Ed. Alan Creighton and Hilda M. Ridley. Toronto: Crucible P, 1938. 163.

Hoffman, Frederick J., Charles Allen, and Carolyn F. Ulrich, eds. *The Little Magazine: A History and a Bibliography*. 2nd ed. Princeton: Princeton UP, 1947.

Horn, Michiel. 'The Forum during the 1930's.' *Canadian Forum* 50.1 (1970): 38–40.

– *The League for Social Reconstruction: Intellectual Origins of the Democratic Left in Canada 1930–1942*. Toronto: U of Toronto P, 1980.

Hornsey, Richard F. 'The Function of Poetry and the Role of the Poet in Canadian Literary Magazines from *New Frontier* through *Delta*.' Diss. U of Alberta, 1975.

Huyssen, Andreas. 'Mass Culture as Woman: Modernism's Other.' *After the Great Divide: Modernism, Mass Culture, Postmodernism*. Bloomington: Indiana UP, 1986. 45–62.

Hynes, Samuel. *The Auden Generation: Literature and Politics in England in the 1930s*. London: Bodley Head, 1976.

Irr, Caren. *The Suburb of Dissent: Cultural Politics in the United States and Canada during the 1930s*. Durham: Duke UP, 1998.

Irvine, Dean J. 'Dorothy Livesay's Perspectives, Retrospectives, and Prospectives: "A Putting Down of Roots" in *CV/II*.' *Contemporary Verse 2* (1999): 65–77.

– 'Editorial Postscript.' Livesay, *Archive* 250–72.

Jones, Douglas [D.G. Jones]. 'The Question of Language Prostitution.' *CIV/n* 4 (1954): 15–16. Rpt. in Collins, *CIV/n* 115–17.

Jones, Margaret C. *Heretics and Hellraisers: Women Contributors to* The Masses, *1911–1917*. Austin: U of Texas P, 1993.

Kalnin, Martha A. 'Flora MacDonald Denison.' *Walt Whitman: An Encyclopedia*. Ed. J.R. LeMaster and Donald D. Kummings. New York and London: Garland, 1998. 179.

Kennedy, Leo. 'Direction for Canadian Poets.' *New Frontier* 1.3 (1936): 21–3.

– 'A Poet's Memoirs.' *CV/II* 2.2 (1976): 23–4.

Killian, Laura. 'Poetry and the Modern Woman: P.K. Page and the Gender of Impersonality.' *Canadian Literature* 150 (1996): 86–105.

Kimmel, David. 'The Spirit of Canadian Democracy: Margaret Fairley and the Communist Cultural Worker's Responsibility to the People.' *Left History* 1.1 (1993): 34–55.

Kimmel, David, and Gregory S. Kealey. 'With Our Own Hands: Margaret Fairley and the "Real Makers" of Canada.' *Labour/Le Travail* (1993): 253–85.

Kittler, Freidrich A. *Gramophone, Film, Typewriter*. 1986. Trans. Geoffrey Winthrop-Young and Michael Wutz. Stanford: Stanford UP, 1999.

Kizuk, Alexander. 'Molly Beresford and the Song Fishermen of Halifax: Cultural Production, Canon, and Desire in 1920s Canadian Poetry.' Davies, *Myth* 175–97.

Klein, A.M. 'Portrait of the Poet as Landscape.' *Complete Poems: Original Poems, 1937–1955 and Poetry Translations*. Ed. Zailig Pollock. Vol. 2. Toronto: U of Toronto P, 1990. 2: 634–9.

Korinek, Valerie J. *Roughing It in the Suburbs: Reading Chatelaine Magazine in the Fifties and Sixties*. Toronto: U of Toronto P, 2000.

Kronfeld, Chana. *On the Margins of Modernism: Decentering Literary Dynamics*. Berkeley: U of California P, 1996.

Lacombe, Michele. 'Songs of the Open Road: Bon Echo, Urban Utopians, and the Cult of Nature.' *Journal of Canadian Studies* 33.2 (1998): 152–67.

– 'Theosophy and the Idealist Tradition: A Preliminary Exploration.' *Journal of Canadian Studies* 17.2 (summer 1982): 100–18.

'A Larger Magazine.' Editorial. *Canadian Magazine* 63.1 (1924): 19–20.

Layton, Irving. 'The Modern Poet.' *First Statement* 1.16 (1943): 4.

– 'Poetry and Politics.' *First Statement* 2.1 (1943): 17–21.

Lazechko-Haas, Myra, comp. 'Court of Comment.' *Impression* 1.2 (1951): 46.

– Editorial. *Impression* 1.1 (1950): 1–2.

– Editorial. *Impression* 1.3 (1951): 45–7.

– *Viewpoint*. Toronto: Ryerson, 1952.

Leahy, David. 'Patrick Anderson and John Sutherland's Heterorealism:

"Some Sexual Experience of a Kind Not Normal.'" *Essays on Canadian Writing* 62 (1997): 132–49.

Lears, T.J. Jackson. *No Place of Grace: Antimodernism and the Transformation of American Culture 1880–1920*. New York: Pantheon, 1981.

Levine, Norman. 'We All Begin in a Little Magazine.' *Thin Ice*. Ottawa: Deneau and Greenberg, 1979. 38–47.

Lewis, Ray. 'To Walt Whitman.' *Songs of the Universe*. New York A. & C. Boni, 1915. Rpt. in *Sunset of Bon Echo* 1.3 (summer 1916): 24.

Litt, Paul. *The Muses, the Masses, and the Massey Commission*. Toronto: U of Toronto P, 1992.

Livesay, Dorothy. *Archive for Our Times: Previously Uncollected and Unpublished Poems of Dorothy Livesay*. Ed. Dean J. Irvine. Vancouver: Arsenal Pulp, 1998.

– 'Art Exhibition at the C.N.E.' *Masses* 1.6 (1932): [10].

– *Call My People Home*. Toronto: Ryerson, 1950.

– 'Canadian Poetry and the Spanish Civil War.' *CV/II* 2.2 (1976): 12–16.

– *Collected Poems: The Two Seasons of Dorothy Livesay*. Toronto: McGraw-Hill Ryerson, 1972.

– *Day and Night*. Toronto: Ryerson, 1944.

– 'The Dispossessed.' *New Frontier* 1.10 (1937): 7.

– *The Documentaries: Selected Longer Poems*. Toronto: Ryerson, 1968.

– 'The Documentary Poem: A Canadian Genre.' *Contexts of Canadian Criticism: A Collection of Critical Essays*. Ed. Eli Mandel. Chicago: U of Chicago P, 1971. 267–81.

– *Dorothy Livesay and the CBC: Early Texts for Radio by Dorothy Livesay*. Ed. Paul Gerard Tiessen and Hildi Froese Tiessen. Waterloo: MRL, 1994.

– Editorial Note. *CV/II* 1.2 (1975): 38.

– Foreword. McCullagh vi–xvii.

– ed. *40 Women Poets of Canada*. Montreal: Ingluvin, 1971.

– *Green Pitcher*. Toronto: Macmillan, 1928.

– 'The Guild of All Arts.' *Masses* 1.6 (1932): [13].

– 'An Immigrant.' *The Worker* 14 March 1936: 4.

– 'In Preparation.' *New Frontier* 1.10 (1937): 7.

– *Journey with My Selves: A Memoir 1909–1963*. Vancouver: Douglas, 1991.

– 'Live-sayings in Reply.' *Canadian Author* 14 (1936): 13.

– *New Poems*. Toronto: Emblem, 1955.

– 'On the Way Out.' Editorial. *CV/II* 3.3 (1978): 2.

– 'An Open Letter to Sir Charles G.D. Roberts.' *Canadian Bookman* 21.1 (1939): 34–5.

– 'The Outrider.' *First Statement* 2.2 (1943): 11–18.

– *Poems for People*. Toronto: Ryerson, 1947.

– 'The Poetry of Anne Marriott.' *Educational Record of the Province of Quebec* 65.2 (1949): 87–90.
– 'Poet's Progress.' *New Frontier* 2.2 (1937): 23–4.
– 'A Putting Down of Roots.' Editorial. *CV/II* 1.1 (1975): 2.
– 'Recent Ryerson Chapbooks.' Rev. of *Hearing a Far Call*, by M. Eugenie Perry, *For This Freedom Too*, by Mary Elizabeth Coleman, *Birds before Dawn*, by Evelyn Eaton, and *Salt Marsh*, by Anne Marriott. *Contemporary Verse* 8 (1943): 13–14.
– 'Rememberings.' *CV/II* 1.2 (1975): 2–3.
– Rev. of *Ann Vickers*, by Sinclair Lewis. *Masses* 1.8 (1933): [12].
– Rev. of *Arena*, ed. John Sutherland, and *Poetry Commonwealth*, ed. Earle Birney. *pm magazine* 1.3 (1952): 61–3.
– Rev. of *Devil Take the Hindmost*, by Edmund Wilson. *Masses* 1.6 (1932): [11].
– Rev. of *When Sirens Blow*, by Leonard Spier, and *We Gather Strength*, by Herman Spector, Joseph Kalar, Edwin Rolfe, and Sol Funaroff. *Masses* 2.12 (1934): 15–16.
– *Right Hand Left Hand: A True Life of the Thirties*. Ed. David Arnason and Kim Todd. Erin, ON: Porcépic, 1977.
– *Selected Poems of Dorothy Livesay 1926–1956*. Toronto: Ryerson, 1957.
– *The Self-Completing Tree: Selected Poems*. 1986. 2nd ed. Vancouver: Porcépic, 1999.
– *Signpost*. Toronto: Macmillan, 1932.
– *The Unquiet Bed*. Toronto: Ryerson, 1967.
– 'V-J Day / Improvisations on an Old Theme.' *En Masse* 4 (1945): 1–2.
– ed. *Woman's Eye: 12 B.C. Poets*. Vancouver: Air, 1974.
'Love the Conqueror Worm.' Advertisement. *CIV/n* 1 (1953): 2. Rpt. in Collins, *CIV/n* 15.
Lowe, Graham S. 'Women, Work, and the Office: The Feminization of Clerical Occupations in Canada, 1901–1931.' *Rethinking Canada: The Promise of Women's History*. Ed. Veronica Strong-Boag and Anita Clair Fellman. 3rd. ed. Toronto: Oxford UP, 1997. 253–70.
Lynch, Michael. 'Walt Whitman in Ontario.' *The Continuing Presence of Walt Whitman*. Ed. Robert K. Martin. Iowa City: U of Iowa P, 1992. 141–51.
MacDonald, Mary Lu. *Literature and Society in the Canadas 1817–1850*. Lewiston: Edwin Mellen, 1992.
MacDonald, Tanis. '"The battle done": Reading the Military Father in the Poems of P.K. Page.' *Canadian Poetry: Studies, Documents, Reviews* 53 (2003): 71–86.
M[ackay], L.A. Rev. of *Day and Night*, by Dorothy Livesay. *Contemporary Verse* 10 (1944): 15–16.

Macnair, Duncan. 'C.A.A. Annual Hibernation.' *New Frontier* 1.5 (1936): 23–4.

MacPherson, Ian. Letter. *Canadian Forum* 19.228 (1940): 313.

Marek, Jayne E. *Women Editing Modernism: 'Little' Magazines and Literary History*. Lexington: UP of Kentucky, 1995.

Marriott, Anne. *Anne Marriott*. Interview with Don Mowatt. Toronto: League of Canadian Poets, 1972.

– 'Appeasers.' *Canadian Poetry Magazine* 10.1 (1946): 30.

– *Calling Adventurers!* Toronto: Ryerson, 1941.

– *The Circular Coast: Poems New and Selected*. Oakville, ON: Mosaic, 1981.

– 'Communication to a Friend.' *Contemporary Verse* 20 (1947): 14.

– 'Holiday Journal.' *Contemporary Verse* 33 (1950): 16–21.

– 'The New Crop of Chapbooks.' Rev. of *The Treasures of the Snow*, by Arthur S. Bourinot, *Three Meridians*, by Geoffrey Drayton, *The Island*, by Katherine Hale, and *Call My People Home*, by Dorothy Livesay. *Contemporary Verse* 34 (1951): 18–20.

– 'Old Maid.' *Contemporary Verse* 24 (1948): 5.

– 'Ottawa Payday, 1945.' *Contemporary Verse* 24 (1948): 5.

– 'Prayer of the Disillusioned.' *Contemporary Verse* 1.1 (1941): 13.

– *Salt Marsh*. Toronto: Ryerson, 1942.

– *Sandstone and Other Poems*. Toronto: Ryerson, 1945.

– *The Wind Our Enemy*. Toronto: Ryerson, 1939.

Martin, Robert K. 'Sex and Politics in Wartime Canada: The Attack on Patrick Anderson.' *Essays on Canadian Writing* 44 (1991): 110–25.

Martin, Robin. *Shades of Right: Nativist and Fascist Politics in Canada, 1920–1940*. Toronto: U of Toronto P, 1992.

Marx, Karl. *Capital*. Vol. 1. New York: Modern Library, 1906.

Massolin, Philip. *Canadian Intellectuals, the Tory Tradition, and the Challenge of Modernity, 1939–1970*. Toronto: U of Toronto P, 2001.

McCourt, Edward. 'Canadian Letters.' *Royal Commission Studies: A Selection of Essays Prepared for the Royal Commission on National Development in the Arts, Letters, and Sciences*. Ottawa: Edmond Cloutier, 1951. 67–82.

McCullagh, Joan. *Alan Crawley and* Contemporary Verse. Vancouver: U of British Columbia P, 1976.

McInnis, Nadine. *Dorothy Livesay's Poetics of Desire*. Winnipeg: Turnstone, 1994.

McKay, Ian. *The Quest of the Folk: Antimodernism and Cultural Selection in Twentieth-Century Nova Scotia*. Montreal: McGill-Queen's UP, 1994.

McKenzie, Ruth I. 'Proletarian Literature in Canada.' *Dalhousie Review* 19.1 (1939): 49–64.

McKible, Adam. *The Space and Place of Modernism: The Russian Revolution, Little Magazines, and New York*. New York: Routledge, 2002.

McKnight, David N. 'An Annotated Bibliography of English-Canadian Little Magazines 1940–1980.' MA thesis, Concordia U, 1992.

McLaren, Floris. '*Contemporary Verse: A Canadian Quarterly.*' *Tamarack Review* 3 (1957): 55–63.

– 'For the Record.' Letter. *CV/II* 1.2 (1975): 27.

McLauchlan, Laura. '"I," "Unknown": Female Subjectivity in Miriam Waddington's Early Life Writing and *Green World* (1945).' *Canadian Jewish Studies* 11 (2003): 53–91.

– 'Transformative Poetics: Refiguring the Female Subject in the Early Poetry and Life Writing of Dorothy Livesay and Miriam Waddington.' Diss. York U, 1996.

McMullen, Lorraine, ed. *Re(dis)covering Our Foremothers: Nineteenth-Century Women Writers.* Reappraisals: Canadian Writers 15. Ottawa: U of Ottawa P, 1989.

McMullin, Stanley. 'Walt Whitman's Influence in Canada.' *Dalhousie Review* 49 (autumn 1969): 361–68.

McMullin, Stanley, and Robert Stacey. *Massanaga: The Art of Bon Echo.* Ottawa: Archives of Canadian Art and Carleton University Press, 1997.

McNaught, Carleton. 'Volume Thirty: In Retrospect (Part III).' *Canadian Forum* 30.351 (1950): 57–8.

'A Message to Our Readers.' Editorial. *New Frontier* 2.5 (1937): [28].

Mitchell, Beverley. '"How Silence Sings" in the Poetry of Dorothy Livesay 1926–1973.' *Dalhousie Review* 54 (1974): 510–28.

Moffatt, Ken. *A Poetics of Social Work: Personal Agency and Social Transformation in Canada, 1920–1939.* Toronto: U of Toronto P, 2001.

Monroe, Harriet. *A Poet's Life: Seventy Years in a Changing World.* New York: Macmillan, 1938.

Morrisson, Mark S. *The Public Face of Modernism: Little Magazines, Audiences, and Reception, 1905–1920.* Madison: U of Wisconsin P, 2001.

Morton, Mary Lee Bragg. '*First Statement* and *Contemporary Verse*: A Comparative Study.' MA thesis, U of Calgary, 1977.

Mount, Nick. 'The Expatriate Origins of Canadian Literature.' *ReCalling Early Canada: Reading the Political in Literary and Cultural Production.* Ed. Jennifer Blair, Daniel Coleman, Kate Higginson, and Lorraine York. Edmonton: U of Alberta P, 2005. 237–55.

– *When Canadian Literature Moved to New York.* Toronto: U of Toronto P, 2005.

Munton, Margaret Ann. 'The Paradox of Silence in Modern Canadian Poetry: Creativity or Sterility?' MA thesis, Dalhousie U, 1981.

Murphy, James F. *The Proletarian Moment: The Controversy over Leftism in Literature.* Urbana: U of Illinois P, 1991.

Nash, M. Teresa. 'Images of Women in National Flim Board of Canada Films

during World War II and the Post-War Years (1939–1949).' Diss. McGill U,
1982.

Nelson, Cary. *Repression and Recovery: Modern American Poetry and the Politics
of Cultural Memory, 1910–1945*. Madison: U of Wisconsin P, 1989.

– *Revolutionary Memory: Recovering Poetry of the American Left*. New York:
Routledge, 2001.

'The New Group.' *Canadian Forum* 15.178 (1935): [back cover].

Norris, Ken. *The Little Magazine in Canada 1925–80: Its Role in the Development
of Modernism and Post-Modernism in Canadian Poetry*. Toronto: ECW, 1984.

– 'The Significance of *Contact* and *CIV/n*.' Collins, *CIV/n* 253–67.

'Old Friends Meet for the First Time.' Editorial. *Crucible* 5.3 (1938): 7.

Olwell, Victoria. 'The Body Types: Corporeal Documents and Body Politics
circa 1900.' *Literary Secretaries/Secretarial Culture*. Ed. Leah Price and
Pamela Thurschwell. Burlington, VT: Ashgate, 2005. 48–62.

Orange, John. 'P.K. Page and Her Works.' *Canadian Writers and Their Works*.
Poetry Ser., vol. 6. Ed. Robert Lecker, Jack David, and Ellen Quigley.
Toronto: ECW, 1989. 221–73.

Page, P.K. 'After Rain.' *Poetry* 89 (1956): 100–1.

– *As Ten as Twenty*. Toronto: Ryerson, 1946.

– *Brazilian Journal*. Toronto: Lester, 1987.

– 'Canadian Poetry 1942.' *Preview* 8 (1942): 8.

– *Cry Ararat! Poems New and Selected*. Toronto: McClelland, 1967.

– 'Giovanni and the Indians.' *Poetry* 89 (1956): 101–2.

– *Hand Luggage: A Memoir in Verse*. Erin, ON: Porcupine's Quill, 2006.

– *The Hidden Room: Collected Poems*. 2 vols. Erin, ON: Porcépic, 1997.

– 'Meeting.' *Contemporary Verse* 25 (1948): 12. Rpt. as 'Find Me' in Page,
Hidden Room 2: 42.

– *The Metal and the Flower*. Toronto: McClelland, 1954.

– *P.K. Page: Poems Selected and New*. Toronto: Anansi, 1974.

– *Planet Earth: Poems Selected and New*. Erin, ON: Porcupine's Quill, 2002.

– 'Stenographers.' *Preview* 11 (1943): 1–2.

– 'Subjective Eye.' *Northern Review* 1.3 (1946): 14. Rpt. in Page, *Metal* 55.

– ed. *To Say the Least: Canadian Poets from A to Z*. Toronto: Porcépic, 1979.

– 'The Verandah.' *Contemporary Verse* 31 (1950): 4–5.

Page, P.K., and Philip Stratford. *And Once More Saw the Stars: Four Poems for
Two Voices*. Ottawa: Buschek Books, 2001.

Panofsky, Ruth. 'Studies in the Early Poetry of Miriam Waddington.' MA
research paper, York U, June 1982. In MWP, box 19.

Parker, Douglas Scott. 'Women in Communist Culture in Canada: 1932 to
1937.' MA thesis, McGill U, 1994.

Parker, George L. *The Beginnings of the Book Trade in Canada*. Toronto: U of Toronto P, 1985.

Paul, Nancy. '"Redressing the balance": Female and Male in the Early Poetry of P.K. Page.' *Essays on Canadian Writing* 58 (1996): 115–35.

Pennee, Donna. 'Canadian Letters, Dead Referents: Reconsidering the Critical Construction of *The Double Hook*.' *Essays on Canadian Writing* 51-2 (1993-4): 233–57.

Philip, Ruth Scott. 'Anne Marriott – Poet of Prairie and Coast.' *Canadian Author & Bookman* 58.3 (1982–83): 11–12.

Pierson, Ruth Roach. *'They're Still Women After All': The Second World War and Canadian Womanhood*. Toronto: McClelland, 1986.

Pitt, David G. *E.J. Pratt: The Master Years 1927–1964*. Toronto: U of Toronto P, 1987.

Poggioli, Renato. *The Theory of the Avant-Garde* [*Teoria dell'arte d'avanguardia*]. 1962. Trans. Gerald Fitzgerald. Cambridge: Belknap P, 1968.

Potvin, Rose, ed. *Passion and Conviction: The Letters of Graham Spry*. Regina: Canadian Plains Research Center, U of Regina, 1992.

Pound, Ezra. *Guide to Kulchur*. 1938. New York: New Directions, 1970.

Prang, Margaret. 'F.H.U. of the *Canadian Forum*.' *On Canada: Essays in Honour of Frank. H. Underhill*. Toronto: U of Toronto P, 1971. 3–23.

Pratt, E.J. 'Comment.' Editorial. *Canadian Poetry Magazine* 1.2 (1936): 5–6.

– 'Foreword.' Editorial. *Canadian Poetry Magazine* 1.1 (1936): 5–7.

– 'News Notes of Contributors.' *Canadian Poetry Magazine* 3.1 (1938): 56.

– 'The Third Year.' Editorial. *Canadian Poetry Magazine* 3.1 (1938): 7–8.

Precosky, Don. '*Preview*: An Introduction and an Index.' *Canadian Poetry: Studies, Documents, Reviews* 8 (1981): 74–89.

Price, Leah, and Pamela Thurschwell, eds. *Literary Secretaries/Secretarial Culture*. Burlington, VT: Ashgate, 2005.

'Prostitutes.' *Woman Worker* 1.7 (1927): 13. Rpt. in Sangster and Hobbs 167–8.

Rabinowitz, Paula. *Labor and Desire: Women's Revolutionary Fiction in Depression America*. Chapel Hill: U of North Carolina P, 1991.

Rado, Lisa, ed. *Rereading Modernism: New Directions in Feminist Criticism*. New York: Garland, 1994.

Rainey, Lawrence S. 'The Price of Modernism: Reconsidering the Publication of *The Waste Land*.' *Yale Review* 78 (1989): 279–300.

Relke, Diana M.A. 'Tracing a Terrestrial Vision in the Early Work of P.K. Page.' *Canadian Poetry: Studies, Documents, Reviews* 35 (1994): 11–30. Rpt. in *Greenwor(l)ds : Ecocritical Readings of Poetry by Canadian Women*. Calgary: U of Calgary P, 1999. 235–55.

Report of the Royal Commission on National Development in the Arts, Letters and Sciences 1949–1951. Ottawa: Edmond Cloutier, 1951.

Ricou, Laurie. 'Into My Green World: The Poetry of Miriam Waddington.' *Essays on Canadian Writing* 12 (1978): 144–61.

– 'Miriam [Dworkin] Waddington: An Annotated Bibliography.' *The Annotated Bibliography of Canada's Major Authors.* Vol. 6. Toronto: ECW, 1985. 287–388.

Ridley, Hilda. 'The Literary Aspirant.' *Dalhousie Review* 24 (1944): 180–3.

Ridley, Hilda, and Laura Ridley. 'The Open Window.' Editorial. *Crucible* 1.1 (1932): 1.

– *The Post-War Woman.* Toronto: Ryerson, 1941.

– 'Sir Wilfrid Laurier.' Creighton and Ridley 164.

– 'A Word to the Poet.' Editorial. *Crucible* 5.1 (1936): 1.

Ridley, Laura. 'Beauty.' Creighton and Ridley 166.

– 'Late Spring in Canada.' Creighton and Ridley 166.

Rifkind, Candida. 'Labours of Modernity: Women, Writing, and the Left in English Canada, 1919–1939.' Diss. York University, 2003.

– 'Modernism's Red Stage: Theatre and the Left in the 1930s.' *The Canadian Modernists Meet.* Ed. Dean Irvine. Ottawa: U of Ottawa P, 2005. 181–204.

Ringrose, C[hristopher] X[erxes]. 'Patrick Anderson and the Critics.' *Canadian Literature* 43 (1970): 10–23.

– '*Preview*: Anatomy of a Group.' MA thesis, U of Alberta, 1969.

Robinson, H.T.D. 'Our U.S. Letter.' *Crucible* 5.2 (1938): 3.

Rose, Marilyn. 'The Literary Archive and the Telling of Modernist Lives: Retrieving Anne Marriott.' *The Canadian Modernists Meet.* Ed. Dean Irvine. Ottawa: U of Ottawa P, 2005. 231–49.

Ryan, Oscar. 'Our Credentials.' *Masses* 1.1 (1932): [1].

R[yerson], S[tanley]. 'Out of the Frying Pan.' *Masses* 2.12 (1934): 6–7.

Sandwell, B.K. 'Among the Poets.' Rev. of *Viewpoint*, by Myra Lazechko-Haas, *The Searching Image*, by Louis Dudek, *It Was a Plane*, by Tom Farley, and *Mint and Willow*, by Ruth Cleaves Hazelton. *Saturday Night* 17 May 1952: 32–3.

Sangster, Joan. *Dreams of Equality: Women on the Canadian Left, 1920–1950.* Toronto: McClelland, 1989.

Sangster, Joan, and Margaret Hobbs, eds. *The Woman Worker, 1926–1929.* St John's: Canadian Committee on Labour History, 1999.

Savigny, Mary. *Bon Echo: The Denison Years.* Toronto: Natural Heritage Books, 1997.

Schultz, Gregory Peter. 'The Periodical Poetry of A.J.M. Smith, F.R. Scott, Leo Kennedy, and Dorothy Livesay 1925–50.' MA thesis, U of Western Ontario, 1957.

Scott, Bonnie Kime, ed. *The Gender of Modernism: A Critical Anthology*. Indiana UP, 1991.

Scott, F.R. 'The Canadian Authors Meet.' 1927. *The Collected Poems of F.R. Scott*. Toronto: McClelland, 1981. 248.

Souster, Raymond. 'Poetry Canada, 1940–45.' *Impression* 1.4 (1952): 67–9.

Spry, Graham, et al. Editorial. *Canadian Forum* 15.176 (1935): 287.

Stevens, Peter. 'The Development of Canadian Poetry between the Wars and Its Reflection of Social Awareness.' Diss. U of Saskatchewan, 1969.

– *Dorothy Livesay: Patterns in a Poetic Life*. Toronto: ECW, 1992.

– 'Out of the Silence and across the Distance: The Poetry of Dorothy Livesay.' *Queen's Quarterly* 78.4 (1971): 579–91.

Stubbs, Roy St. George. 'This Man of April.' Rev. of *The Shrouding*, by Leo Kennedy. *CV/II* 2.2 (1976): 20–2.

Sutherland, John. 'Anne Marriott's Native Realism.' Rev. of *Sandstone and Other Poems*, by Anne Marriott. *Northern Review* 1.1 (1945). Rpt. in Sutherland, *Essays* 100–1.

– 'A Criticism of "In League with Stones."' *First Statement* 1.4 (1942): 2.

– 'Crucible's Standard of Poetry.' *First Statement* 1.15 (1943): 10. Rpt. as 'Against Bad Poetry' in Sutherland, *Essays* 24.

– Editorial. *First Statement* 1.14 (1943): 10.

– *Essays, Controversies, Poems*. Ed. Miriam Waddington. Toronto: McClelland, 1972.

– 'First Statement Books.' Editorial. *First Statement* 2.10 (1944–5): 1.

– 'First Statement Groups.' *First Statement* 1.16 (1943): 9.

– 'First Statement Opinions.' *First Statement* 1.17 (1943): 6–8.

– *The Letters of John Sutherland, 1942–1956*. Ed. Bruce Whiteman. Toronto: ECW, 1992.

– 'A New Organization.' *First Statement* 1.13 (1943): 1.

– 'The Past Decade in Canadian Poetry.' *Northern Review* 4.2 (1950–1): 42–7. Rpt. in Sutherland, *Essays* 70–6.

– 'P.K. Page and *Preview*.' *First Statement* 1.6 (1943): 7–8. Rpt. in Sutherland, *Essays* 96–7.

– 'Production of the New Literary Magazines.' *First Statement* 1.8 (1942): 1.

– Rev. of *Direction*, ed. Raymond Souster et al. *First Statement* 2.5 (1944): 18–19.

– 'The Role of the Magazines.' *First Statement* 1.15 (1943): 1. Rpt. in Sutherland, *Essays* 22–4.

– 'The Role of Prufrock.' *First Statement* 2.1 (1943): 19–21. Rpt. as 'Prufrock: Mystification Misunderstood' in Sutherland, *Essays* 29–31.

– 'We Go to Press.' Editorial. *First Statement* 1.20 (1943): 1. Rpt. in Sutherland, *Essays* 28–9.

Swallow, Alan. Introduction. *American Writing 1943: The Anthology and Year-book of the American Non-Commercial Magazine*. Ed. Alan Swallow. Boston: Bruce Humphries, 1944. 7–15.

Swann, Jane. 'Mapping the Mind's "I": Vision, Perception, and Complicity in the Early Poems of P.K. Page.' *Studies in Canadian Literature* 30.1 (2005): 181–97.

Thompson, Lee Briscoe (J. Lee Thompson). *Dorothy Livesay*. Twayne World Authors Ser. 784. Boston: Twayne, 1986.

– '"Emphatically Middling": A Critical Examination of Canadian Poetry in the Great Depression.' Diss. Queen's U, 1975.

Tiessen, Paul. 'Dorothy Livesay, the "Housewife," and the Radio in 1951: Modernist Embodiments of Audience.' *The Canadian Modernists Meet*. Ed. Dean Irvine. Ottawa: U of Ottawa P, 2005. 205–28.

Tiessen, Paul, and Hilda Froese Tiessen. Introduction. Livesay, *Dorothy* xi–xxviii.

Tippett, Maria. *Making Culture: English-Canadian Institutions and the Arts before the Massey Commission*. Toronto: U of Toronto P, 1990.

'To All Subscribers and Readers of Masses.' Editorial. *Masses* 1.6 (1932): [14].

'To Our Readers.' Editorial. *Canadian Forum* 26.313 (1947): 245.

'To Our Subscribers.' *Contemporary Verse* 1.4 (1942): 2.

Trachtenberg, Alan. 'Walt Whitman: Precipitant of the Modern.' *The Cambridge Companion to Walt Whitman*. Ed. Ezra Greenspan. Cambridge: Cambridge UP, 1995. 194–207.

Trehearne, Brian. *Aestheticism and the Canadian Modernists: Aspects of a Poetic Influence*. Montreal: McGill-Queen's UP, 1989.

– 'Critical Episodes in Montreal Poetry of the 1940s.' *Canadian Poetry: Studies, Documents, Reviews* 41 (1997): 21–51.

– *The Montreal Forties: Modernist Poetry in Transition*. Toronto: U of Toronto P, 1999.

The Vancouver Poetry Society, 1916–1946: A Book of Days. Toronto: Ryerson, 1946.

Vipond, M[ary]. 'The Canadian Authors' Association in the 1920s: A Case Study in Cultural Nationalism.' *Journal of Canadian Studies* 15.1 (1980): 68–79.

– 'The Image of Women in Mass Circulation Magazines in the 1920s.' *The Neglected Majority: Essays in Canadian Women's History*. Ed. Susan Mann Trofimenkoff and Alison Prentice. Toronto: McClelland, 1977. 116–24.

Vulpe, Nicola. 'This Issue Is Not Ended (An Essay in Lieu of an Introduction).' *Sealed in Struggle: Canadian Poetry and the Spanish Civil War / An Anthology*. Ed. Nicola Vulpe with Maha Albari. [N.p.]: Centre for Canadian Studies, Universidad de la Laguna, 1995. 21–65.

Waddington, Miriam. Afterword. Waddington, *Collected Poems* 411–16.

– 'Apartment Seven.' Waddington, *Apartment* 15–35.

– *Apartment Seven: Essays Selected and New*. Toronto: Oxford UP, 1989.

– *Collected Poems*. Toronto: Oxford UP, 1986.

– ed. *The Collected Poems of A.M. Klein*. Toronto: McGraw-Hill Ryerson, 1974.

– *Green World*. Montreal: First Statement P, 1945.

– Introduction. Sutherland, *Essays* 7–15.

– 'John Sutherland: All Nature into Motion.' Waddington, *Apartment* 108–19.

– Letter. *Canadian Forum* 35 (1955): 207–8.

– *The Season's Lovers*. Toronto: Ryerson, 1958.

– *The Second Silence*. Toronto: Ryerson, 1955.

– 'Social Worker.' *First Statement* 1.13 (1943): 10. Rpt. as 'Folkways' in Waddington, *Collected Poems* 32.

Waddington, Patrick. 'First Statement Opinions.' *First Statement* 1.16 (1943): 5–7.

Wallace, Joe. 'How I Began.' Interview with Dorothy Livesay and Alan Safarik. *CV/II* 1.1 (1975): 35–42.

'Weekly "New Masses."' Editorial. *Masses* 2.11 (1934): 3.

Weiss, Mona. 'My Fellow Stenos.' *Masses* 1.4–5 (1932): [10].

Whiteman, Bruce. '*Here and Now*: A Note and an Index.' *Canadian Poetry: Studies, Documents, Reviews* 18 (1986): 77–87.

– Introduction. Sutherland, *Letters* ix–xxxv.

Whitman, Walt. *Leaves of Grass: Comprehensive Reader's Edition*. Ed. Harold W. Blodgett and Sculley Bradley. New York: New York UP, 1965.

– 'Ventures, on an Old Theme.' [c. 1882]. *Complete Poetry and Collected Prose*. Ed. Justin Kaplan. New York: Library of America. 1055–88.

Whitney, Patricia. 'First Person Feminine: Margaret Day Surrey.' *Canadian Poetry: Studies, Documents, Reviews* 31 (1992): 86–92.

– 'From Oxford to Montreal: Patrick Anderson's Political Development.' *Canadian Poetry: Studies, Documents, Reviews* 19 (1986): 26–48.

Wilkinson, Anne. *The Tightrope Walker: Autobiographical Writings of Anne Wilkinson*. Ed. Joan Coldwell. Toronto: U of Toronto P, 1992.

Williams, Andrea. 'Flora MacDonald Denison and the Rhetoric of the Early Women's Suffrage Movement in Canada.' *The Changing Tradition: Women in the History of Rhetoric*. Ed. Christine Mason Sutherland and Rebecca Sutcliffe. Calgary: U of Calgary P, 1999. 173–82.

Williams, Raymond. 'Culture Is Ordinary.' *Conviction*. Ed. Norman McKenzie. London: MacGibbon and Kee, 1958. Rpt. in *The Raymond Williams Reader*. Ed. John Higgins. London: Blackwell, 2001.

– *Marxism and Literature*. Oxford: Oxford UP, 1977.

- 'Means of Communication as Means of Production.' *Problems in Materialism and Culture: Selected Essays*. London and New York: Verso, 1980. 50–63.
- *The Politics of Modernism: Against the New Conformists*. Ed. Tony Pinkney. New York: Verso, 1989.

Willmott, Glenn. *Unreal Country: Modernity in the Canadian Novel in English*. Montreal and Kingston: McGill-Queen's UP, 2002.

Wilson, Ethel. 'Of Alan Crawley.' *Canadian Literature* 19 (1964): 33–42.

Wilson, Milton. 'Turning New Leaves.' Rev. of *Pressed on Sand*, by Alfred Purdy, *The Second Silence*, by Miriam Waddington, *Europe*, by Louis Dudek, and *In the Midst of My Fever* and *The Cold Green Element*, by Irving Layton. *Canadian Forum* 35 (1955): 162.

Woodcock, George. 'Recent Canadian Poetry.' *Queen's Quarterly* 62 (1955): 114–15.

- 'Transmuting the Myth: Dorothy Livesay and the 1930s.' *Northern Spring. The Flowering of Canadian Literature*. Vancouver: Douglas, 1987. 235–45.

'Your Task and Ours.' Editorial. *Masses* 2.12 (1934): 3.

Index

Miriam Waddington, 250–1; Joe
Wallace, 255
Communist Party of Canada
(CPC) and, 252, 253
Communist Party of Great Britain
and, 252
feminism of, 252
Labour Progressive Party (LPP)
and, 253
LPP Cultural Commission and,
253, 256
Massey Commission and, 225,
251, 253–5
on modernism, 250–1
nationalist leftism of, 225, 254
periodicals and: *Canadian Forum*,
252; *Canadian Tribune*, 76,
252–3; *Horizons*, 271; *New Frontier*, 76, 252; *New Frontiers*, 26,
182, 198, 225, 249–57; *Rebel*, 252
scholarship on, 9, 251, 271
Spirit of Canadian Democracy (ed.),
250–1
Farrell, Mark, 213
fascism, 37–8, 56, 63, 199
Federation of Canadian Writers
(FCW), 293–4n6
fellow-travellers, 34, 36, 38, 39, 46,
57, 58, 60, 69, 76, 151, 265
Felski, Rita, 10, 275n2
feminism, 7, 8, 10, 11, 16, 19, 26, 27,
28, 88, 120–1, 122, 127–8, 131, 132,
176, 181, 185, 197, 212, 252,
259–62, 266, 269, 270; bourgeois,
41–2; proletarian, 26, 194; reform,
187; socialist, 11, 165; suffragist,
11, 26, 42, 187, 191, 194; utopian,
189
Ferne, Doris, 4, 15, 79, 84, 85, 95,
102, 296n1, 282n13, 289n5

Fewster, Ernest, 83, 282n11
Fiddlehead, vii, 124, 125, 223, 259,
270
Fiddlehead Poetry Society, 221
Filewod, Alan, 279n28
Fireweed, 27, 260
First Statement, vii, 10, 15, 16, 18, 22,
58, 87, 123, 126, 127, 128–9,
129–30, 132–3, 139, 144, 145,
146–58, 159, 161, 163–4, 165, 166,
184, 209–10, 217, 218, 222, 230,
235, 286–7n1, 289n15, 293n5,
293–4n6
First Statement groups, 129, 132,
146–8, 150, 152–3, 164, 265
First Statement Press, 25, 132, 133,
148, 158, 220, 276n3
First World War, 9, 67, 68, 281n8
Fisher, Neil, 132, 286n1
Foley, Barbara, 35
Forerunner, 189
Foster, Robert, 269
Fox, Gail, 259
Francis, Wynne, 3, 9, 12, 16, 17, 18,
226, 227, 259, 247, 286–7n1
Franco, Francisco, 74
Frye, Northrop, 167, 212, 215, 217,
290n17, 291n22, 293n5
Full Tide, 83, 84
Funaroff, Sol, 53
futurism, 27, 199

Gallagher, Jackie, 243
Garrow, A.B., 228
Georgian poetry, 82–3, 92, 280n2,
281n8
Gerson, Carole, 8, 11
Gilbert, Sandra M., 275n2
Gill, Eric, 228
Gilman, Charlotte Perkins, 189, 191

women's suffrage, 11, 26, 42, 185–6, 187, 191, 192, 194, 206
Woodcock, George, 32, 167, 291n22
Woodsworth, J.S., 39
Woolf, Virginia, 199, 247, 252
Worker, 32, 48, 49, 195, 277n17
worker-poets, 53, 54
workers, 34, 35, 37–8, 39, 40–1, 42, 45, 51, 52, 55, 57, 67, 113, 196, 202, 276n5; feminized, 39; immigrant, 48; industrial, 35, 71; office, 42–3, 44, 105–6, 130, 134–45, 288n13; sex, 195–6, 197; social, 121, 149, 150, 165; women, 138, 139, 140, 143
Workers' Experimental Theatre, 54
workers' press, 33, 53–4

workers' songs, 33, 40, 54, 65
Workers' Unity League (Toronto), 47
worker-writers, 35, 45, 53
Wreford, James, 250
Writers' Craft Club (WCC), 203–4, 205, 207, 208, 265, 293n1

Yellow Book, 228, 229
Yes, vii
Young Communist League (YCL), 47, 76
Young Worker, 279n26

Zynchuk, Nick, 48, 277n17, 278n21

STUDIES IN BOOK AND PRINT CULTURE

General Editor: Leslie Howsam

Bart Beaty, *Unpopular Culture: Transforming the European Comic Book in the 1990s*

Benjamin C. Withers, *The Illustrated Old English Hexateuch, Cotton Ms. Claudius B.iv: The Frontier of Seeing and Reading in Anglo-Saxon England*

Mary Ann Gillies, *The Professional Literary Agent in Britain, 1880–1920*

Willa Z. Silverman, *The New Bibliopolis: French Book-Collectors and the Culture of Print, 1880–1914*

Lisa Surwillo, *The Stages of Property: Copyrighting Theatre in Spain*

Janet Friskney, *New Canadian Library: The Ross-McClelland Years, 1952–1978*

Janice Cavell, *Arctic Exploration in British Print Culture*

Elspeth Jajdelska, *Silent Reading and the Birth of the Narrator*

Dean Irvine, *Editing Modernity: Women and Little-Magazine Cultures in Canada, 1916–1956*